P9-DZA-242

"There is a small number of people in every generation who are forerunners in thought, action, spirit, who swerve past the barriers of greed and power to hold a torch high for the rest of us. Frances Moore Lappé is one of those. Her writing has done that again and again. Here, in her latest work, she brings the familiar eloquency of expression, simplicity of language, poetic and passionate, to our nation's most urgent problem, the reclaiming of democracy."

—**Howard Zinn,** author, *A People's History of the United States*

"Make no mistake, this is a very powerful book, and its scope and vision are huge. In this century you will see the job of citizens is to keep their mouth open and their capacity to be heard in every discussion that will shape their lives. This is a book about finding our voices where all concerned about democracy are no longer merely passive onlookers but dedicated participants. *Democracy's Edge,* thank God, is beautifully written. It gives us the language we need to reclaim our democracy and for seeing where our real democracy lies: in the grass roots, in the communities where creative solutions to social problems are aplenty. Please, please, please make this audacious book a priority, for it is written with the most careful and tender feelings about what we are all so near to losing—our democracy."

—**Dame Anita Roddick,** founder, The Body Shop

"America is lost in a gnarled thicket of bought politicos, corporate con men, and media hucksters. But we're lucky: Lappé has drawn the map that will get us out alive. Read it and get going."

—**Greg Palast,** author, *The Best Democracy Money Can Buy*

"Our country is suffering from a serious 'democratic deficit,' a widening gulf between public opinion and public policy—and what ails America necessarily ails the world. A great many people do not like what is happening to their lives and their country, and what is being done in their name, but feel isolated and helpless, victims of forces beyond their control. With the clear thinking, plain talk, and penetrating insight that we have come to expect from her work, Frances Moore Lappé confronts these fundamental problems directly and constructively. The book is both a guide to the perplexed and a guide to action."

—**Noam Chomsky**

"Lappé is a pioneer in democratic thought and action."

—**Cornel West,** University Professor of Religion, Princeton University

"Extraordinary. Frances Moore Lappé, the brilliant woman who broke open the story of global hunger with her *Diet for a Small Planet,* has now burst forth with a provocative and exciting new approach to reviving democracy. She reminds us that a robust and wholesome democracy is what delivers a good life to a nation's citizenry. Her challenge to us is to reinvigorate our thinking, to take individual actions, and to participate every day as citizens. She offers hope for those of us who believe that civic society is at the root of a healthy government."

—**Amy Domini,** founder and CEO, Domini Social Investments

"Frances Moore Lappé believes deeply that true democracy is more than simply a set of institutions or a political system. It is the active engagement and voice of ordinary citizens in the decisions that shape their lives and communities. *Democracy's Edge* is an exciting and hopeful account of the rebirth of a living American democracy as people connect with each other around the country to solve problems and build a better society. An important part of that rebirth is a new and growing movement by people of faith who are putting their faith into action for the common good."

—**Jim Wallis,** author, *God's Politics,* and editor and convener, Call to Renewal

"I am invigorated by this book. Lappé's idea of drawing the corporation into democracy's fold is a challenge I hope all of us will take up as our own. There is no more important task for us to embrace today."

—**Marjorie Kelly,** editor, *Business Ethics,* and author, *The Divine Right of Capital*

"With an abundance of inspiring, well-told stories, Lappé sweeps away the disempowering myth that an individual can't make a difference and demonstrates that democracy is a living practice. Essential reading for all who believe that democracy in America would be a good idea."

—**David C. Korten,** board chair, *YES! A Journal of Positive Futures* and author, *When Corporations Rule the World*

"Frankie Lappé has a gift for synthesizing complex ideas into accessible and inspiring simplicity. *Democracy's Edge* is an excellent primer on what our democracy was intended to be, where it went astray, and what needs to happen (and is in fact already happening below the radar of mainstream media) for democracy to come alive. Read, take hope, and take action!"

—**Nina Utne,** chair, *Utne Magazine*

Democracy's edge. It's not an easy place to be, but here we are—on the razor's edge, at risk of losing our hard-won democracy. Yet at the very same time, all around us, Americans are pushing forward democracy's edge—its edge of inclusion, discovery, and innovation. Fortunately, their breakthroughs also give us an edge, just what we need now to meet our toughest challenges.

Also by Frances Moore Lappé

You Have the Power: Choosing Courage in a Culture of Fear (with Jeffrey Perkins)

Hope's Edge: The Next Diet for a Small Planet (with Anne Lappé)

The Quickening of America: Rebuilding Our Nation, Remaking Our Lives (with Paul Martin Du Bois)

Diet for a Small Planet

Taking Population Seriously (with Rachel Schurman)

Rediscovering America's Values: A dialogue that explores our fundamental beliefs and how they offer hope for America's future

Betraying the National Interest (with Rachel Schurman and Kevin Danaher)

World Hunger: Twelve Myths (with Joseph Collins, Peter Rosset, and Luis Esparza)

What to Do After You Turn Off the T.V.

Nicaragua: What Difference Could a Revolution Make? (with Joseph Collins and Paul Rice)

Now We Can Speak (with Joseph Collins)

Aid as Obstacle (with Joseph Collins and David Kinley)

Mozambique and Tanzania: Asking the Big Questions

Food First: Beyond the Myth of Scarcity (with Joseph Collins and Cary Fowler)

DEMOCRACY'S EDGE

To the reporters and editors of
the American News Service (1995–2000),
whose stories in over three hundred newspapers nationwide
inspired readers to the possibilities of living democracy,
especially Emily Bernheim, William Bole, Mieke Bomann,
Paul Bush, Mary Ann Carr, Mary Ann Comfort, Marcia Duffy,
Paul Karr, Mark Lewis, Jane Braxton Little, Linda Lutton,
Robert Preer, Peter Seares, Gustav Spohn,
Darren Waggoner, and Nancy Weil

DEMOCRACY'S EDGE

Choosing to Save Our Country by Bringing Democracy to Life

FRANCES MOORE LAPPÉ

with the assistance of
Rachel Burton, Anna Lappé,
and Hope Richardson

JOSSEY-BASS
A Wiley Imprint
www.josseybass.com

Published by Jossey-Bass
A Wiley Imprint
989 Market Street, San Francisco, CA 94103-1741 www.josseybass.com

Jossey-Bass books and products are available through most bookstores. To contact Jossey-Bass directly call our Customer Care Department within the U.S. at 800-956-7739, outside the U.S. at 317-572-3986, or fax 317-572-4002.

Jossey-Bass also publishes its books in a variety of electronic formats. Some content that appears in print may not be available in electronic books.

Library of Congress Cataloging-in-Publication Data

Lappé, Frances Moore, date.
Democracy's edge : choosing to save our country by bringing democracy to life / Frances Moore Lappé, with the assistance of Rachel Burton, Anna Lappé, and Hope Richardson.—1st ed.
p. cm.
Includes bibliographical references and index.
ISBN-13: 978-0-7879-4311-0 (alk. paper)
ISBN-10: 0-7879-4311-8 (alk. paper)
1. Democracy—United States. 2. Political participation—United States.
3. United States—Politics and government. I. Title.
JK1726.L36 2005
320.973—dc22

2005024330

Printed in the United States of America
FIRST EDITION
HB Printing 10 9 8 7 6 5 4 3 2 1

CONTENTS

Acknowledgments ix

The Path xi

PART ONE

Living on Democracy's Edge **1**

Our journey to the edge and the forces making possible an invisible revolution of hope

1. The Frame 3
2. The Long Arc 13
3. Power Is Not a Four-Letter Word 29

PART TWO

Democracy Growing Up **49**

Outgrowing four beliefs that stymie us and discovering that power, even corporate power, isn't so stuck after all

4. Our Coat 51
5. The Elephant 77

PART THREE

Democracy as a Verb **109**

It's not what we have, it's what we do. Americans seize the rewards of self-direction

6. Attention 111
7. Action 151

8. Choice 183
9. Voice 219

PART FOUR
Democracy in Our Bones **249**
Americans create a culture of empowered, connected people

10. Learning 251
11. Security 277
12. The Invitation 309
Two Frames for Democracy 319
Toward a Language of Democracy 321

Notes 325
Entry Points for Living Democracy 405
The Author 451
Index 453

ACKNOWLEDGMENTS

As I was completing this book, scientist and environmental protector Marc Alan Lappé, my former husband, passed on. Because Marc so wholeheartedly encouraged me in writing my first book, I am indebted to him for all that has flowed from it, including *Democracy's Edge*. Thank you, Marc, for the powerful intellect and healing grace you brought to our wounded planet.

The insights and attention of many talented collaborators made the writing of this book an experience of its message.

First are the inestimable contributions of the three women whose names appear on the title page: Rachel Burton brilliantly and cheerfully offered editorial feedback and oversaw the research and coordinated our "TeamDemocracy" volunteer researchers and editorial responders. Anna Lappé graciously provided overall feedback as well as expert help in the interviewing for and the crafting of Chapters Eight and Nine. Small Planet Institute Fellow Hope Richardson contributed in-depth research assistance, particularly for Chapters Four and Six, as well as careful and creative editorial feedback. Thank you Rachel, Anna, and Hope. What a joy it's been to work with each of you.

TeamDemocracy provided invaluable research and feedback on the flow and message of the book. Thank you, David Barnes, Zenia Dacio-Mesina, Wendy de Heer, Jim DeLorenzo, David Erlbaum, Jyoti Gupta, Mindi Hertzog, Stephen Lappin, Julie Claire Macé,

Thomas MacMillan, Caitrin McKee, Deesha Narichania, and Ginny Pidot. Your commitment to the project spurred me on.

Others to whom I am indebted for research help are Katie Cartier, Jovana Davidovic, Ellen Gray, Michael Johnson, Sierra Pettengill, and Leslie Wittman. I am grateful for the excellent editorial suggestions of my dear friends Diana Beliard and Susan Kanaan. A number of colleagues kindly went the extra mile to offer feedback, including Robert Hinkley, Marjorie Kelly, Tom Linzey, Mark Schultz, Michael Shuman, Timothy Smith, Judy Wicks, and Sheila Wilensky. Thank you for your generosity.

Thanks to Benjamin Barber, whose writing about "strong" and "thin" democracy helped shape my thinking. I am indebted to my insightful editor Dorothy Hearst and her Jossey-Bass colleagues, who poured their hearts and souls into this book, and to my world-class publicists, Jane Rohman and John Bianco.

Family and friends pitched in too. Thank you, Anthony and Clarice Lappé, for your encouragement and practical help every step of the way, and thank you, Linda Pritzker, for your steadfast belief in me and the importance of this message over two decades. My thanks, too, to dear friends Hathaway Barry, Ginny Benson, Sylvia Blanchet, Sue Bumagin, Mary Ann Carlson, Sarah Conn, Andrea Diehl, Mark Finser, Paul Korn, Paul Lacey, Mishy Lesser, Joshua Mailman, Nancy Moorehead, Jeff Perkins, Rose Pritzker, Susannah Rowe, Aaron Stern, Jan Surrey, Judith Thompson, Kaethe Weingarten, Monroe and Carol Whitaker, Anna Whyatt, and others who buoyed my spirits through this complex project.

Finally, Dick Rowe—your unwavering enthusiasm, your countless astute suggestions, your cheerful willingness to lend your creativity and technical savvy—whatever it took—at any moment. Not to mention the green ribbons! You make the journey fun.

I am grateful to each of you for believing in the power and possibility of living democracy.

Cambridge, Massachusetts Frances Moore Lappé
August 2005

THE PATH

To save the democracy we thought we had,
we must take democracy to where it's never been.

This book asks a lot. It asks us to hold in our hearts two seeming opposites, and that's awfully hard for human beings.

Most of us love to settle in with a judgment, to name our experience good or bad and be done with it. But this extraordinary moment in human history calls us to stretch our hearts—and our minds—to hold this era's pain as well as its promise.

We can acknowledge the terrifying, rapid degradation of democracy's core institutions and values: that human beings are being tortured in our name, that U.S. elections fail internationally recognized fairness standards, that government-made "news" is passed on to us as the real thing by corporate-controlled media, and that even here in America, the world's richest country, poverty cuts years off people's lives.[1]

And at the very same time, we can perceive and then pour ourselves into the emerging, powerful practice of democracy that this book explores and celebrates: Americans in every walk of life discovering power within themselves to stay true to democracy's core principles and to create solutions to our toughest problems.

I believe it's possible to hold both truths.

This book is about how I believe we got to this precarious place, democracy's edge, and now that we're here, how very personally we might choose to respond.

looking for patterns

I flash back to a favorite memory of my Fort Worth, Texas, childhood: lying in my bedroom listening to my parents and their friends in the kitchen down the hallway. With coffee and conversation percolating, they taught me what grown-ups do. They talk—a lot—to make sense of the world. That's how they figure out what to do to make things better.

My parents and their friends in the 1950s sought to make sense of the world—to see patterns of causation—in part by identifying the evils of Nazism and Soviet-style communism. They saw the suffering caused by these two thought systems, and when the church my parents co-founded sponsored a family who had escaped communist Hungary, they witnessed the pain up close.

My parents assumed that America was free of any such grand "ism" that could enslave us. Like their friends and most Americans, they believed our basic operating system to be just fine: the market economy plus electoral democracy gives us what we need to thrive—forever.

I absorbed the notion that we live in a country that had figured out the basics. America had not only a proven-the-test-of-time democratic government but widely shared core values that we could rely on to smooth the remaining rough edges—persistent poverty, racism, violence, corruption. Our biggest remaining task and obligation, I learned, was to share our success formula with poor people still struggling overseas; so in my first year of college I trained to become a Foreign Service officer to do just that.

Then came the first big jolt—the war in Vietnam. While I'd previously trusted my parents' support for Lyndon Johnson and the war, once on my own I began trying to understand its roots for myself. I concluded that "my" government was lying to me. This shock was intensified by others—the assassinations of the Kennedys and Martin Luther King Jr. All led to a sense that something was profoundly amiss and more than rough edges needed attention here at home.

My internal disquiet led to my first job—helping welfare recipients in Philadelphia secure the federal benefits due them. Within a year, the poverty-stricken mother with whom I worked most closely died suddenly in her forties of a heart attack. Lilly had at least one child with asthma and worried every day about whether she could feed and clothe her kids.

I was convinced that poverty killed Lilly, and I doubted that what I was doing addressed the roots of her untimely death. I was twenty-four.

Soon I'd concluded that our challenge was not just cleaning things up piecemeal—a bit of racism here, poverty there. My gut told me something systemic was really off: core assumptions of our society needed reworking.

To dig up those assumptions, I started with a single question, a pretty straightforward one:

Why hunger in a world of plenty?

To answer it, I had to peel away layer after layer of causation until finally it dawned on me. Hunger isn't caused by a scarcity of food. It is caused by a *scarcity of democracy*.

Huh?

Democracy? Food?

Have I grabbed your attention? The puzzle certainly grabbed mine, as I struggled to understand the irrationality of hunger amid plenty for my first book, *Diet for a Small Planet*, in 1971. Ultimately, this cruel paradox forced me to see that a society could have all democracy's formal trappings—adding up to what I call "thin democracy"—but still lack its heart and soul.

A nation may have on its books the most elegant structure of democracy anywhere and still, I realized, not have a society in which all, or even most, people have the essentials they need to thrive, or even to survive. Think only of the "democracies" of India, Philippines, or Guatemala, where vast numbers live trapped in destitution. Or consider that the old Soviet Union had a superb bill of rights—on paper.

The heart of democracy, I finally came to understand, is *voice*—the capacity of citizens to have a say in those critical choices shaping their lives and their futures. Since all life seeks to further life, no living creature *chooses* to go hungry. Hunger is therefore proof that certain citizens—huge numbers of us today, even in the United States—have no effective voice. The very existence of hunger belies democracy's promise.

Wanting to awaken people to the human-made causes of hunger, in 1975 with Joseph Collins I co-founded the Institute for Food and Development Policy (Food First). As I look back over the early years, I can now see that much of my thinking was grounded in a sense of "what's right"—what is ethical and good. It is wrong for some people to be denied food while others are drowning in surplus, wasting, as we do in the United States, almost half of all that's grown.[2]

What could be more obviously wrong?

But gradually, my grounding began to shift, or certainly to widen.

In 1990, I left Food First because I wanted to cut beneath all the issues—hunger, the environment, violence—to the underlying question of democracy itself. My hope was to show others not a blueprint but a pathway, not some idealized form of democracy but examples of regular Americans moving us in the direction of its fuller, more effective practice.

To do this work, I co-founded the Center for Living Democracy (1990–2000) and with Paul Martin DuBois co-authored in 1994 *The Quickening of America*.

I had no idea this book would forever change the way I see the world.

In our research we expected to dig up a few evocative stories revealing a first stirring of what I had come to call Living Democracy—citizens finding their voices to co-create solutions to public problems. But the handful grew to hundreds, many hundreds, so vast in number that we couldn't possibly squeeze them into one book. Knowing that the corporate media don't typically see these breakthroughs as "news," we felt we had to make them news. Only then could they spread.

We figured that if Americans could read about, and see, others like themselves engaged in their communities—out there building what *they* want—then they'd believe themselves capable of doing it, too. To create this kind of democratic "social multiplier effect," in 1995 we at the Center decided to start our own national news service. We called it the American News Service (ANS) to proclaim that these stories—ultimately sixteen hundred original solutions-news stories—are not "alternative," not on the sidelines of American culture. They are at its center. They tell perhaps the most important story of all—what regular people are doing about the biggest, most pressing problems of our time.

ANS lasted only five years, but in its short life published stories in nearly half the biggest U.S. newspapers, including *USA [Today] Weekend* and the *Boston Globe*. You can read these stories via our Web site.[3]

Today, looking back on my years as founding editor of the American News Service, I realize what changed for me: I came to see pattern not just in the causes of suffering but also in the solutions emerging. Within desperate examples of engagement I saw common lessons giving shape to a new concept of democracy itself, perhaps to democracy's next historical stage. In this way, I came to appreciate not just the rightness of democracy—the rightness of its inclusivity and fairness—but its power.

Without this power—without the edge Living Democracy gives us—we *are* lost. Thus rethinking the meaning of democracy is not something that would be "nice"; it is the only way to save what we hold most dear. Living Democracy is not a luxury. It is not something that's great for good times. It is what we most need in these perilous times.

Over all these years you might say I've just been trying to do what my parents did around our kitchen table with their friends: trying to make sense of the world, stripping away layers to get at root causes so that I might help make things better.

I believe that all of us are capable of identifying causal patterns, but more than that I believe that doing so is essential. Without this work we feel powerless. Unable to see the patterns creating the catastrophic losses we face today, we're apt to grasp for anything—any act of charity, any protest, any good cause. Or any rationale to retreat into our private worlds. Or simply to sink into despair.

Once we recognize causal patterns, we become powerful. We're able to identify personal entry points and join with others for clearer vision and effectiveness. Our considered actions can then begin to shift entire patterns toward health.

This book is about both patterns and entry points. Part One probes the myths and practical obstacles that block Americans from jumping in—along with new ideas and practices to free us. Part Two looks at the bigger picture—four assumed "givens" about economic and political life that have locked American society in a downward spin—and contrasts them with a new framing of possibility. Part Three telescopes in to show how Americans are transforming democracy into a living practice, from economics and politics to food and the media. Finally, Part Four traces the contours of a culture of connection now being woven—one strong enough to break the grip of fear and to enable effective learning and real security.

Three offerings close the book. "Two Frames for Democracy" contrasts the dominant understanding of democracy with the emergent Living Democracy frame and "Toward a Language of Democracy" suggests new terms to more effectively communicate the emergent frame. These can be copied and used as handouts. "Entry Points for Living Democracy" is a resource guide to help you connect.

In all, I invite you to rethink long-held, disempowering assumptions and offer, I hope, fresh conceptualizations of power within reach of each of us. One thing I promise: after meeting the people in this book, you'll never again see your country or your possibilities for personal happiness in the same light.

Welcome to life at democracy's edge.

DEMOCRACY'S EDGE

PART ONE

LIVING ON DEMOCRACY'S EDGE

I'm hooked for life!

PAM EMIGH,

after joining a Pennsylvania citizens' effort to stop mining companies from degrading the land

Out of sight of most of us, millions of Americans are satisfying their deep needs for connection with each other and expanding their capacities for effectiveness in the larger world. They are showing us how democracy can become more than a set of unapproachable, distant institutions—how it can become the rewarding way of life I call Living Democracy.

And none too soon!

The indignities and misery of economic insecurity and deepening poverty, the devastation of our ecological home, and the assault on our basic freedoms are of such magnitude that the emerging, more powerful practice of democracy may be our last, best hope.

Chapter One, "The Frame," challenges prevailing wisdom about the core crisis facing our nation. Chapter Two, "The Long Arc," reminds us of competing currents in our culture's history that have taken us to democracy's edge and points to underrecognized common ground on which we can now walk to move that edge forward. Chapter Three, "Power Is Not a Four-Letter Word," invites us to discard long-held, stifling assumptions about power, self-interest, and public life and to embrace liberating alternatives that are already proving effective.

1

THE FRAME

discovering democracy's power

It is far too late and things are far too bad for pessimism.

DEE HOCK[1]

Contemporary social critics see America divided—left versus right, conservative versus liberal, religious versus secular. I disagree and even find these framings destructive. They deflect us from the most critical and perhaps the only division we have to worry about.

It is that between those who believe in democracy—honest dialogue, basic fairness, mutual respect, inclusivity, and reciprocal responsibilities—and those who do not. In the latter category are those willing to put ends over means, violating these core principles in pursuit of an ultimate goal.

Antidemocrats here or abroad include those willing to demonize opponents and even to kill innocent people in pursuit of political power, an idealized future, or a superior afterlife.

At home they include members of our own government who allow illegal detention and torture of captives, arm known tyrants, meet secretly with private interests to hash out the public's business, bar congressional colleagues from hearing rooms, interfere with voting by citizens likely to disagree with them, remove vital information from government Web sites, disguise government propaganda as real news, and employ Orwellian labels to mislead us.[2]

All are justified by perpetrators as necessary tactics to move us to their idealized future.

In the past two centuries, we human beings have proved to ourselves something vital to our survival: that we have the capacity to make democracy work. Within democracy's framework of values, we *are* able to address even our biggest problems by working creatively with—and even gaining from—differences of opinion and culture.

Thus the only real threat we face now is that to democracy itself.

Democracy—negotiating interests by relying on fair play, honest dialogue, and mutual respect—is powerful, I will argue; yet it is also fragile. Democracy can "easily be lost, but is never fully won," Judge William Hastie once observed.[3]

Social creatures, we humans are easily molded by those around us. Once the bullying begins, once dishonesty appears to succeed, it can quickly avalanche toward fascism, the term I use for a society ruled by the power of wealth and fear.

Glancing back over the twentieth century and now the early twenty-first, we see just how startlingly malleable we humans are. The Holocaust. Pol Pot. Bosnia. Rwanda. Abu Ghraib. Darfur. We see decent people commit unthinkable acts. We see decent people silent in the face of unthinkable acts.

Once acknowledging the potential for brutality in each of us, we become incapable of locating evil in "the other"—in everyone else but not in ourselves. It is, yes, a terrifying thought, but also liberating, for this admission helps us appreciate the power of the culture we ourselves create to bring forth either the best or the worst in human beings.

And from there the survival task for humanity is clear: it is to envision and create institutions, from our schools to our media to our businesses, that foster our democratic selves—people able to feel and express empathy and to see through the walls of race, culture, and religion that divide us, people who know how to exert power while maintaining relationship.

This book is an invitation to engage in that vital task. It is more than a call to resist our downward slide. It is an invitation to stand up energetically for democracy in the biggest and littlest ways. It is an invitation to hone our democratic selves and therefore to strengthen a kind of courage that doesn't come easily to most of us—certainly not to me.

Yet as much as this book invites us to the difficult—to uncertainty and to risk—it also invites us to the reward: to the personal power, connection, learning, and fulfillment that is the promise of Living Democracy.

my love affair with democracy

Here and in "The Path," I've shared with you a glimpse of the thinking that has propelled my journey. Now I want to share why I've given not only my head but also my heart to democracy.

As a young woman, I thought I grasped the worsening global crisis. It seemed all too obvious to me. I saw it as needless, life-stunting hunger, relentlessly concentrating wealth, and escalating violence.

But gradually it sank in on me, and then, one day, I had an epiphany: These problems aren't the crisis. They're all solvable. In most cases, solutions are already widely known.

The crisis is our *feeling of powerlessness* to address them.

And this is true because we've blinded ourselves to the most powerful tool we have. That tool is democracy.

I'd be surprised if my epiphany bowls you over! If you're like most Americans, the word *democracy* is a yawn; it's boring, wrapped in duty or perhaps hypocrisy. You've learned to see democracy not as alive and fluid but as dead and rigid—as a collection of inherited structures far removed from our daily lives.

We don't have to look far to see where some of these notions come from. Think back to your middle school classroom. What did you learn about democracy? In Texas public schools in the 1950s, I learned that it was secret ballots, multiple parties, countervailing powers. If these structures are in place, *voilà*—democracy! Preparing for citizenship meant memorizing how a bill becomes law or reciting the Gettysburg Address. Sure, rough edges—the legacies of racism and poverty—will always need smoothing. But democracy is what we already *have*, certainly not something we *do*.

Moreover, we're made to believe that we like it this way—that we *prefer* to leave our futures to others. Only a few oddballs care about contributing to something bigger than themselves. You know, those *activists*.

And expectations have continued to shrink. Recall that after 9/11, when our hearts were torn open, releasing an outpouring of desire to help, President Bush told us that our real job was to go shopping.

Also likely is that for many Americans, democracy reeks of weakness—something "good" and "just" but not necessarily strong. Especially today when our government defines our fight against terror as "permanent war," democracy may hardly seem up to the task. Some may doubt that democracy could ever be tough enough to win out against extremism rising around the globe—those willing to kill themselves, kill civilians, and send others to die to advance their absolute truths.

To me, this perception of democracy is the central and most tragic error of our time.

Yet the doubters are probably right about one thing. Thin democracy *is* weak. It is weak because it's hard to take seriously. True, some Americans are willing to risk their lives for a system that doesn't offer them fair opportunity at home (or even adequate armor over there!) and caters to an ever smaller wealthy minority. But willingness to sacrifice can change: Whether in the voting booth or on the battlefield, it is hard to keep standing up for something called democracy that you know in your heart excludes you.

Some extremists hold out the glorious prospect of a theocratic state. Its moral rationale and promise of otherworldly salvation can understandably look awfully good to many of the world's downtrodden. The purity of this grand idea inspires even some who are educated and better-off—as many suicide terrorists are.

Can thin democracy rooted in a narrowly individualistic, material view of life compete? I have my doubts.

By contrast, Living Democracy respects and builds our capacities to create community, not just consume things. It is an uplifting, inclusive vision that calls forth the best in us and justifies our devotion, including a willingness to sacrifice. Thus, bringing democracy to life as the Americans featured in this book are doing may be the only path to a society robust and resilient enough to resist extremism of all stripes.

"THIN DEMOCRACY" FAILS TO ENGAGE US

- In most presidential elections in the past seventy years, barely half of eligible voters actually cast a ballot.[4] Voter turnout here is 63 percent of that in Western Europe.[5]
- Thirty-three percent of voters said they didn't care who won congressional elections in 2000.[6]
- Only 3 percent of Americans worked for the election of a political party in 2002.[7]
- U.S. elections fail to meet internationally recognized fairness standards.[8]
- Between 1973 and 1993, the number of Americans writing to Congress dropped by 23 percent, and the number attending a political rally or speech dropped by 34 percent.[9]
- The share of Americans who feel that "the government is run by a few big interests looking out only for themselves" more than doubled between the mid-1960s and the mid-1990s to reach 76 percent.[10]
- Lobbyists in Washington outnumber members of Congress by fifty-six to one, tripling since 1996.[11]

"THIN DEMOCRACY" FAILS TO SERVE US

- *America is dividing*. The United States underwent the largest wealth transfer in our history during the 1980s and 1990s. Net worth of the top 1 percent rose by 63 percent while those of the bottom 40 percent dropped by 44 percent.[12]
- *Americans are working but still poor*. One in five jobs in the U.S. cannot keep a family of four out of poverty and provides few or no benefits. The buying power of the minimum wage has sunk by 25 percent in twenty-five years.[13]
- *Americans are facing financial disaster*. Just since 2000, personal bankruptcies are up by a third, half of them estimated to be trigged by paying for a health crisis (and three-quarters of those bankrupted by illness were "covered" by health insurance!).[14]
- *Americans are dying from poverty*. Eighteen thousand Americans die unnecessarily each year because they lack health insurance, estimates the Institute of Medicine.[15] Our health care failure means that the United States—one of the world's richest countries—ranks forty-second in infant survival.[16]
- *Americans are going hungry*. Thirty-five million Americans—equivalent to the entire population of Canada—live in households so poor they're often not sure where their next meal is coming from.[17]
- *Our government is failing to protect our health*. Pollution is so bad that over half of Americans live where air quality falls below Environmental Protection Agency minimum standards.[18]

Thus thin democracy can't work. It isn't working.

We can see it now, and we can begin to embrace a fuller, richer practice of democracy. It is not only the most powerful tool we have, but in many ways still invisible to most of us, it is becoming more so. The people whose stories this book tells, and millions like them, are redefining democracy as a culture more fully tapping the vastly underused potential of "regular people."

democracy's strength

So democracy for me is hardly a yawn; it is a glorious concept that makes my heart sing. It conjures up a world of human striving, a journey in which we human beings keep on risking belief in ourselves.

Not in any abstract sense, but in my very bones, I have come to appreciate its power. That appreciation has grown as I've seen ever more clearly that our top-down strategies can't fix our problems, whether they be homelessness, joblessness, environmental devastation, faltering health care, failing schools, AIDS, or discrimination. They can't be solved simply by giving orders or by applying new technologies. They're complex and interrelated; they touch us all.

Solutions therefore depend on *widening the circle of problem solvers*—embracing those most directly affected—for engagement brings with it at least these three essentials to success:

- The experience and insight of the people closest to the problem
- The creativity that emerges only when diverse perspectives meet
- The commitment to actually "making it happen" that arises when the people involved know that their voices are heard and "own" the plan of action

Living Democracy brings these core insights to life to create a culture of mutual accountability. Citizens are no longer mere spectators or complainers. We hold ourselves as well as authorities accountable for solutions.

Living Democracy is not just righting a particular injustice that limits people's freedom. It's changing how decisions are made.

"The key is citizens getting a seat at the table and a voice in the decisions, regardless of what the specific issue is. That's the issue behind the issues," Ken Galdston, a friend and lead organizer of a broad-based citizens' organization in New England, told me.

To take the next step, to push democracy's edge, we surely need help—help in imagining what is only barely coming into being. In these pages, I try to offer some, asking only that we allow ourselves to imagine the way that comes naturally to most people—from the sparks others ignite in us:

- From the ingenuity and courage of those saying no to our increasingly centralized, inefficient, unfair economy and igniting a more human-scale, efficient, and just one
- From those dismayed by our degraded media, excluding the voices of most Americans, and becoming media makers themselves
- From those alarmed by the failure of their children's schools and remaking them so that their kids love learning and contribute to their communities
- From those fed up with top-down, money-driven politics and rewriting the rules so that citizens find their place at the center of public problem solving
- From those frightened by the current approach to security and discovering the power of community connectedness to reduce violence and enhance peace of mind.

They're demonstrating that democracy is not a separate, distant sphere—something done *to us* or *for us* by faraway forces. It is part of the very essence of the good life, fulfilling our deep needs for meaning and community and for meaning in community.

Yes, we live in paradoxical times. Social and environmental decline is almost too much to bear. Yet at the same moment, startling breakthroughs across a diverse range of communities and problems point to root causes and real solutions.

They tell us our challenge is not simply to reclaim what's been lost. It is to push democracy's edge. We learn that to save the democracy we thought we had, we must take democracy to where it's never been.

2

THE LONG ARC

tracing democracy's journey

The arc of the moral universe is long,
but it bends toward justice.

MARTIN LUTHER KING JR.[1]

One evening not long ago, I wandered alone around "old Philadelphia." As dusk fell, I caught a glimpse of Constitution Hall, the Liberty Bell, and the fine brick home of one of the Constitution's signers. Nearly two million Americans visit here each year to pay homage to those responsible for the liberty and opportunity we enjoy.[2]

But while many of us may imagine that we have largely our Founders to thank—those august gentlemen who gathered in Philadelphia that hot summer of 1787—our democracy has actually been in a continual process of development for more than two centuries. Our nation's first black federal judge, William Hastie, nailed it: "Democracy is a process, not a static condition."[3]

For me, it helps to think of our history as a journey with two competing strains, one pushing democracy forward, one impeding it. To orient us on this journey, here I'll briefly touch on both.

Remember first that in the eyes of our Founders, only about a tenth of the population—white, male property owners—were fit for democracy.[4] Thus for opportunities to have our voices heard today, we can salute those among our forebears who were willing to stand up against slavery, to march in the street claiming that even women could be trusted with the vote, and to sit in at lunch counters in Mississippi to secure civil rights protections for black Americans. Democracy has also deepened and become more accountable, more life-enhancing, thanks to those who brought the end of child labor and won the eight-hour workday, those who made public places accessible to people with disabilities, and those who have fought to end second-class citizenship for gays and lesbians.

Each of these citizen movements has widened the circle of people deemed worthy of being heard. Each declares, in effect, that democracy is about *inclusion*, about voice—all of our voices—and about *deliberation*, about citizens themselves coming together, partnering as needed with government and business, to get the job done.

This democratic current is always bubbling, even surging, despite the darkness of the time.

Yet in this moment, the opposing antidemocratic strain is ascending. It has deep roots, too—for many of our forebears profoundly mistrusted democracy.

mistrusting democracy

Over two hundred years ago, Alexander Hamilton, a framer of the Constitution, lay awake worrying about the "imprudence of democracy" and the "turbulent and changing" disposition of the masses.[5] Those fearful of citizen power in real democracy have used all sorts of grand ideas to disenfranchise us.

One can be traced way, way back to the era after Isaac Newton (1643–1727) convinced his contemporaries there were immutable laws governing the physical universe. Soon some began to think, *aha!* there must be parallel laws governing our human interactions. If we could only discover them, what a relief! Human beings could just let these laws decide outcomes, let them determine the shape of our societies. Then we'd be off the hook! (Or, well, powerless, depending on how you look at it.)

And over the centuries, some protagonists in the antidemocratic historical strain have convinced themselves that there are indeed such "laws"—rules governing property and market exchange that are virtually God-given.

After the late eighteenth century, when Adam Smith (1723–1790) came up with the notion of an "invisible hand" guiding the market, such fixed-rules proponents leapt on it. Smith simplifiers ripped his "invisible hand" metaphor from its context—from his assumption of deep human bonds he called "moral sentiments," among which he believed our passion for justice to run deepest.[6] Discarding any understanding that a just human society is necessary for a market to work, they put forth the "free market" as a natural state, one that exists automatically—if only humans don't interfere.

Adam Smith neckties, I understand, were big in the Reagan White House.

Also undermining democracy within this historical current are those who have oversimplified John Locke (1632–1704) in an effort to convince us that property rights—in which corporations wrap themselves—are also sacrosanct, springing up spontaneously and inherently just, rather than a human invention that can be used for good or turned against us.

Three centuries hence, we can trace this suspicion of democracy all the way forward to today's Far Right.

As the third millennium dawns, we face a stunningly radical assault on democracy's bedrock values.

One is the rule of law. In 2003, the George W. Bush administration attacked Iraq in defiance of international law and then claimed not to be bound by the Geneva Convention in its treatment of certain international prisoners. And just when we were told that the U.S. use of torture had been limited and its perpetrators punished, early in 2005 new documents forced us to recognize that the horrors committed in our name have been widespread.[7]

Another democratic value under attack is honest dialogue, whether with citizens or within Congress. In George W. Bush's first term, Democratic members of Congress were given forty-eight hours total reading time to consider key legislation of more than 2,900 pages, authorizing more than $1 trillion in spending.[8] In an unprecedented breach of congressional protocol, Democrats have been consistently barred from conference rooms where bills are ironed out.[9]

In what unfortunately was not a moment of ironic comedy, the Bush campaign ousted three teachers in Oregon from an October 2004 rally and threatened them with arrest for wearing T-shirts bearing the words "Protect Our Civil Liberties."[10] And in early 2005, we learned how thoroughly the Bush White House had degraded "town hall meetings" from honest give-and-take to rehearsed theater.[11]

Even more basic, perhaps, the Far Right has targeted democracy's core premise that government is citizens' tool to ensure fair opportunities and protection from harm—the bases both of our personal freedom and healthy communities.

George W. Bush's administrations have diluted the Clean Water Act so that it no longer applies to 60 percent of our major waterways, refused to raise the minimum wage so that it continues to lose purchasing power, and cut funding for police and programs helping poor working families. At this writing, the administration seeks to privatize Social Security and to slash funds for affordable housing, child care for low-income working parents, energy assistance, and nutrition.[12]

Doubting that citizens are capable of self government, this strain in our history is peopled by those seeking to transfer as many decisions as possible from the public realm, where decisions are made by deliberation, to the marketplace, where only money talks. Today that means the transfer of vital democratic functions to corporations—from running our public schools to sponsoring our presidential debates.

I've stressed historical continuity, and yet I'm aware that overemphasizing it could shield us from seeing something quite painful: that those at the center of power today are, in their extreme antidemocratic stance, an aberration, not a continuation of Republican or conservative politics. What we're experiencing is not differences, say, about the role of government versus voluntary activities but a difference between those who live the democratic process and those who do not.

The threat to democracy is especially grave because the anti-democrats' control is virtually unchecked: A small group now dominates the party in control of both houses of Congress and often prevails in the Supreme Court.

President Reagan and the senior President Bush regarded those who form the tight circle around George W. Bush—Paul Wolfowitz in particular—as extremists, reports Ray McGovern, a CIA analyst who served Presidents Kennedy, Johnson, and Reagan. At the time, he reports, they were even dubbed "crazies."[13]

The term *neoconservative*, often used to describe this inner circle, is therefore profoundly misleading.

Our government has been taken over not by conservatives but by a "revolutionary" power, warns the Princeton University economist and *New York Times* columnist Paul Krugman. In *The Great Unraveling,* he argues that those in control in Washington today regard hard-won social protections that Americans have long seen as essential to a healthy, inclusive democracy—including Social Security, unemployment insurance, and Medicare—as "a violation of basic principle."[14]

If only we could dismiss Krugman as an alarmist. But he's a sober-minded academic, and he's really worried.

The tactics employed by the Far Right reflect an explicit strategy. In 2000, the leading Republican congressman who became majority whip, Tom DeLay, distributed a pamphlet to all his Republican colleagues titled *The Art of Political War: How Republicans Can Fight to Win.* Its author, David Horowitz, writes, "Politics is war conducted by other means. In political warfare you do not fight just to prevail in an argument, but to destroy the enemy's fighting ability. . . . In political wars, the aggressor usually prevails."[15]

With the help of courageous social critics, we can now see that the current assault on democracy is intentional.[16]

It is being carried out by those in power who are not playing by rules most of us thought to be America's foundation.

For me, David Brock's 2002 book *Blinded by the Right* was a jarring wake-up call. Once a Far Right insider himself, Brock recounts his experience of the mean-spirited, ends-justify-means mind-set of this group that is—chillingly—convincing. He depicts people willing to go to any lengths, including deliberately misleading others (as Brock himself did in his character assassination of Anita Hill), to vanquish enemies.[17] His later work makes clear that the Bush administration's payments to news commentators to push its policies are part of a no-holds-barred strategy.[18]

This assault on democratic principles by our elected representatives is, however, only one dimension of the crisis of democracy upon us. Unelected corporate power has grown dramatically in recent decades.

Corporations at the pinnacle fully grasp that their interests lie with the Far Right. Despite the narrow gap in Congress between Republicans and Democrats, in the 2004 presidential election top-giving corporate political action committees favored Republican candidates ten to one.[19] And they have been richly rewarded. The fifth largest contributor to the Bush's two presidential campaigns was the credit card giant MBNA Corporation, which in 2005 prevailed in its eight-year lobbying effort for a law limiting personal bankruptcy relief, even when caused by medical catastrophe.[20]

The lesson? Thin democracy's weakness puts it always at risk of takeover by private interests and extreme minorities, left or right.

the blinding myths

To grasp why more Americans aren't in open revolt, think of the culture's dominant message—bombarding us through advertising and media portrayals: We humans are nothing but selfish, calculating schemers in the marketplace. "Greed is good," we heard in the Reagan 1980s. And since then, advertising and other media messages have intensified, all telling us we're only capable of looking out for Number One.

Believing this shabby caricature of our nature, of course any thought of coming together to deliberate and choose what's best for all of us—democracy—seems naïve: After all, our selfish little selves will always subvert the process.

It follows then like night follows day that the more of life's choices we let the marketplace decide the better—even the ownership of life itself, including genes and seeds. So what if economic power becomes a bit tight? That's just a necessary trade-off . . . or so goes the theory.

And what theory is that?

It's hard to see it as "theory" because it is now the air we breathe. Ronald Reagan called it "the magic of the market," and since his time, conservatives (an unfortunate misnomer, since their ideology is not "conserving" our environment and is breaking with our democratic past) have drummed home a clear message: our government is not a tool for citizens to use to express our values and create a society that works for us all. No, the government is our enemy; "the market" is our salvation.

In 2001, Grover Norquist, a powerful voice of the Far Right in Washington's inner circle, said he'd like "to cut government in half in twenty-five years, to get it down to the size where we can drown it in the bathtub."[21]

And many Americans are cheering: Yes, yes, drown that big, bad bogeyman.

Only . . . wait a minute.

the antigovernment myth

The Far Right has certainly perfected antigovernment and promarket rhetoric, but its actions are something else again. It is *not* against government per se.

The Bush administration has expanded the federal budget—with a huge military buildup benefiting the military-industrial giants (causing Halliburton's profits to double in the last two years alone).

We now spend nearly as much on the military as the rest of the world combined. And a drug benefit in the 2004 Medicare bill gives pharmaceutical companies a $700 billion bonanza in the coming decade.[22]

In all, the federal budget has grown twice as fast during the Bush years as it did in the Clinton nineties.[23]

While proclaiming fierce antigovernment and promarket allegiance, the administration increased spending so much that by 2005 the United States slipped for the first time below the top ten countries in the *Wall Street Journal*–Heritage Foundation's Index of Economic Freedom.[24] The index ranked as freer Denmark, for example, which the Far Right here tars as "socialist." The media ignored the U.S. slippage because, I believe, it did not support the prevailing myth.

The Far Right's "get government off your back" language also hides its USA PATRIOT Act initiatives to extend government power, including access to medical histories, library records, school transcripts, bank statements, Internet usage, and travel plans. The government can now wiretap or secretly search anyone's home without probable cause of illegal activity.[25]

While increasing federal spending, the Bush administration has slashed federal revenues with $276 billion in tax cuts—three-quarters of which went to the wealthiest 20 percent among us.[26] In this way, President Bush has racked up an unprecedented national debt, one so huge that interest alone—three-fourths owed to foreigners, mostly Chinese—eats up each year one-third as much as we spend on a swelling military. The debt burden now amounts to what *New York Times* columnist Nicholas Kristof calls a "birth tax" of $150,000 on every newborn American.[27]

What a perfect setup.

Increasing expenses but cutting revenue, the Bush administration bankrupts government. So President Bush can now say with a straight face that there is no money for affordable housing, job training, Social Security, environmental protections, or community development.[28]

The Far Right doesn't oppose big government. I hope these numbers make that clear. What they oppose is the democratic premise that citizens use government as our tool to provide basic security for ourselves and express solidarity with our neighbors—through protections against catastrophic job and health loss—and as our means to ensure fair educational and job opportunities. Both are essential to strong communities and thus to freedom itself.

This security-plus-opportunity premise of democracy is what Franklin Roosevelt was getting at when in his 1936 inaugural speech, he quoted an English judge: "Necessitous men are not free men."[29]

the myth of government versus market

The Far Right's antigovernment, promarket ideology also blinds us to the ways in which a market, or at least a well-functioning one, *needs* democratic government. The market and government aren't enemies; they are essential democratic friends.

In Far Right rhetoric, the market functions freely and efficiently, untainted by interference from the always destructive government. But in capitalism, wealth accrues to wealth; that's just what it does—and in the last twenty years at a virtually unprecedented pace. Left to its own devices, therefore, the market undermines the very competition for which it is so prized.

Jaws dropped at the size of the $13 billion Standard Oil–Gulf Corporation merger in 1984.[30] Sixteen years later, no one blinked when the merger between America Online and Time-Warner created a $350 billion company.[31] Today in most major industries, so few companies dominate sales that a truly competitive market is increasingly an illusion.[32]

And at the same time, the tightening grip on individual assets means that more and more Americans are cut out altogether. The top 1 percent control more wealth than the bottom 95 percent put together, and thirty-five million of us are too poor to meet even many of our essential needs through the market.[33]

In the 1980s, on the University of California's Berkeley campus, I had the opportunity to debate the free market's *numero uno* champion, Milton Friedman, author of *Capitalism and Freedom*. "Dr. Friedman," I said, "with all due respect, the market serves human freedom, *but only on one condition*—that we can participate in it! It serves freedom, therefore, in exact proportion to the breadth of the distribution of wealth, and it takes democratic government to ensure that breadth."

But the myths persist, blinding Americans to the fact that a government overpowered by corporate interests cannot maintain a fair marketplace. As Robert Kennedy Jr. has written, "Corporate capitalists don't want free markets, they want dependable profits, and their surest route is to crush the competition by controlling government."[34]

Lest my critique sound extreme, note that we've been warned of precisely the predicament we now face by many esteemed Americans, both Republicans and Democrats.

Thomas Jefferson late in life warned us against the usurpation of citizen power by "the aristocracy of our monied corporations."[35] And by the twentieth century, presidents of both parties awakened to what Jefferson feared. In accepting the Democratic presidential nomination in 1936, Franklin Roosevelt decried giant corporations—what he called "economic royalists"—as the new threat to our freedom because "they had concentrated into their own hands an almost complete control over . . . other people's lives." His call to action was clear: "Our allegiance to American institutions requires the overthrow of this kind of power."

Two and a half decades later, a Republican, President Dwight Eisenhower, warned Americans in his farewell address about the "acquisition of unwarranted influence" within government by the "military-industrial complex." He added, "The potential for the disastrous rise of misplaced power exists and will persist."[36]

Even with his amazing foresight, I doubt that Eisenhower could have imagined a Halliburton today, with billions in no-bid contracts for work in Iraq, getting caught overcharging taxpayers over a hundred million dollars and still being rewarded with huge bonuses.[37]

the arc extends

At the same time, this book argues, movements are alive that not only seek to restore the long arc of justice but are potentially extending it to democracy's next historical stage—a more inclusive, pervasive, vibrant democracy.

How can this be?

Given the mighty antidemocratic forces in ascendance, could it be that at the very same time, a more powerful understanding and practice of democracy is emerging in America?

Yes, I believe it is. Here are my best guesses to at least some of the impetus feeding the emergence of Living Democracy.

One is simple: the alarm is sounding. It's harder and harder to block out the bad news of where the thin, anemic understanding of democracy has taken us.

We have only to ponder the multiple assaults on our health and well-being, such as those in the box in Chapter One. Then let sink in the tragedy of eleven million American children facing hunger in a country in which obesity ranks among the greatest health threats and wages are so low that one in four working families faces financial hardship.[38] In the face of all this, a new sense of urgency is enabling many to take new risks and to seek solutions themselves.

Plus, awareness is spreading that is emboldening many Americans. They are now seeing that "those up there"—you know, the folks who are supposed to be "taking care of business"—aren't.

The 1980s savings and loan scandal and the 1990s implosion of corporate giants like Enron and Tyco revealed shocking arrogance and ethical blindness.

Then the current Bush administration convinced Americans to go to war in part by falsely linking Iraq to al-Qaeda terrorists and by relying on "worthless or misleading" intelligence and analyses "riddled with errors," according to even the Bush-picked review panel.[39] With no plan to secure the peace, the administration sent our troops into battle, exposing them to U.S.-deployed depleted uranium, while allowing hundreds of tons of Iraqi weapons to fall into the hands of insurgents.[40]

Shocking developments like these have forced Americans to face up to bad faith at the highest levels. Ironically, though, the very failures of those at the top may be empowering the rest of us—as their shortcomings demystify authority.

Perhaps more and more people are asking, Could we—everyday people using our common sense and our own moral grounding—do worse? Maybe we could do better!

Paralleling the demystification of authority at the top is a third development essential to Living Democracy—a deepening appreciation of the capacities of those at the "bottom." With, as you will see, "regular people" stepping out in their communities—becoming knowledgeable in arcane matters from banking to federal communications policy—our expectations grow as to the legitimate role of those without official authority.

This radical shift in perception is so pervasive, happening on so many levels, that it's hard to identify it for the revolution it is. Some measure it in the explosive growth of citizen organizations, now totaling two million in the United States alone and growing worldwide.[41] In just one decade, the 1990s, they jumped 60 percent.[42] And they're being noticed: More national governments, as well as the United Nations, are inviting citizen representatives to the table.

Other, more subtle changes are making way for democracy to move into a more powerful stage.

A quiet sea change has occurred over at least the last forty years—perhaps its beginning best marked with the 1962 release of Rachel Carson's *Silent Spring*.[43] Ecology is becoming the dominant metaphor of our time—teaching us that the nature of life is relationships and never-ending change. From the ozone hole—now the size of a continent—to the greenhouse effect—already causing weather mayhem—we experience ecology's dual lessons of interconnectedness and continual change.

Ecology teaches us that there is no single action, isolated and contained. All actions have ripples—not just up through hierarchical flows but out through webs of connectedness in what we might think of as lateral flows. Scientists for the first time have tools to understand that "all living systems are self-organizing networks," as physicist Fritjof Capra explained to me.[44]

Beneath our awareness, perhaps, these lessons seep into popular consciousness, telling us that our acts do matter, all of them. How much more motivating is this ecological worldview than the now discredited mechanistic view of society, in which we're each isolated, encapsulated egos trapped within our own self-created boxes!

Moreover, in piecing together why democracy might be moving into a new historical stage of greater inclusivity and participation—despite frightening signs of regression—we can't overestimate the communications revolution: computers and the Internet. The layperson's access to information and knowledge is exploding. It's tough now for those in power to keep secrets—whether it is details of what the government didn't do to prevent 9/11, which energy company execs sat down with Vice President Cheney to craft energy policy, or who paid for Tom DeLay's $70,000 golfing trip to Scotland's legendary Saint Andrews links.[45]

"Transparency"—that's the new buzzword. Citizens are demanding that governments and corporations make visible everything from stockholders' votes to the chemicals they use in production. But before the era of computers and the Internet, citizens had no practical way to make use of these vast quantities of data.

Not so today.

Consider the impact of the 1984 "right to know" law, passed after thousands died and hundreds of thousands were injured in the chemical release disaster at the Union Carbide factory (now owned by Dow) in Bhopal, India. Under this law, manufacturers and federal facilities must report how much of certain chemicals they release, and the Environmental Protection Agency publishes the data—the

Toxics Release Inventory—on the Internet and elsewhere.[46] Now citizens have critical information to hold polluters accountable. In arguably the most polluted communities in America, the Louisiana Environmental Action Network—thanks to the data—has successfully sued the EPA for not following the Clean Air Act.[47]

We can even click and see what might be harming us. Just visit, for example, http://www.scorecard.org, key in your ZIP code, and find out exactly who is polluting your town and what is spewing into your water and air. When I did this, I was in for a shock: I discovered that a company I jog by regularly ranks among my county's top twenty polluters.

The impact of the Toxics Release Inventory has been striking: in the seven years after its launch in 1988, releases of listed chemicals dropped by 45 percent.[48] Citizens' use of those newly usable cold data can take part of the credit.

the myth of blue versus red

Living Democracy's emergence has yet another source of energy.

Even as the pundits keep drumming into us that we're a nation deadlocked—red states versus blue states—the many openings as well as the threats I've just described tell another story. They are generating significant common passion for change among a majority of Americans.

We often hear that Americans' moral concerns focus on the rights of gays to marry and of women to obtain abortions—two matters that often divide. Actually, reports a 2005 poll, we're twice as likely to cite greed, materialism, and poverty as the country's most urgent moral crises—matters that could unite.[49]

In an extensive national survey in 2000, doing "whatever it takes to protect the environment" was important to Americans in both red and blue states—64 and 70 percent, respectively.[50] In early 2005, fifty-one evangelical Christian groups released an impassioned call for government and citizen action to avert global warming and save the environment.[51]

Exactly the same proportion of Republicans and Democrats (61 percent) said in a 2004 poll that lowering health care costs should be a top priority for the country. Fully 72 percent of us agree that "the government should provide universal health care, even if it means repealing most tax cuts passed since Bush took office," according to a 2003 Pew poll.[52]

Another survey found that neither red nor blue state residents place a high priority on increasing defense spending.

That survey also reveals almost the same proportion of red and blue staters (62 and 64 percent) agreeing that corporations wield too much power.[53] Another survey shows almost 90 percent of us think that corporations hold too much sway in Washington.[54] A lot of common ground there!

Beyond any specific issues, most Americans, whether red or blue, would be appalled, I believe, by the antidemocratic tactics of the Far Right—if they knew.

So let's ditch notions of an unbridgeable divide. Widely shared perceptions about deep, systemwide problems open possibilities for dialogue and unified action among tens of millions of now disaffected Americans.

I opened this chapter with Martin Luther King's evocative words, reminding us that the arc of the moral universe is long, but it bends toward justice. And I'll bet ours isn't the only era in which it has been hard to track the arc at all, because history seems to be simultaneously moving in two opposing directions.

Today, one direction, driven by fear and suspicion, is ripping our society apart as wealth concentrates and fair-opportunity guarantees and security protections are under attack—along with the retrenchment of fundamental civil liberties. This book is primarily about the other dynamic—about real, undeniable signs of Living Democracy emerging, democracy practiced by citizens who understand that freedom is possible only in strong communities. To use political philosopher Harry Boyte's felicitous phrase, they are claiming their voices to define freedom as "the liberation of talents."[55]

3

POWER IS NOT A FOUR-LETTER WORD

reframing the big ideas that stop us

If an American were condemned to confine his activity to his own affairs, he would be robbed of one half of his existence; he would feel an immense void in the life which he is accustomed to lead.

ALEXIS DE TOCQUEVILLE, 1835[1]

Today our culture tells us de Tocqueville is wrong; it's precisely by pursuing our "own affairs"—our intimate love lives, the cool new car, the bigger house—that we'll fill the void. But have we been looking for happiness in all the wrong places, or at least ignoring some key ones?

Living Democracy presumes needs not met in this relentless material quest or even in our private lives—large needs that often go unrecognized. Ignoring them might help explain why depression rates have climbed steadily over the last half century.[2]

So maybe de Tocqueville was on to something when he predicted the "immense void" we'd feel if deprived of rich engagement in wider communities.

Recently, social scientists, even one of Britain's leading economists, began studying not just what makes us sick but what makes us thrive. Investigating happiness itself—imagine that!—they are discovering that once our basic needs are met, having more stuff contributes little to our happiness. More important are our relationships, feeling truly engaged, and finding meaning in life. Looking out for Number One fails the happiness test: Showing and feeling gratitude and doing things for others—that's what makes us happy.[3]

The mid-twentieth-century psychologist and social philosopher Erich Fromm wrote eloquently about humans' deep need to count, to "make a dent" in the larger world. Remaking Descartes's famous line, Fromm wrote, "I am, because I effect."[4]

In bringing our gifts to common pursuits, we experience the joy of discovering we can make that "dent" and we experience the satisfaction of growing as we reshape ourselves through interaction with others unlike ourselves. Another of the twentieth century's celebrated psychologists, Abraham Maslow, urged individuals to develop such a wider circle of identifications—what he called the "more inclusive Self."[5]

This outward-reaching aspect of the human personality, a premise of Living Democracy, is not just wishful thinking: New brain research reveals that we evolved to function in community.

Scientists at Emory University in Atlanta used MRI scans to detect brain responses. While subjects played the simulation game Prisoner's Dilemma, used by social scientists to study cooperative and competitive behavior, researchers saw that the brightest signals arose when subjects were cooperating. The signals showed up "in those neighborhoods of the brain already known to respond to desserts, pictures of pretty faces, money, cocaine and any number of licit or illicit delights." These responses, said the scientists, suggest "that we're wired to cooperate with each other."[6]

So we shouldn't be surprised by the findings of John Drury, a professor of social psychology at Britain's University of Sussex. His in-depth interviews revealed heightened feelings of empowerment, connectedness, and well-being in people recently engaged in political action. "These emotions are not only psychologically good but they are linked with the absence of depression, anxiety and stress," he said. "Collective action can therefore be a life-changing, uplifting, and life-enhancing experience."[7]

To convince human beings to deny such key aspects of our nature takes a lot. But nonstop commercial messages are pretty good at it. Equally disempowering is the long-standing cultural belief that only *certain* people—the upper class, the experts, the officials—have what it takes to make decisions, not regular people, as we imagine ourselves to be.

If we buy into these notions—that we're no more than selfish accumulators unable to find joy in common purpose beyond our intimate circles or that we simply don't qualify as decision makers—it *is* hard to believe that democracy is possible. And it is very easy to feel depressed.

To bring democracy to life, we can consciously counter these false messages—both external and internal ones.

One false message presumes that power is a "thing" and tells us that we're crazy to think regular people can have any at all because corporations and governments have already grabbed so much.

We tell ourselves that getting involved just isn't worth the trouble. In fact, it is a drag, a grand hassle. And anyway, we assume we have no time for anything that's not paying the bills.

Finally, many of us are convinced that we are the only ones who care. Others, we imagine, are so apathetic or self-centered that if we were to get involved, no one would join in. We'd be alone. So what's the point?

Put these dreary ideas together and we *are* sunk!

But the world this book reveals defies each of these ideas about ourselves, our neighbors, and the social order. Americans are revealing aspects of ourselves too long overlooked: our needs for genuine connection with our neighbors and for effectiveness and recognition in the larger world.

So Living Democracy doesn't require remaking human nature; it does require rethinking several narrow and—we are now learning—false ideas about our social nature. In particular, it means rethinking public life, power, and self-interest. Here I take each one in turn, drawing from many sources but especially from the philosophy of public life developed by the extensive citizen organizing network, the Industrial Areas Foundation.[8] A box in Chapter Seven provides a thumbnail sketch of its approach.

rethinking what's public and what's private

Americans rarely see themselves as having public lives. Public life, we imagine, is what celebrities and officials have. Us? No, our lives are private. And most of us want to keep it that way.

I once used as a "focus group" some unsuspecting dinner party guests at a friend's home. I asked, "What is public life?" And someone answered, "It's what you go into if you want your private, even your sex life, to be fully investigated!"

I groaned, realizing just how big the challenge is.

The challenge may be as big as seeing the invisible. Though few of us realize it, we already *have* public lives. As the illustration shows, each of us plays many roles—worker, consumer, viewer, employer, supervisor, client, voter, opinion giver, student, service recipient, critic, contributor, leader, participant. Even many roles we think of as private—parent, for example—have vast public consequences. Personal choices we make daily—what we eat, where we shop, how much we drive—have far-ranging economic, societal, and ecological impacts.

Many people assume that we affect this larger world only if we make conscious (read "politically correct") choices to, say, boycott one company and buy from another. But in fact, *all* our choices count. Choosing without thinking, we have *just as much impact*—only we're likely to choose the status quo, speeding the downward spiral.

The influence we have in our public lives is, moreover, growing. We each touch many more people than our forebears did. Think about earlier generations for whom work was largely circumscribed by home and farm. How many new people did they

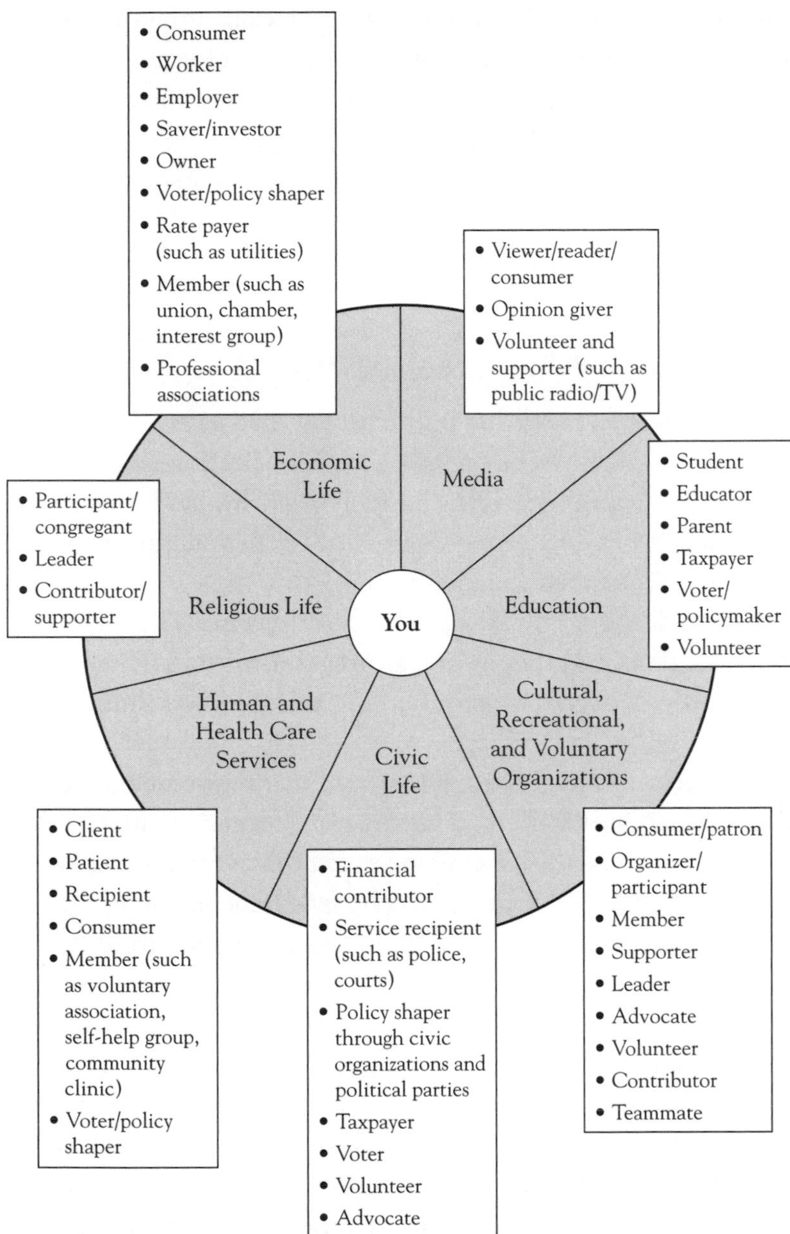

Our Public Lives: Some Key Roles

meet in a week, if any? Now think about how many new people you encounter in a week's time. Multiply that number by two thousand and you'll have roughly the number of people you'll relate to during a forty-year work life. If your guess was a modest five, that's ten thousand people—more than in most towns in America.

In every core aspect of contemporary life, we are engaged in complex public relationships.

what's good about power

For some people, public life is strictly defensive. How can I protect myself from others' decisions—the dumping of toxic wastes, the outsourcing of American jobs, the location of a highway? But more and more people are discovering they can shed their victim status and make things happen. Suddenly, public life isn't an unpleasant, defensive duty. As Pam Emigh of the Pennsylvania Environmental Network described the joy of realizing that she had the power to stop mining's degradation of her community, she told me, "I'm hooked for life."

Americans are becoming involved in a new breed of citizen organizations, such as Kentuckians for the Commonwealth (KFTC), which proudly boasts a membership of 2,500, actively addressing concerns from toxic dumping to open government.

Jean True, a leader in KFTC in the 1990s, admitted, "I was home raising kids for ten years. I didn't know anything about politics. I thought my only job was to vote." When we asked Jean to tell us why she joined KFTC, she responded, "It's just the fun! That you can get together some regular people, go to the capitol, and make changes in state policy. . . . We have a great time doing what we do, going toe to toe and head to head with state legislators. We sometimes know more than they do! It's the fun of power—the ant knocking over the buffalo."

It's also a very different notion of power than most Americans hold. When, for example, a Massachusetts teacher I know asked his tenth graders to blurt out the first words that came to mind on hearing the word *power,* they said, "money," "parents," "guns," "bullies," "Adolf Hitler," and "Mike Tyson." And in my workshops with adults, I've heard those words, plus "force," "police," "law," and "politicians." Often "men" pops out, too.

As long as we conceive of power as the capacity to exert one's will over another, it *is* something to be wary of. Power can manipulate, coerce, and destroy. And if we are convinced we have none, of course power looks negative.

"People think, power, oh, that's bad. But powerlessness—that's really bad," observed Margaret Moore of Allied Communities of Tarrant (ACT) in Fort Worth, Texas, which has successfully taken on challenges ranging from jobs to school reform. In fact, power simply means our *capacity to act*. "Power is necessary to produce the changes I want in my community," Margaret told me. I've found many Americans returning power to its original meaning—from the Latin *posse*, "to be able."

To participate in power is to stop blaming and to become a problem solver.

But that's hard to do if we also see power as something fixed—what we contend for, not something we develop together. But the people you meet in this book embody a different concept. Some call it *relational power:* if power is our capacity to get things done, then even a moment's reflection tells us we can't create much alone. *Relational* suggests that power can expand for many people *simultaneously*. It's no longer a harsh, zero-sum concept—the more for you, the less for me. The growth in one person's power can enhance the power of others.

"Before we began to think about organizing ourselves, we'd tell officials, 'You solve it,'" said Dulcie Giadone, who in the 1990s headed Hartford Areas Rally Together, a broad-based citizen organization in Connecticut. "But they didn't solve it," admitted Dulcie—a preschool teacher who had never before taken a leadership role. So she rethought power: "What can we offer to make a difference?" A string of successes followed—from shutting down a drug-plagued apartment building to home ownership access for low-income residents.

Implicit in this understanding of power, Living Democracy builds relationships based on mutual accountability, not one-way force.

power in relationships

What Dulcie Giadone and many others are realizing is that power is not exclusive to public officials or so-called experts. Because power always exists in relationships, someone has the power to create, to block, to enable, to oppress *only insofar as* other people accept, respond to, or honor that power.

"We're the ones who let them roll over us," said Pauline Thompson of Kentuckians for the Commonwealth, as she acknowledged her part in enabling coal companies and toxic waste disposers to defile much of the Bluegrass State.

Understanding power as a relationship need not blind us to the very real power imbalances based on wealth, status, prejudice, and long-existing "connections." But grasping that power is always a relationship enables us to find ways to shift the balance.

The Reverend Terry Boggs, a leader in Allied Communities of Tarrant in the 1990s, told us that when Texas Wesleyan College announced it was moving to a more upscale part of town, the college was reacting to the neighborhood's decay. But if the college pulled out, the neighborhood had virtually no chance of recovery; the campus provided the last point of stability on which to rebuild the neighborhood.

So ACT leaders and members—mostly moderate- and low-income blacks, whites, and Hispanics—contacted the board of trustees and the college's president. "To prepare, we conducted a two-and-a-half-hour role play," Terry recalled. "We went over every eventuality. We were ready! At the appointed hour, all of us—

fifteen laypeople and pastors—arrived at a parlor off the president's office. There we saw chairs lined up in two rows, all facing a table where the president was to sit. Immediately, we started rearranging the furniture so that we could sit in a circle."

ACT organizer Perry Perkins explained what happened next: "At that point, the president's assistant walked in. 'What are you doing?' he asked. We said, 'We want a meeting. We don't want a lecture!' We were polite, but our actions communicated that we were an organization with power. We deliberately created a certain tension. Our action produced some discomfort that the president and his assistant had to deal with. We created a 'public moment' that focused people's attention."

The meeting worked, and the college ended up recommitting itself to the community. In its disciplined initiative, ACT had remade the power relationship—not through nastiness but by creating enough tension to make those with more power aware that they had to take seriously the voices of those they had perceived as powerless.

Typically, Americans think of power in the form of money, the law, force, and status. But once we understand power as a relationship among people, many new sources open up.

building relationships to build power

"Our members simply sit in the homes of their neighbors or meet with each other after a church service. They listen to each other for thirty or forty minutes. It's called a 'one-on-one.'" That's how organizer Ken Galdston of the InterValley Project in New England described his group's primary approach to building power.

"We don't go in and say, 'We're canvassing your neighborhood to find out what you don't like.' Instead, we approach people with questions like 'How long have you lived here? What forces and people shaped your life? Where do you work? What's happening in your company? What do you think about TV?' They begin to build a relationship."

"People have less time for each other," Ken said recently. "They're working more; there's more mobility. So within our six member organizations—each made up of twenty-five or more congregations and unions—we put a lot of emphasis up front on relationship building. In six to eight weeks, our congregations may help bring about as many as nine hundred new one-on-one relationships," said Ken. "That itself goes a long way toward helping people see what they have in common with each other."

A relationship of trust begins—a far cry from simply asking people to sign on to your campaign.

Relationships of diversity build power, Ken argues. In InterValley's meetings, "maybe twenty people have roles," he said. "Some are suburban folks whose ancestors may have come over on the *Mayflower*, while some just arrived from the Dominican Republic. There's power in this—it's that sense that 'I'm in this with other people,' that sense of solidarity."

Relationship building creates power in part because it transforms people's sense of themselves. "My organization saw qualities in me that I didn't see in myself," said Elena Hanggi, a homemaker and part-time hospital aide when the Association of Community Organizations for Reform Now (ACORN) knocked on her door. In a few years, she rose to become an effective national leader in ACORN.

the power of knowledge

Discovering power within themselves, those who've never before been involved in public life often come to a startling realization: the people to whom we have so often deferred are frequently less knowledgeable and competent than we've assumed.

The national citizen organization ACORN long suspected that banks in many cities were discriminating against low-income people of color. How did ACORN counter while building its own power? By doing its own study of twenty banks in ten cities, discovering that the percentage of whites who got mortgages was much higher than that of equally qualified blacks. In the early 1990s, that research itself—published in a number of major newspapers—had national impact.[9] Immediately, many banks announced new efforts to reach minority borrowers.[10] To achieve this victory, ACORN members had to learn a lot about the intricacies of banking. "These folks know more about banking than the finance professors I know," remarked a finance professor who attended an ACORN meeting.

power in organized numbers

When groups like these turn out hundreds or even thousands of members to a meeting or an "action" (their shorthand for a public confrontation with a public official or institution), decision makers listen.

"We got thirteen thousand people out for our meeting on school reform," said the lead organizer in California for the Industrial Areas Foundation, a national network of congregation-based citizens' organizations founded in Chicago in the 1940s by Saul Alinsky. "That's what established our credibility on the issue of failing schools."

People's willingness to turn out is visible evidence of their commitment to act.

power in humor

Drama, surprise, and humor tend to "shake things up." They help people see old issues in a new light—that's part of what gives them power.

In the 1990s, Daymon Morgan, then in his sixties, seemed to me to be the classic farmer figure, overalls and straw hat included. He was also chairman of Kentuckians for the Commonwealth. With a broad grin, Daymon described a KFTC skit at the state capitol in Frankfort.

Members carried a bed into a legislative hearing room. In it were Daymon and others wearing stocking caps. Some were dressed in costume to represent the state's biggest coal and waste companies; others, the legislators. And under the covers they passed large wads of fake cash. The message of "who was in bed with whom" was quite clear: corporations control the legislators' votes. The media loved it, flashing the images across the state and helping KFTC win a big victory limiting corporate influence.

In a similar vein, in the 2004 election, Billionaires for Bush used street theater and a light touch to bring attention to the influence on politics of the superwealthy.

power in discipline

Since the late seventies, the Youth Action Program in New York City has been involving poor teenagers in a self-governing training program in the construction trades. These young people taught me a great deal about the power of discipline.

"When we were organizing to appear at the city council, calling for jobs for young people, we practiced every Wednesday night for three months," said a Youth Action organizer. "We practiced walking in an organized way, in single file, filling up every successive seat in a row rather than flowing in to the council in an undisciplined way. We practiced standing in unison and clapping together at the close of every speech of one of our supporters. Nobody wore hats or chewed gum. We knew that this degree of self-discipline, implying no threat but demonstrating internal unity, would have an impact. It did.

"We knew that the more respectful the group, given how scared white society is of black and Latin young people, the greater the power of the group. They would inspire respect, trigger surprise, and in fact generate gratitude, because people with the right to be mad are reaching for alliances instead of attacking."[11]

These young people succeeded. They won millions in city funds for job-training programs that have benefited hundreds of youth. The Youth Action Program approach has spawned over two hundred similar ones, now linked through YouthBuild USA in Boston.[12]

power in vision and in tapping human compassion

In 2004, the Greater Boston Interfaith Organization, made up of sixty congregations, discovered that among its members were Haitian immigrant nursing assistants facing painful discrimination on the job—some so severe it interfered with the care they could give nursing home residents, many also members of its congregations.

So the group invited Massachusetts Attorney General Thomas Reilly to a meeting, a rather large one: seven hundred of its congregations' members turned out.

"One told the attorney general how she had been fired when someone misheard her Haitian accent. Another, in tears, described the humiliation of being spit on by a resident's daughter," Eddly Benoit, the young first elder of Boston's largest Haitian church, reported.

"It was impossible not to be moved by the testimonies."

"No one knew what the attorney general would do," Elder Benoit added. "His staff had told us there was little he could do. We all literally held our breath.

"The attorney general started by telling his own story—his memory of the discrimination his mother, an Irish immigrant, experienced. He made the connection. And then he surprised us, his staff, and perhaps even himself. He committed to write a formal advisory on the rights of immigrant workers and send it to every nursing home in the state.

"The on-the-job impact was immediate, and the women who spoke at that meeting became local celebrities," Elder Benoit said.

His story reminds me of something I'd been told years ago after a similar encounter set up by Orange County Congregation Community Organizations, in California. "Even the most cynical, indifferent, hard-bitten official responds to human pain when it's communicated without subjecting them to personal attack," Rabbi Moshe ben Asher had said. Rabbi ben Asher and Elder Benoit are both talking about the power of innate human compassion—unleashed.

One can, of course, *individually* gain the power of wealth simply through a big inheritance or a lucrative investment. One can acquire power in an official post with top-down authority. Not so the types of power flourishing in the lives of the people who appear in this book. These sources of power grow from within and become stronger as we relate to others, relate not in just any old way but from a new understanding of self-interest to which I now turn. We build power in our daily interactions in the schools, businesses, and other institutions that shape us and that are in turn shaped by us.

TWO WAYS OF THINKING ABOUT POWER IN PUBLIC LIFE

Power Is	*Power Can Be*
Zero-sum. It strengthens some people at the expense of others. It divides what already exists.	Mutually expanding. It builds the capacities of all involved. It is creative, involving new sources and new possibilities.
A one-way force: either you have it or you don't. It's the powerful versus the powerless.	A give-and-take, two-way relationship. No one is ever completely powerless because each person's actions affect others.

Limiting, intimidating, and scary.	Freeing.
Controlling.	Collaborative.
Rigid, static.	Dynamic, always changing.
Derived mostly from laws, status, force, and wealth.	Derived from relationships, knowledge, experience, numbers, organization, creativity, vision, perseverance, discipline, and humor.
All about what I can do or get *now*.	Concerned with how decisions get made and how power is built *over time*.

self-interest, not selfishness

Our culture drums into us two diametrically opposing messages about why anyone might want to get involved in the wider world. First, it's *go get what's yours*—stand up for your rights! In the next breath, it's *squelch your own interests*, become a minor-league Mother Teresa and sacrifice on behalf of those less fortunate. In both messages, self-interest is assumed to mean selfishness. The only question is whether we should assert or suppress it. But *both* messages need rethinking.

Self-interest isn't selfishness; it is what we legitimately bring to public life. Self-interests are our passions—what we care most about: family, security, health, faith, and professional development, as well as broader passions such as protecting the natural world.

In this light, distinguishing between one's self-interest and one's values is tricky. Maybe we should just stop trying.

Equally true, many people *want* to help others when suffering is spreading all around us. Helping feels good. In fact, a recent study of over three thousand people uncovered a "helpers' high." Fully 95 percent of volunteers report that after helping others, they feel better both emotionally and physically. They have more energy and enjoy a feeling of serenity.[13]

But service alone does not create strong communities; strong communities aren't divided between givers and receivers. Although helping can meet a real need, it's not enough. If we want to uproot what's created the need in the first place, we have to focus on building people's capacities for problem solving.

"Never do for others what they can do for themselves" has become the credo of the Industrial Areas Foundation, among the more effective national networks of citizen organizations, highlighted in Chapter Seven. In the 1990s, its lead organizer in the Southeast, Gerald Taylor, approached pastors and lay leaders in white churches to join Shelby County Interfaith. He told them bluntly, "Don't do this if you think you're going to help those poor black folks. They don't want your help."

"The whites were shocked," Gerald remembers. Instead, Gerald encouraged them to examine their own interests and ask themselves what they would get out of joining the effort. When we make ourselves servants, we not only ignore our own needs but often presume that we know what others need and fail to really listen.

It's hard even to define one's self-interests without interacting with others. As the philosopher Bernard Crick observed, "The more realistically one construes self-interest, the more one is involved in relationships with others."[14] And certainly it's often impossible to realize our self-interests without incorporating those of others. So effectiveness in public life depends on developing relational self-interest—our own interests as they are linked to those of others.

Relational self-interest isn't always easy to see. It evolves as our awareness grows.

"Let's face it. When we started, everyone was a NIMBY [believer in "not in my backyard"]. Well maybe not everyone—just 99.5 percent of us!" said Diana Steck, a young woman who developed an active public life through the Pennsylvania Environmental Network. In front of her colleagues, she described how many of them began with a narrow view of their own interests: "People come in [to the Environmental Network] asking what you can do to help me with my problem. It's self-preservation. But something happens along the way. People think they are totally alone. But they discover they are not alone. They see the problem is much bigger than their problem. Their view broadens. It's a definite process."

COMPARING THREE REASONS FOR ENTERING PUBLIC LIFE

Service	*Selfishness*	*Relational Self-Interest*
Reflects the belief "I want to do for others."	Reflects the belief "I have to look out for myself."	Reflects the belief "I want to live well and fully in a community that works."
Is reactive to others (focuses on what others need).	Is reactive to internal needs and unreflective (focuses on what I need).	Is proactive and reflective (focuses on all I care about—family, faith, career, justice, and other important matters).

Cont'd

Service	*Selfishness*	*Relational Self-Interest*
Is defined by me.	Is defined by me.	Develops from dialogue and interaction with others.
Develops empathy but can foster paternalistic attitudes.	Provides short-term material or other gains.	Develops reflection, empathy, critical thinking, knowledge, and hope.
Sometimes offers recognition.	Sometimes offers visibility.	Offers recognition, visibility, and meaningful relationships.
Can increase self-respect.	Does not increase self-respect.	Increases self-respect and respect from others.
Permits limited creativity; can relieve immediate suffering but sometimes fails to address the roots of that suffering.	Permits limited creativity; shapes communities in ways that often have negative consequences.	Permits unlimited creativity; shapes community life in ways that benefit long-term community health.

■ ■ ■

Shedding the disempowering ideas blocking the emergence of effective democracy doesn't happen simply by deciding to act—though that's the beginning.

Becoming powerful is something we learn, like baseball or ballet. We learn by doing and by reflecting on our doing. Yes, human beings are innately social creatures, highly dependent on one another, but we're not born *effective* social creatures. While virtually all of us have the potential to listen, to communicate well, to imagine ourselves in the shoes of others, to resolve conflict creatively, and to envision a better society—we do not all realize that potential.

To manifest power means learning—not just when we're kids in school but as a lifelong journey. On our Web site you'll find some initial suggestions for learning and practicing ten "arts of democracy"—from active listening to creative conflict.[15] We gain power as we hone the arts of engagement, not as an onerous duty, but as a key to the joy of living.

Living Democracy presumes a capacity for human attention far beyond what the dominant worldview takes for granted. In the old understanding of democracy, we can sleepwalk. We can trust the magic of the market, and we can (optionally) vote. But in the more powerful new democracy emerging, we pay attention to the consequences of our actions. We pay attention not just because we should. We pay attention not because someone tells us to. We pay attention because the more we do, the richer our lives become and the more we discover that we truly can create the world we want.

PART TWO

DEMOCRACY GROWING UP

You too are merely approaching democracy.
But you have one great advantage: You have been
approaching democracy uninterruptedly
for more than 200 years.

VACLAV HAVEL[1]

Despite breathtaking change popping up all around us—from the overthrow of apartheid to the shock of 9/11—sometimes things still feel stuck.

Life is change, we know that. But it can be hard nonetheless to see that yes, as a people, we are stretching the fabric of rules and expectations that once fit us. And we are easing—inch by inch—into a newer, more fitting garment.

In Chapter Four, "Our Coat," I look at four "measures" of the old—four assumptions that have come to define our economic and political life—and suggest how each is being altered, remade to fit new realities. We assume, for example, that a free market equals capitalism equals democracy when the meaning and shape of each of these organizing principles is actually in play, taking new forms to meet new challenges.

From there, in Chapter Five, "The Elephant," I zero in on the knot at the center of our economic life—the corporation. Corporate power can feel huge and immovable. But even at this epicenter, more is in motion than meets the eye.

4

OUR COAT

new times, new measures

We might as well require a man to wear still the coat which fitted him as a boy, as civilized society to remain ever under the regimen of their barbarous ancestors.

THOMAS JEFFERSON, 1816[1]

Jefferson reminds us that history doesn't stop.

We create our world from moment to moment. But not just any whichaway. We create our world from the templates we carry around in our heads and bring to life through our society's institutions and our everyday habits. Thus to experience our power to bring forth the strong, healthy communities we want, we must raise those templates to conscious awareness. We can then contrast what we assume to be "given" with the deeper reality of change that might not meet the eye.

Here I'll consider four of the "givens" that shape American society. They span both political and economic life—two realms that we typically imagine as separate but are in fact inseparable. They are, to use Jefferson's charming metaphor, the measures that define our coat. We'll see that none is as fixed as we thought.

FOUR CONSTRICTING MEASURES

Misfit One: Just two political parties—that's the American way.

Misfit Two: We can't limit campaign spending—that's denying free speech.

Misfit Three: Leave the market alone! The free market brings us all prosperity.

Misfit Four: To keep generating wealth, corporations must consider only the financial bottom line.

misfit one: just two political parties—that's the american way

It was November 1, 2004, and I was standing on a suburban Philadelphia commuter train platform passing out campaign flyers when a young man in a suit brushed by me with a nasty scowl on his face. "They're all crooks," he muttered.

This fellow, I can say with confidence, wasn't about to rush to the polls the next day. He was telling me I was wasting my time because neither party was any good. And likely he felt there wasn't much he could do about it. Americans go along with a two-party premise despite half of us saying, in a recent survey, that we'd really like more than two choices on the ballot.[2]

Perhaps these Americans feel that two parties aren't enough to capture the breadth of American sentiments. Or since almost two-thirds of Americans believe that corporations wield too much power, maybe we feel that both major parties are more beholden to them than to us.[3]

I recall meeting President Julius Nyerere of Tanzania on a visit there in the late 1970s. He teased me about my country's political system while defending his own one-party state. "You Americans, you have a one-party state, too," he said laughing, "only in your typical, extravagant American style you insist on having two of them!"

I had to laugh, too, although I do see significant differences between the two major parties. Nonetheless, I admit to sharing a bit of the brusque Philadelphian's disdain—the sense that neither really represents me.

The problem is that plenty of Americans critical of both parties get worried when a third-party candidate, such as Ralph Nader, jumps in. They rightly fear that voting for him or any third-party candidate could end up putting in office the *less* desirable major-party candidate.

While many Americans feel stuck, it's worth noting that our two-party stranglehold is an anomaly. In Germany, five major parties participate in parliament; in Sweden, it's seven parties; and in the Netherlands, eleven. In fact, in most of Western Europe, the former Soviet Union, and in a majority of the emerging democracies of Eastern Europe, a party can win a certain minimum of the national vote—in some countries as low as 4 or 5 percent—and still participate in the government.

Europe's much higher voter turnout may mean that citizens there feel freer to vote their conscience without fearing their votes will be wasted. Considering all this, you might not be surprised that none of the dozens of countries moving to a representative form of government over the last half century have opted for the U.S. two-party, winner-take-all approach.

But even if America is not about to embrace a parliamentary, multiparty system, are we stuck?

What if here, right now, you could vote for a political party addressing issues you care most about *and* not have to risk "wasting" your vote on a sure-to-lose third party? Or even worse, worrying that your vote could help elect the less desirable of the two major-party candidates? Might you just go for it and become a voter again?

Many people living in New York State are, including some who haven't voted for decades. That's what the seven-year-old Working Families Party is discovering. Its membership—mainly working-class and low-income people concerned about deteriorating wages, housing, health care, and schools—has been growing each year.

And so has its clout. With us, says the party's official literature, you have a "protest vote that counts."

The Working Families Party attributes its success to what it calls its "secret weapon": *fusion voting,* which permits candidates to appear on more than one party's ballot line. Fusion—also known as cross-endorsement—was common in America until the end of the nineteenth century. It's now legal in seven states and up and running in New York and Connecticut. With effort, it could spread.[4]

"Fusion" means the Working Families Party can run its own candidate chosen by members to fight for their priorities or it can put another party's candidate on its ballot line. For the most part, the party has cross-endorsed Democrats, but occasionally it's backed a Republican. It has also run its own candidates when there seemed to be a fighting chance of victory.

Main-party candidates see that Working Families' votes now sometimes provide the victor's edge. To a main-party candidate whose victory in part relied on votes tallied on the Working Families line, the party can convincingly argue that he or she should pay attention to the concerns of its voters.

Without its own ballot line, the concerns of the Working Families Party would remain invisible. With them now made visible, the political landscape starts to shift.

In 2004, the Working Families Party's efforts succeeded in raising the statewide minimum wage for all workers, meaning that *one million* of New York State's low-wage workers got a $2-an-hour pay raise. Republican Governor George Pataki vetoed the bill, but remarkably, a majority-Republican Senate overrode him—something that could never have happened without the broad grassroots support the Working Families Party had drummed up.

"People would get excited when we gave them something that they could do," said Patrick Welsh, head of the Westchester County chapter of the Working Families Party. "Our members went door to door. We'd say to people, 'Here's a pen and a blank piece of paper. Say, "Dear Senator," and write a letter in your own words.' We'd tell them, 'This letter is worth five hundred typewritten form letters.'"

Elsewhere, the party has tipped the balance for campaign finance reform and new state health and education investments. And Working Families was key to breaking a thirty-year gridlock over rewriting the state's harsh and impractical drug-sentencing laws.

Last summer, I greeted the executive director of Working Families, Dan Cantor, outside his office on Third Avenue in Brooklyn. At that moment, my daughter Anna, who lives only blocks away, pulled up on her bike.

"Great to meet you," she said. "You guys really helped me in the last election. I didn't know enough about all the candidates for local and state offices, but I share the values of the Working Families Party. So I voted straight WFP."

Dan beamed. "That's just what we want people to do!"

"I believe people are decent," Dan, a warm but serious man in his forties, told me. "They want things to be better, but they feel manipulated," he added, as the elevator climbed to his no-frills fourth-floor office.

"To get involved, people need to trust that they are getting good information. And they trust other people like themselves."

The Working Families Party was founded by people "just like themselves," said Dan, who's been executive director since the beginning. Those founders include the Association of Community Organizations for Reform Now (ACORN), with 175,000 low-income members nationwide; the union movement; and former members of the New Party.

In the late 1990s, Dan said, people asked, "Wouldn't it be nice if workers had a party of their own?" The party now has roughly five thousand dues-paying members, another forty thousand onetime contributors, and twenty thousand registrants, plus—the most important piece of the effectiveness puzzle—seventy affiliated organizations across the state.

With each statewide election, the WFP share of the vote inches up. In 2003, the party helped garner enough votes to assure victory for all thirty-three candidates it endorsed in New York City elections; and in ten contests, it provided more than 10 percent of the votes. That year, the WFP also elected its own New York City council member, the first win for a third party in over a quarter century.[5]

Before Working Families, "I was a Democrat," Larry DeAngelis, forty-six, told me, "because there was no other place to go. But I could see, [the politicians] talk great to get your vote, but once in office, they forget about you."

Larry works for the Communications Workers of America, and when the union helped create the Working Families Party, "I realized," he said, "now I could reach our members on issues they cared about—their families' basic security."

I pushed Larry as to why he couldn't do this as a Democrat.

"Most people are disgusted with both parties. No matter what they do, they feel their voice doesn't count. But the Working Families Party option gives me a way to talk about universal health care, progressive taxes, raising the minimum wage, housing. It gives me an 'in' to incite them enough to start believing again.

"In the WFP, you can be a Republican and hate Democrats and never vote for one. But if you really believe in an issue, you can vote WFP.

"This is a big part of my life now. I even ran for office and got 46 percent of the vote in a Republican district.

"I've really grown as a person," Larry volunteered. "Knocking on doors, I've met people I would never have had the opportunity to meet. You go into some parts of this county, and you see the unemployment, the terrible housing. And you see that people have just lost faith in the system.

"I can talk to a hundred people, and if their eyes light up—even two of them—it's like somebody's being reborn. I just got a call from an old friend. He said, 'I told you I was going to do it, and I did. I voted.' This was the first time in twenty-two years," Larry told me with unmistakable glee.

Back with Dan Cantor in his sunny Brooklyn office, what he really wanted me to understand is that the Working Families Party is not just a set of good ideas and a ballot line. It is people.

"Our party is based on organized groups of people, people who are learning that democracy means not just freedom from something but freedom to participate. To be heard," he said.

"People love to learn stuff," he added. "We brought all the chapter leaders together for a weekend seminar. We learned the skill of targeting voters, electoral planning, fundraising, lobbying. They feel like they are 'on the inside' for the first time.

"Our interviews with candidates where we decide whom to endorse are open to members. Sometimes eighty show up. They tell their stories. They have a sense of power.

"We know the other side has endless cash. The only thing we have is skill, determination. And now that we can turn out as much as 10 percent of voters on our ballot line, the candidates get to be attentive."

Dan told me that he'd been trying to make democracy work since he graduated from Wesleyan University in 1977. And what he's learned is that "we have to change the rules of the game." Starting where fusion voting is already legal, we "could have a Working Families Party in five, six, seven states. Instantly, we'd have a real effect on the Democratic Party."

On the train heading back to Massachusetts the next day, I felt like one of those "born-again citizens" that Larry DeAngelis ignited, wondering how my state could get our own Working Families Party off the ground.

Fusion voting is just one innovation that's springing us free from the two-party lockdown.

Another is instant run-off voting, also a way to escape the danger that voting one's heart could actually help elect the candidate you least want. In an instant run-off, voters mark their top two or three choices on the ballot. If no candidate has a majority, the candidate with the fewest votes is cut out, and all ballots get counted again. This time, ballots whose number-one choice was dropped now get the next-favored one counted. This continues until there's a clear majority winner.

Australia, Ireland, and the United Kingdom use the instant run-off, and now five American cities have joined them, including San Francisco. With it, citizens can "vote their hopes, not their fears," says former congressman John Anderson, once a third-party candidate himself.[6]

These strategies—instant run-offs and new parties built with fusion voting that involve and represent working people—aren't pie in the sky. They are already offering wider choice on election day and helping pry the dominant parties from the corporate grip.

misfit two: we can't limit campaign spending— that's denying free speech

Almost nine out of ten Americans believe that big companies have too much influence on Washington politics, according to a recent Harris poll.[7] And we're aware that part of the power they wield comes from helping decide who gets elected in the first place.

The more costly campaigns become, the more weight corporations and wealthy individuals carry.

Spending by congressional candidates has doubled in just ten years, to over $1 billion.[8] And in 2004, presidential candidates and their national conventions spent another $1 billion, up by more than half in only four years.[9]

Smaller contributions—$200 or less—shrank from a third to about a fifth of campaign contributions between 1996 and 2000. Donors of gifts exceeding $200 rose in importance, providing over four-fifths of the total. They represent *just one-quarter of 1 percent* of all Americans.[10]

And the big bucks work their magic: In the 2004 Senate race, 91 percent of winners outspent their opponents, and in the House of Representatives, it was 95 percent.[11]

For so many Americans, money in politics is such old news that even numbers like these hardly cause a stir. How to make the threat real?

In 2003, a CBS *60 Minutes* exposé showed journalists waltzing right through open gates to tanks of deadly chemicals at one of the fifteen thousand chemical plants in America, many of which lack security against terrorists. If those tanks were hit, millions would die, but how many Americans realize that federal oversight of these high-risk plants was quashed by the lobbying of the $450 billion chemical industry?[12]

Or consider that throughout the 1990s, pharmaceutical manufacturers poured more than $108 million into campaigns for federal candidates and their parties while the Food and Drug Administration approved twice as many drugs in half the time it used to take to review them.[13] Meanwhile, the number of drugs recalled for safety concerns has spiked, and hundreds of people have died while taking drugs that were later pulled from the market.[14]

Corporate influence in Washington hurts us in countless ways, but one is especially direct: tax breaks, subsidies, and other welfare for corporations and wealthy special interests cost each American household $1,600 a year![15]

For decades, citizen reform groups such as Common Cause and Public Citizen have struggled to limit the influence of money in politics through legislation. But as soon as reformers would slap closed one loophole, another would pop open! Because cleanup efforts have so far failed to remove money's grip on our democracy, some Americans throw up their hands. In the end, many resign themselves to "the best democracy money can buy," as in the title of Greg Palast's best-selling book.[16]

Making the challenge of real reform more difficult still, the 1974 Supreme Court ruling *Buckley* v. *Valeo* declared that caps on campaign expenditures "limit political expression at the core of our electoral process and of First Amendment freedoms."[17] In this ruling, the Court conflated the right to spend and the right to speak, with the result that only the sound of money gets heard.

Over time, though, citizens have learned what doesn't work—caps on contributions—and have found what *does:* a more democratic approach, one removing private wealth from the picture altogether. In six states, citizens are proving that we do not have to settle for the best politicians money can buy.

"Clean money, clean elections" laws or citizen initiatives have passed in Arizona, Maine, New Mexico, North Carolina, New Jersey, and Vermont.[18]

Now in races for state offices in Maine and Arizona, the state provides money for candidates who commit not to use private funds—except for a little seed money to get started. In these two states, which have pioneered "clean money" elections, candidates must collect a certain number of $5 contributions from voters in order to get on the ballot. In Arizona, it's four thousand contributions of $5 each for a gubernatorial candidate and 210 contributions of $5 each for a state legislative candidate. The grassroots, meet-the-voters effect of these laws is a sharp break with the norm in most states, where candidates court only a wealthy elite.

The impact has been astonishingly quick and measurable.

In the four years after the 1998 clean elections law passed, the number of candidates and voter turnout in Arizona went up by a quarter, and the number of minority candidates rose substantially.

In 1998, in eight out of ten races, candidates with the larger war chest won, but by 2002, only 2 percent of races were affected by disparate funding.[19]

Only four years after the reform, fully half the members in Arizona's house of representatives were men and women who'd taken the "clean money" path, accepting only public funds. Since four-fifths of Arizonans believe that contributions influence votes, one can now assume that Arizonans feel they've at least gotten half their representatives back—looking out for them, not for wealthy contributors' interests.

In Maine, the effect has also been immediate: After dropping for years, the number of candidates seeking legislative seats has been rising since public financing kicked off in 2000. Today 83 percent of the state senate and 77 percent of the house are made up of legislators who ran clean.[20]

"All the trucking companies were in my committee room. But I know I haven't taken a penny from the companies and they know that, too," the chair of Maine's senate labor committee, Beth Edmonds, told a reporter in 2003. She was describing the effect of clean elections on her during debate on a bill to require trucking companies to pay drivers overtime. "None of them have any ownership of me," she said.[21]

Who knew? Most Americans still see campaign finance reform as a cruel joke.

Not Marge Mead of Sun City, Arizona. Marge, seventy-five, a mother of eight with ten grandchildren, took her first college class when she was forty-two and got her master's degree at fifty-one. After years of teaching, "I was tired of correcting freshman compositions," she told us, "so I retired, and my husband and I moved here." She felt like a fish out of water until she attended a meeting of the Sun City Democratic Club; soon Marge became a precinct and state committee person. She joined the League of Women Voters.

In 1996, several League leaders were going to be away for the summer, and Marge was asked to fill in at meetings to shape a law to clean up campaigns. "I was pretty ignorant about details of the law," Marge said, "and ignorant about politics in general."

But she felt strongly about money's corrupting power, about what she called "candidates selling their souls." She summed up the problem this way: "It stands to reason that there's going to be quid pro quo. Big campaign donors aren't in it for altruism. They don't consider their money a contribution; they consider it an investment." (And a pretty sound one, too.)

So Marge went to the campaign finance reform meeting as a stand-in.

"I walked in and said, 'Who's taking notes?' 'Well, we're all taking notes here and there.' And I said, 'You should have someone taking minutes because this is a historic happening. And you can't remember all the nuances of discussions.' So they asked, 'Will you take the notes?' Being an old secretary, I knew shorthand and typed quite well. So I became the secretary."

Marge's insistence on having formal minutes may be the act that launched what she called her "latest incarnation, that of political activist"—a citizen leader in a critical battle for democracy.

"I was in awe of all the ramifications of writing an initiative we hoped would become law," she told us. "It was a new concept and rather radical. I was amazed at the dedication of other members of the coalition.

"At first, I felt insecure. The law is complicated. But I traveled all over the place, talking to various groups, church groups. I went to Glendale Community College, where I had been an instructor, and talked to social studies classes. It was exhilarating, and I became increasingly confident."

To bring the Clean Elections Act to a vote, the coalition backing it had to collect 10 percent of the number of votes cast for governor in the previous election—that was 112,961 signatures. "We collected the signatures, and when it came to the vote, we squeaked by with 51 percent," Marge said.

The law took effect in 1998, and for the first time, "clean" candidates went door to door to collect small contributions.

"When I went out in my precinct," Marge said, "and asked for $5 contributions, candidates walked with me. People would open their doors and say, 'Here's an actual live candidate!'

"These contributions mean people feel invested: 'I've given $5; I have every right to contact this person if he or she gets elected.' People are more apt to vote because they're invested. They're more apt to vote because there's more than one name on the ballot; there's competition."

Predictably, wealthy narrow interest groups, accustomed to buying the attention of politicians, have battled clean elections every step of the way. In Arizona, bankers, developers, and corporate lobbyists—calling themselves No Taxpayer Money for Politicians—spent half a million dollars trying to get a dubiously worded question on the 2004 ballot to kill clean elections.[22]

They failed.

Now armed with proof of clean elections' impacts, citizens are pursuing initiatives in more than thirty states and already crafting legislation in fifteen.[23]

Though still invisible to most Americans, the clean elections movement is gaining momentum. Will Americans soon be forced to pack in their cynicism?

misfit three: leave the market alone! the free market brings us all prosperity

The idea of the "free market" is about as American as apple pie; and that's a big problem because—sit down, hold on—there is no such thing.

The free market doesn't exist.

Of course, market exchange is as old as human society. What doesn't exist, as noted in Chapter Two, is an automatic mechanism—the "magic of the market," in Ronald Reagan's alluring words—that emerges and functions on its own to create prosperity for all. In complex societies like ours, markets that work to create wealth for all are the product of democratic governments. The market *depends on* truly representative government—an obvious point that is lost on those who see the market and government in eternal battle.

Also, a market can be organized in various ways, but here we've been taught that there's only *one* way: Make business decisions using a single criterion—maximum return to shareholders. So every decision returns wealth to people who already have it.

Hmmm. Didn't anyone play Monopoly as a kid?

Why would anyone be surprised that the richest 1 percent of American households now control more wealth than the bottom 95 percent combined?[24] Or that five people—members of the Walton family, who own Wal-Mart—have in only forty-three years come to own more assets than the yearly income of a quarter of a billion people![25] With shareholder return as the single driver of the market, wealth accumulates to the point that many people are too poor to participate in the market at all.

We've been made to believe that this game of concentration—corporations growing bigger and bigger by gobbling up others—"is fundamental to the success of capitalism because it weeds out the weak and allows the fittest to survive," Robert Hinkley, an investment lawyer, stressed to me. "The theory," he says, "is that all this results in lower prices for everyone and from this society benefits." But he went on, "What it really does benefit is a select few who know how to play this new game while it threatens almost everyone else."

The truth is, the market depends on us—on our acting as citizens to create the conditions for it to work.

Throughout our history, citizens in values-based political movements have risked their livelihoods and their lives to establish democratic "boundaries" around the market. They've put a floor of decency under workers' wages—both because it is morally right and, of course, because, as Henry Ford understood, poorly paid workers can't expand the market, they can't buy what they produce.

The understanding that a market needs value corrections because it doesn't, *by itself*, lead to fair or sustainable outcomes goes back at least to biblical times, when at "jubilee" every seven years, property got redivvied up. In our own history, Thomas Jefferson's distress at extreme inequality, which he said brought "misery to the bulk of mankind," led him in 1785 to argue that "legislators cannot invent too many devices for subdividing property."[26]

Just over one hundred and fifty years later, Franklin Roosevelt sounded a similar note, declaring that equal opportunity in the polling place isn't enough for democracy, that citizens "must have equal opportunity in the marketplace," which government must ensure.[27]

That was 1936, and for more than four decades, advances to equalize economic opportunity can be counted in unemployment insurance, GI loans, medical help for elders and poor people, college loans, job training, job stimuli, food stamps, Social Security, veterans' benefits, the minimum wage, and more. Even the interim Iraqi constitution that the U.S. helped write calls on government to provide "employment opportunities to the people."[28]

But for the past thirty years, we've heard a particularly strident and insistent countermessage of the antidemocratic current described in Chapter Two: "Taming the market is un-American."

Some hear that drumbeat in a 1971 rallying-the-troops memo by Supreme Court Justice Lewis F. Powell. Any alternative to the unfettered market meant "bureaucratic regulation of individual freedom—ranging from that under moderate socialism to the iron heel of the leftist or rightist dictatorship," he wrote in a stern warning to the U.S. Chamber of Commerce.[29] He singled out Ralph Nader as a particular threat, though at the time all Ralph had done was save us from exploding Corvairs.[30]

Powell's call to action spawned a master plan to convince Americans that *any* measure to keep in check vast accumulations of wealth or *any* policy to ensure wide access to the market—from the minimum wage and capital gains taxes to inheritance taxes and antimonopoly action—is not only counterproductive but virtually immoral.

Far Right foundations and their wealthy donors have gone all out to convince us these freedom-enhancing policies are actually bad for us, pouring $1 billion into Far Right, tax-exempt think tanks and media campaigns in the 1990s.[31] Plus over $35 million a year is poured into spreading the message on college campuses through, for example, student newspapers—and tens of millions more into academic programs.[32]

But as attacks on democracy's foundation intensify, many newly activated citizens are reviving the tradition that sees economic opportunity as being just as essential to our freedom as political rights.

They are angry that working full time in the world's richest country isn't enough to live in dignity and health. One out of every five jobs in the United States will not lift a family of four out of poverty, and more than a quarter of all working families are low-income.[33]

Citizens across the country are saying that if "the market" doesn't offer workers a wage on which families can live in dignity, then it's up to the government to ensure that it does. But the federal government has let the minimum wage lose more than a quarter of its value in the last twenty-five years.[34]

This setback has sparked a grassroots movement that I, for one, could never have predicted a decade ago. It is the campaign for "living wages" above the federal minimum, what the Working Families Party has pursued so successfully.

In Los Angeles, a successful living wage campaign lifted ten thousand people above the poverty line; and it turns out, all taxpayers benefit.[35] The Los Angeles law, says one study, could cut in half public subsidies to workers and their families whose wages were so low that they couldn't afford health care and other basics.[36]

I'll tell more of this story in Chapter Seven.

Citizens are also taking another, parallel track to make sure that government protects values that the market cannot. They are deeming certain activities off limits to corporations. Passing laws or state constitutional amendments, they are putting "values boundaries" around the market, saying that some things—hair dryers and cars—may be commodities, but other things aren't. Land, our health, and thriving rural communities are too central to our nation's well-being to be treated as commodities.

That's the spirit I picked up talking with local farmers over many cups of coffee at Little Oscar's diner near Minneapolis in early 2004. Their clear sense of their democratic right to say no to huge, corporate factory hog and dairy operations impressed me. They see these behemoths unfairly driving family farmers under and polluting air and water. As Minnesotans, they know the risks: In 1997, just one manure leak at a corporate hog factory farm killed 690,000 fish in their state.[37]

These rural citizens, many lifelong Republicans, are building their power through the grassroots Land Stewardship Project.[38] They told me they've stopped twenty-nine factory farms in eight years.

Now agribusiness corporations are trying to go over their heads, lobbying the state legislature to repeal townships' rights to choose family farming. Fighting back, they made clear that the issue is not just farming or even their livelihoods. The issue is democracy, as I take up again in Chapter Eight.

In defense of family farms—the most efficient farming system—nine states have passed laws or constitutional amendments blocking nonfarm corporations from owning farmland. In 1982, citizens of Nebraska—despite corporate opponents who outspent them fifteen to one—amended their state's constitution to read, "No corporation or syndicate shall acquire . . . title to real estate used for farming or ranching in this state, or engage in farming or ranching."[39] And for more than two decades, Nebraskans have successfully fought off attacks on this constitutional protection.

Counties in states with such anticorporate farming laws enjoy less unemployment, fewer impoverished families, and more farm income than those without, says a recent study.[40]

No surprise, then, that in other states, citizens are striving for similar protection.

To those in South Dakota in the late 1990s, farmer Charlie Johnson, forty-seven, told us, "It became clear the legislature wasn't going to do anything to protect farmers, and more importantly, to protect the environment."

So Charlie said, "Enough people finally got to the point of saying, 'Well, we're probably going to have to do it ourselves.'"

In May 1997, Charlie's organization, Dakota Rural Action, and allied groups proposed an initiative like Nebraska's to amend the state constitution. To get it on the ballot, they had only six months to gather the signatures of one out of every ten people who voted in the last election—more than thirty-two thousand signatures.

"I literally drove a tractor with one hand, talking and driving at the same time, racking up $800 cell phone bills," Charlie told us.

Two weeks before the deadline, they only had half the required signatures.

"It didn't look good for the home team, quite frankly. Then a story about the initiative appeared on the front page of the Sioux Falls *Argus Leader*.

"All of a sudden the rain came down from heaven! I think people must have realized that they had petitions sitting around in their desk drawer, or in the car, or in their purse. The mailboxes were just filling up with petitions. About a day out from our deadline, we met our goal.

"The other stroke of luck we had earlier in the campaign was that Garth Brooks came here and did nine or ten performances. We had to stand out in the snow and the rain on the sidewalks getting people as they were going into or out of the concert. Some people said we wouldn't have won without Garth Brooks!

"We had a lot of unsung heroes. Bill Sorenson was one, a former very active Republican from Sioux Falls. He was probably in his early eighties, but every day for six months he gathered signatures—at the post office or the courthouse. I think out of the thirty-three thousand signatures that we gathered, he was personally responsible for about six thousand of them.

"We won by 59 to 41 percent, and we won in all but two counties," said Charlie. "We had a huge amount of support."

Then, during the writing of this book, a court decision struck down the amendment—to Charlie's great disappointment.

Despite Dakota Rural Action's appeals in early 2004, the U.S. Supreme Court refused to consider the case. Corporate farm groups, led by the South Dakota Farm Bureau, joined with utility companies to convince the judges that concern about impeding "interstate commerce" outweighed South Dakotans' expressed interest in protecting family farming and the environment.[41]

Groups like Dakota Rural Action are not giving up, though. They're now working to beef up county zoning and to pass ordinances requiring that farm corporations put up bonds to cover harm they might do to the community. They're also helping build up family farm marketing and processing cooperatives to protect their interests.

From urban living wage campaigns to rural anticorporate takeover initiatives, citizens across political affiliations are coming together not to do away with the market but to ensure that it promotes healthy communities.

The market, it turns out, depends on us.

misfit four: to keep generating wealth, corporations must consider only the financial bottom line

It's been the gospel of capitalism: business focuses strictly on immediate profits for shareholders; it succeeds and then we all thrive in the wake. But with ice caps melting and hunger stunting millions, more and more people no longer swallow the "we all thrive" part of this equation.

In a recent survey in twenty-three countries, two out of three respondents said they "want companies to go beyond their historical

ARE CORPORATIONS OUT OF SYNC WITH AMERICA'S VALUES?

In 2000, a *Business Week*/Harris Poll asked Americans which of these two propositions they support more strongly:

1. "Corporations should have only one purpose—to make the most profit for their shareholders—and pursuit of that goal will be best for America in the long run."
2. "Corporations should have more than one purpose. They also owe something to their workers and the communities in which they operate, and they should sometimes sacrifice some profit for the sake of making things better for their workers and communities."

What's your guess as to how Americans responded?*

*95 percent of Americans chose option 2.[43]

role of making a profit, paying taxes, employing people and obeying all laws; they want companies to contribute to broader societal goals as well."[42]

Now it might be because I lived most of my adult life in Northern California—home to thousand-year-old redwoods, falling fast to fatten lumber company profits—but I would have pegged lumber companies as the last to acknowledge, much less act on, this broader sense of responsibility.

Worldwide, only 20 percent of old-growth forests remain, and in the United States, it's less than 5 percent. And even that is shrinking fast: every year, says the United Nations, an area the size of the island of Great Britain (England, Wales, and Scotland) is cut down.[44]

Aware of a global environmental crisis, 70 percent of Americans say they would prefer buying from companies with ethical environmental practices.[45] But how can regular citizens get across to companies that they should respond to these customers and that their responsibilities go far beyond shareholders?

For two decades, the Rainforest Action Network has been trying to figure it out. In 1998, RAN, a fifteen-thousand-member citizen action organization based in San Francisco supported by hundreds of thousands of unpaid volunteers around the world, targeted the home improvement colossus Home Depot.[46]

The way to get to logging companies was through their customers, RAN figured; and each year Home Depot sells wood worth $8 to $9 billion, much of it from old-growth and biologically fragile forests.

Rainforest Action hired a young man from New Jersey, Michael Brune, now thirty-three, to figure out how to get Home Depot to stop using old-growth wood.

Mike's environmental passion, he told me, got stirred as a teen. "I grew up on a barrier island off the Jersey coast, and the most exciting thing in the summer was going to the beach with my friends. But the summer I was fourteen, the beach closed. You couldn't even walk on the sand because of sludge and hypodermic needles. It sure ruined my social life! It affected my dad's business, everything. We were all outraged," Mike said.

"Then Greenpeace organizers came to help townspeople get the pollution stopped. And we did. It was a dramatic improvement in all our lives."

Now, years later, as leader of RAN's old-growth campaign, Mike led yearlong protests that even slowed the opening of new Home Depot stores. "Almost all of our ideas and most of our activities for the campaign came from thousands of volunteers—students, retirees, scientists—who want to be part of a global movement to protect old-growth forests," Mike told me.

But sometimes RAN got help from Home Depot insiders too. One manager confessed to Mike that "I make a good living, but I don't want to be on the wrong side of history. I want to take my daughters to see the rainforest in Ecuador someday; I want it to still be there. How I can help?"

So he slipped Mike information about where the company's wood was coming from, and he also turned over the secret code for using store intercoms, the ones in every Home Depot aisle.

Soon Home Depot shoppers began hearing a surprise intercom message: "Attention shoppers! There's a special in aisle 23 on products made from old-growth timber."

Home Depot was not amused and continued to resist demands for change.

Then came the culmination of RAN's campaign. It was the spring of 1999, and RAN's allies, As You Sow Foundation and Trillium Asset Management, placed a resolution before Home Depot stockholders that would require the company to phase out endangered wood. At the stockholders' May meeting, the "old-growth resolution" received just under 12 percent of shares voted—more than RAN expected but not a home run.

Soon, though, Mike told me, they got the word in confidence from an executive in Home Depot: After the meeting, Home

Depot's CEO, Arthur Blank, told his top executives that he didn't want to see any protesters at the next meeting. He even acknowledged that the protesters were making good points.

"Then one day in August it happened," Mike said. "A fax appeared in our office from Home Depot announcing its policy to halt buying old growth. We were completely shocked.

"We had a big party and then took out an ad in the *New York Times* to congratulate and thank them. Sure, we can be confrontational, but we want to acknowledge environmental leadership when we see it."

And in less than a year, RAN had gotten eight of ten of Home Depot's competitors to commit to the same standards. Next, logging companies became the target. And although this time it took RAN three years, they've begun to budge. They had to if their customers were looking for ethically harvested wood.

Responding to RAN's pressure, in 2003, the world's sixth largest forest-products company, Boise Cascade, became the biggest American company of its kind to announce that it would withdraw from old-growth forests here and move toward exiting all endangered forests worldwide.

Astounding to me, the company committed itself to abide by guidelines, in its words, "mapped by major conservation organizations and others through a consensus-building process."

Since 1985, RAN says, it has helped over four hundred companies—from Burger King to Bank of America—introduce environmental ethics to their bottom line.

After Boise, RAN set its sights even higher—on the world's third largest forest product company, Weyerhaeuser, which yearly logs seventy thousand acres on public (citizen-owned) land.[47]

RAN's tactics included nonviolent direct action—such as unfurling a huge, 2,500-square-foot "Wake Up Weyerhaeuser!" banner in downtown Seattle—ads, and of course, shareholder resolutions.

Part of Mike's job is sitting down at the negotiating table with Weyerhaeuser executives. I wondered aloud as to why a company as big and powerful as Weyerhaeuser would even bother to respond to a call from RAN, much less sit down and talk. But Mike reminded me: it's RAN's persistence—its campaign to get Mitsubishi to act lasted six years—and a growing grassroots movement that have built its power. The company knows RAN is not going away.

Weyerhaeuser not only agreed to come to the table but has flown top-echelon representatives to RAN's headquarters with a mutually acceptable mediator.

I confessed it was a bit of a stretch imagining a person so young and outside the world of big business going head to head with one of the planet's biggest corporations.

"I have to suspend all that talk in my head that I'm only thirty-three years old," Mike told me, hopefully not offended by my confession. "I have to forget that I didn't have decades of corporate training or know a lot about the industry.

"All that we really carry into the room is our pure sense—and scientific knowledge—that this is what the world needs.

"We like to go hard on the issues and soft on the people," he added. "We don't approach these negotiations with a desire to win so much as to find a way for [the companies] to win by addressing the earth's needs.

"To most of these executives, it's like, oh, yeah, the environment. Like it's the opera or UNICEF. The environment is just another cause. Most want to be good people, but they're not ready to roll up their sleeves and turn their company around. So our goal is to get the change started. And then keep it going.

"We're not finished with Boise or Home Depot. As good as the new policies are, neither company has yet achieved sustainability."

I explained to Mike my notion that any of us can learn the arts of democracy, such as negotiation, if we put our minds to it. So I was curious about whether he'd trained for these high-stakes encounters.

"Oh, yes, for meetings, I do a fair bit of preparation. There's one guy, Bill Ury, who is a personal hero. He does trainings with us, based on his book *Getting to Yes*. He teaches us how to use conflict, how to use agitation to get to a point of resolution, even collaboration.

"The biggest challenge, with Boise Cascade or anyone, is really trying to get inside the skin of people on the other side of the table, to deeply understand their perspective. Then we can couch our issues in ways they'll understand; it's what I do with my wife. It's basic human stuff."

Michael Brune understands that corporations' insistence that they can only act on what will bring their shareholders the biggest, most immediate return becomes untenable once we acknowledge the interconnectedness of life. With a little help from a lot of distressed citizens, Boise finally began to get it, too. Now the company's official environmental pledge begins by noting that Boise's success depends on "sustaining the resources that underlie the products," as if this were the most commonsense observation in the world.

After talking with Mike, I found myself wondering how those Home Depot shareholders now feel, all the ones who voted against that no-old-growth wood resolution. Sheepish, I hope.

As the following two chapters explore, the seemingly fixed and immovable core capitalist notion that short-term, shareholder return reigns supreme is beginning to crack.

NEW TIMES, NEW MEASURES

One: Citizens are effectively challenging the two-party straitjacket.

Two: Citizens are kicking big money out of politics, one state at a time.

Three: Citizens are putting boundaries on where the market can go in order to safeguard community health and even the market's health.

Four: Citizens are showing corporations that they must embrace values beyond highest immediate dollar return and can even prosper at it.

Continuing to view as immovable the four imagined "givens" surfaced in this chapter means denying ourselves full citizenship; failing to challenge them means that solutions to our most pressing human and environmental problems remain beyond reach.

Thankfully, yet unknown to most of us, people like Dan and Larry in New York, Marge in Sun City, Charlie in South Dakota, and Mike in San Francisco are finding the confidence and building the skills to crack these old, disempowering ideas. They are showing us that it's possible to reclaim politics from corporate manipulation and to place market exchange within boundaries that respect community values.

Their courage is proving to be contagious.

5

THE ELEPHANT

corporate power & the shape we give it

The corporation is an evolving entity,
and the end of its evolution is by no means in sight.

EDWARD S. MASON,
ECONOMIC ADVISER, TRUMAN WHITE HOUSE, 1968[1]

Chapter Four explored four framing "measures" constricting our society's well-being and showed how each touches on economic life—whether it's money corrupting politics or dogma destroying the market.

At the center of it all is a particular way of organizing economic life we call The Corporation. Over time, it's grown to become the proverbial elephant in our collective living room. That huge, awkward thing right in our faces, the one whose influence few want to own up to, much less challenge. Most of us aren't even sure how it got there, right in the middle of things.

With eighty-two corporations controlling over a third of our economy of 297 million people, and the sales of just one, General Motors, bigger than any GDP of 190 countries, the corporation can feel omnipresent, monolithic, unstoppable.[2]

In just the past decade, "eleven thousand independent pharmacies closed, and chain drugstores now account for more than half of all pharmacy sales," laments Stacy Mitchell, author of *The Hometown Advantage*. "More than 40 percent of independent bookstores closed during the same period. Barnes & Noble and Borders capture half of all bookstore sales. Local hardware stores are disappearing too as Home Depot and Lowe's now own nearly 45 percent of that market. Five firms now capture about 45 percent of grocery sales nationwide. Blockbuster rents one out of every three videos. . . .

"Most striking of all," she adds, "a single firm, Wal-Mart, controls more than nine percent of *all* U.S. retail sales. It is now the largest grocer as well as retailer in the country and captures more than one-third of the U.S. market for numerous products from dog food to diapers."[3]

The elephant seems to be swallowing everything in sight.

But what might happen if we were to see the corporation not as an "it" but rather as a pattern of relationships created moment to moment by our own beliefs and behaviors? What would change if we were to recognize that it exists in the middle of our living room because we keep walking around it, as if it really lives apart from us?

What could change if we realized that the corporation and the rules of property by which it functions are *of our own making*?

Thomas Jefferson and Benjamin Franklin were clear on this point. "Private property . . . is a Creature of Society," Franklin wrote in 1789, "and is subject to the Calls of that Society, whenever its Necessities shall require it."[4]

To Jefferson, property is governed by man-made laws, whereas access to the essentials of life is a "natural right," which takes priority. "Whenever there is in any country, uncultivated lands and unemployed poor," he wrote in 1785, "the laws of property have been so far extended as to violate natural right."[5]

■ ■ ■

But if on reflection you are a bit bewildered that our nation's Founders, in all their wisdom, didn't put some rules into place to prevent today's concentration of economic might—the modern corporation—I sympathize. Consider, though, how different things looked to them. At our nation's founding, the threat of economic tyranny—one person depriving another of life's economic necessities—was almost unthinkable: America's unique geographic endowment, our vast and fertile unsettled land, meant that any able-bodied soul could turn hard work into food and income.

Plus, democratic theory has lacked any framework for understanding the role of today's corporations in our public lives. "The large private corporation," writes the Yale political philosopher Charles Lindblom, "fits oddly into democratic theory. Indeed, it does not fit at all."[6]

Political theory has no place for entities that call themselves private but influence public opinion and the pace and safety of our workdays, our livelihoods, the air we breathe, the water we drink—in other words, that more powerfully determine our well-being than governments do.

Sometimes I wonder, though, whether corporations' splashing their names on our precious civic spaces—such as Houston's ballpark, "Minute Maid Park" (admittedly, an improvement over "Enron Field")—will speed up our awakening to their public nature.[7]

Our Constitution doesn't mention corporations. Why would it? How could our forebears have foreseen a populace transformed from the small, independent shopkeepers and farmers of their time into what we are today—employees of corporations with resources and influences over our lives so vast that they dwarf those of local and state governments and even those of entire nations?

To give credit where credit is due, though, Thomas Jefferson did at least foresee a misfit, as noted in Chapter Four. He feared "the aristocracy of our monied corporations," imagining the scary possibility that without built-in rules of democratic accountability, some economic players—the biggest—would run roughshod over the rest of us.[8] He got so worried, in fact, that he sought to include in our Bill of Rights protection against "monopolies in commerce," which as early as the 1790s he identified as a threat to freedom.[9]

His concern was ignored.

Jefferson failed, but we don't have to. He had worries; we have evidence.

We've seen Enron steal almost $2 billion from West Coast utility users and another $3 billion from the pensions of its own employees, as well as cause funds on which people of modest means depend to lose $50 billion when Enron stocks tanked.[10] We've sat by, unknowingly, while corporations have put three thousand chemicals—and those include only what the Environmental Protection Agency calls high-production-volume chemicals—into our air, water, and soil, with fewer than *half* ever tested for toxic effects on us.[11] And in the last few years, we've seen pressure from the coal and other industries succeed in gutting long-standing clean air laws, even as asthma rates have doubled in the last two decades.[12]

"PRIVATE" CORPORATE CONCENTRATION AND SOME PUBLIC CONSEQUENCES

- *Public giveaways enrich corporations*. Corporate influence has led our government to sell at $5 an acre or less a total of 3.5 million acres of public land—equal in size to Connecticut—containing billions of dollars' worth of minerals.[13] Through patenting or royalty-free mining, it's given away over $245 billion in public mineral reserves.[14]
- *Corporations avoid taxes so we take on more*. In 1940, businesses and individuals split the federal income tax bill equally; today corporations contribute less than 14 percent.[15] Plus, the federal government gives $125 billion to corporations in subsidies—equal to the federal income taxes paid by sixty million individuals.[16]
- *Global warming—we all pay*. In pursuit of private ends, corporations account for almost half—not even counting transportation—of the United States' emissions of

the main greenhouse gas, carbon dioxide.[17] By 2050, worldwide damage from the resulting global warming will cost $300 billion each year.[18]

- *Hazardous water cleanup—we will pay.* Agribusiness and chemical and petroleum corporations pump trillions of gallons of untreated wastewater, some of it hazardous, each year into eight hundred thousand underground "injection wells" around the country.[19]
- *Profits increase but workers' wages don't.* Since 2001, corporate profits have increased by 40 percent, but wages have stagnated.[20] In part as a consequence of lagging wages, Americans now put in 184 more hours a year than in 1969, and parents have 22 fewer hours a week to spend with their children.[21]
- *Concentration means drug companies profit at our expense.* By the 1990s, drug company profitability had jumped to nearly four times the Fortune 500 median, and Americans now pay twice as much as Europeans do for identical drugs.[22]
- *Low corporate wages make the public pick up the tab.* The country's largest employer, Wal-Mart, earns profits of $6.6 billion annually yet pays wages so low that its employees are entitled to $2.5 billion in public benefits.[23]
- *When unions are attacked, workers lose protection.* Median salaries of unionized workers are 25 percent higher than those of nonunionized workers.[24] But growing corporate power has unleashed increasingly cutthroat antiunion tactics. The result? Five decades ago, almost 40 percent of private sector workers were protected by unions; today, 8 percent are.[25]

the elephant grows yet remains perpetually immature

"When I first got out of law school in 1978," Robert C. Hinkley, a former New York attorney, told me, "hostile takeovers were still considered ungentlemanly by most Wall Street law firms and investment banks. But companies that did participate started to see how much they could gain."

Soon they "started to realize how much money they could make serving this market," said Bob. "So we now have an entire industry of well-paid financial managers trying to spot the next takeover targets. It's an eat-or-be-eaten world."

Bob is describing the Wall Street world since Reaganomics took hold in the 1980s. With Washington's friendlier view toward monopoly, corporate coupling flew into high gear. Mergers and acquisitions exploded in the 1990s, growing sevenfold from 1994 to 1999 to $1.4 trillion.[26]

Perhaps we shouldn't be surprised: all government resources used to protect us against monopoly power, $211 million, amount to what one big corporation spends just to launch a couple of new soft drinks.[27]

So what's my problem with an ever-bigger elephant?

Most obvious is that the bigger it grows, the more resources it has to twist democratic politics to its private ends and the more muscle to block workers' efforts to look out for their own interests through trade unions.

In addition, two "givens" of our economy help the elephant grow and shape its behavior, with alarming consequences for the rest of us.

For one, as currently organized, the corporation doesn't have to pay many of its bills. I know this sounds strange, but it doesn't have to pay for much of what it uses in, for example, clean air or water; and it doesn't have to clean up after itself. Economists call "externalities" these massive costs passed on from corporations to all of us. I've enumerated just a few of these "public consequences" of private power in the earlier box on corporate concentration.

Economists make externalities sound inevitable, but as we'll see, they aren't. They exist in large measure because we've set it up so that the corporation enjoys many rights and protections but lacks corresponding built-in obligations.

Second, unlike the other kind of elephant, which has a very good memory and strong community loyalties, all this elephant knows is short-term, self-centered thinking. What our society most needs, however, are long-term investments in such things as higher wages, worker training, renewable energy, and conservation.

The pressure against long-term investment is mighty. It's felt in the relentless expectations of Wall Street—whether the corporation's performance meets what financial analysts expect, quarter by quarter. I got a close-up look at this pressure because my partner, Richard R. Rowe, was the CEO of a large publicly traded company during the roaring 1990s.

"You live or die in any deviation from those expectations," Richard told me. If you don't meet "the numbers, you're at risk—of losing your job, of a hostile takeover, or of going bankrupt because financing dries up," Richard said. And rewards for meeting those expectations? A personal bonus—perhaps in the millions—lower-cost loans, and an improved position to buy other companies with your stock.

The speedup in corporate stock turnover has magnified this already destructive short-term pain-or-reward cycle. In the 1970s, 15 percent of stocks changed hands each year. Today it's more than half. "If you miss projections by a penny, the Street reacts," Richard said. "Your company instantly loses millions of dollars of value. The market is so bloody reactive. It's like an immature child; no adult behaves that way."

So fewer and fewer decision makers, farther and farther removed from our communities, come to control—reactively—everything from drugs to books to food.

Yet Americans have no framework with which to conceive of these unelected economic entities with power greater than elected governments. (It wasn't supposed to happen this way.) Moreover, the phrase "free market" is repeated so glibly so often that we become blind to how centrally controlled the market now is.

But it's not just the elephant's size and might that stumps so many. It's that we can't imagine something else—and we can't create what we can't imagine.

To feed our imaginations, the next chapter asks, what would a democratic economy look like? But first we must clear the way by recognizing that this elephant, the giant corporation, didn't just move in on us. We human beings built it.

The corporation takes its shape in five ways. In each, a mounting sense of urgency is triggering new ferment, demonstrating that what we made we can remake so that it no longer destroys what we love, what sustains us and our communities.

FIVE WAYS THE ELEPHANT TAKES ITS SHAPE

1. Statutes define a corporation's purpose, giving its board its marching orders.
2. Court decisions define corporate rights and protections.
3. Laws citizens enact through their representative bodies set "values boundaries" around the actions of corporations.
4. Shareholders' actions influence corporate choices.
5. A culture's norms and expectations shape corporate behavior.

None of these is fixed.

1. *Shaping the elephant: Statutes define a corporation's purpose, giving its board its marching orders.* Because corporations place maximizing shareholder return foremost—or at least claim to, even when managers are the big winners—I'd long assumed that the corporate statutes *require* directors to put shareholders' immediate gain first, without exception. In preparing this book, I read in an otherwise credible source that this mandate is even enshrined in federal law.

I was wrong and my source was wrong.

There is no federal law; corporations are chartered by state statutes. And no state instructs directors only to consider *short-term* shareholder interests. Short-term performance pressure, to keep stock prices up at all costs, comes in part from the threat of hostile takeovers if stock prices dip and from executives' fear of losing their jobs, as Richard Rowe noted.

In fact, it turns out that state statutes governing corporate charters are not set in stone.

The heightened threat of hostile takeovers, starting in the 1980s, encouraged more than forty states to amend their corporate statutes to bolster a corporation's defenses. The new wording permits corporate boards to consider the impact of their decisions on broader constituencies such as workers and the community—sometimes called stakeholders.[28] For example, in Pennsylvania, directors are explicitly not required to put the interests of one group—even shareholders—first.[29]

Skeptics may laugh, and they do, noting that corporate boards have not acted on this new "permission" to consider broader interests. On average, they ask, haven't corporations become even more reckless in their disregard of people and the earth?

Granted, on average. So far.

But what these statute changes *do* prove is that the corporation's marching orders, the statutes defining it, aren't diamond-hard. They can crack. They are alterable. Some citizen reformers argue that even if the changes so far lack teeth, altering corporate statutes *can* have real impact. They insist that holding corporations to community protection standards after the fact—as our environmental and workplace safety agencies are supposed to do—can never get us there. The DNA of the corporation must change, they argue, so that built into its purpose is consideration of the effects of its actions on the broader community.

Bob Hinkley is one insider whose experience drove him to this conclusion. He is the securities lawyer introduced earlier who in 2003 made his point with purposeful drama: he incorporated a company in Virginia under the name Licensed to Kill, Inc., with a charter explicitly stating that its purpose was to market tobacco products in a way that would kill nearly five million people worldwide every year.

When news leaked out, people got upset. So the Virginia State Corporations Commission defended itself, saying, "There was nothing we could do about it."[30]

Bob's point is that it *should* be able to do something about it!

So he and his allies are working, in effect, to insert a "do no harm" clause into corporate statutes. His reworded statute, what he calls "the Code," would allow the corporation to continue to focus on its shareholders' interests, "but not at the expense of the environment, human rights, the public health or safety, the communities in which the corporation operates or the dignity of its employees."[31] Bob and fellow reformers have helped introduce this approach in three state legislatures—in California, Minnesota, and Maine.

"These twenty-eight words in the Code would take away corporate directors' excuse for antisocial behavior—that they are only serving their shareholders. This change would make everyone in the corporation aware that their jobs consist of more than just making money," Bob maintains.

He draws a parallel with the securities industry. "Companies are forbidden by law to falsely represent themselves when selling their stocks or bonds to the public. And the approach is largely self-enforcing. They are very cautious. They don't like to take risks by even getting close to the line because they don't want to risk attracting a lawsuit—even one they might win." With a charter change requiring corporations to do no harm, a similar logic could come into play to affect corporate behavior.

The challenge to corporate myopia is taking off abroad too. In late 2004, Robert Debus, the attorney general of New South Wales, Australia, argued that it is "morally wrong" for corporations to use responsibility to shareholders as an excuse for betraying workers and the environment. What set Debus off was an asbestos maker using its shareholders' interest as its defense for not providing adequate compensation to workers sickened by its products. Debus seeks to remove that defense.[32] Now a government committee is taking up the question of whether Australia's Corporations Act should be revised to require directors to consider the broader community when making corporate decisions.

All this means that statutes giving the corporation its marching orders—and contributing to its narrow, antisocial focus only on shareholders' gain—are open to change. Indeed, a challenge is under way.

BURYING THE MYTHS THAT FEED THE ELEPHANT

- *Shareholders are not owners in any usual sense.* In a recent letter to ExxonMobil, an owner of the company's stock worth $470,000 wrote plaintively: "If the shareholder's vote does not count, how does that make the shareholders the owners of the company?"[33] The answer is, they aren't: most shareholder votes are nonbinding.
- *Less than 1 percent of the dollars traded on Wall Street fuels corporate operations.*[34] More than 99 percent simply moves from one speculator to another as half of all

stocks change hands within a year, often within hours. Corporate operations rely on borrowing, selling new stock, and retained profits.

- *Corporate directors often do not operate even in the interests of shareholders, much less the larger society.* Directors often rubber-stamp decisions to best enrich corporate management, leaving shareholders and pension holders the big losers. Witness Enron, WorldCom, Qwest, and Adelphia, to name a few. Directors of top U.S. corporations have let the ratio of average CEOs' compensation to workers' pay shoot up to 531 to 1—*thirty to fifty times* the norm in Europe and Japan.[35]

For an elegant argument on these and related points, see Marjorie Kelly, *The Divine Right of Capital* (San Francisco: Berrett-Koehler, 2001).

2. *Shaping the elephant: Court decisions define corporate rights and protections.* Over time, courts have wrapped corporations in many constitutional protections that real people enjoy. Now this might sound silly, for anyone can see that corporations aren't human beings.

Corporations are "artificial beings," observed the revered chief justice, John Marshall, in 1819.[36] They are legal constructs, they are immortal, and in many ways they shield the actual flesh-and-blood people involved from responsibility.

In the early 1800s, corporations were public inventions chartered by towns and states to carry out specific tasks, including road and canal building, for specific rewards. They possessed only the "properties which the charter of creation confers," wrote Marshall.[37] When their projects were completed, that was it. Their charters ended.

But railroad and other industrial giants pushed through the courts—beginning in the late nineteenth century and continuing today—a series of decisions giving corporations many rights belonging to real people.[38] They include free speech, freedom from unreasonable search, and the right to a speedy and public trial by an impartial jury, as well as protection from being prosecuted twice for the same offense.

The Fourteenth Amendment, passed in 1868, declares, "Nor shall any state deprive any person of life, liberty, or property, without due process of law; nor deny . . . equal protection of the laws." Its intent was to protect African Americans. But in the first few decades after its passage, over half of the six hundred cases citing it involved corporations and in only twenty-eight were African-Americans the principal party.[39]

These constitutional protections awarded to corporations—without citizens' becoming aware or debating the consequences—form a huge barrier to democracy.

Corporations have, for instance, used the Fourth Amendment's protection against "unreasonable search and seizures" to resist unannounced inspections of manufacturing plants, without which it is virtually impossible to ensure crucial environmental and worker protections.[40] In 1996, Vermonters overwhelmingly backed a state law requiring milk to be labeled if containing the questionable bovine growth hormone, Monsanto's rBGH. But grocery chains killed it, claiming that labeling violated their constitutional right "not to speak." [41]

Perhaps most devastating for democracy, corporations have successfully claimed free speech rights equal to those of citizens to influence the laws of the land. A 1978 Supreme Court case decided just after President Nixon appointed Justice Lewis Powell—whose searing probusiness memo I quoted in Chapter Four—assured corporations such rights even on matters having nothing to do with their business interests.[42]

Corporations have taken not just the right to *influence* lawmaking—with fifty-six paid lobbyists now in Washington for every elected officeholder—but even the right to *initiate* and organize lawmaking to benefit them.

In 2003, Contra Costa County, east of San Francisco, passed an ordinance to limit grocery sales at Wal-Mart's biggest stores in unincorporated areas. Wal-Mart's enormous wealth meant it could hire professional signature gatherers—paying them more than their own store employees!—and mount an expensive advertising campaign to place a referendum on the ballot to overturn the ordinance. In 2004, Wal-Mart won.[43]

Combining their constitutional protections intended for real people with their vastly greater resources compared to real people, corporations can trump the values, interests, and desires of communities.

One beautiful early spring evening in 2004, I headed southeast from Pittsburgh. My destination—Chambersburg and the home and workplace of attorney Tom Linzey in a newly converted dental office. Tom, thirty-six, is the powerfully articulate, outside-the-box founder of the nonprofit Community Environmental Legal Defense Fund. Enjoying a lasagna dinner, I chatted with members of a local citizens' group fighting a company that's threatened to construct a large limestone quarry and two plants within nine hundred feet of a grade school and many homes.

Around the table sat a half dozen of us, including Tom in shorts and T-shirt. Others were members of Friends and Residents of Saint Thomas (FROST) who were upset about the quarry—including a fellow in the dairy business, a teacher, and a new township supervisor, Frank Stearn, who reminded me a bit of Dick Cavett. He and his wife run the electronics store in town.

At the last minute, FROST chose Frank, a Republican, as their man to run for supervisor as a write-in candidate on an antiquarry platform. To the group's surprise, he won. But within months, the quarry company sent a threatening letter to the township supervisors, arguing that if as a supervisor Frank were to speak or vote on the quarry, the company's constitutional right to due process would be violated.

"It was very chilling. . . . It's your first day on the job, you come to work, and what you've run into is this kind of sledgehammer in your forehead," Frank told David Brancaccio on PBS *Now* in early 2005.

Initially, I thought I'd misunderstood. How could this happen in America? A corporation's threat silencing an elected official's voice on a public issue? But, I learned, it was true.

Frank recused himself on any matter related to the quarry.

Turning to Tom's law firm for help, the FROST group sued the company because its threats, backed up by its deep pockets, had robbed Saint Thomas citizens of their right to self-government. FROST also lodged a complaint against the state for violating the constitution by granting corporations rights that "abridge the privileges" of citizens.[44] The state rejected the complaint.

Sitting there at supper, taking in the budding trees I could see through a big patio door, I kept reminding myself that all great historical movements start modestly. No doubt Susan B. Anthony and Elizabeth Stanton sat plotting around many kitchen tables, too, although probably not in shorts.

So here we are, well over a hundred years after corporations began accumulating constitutional protections, with rural Pennsylvanians, among others, waking up and saying, in effect, "Wait a minute. Corporate rights cannot trump citizens' rights. What a crazy idea that is."

Later I talked with a farmer, Mik Robertson, forty, one of the 479 people living in Licking Township on the other side of the state north of Pittsburgh. He's a township supervisor, and the first time I tried to reach him, the road noise was so loud I could hardly hear. Soon I learned that in Licking being a supervisor means you're part of the town's snow-removing road crew.

Two years ago, Mik knew nothing about the legal rights of corporations. (Although, fortunately for his little town, he did know something about toxic contamination, having worked as a geologist.) But his legal education began when Licking was in a face-off with companies that apply sewage sludge—or "biosolids," as the companies prefer to call it—as fertilizer.

In 2002, Licking, along with scores of other townships, had adopted an ordinance requiring companies bringing in urban sewage sludge, from household and human waste, to register and pay fees. That way, the towns could inspect the sites and test the sludge to make sure it met state safety regulations. Concern was growing that sewage sludge could make people sick; it had been implicated in several mysterious illnesses and even deaths in Pennsylvania and elsewhere.[45]

Townships aren't allowed to set standards, Mik told me. That's in the state's hands. "All we can do is require testing." But for Mik, the state standard is far too lenient. From prior work as a geologist, Mik remembered that surface soils at hazardous waste sites had to be brought to no more than twelve parts per million of arsenic, for example. But in Pennsylvania, sludge for farm fields was allowed to have an arsenic concentration six times greater than that.

Mik was troubled.

Then, to add insult to injury, giant sludge-spreading companies sued tiny townships, including Mik's. The $300 million company Synagro Inc. in 2002 had claimed that even a nearby township's *testing* ordinance violated its constitutional rights. The township was forced to spend tens of thousands of taxpayer dollars defending its testing ordinance. It lost, Tom Linzey informed me later, and was forced to pay the corporation's attorney fees.

"But our township's code obliges supervisors, as it says, to 'secure the health, safety and welfare' of the citizens," Mik said. "So in 2003, to protect our original ordinance challenged by the corporation, we had to pass another one." It says simply that in Licking Township, "corporations shall not be considered to be 'persons' protected by the Constitution of the United States or the Constitution of the Commonwealth of Pennsylvania."

Mik's township and others are getting help from Tom Linzey's outfit in Chambersburg.

It was sinking in on me. Here a tiny, staunchly Republican township was thumbing its nose at over a hundred years of legal precedent. I asked Mik if he realized that he and the two other supervisors who unanimously approved the Corporate Rights Elimination Ordinance were making history.

Mik shot back: "We're not making history. History was made 225 years ago when the documents founding this country were written. The Founders said clearly that all men are created equal. Our basic protections were meant to apply to people. It's corporations that have twisted the meaning, through interpretations by the courts. What we're doing is simply a return to the very basis of America."

A year before Licking's action, nearby Porter Township had passed the country's first legally binding ordinance declaring corporations not to be "persons" with constitutional protections. By 2004, three municipalities in California had passed resolutions opposing constitutional rights for corporations.[46]

These localities felt pushed to the wall, forced to protect themselves by stripping corporations of legal personhood standing. But since most of us never thought of corporations as persons in the first place, declaring corporations nonpersons may be mystifying or even seem wacky.

These courageous people are, however, doing us a great service.

Their challenges wake us up to what's been lost by allowing the line to blur between a legal entity shielded from significant liability, narrowly interested and often gargantuan in size—the corporation—and real citizens.

The differences are huge. For one, democracy depends on citizens with loyalties—unlike those of corporations—that extend far beyond the monetary or even the material. The essence of citizenship is considering the present and future well-being of the wider community, as well as one's own. And there's plenty of evidence that's what American voters try to do.[47]

Corporations are useful tools for generating wealth, and they need certain legal protections to function. But democracy is dead if corporate interests trump the interests and values of citizens. Now coming to light, this travesty—the corporation's use of constitutional protections to overpower and silence citizens—may ignite new fires under Americans to retake our elected bodies from the corporate pocket.

Mik and Frank and other brave Pennsylvanians are telling us it's high time. It's high time we saw the danger to democracy in court decisions conferring rights intended for citizens on what Justice Marshall observed are "the mere creature of law." It's high time we engaged in the long-overdue debate about the appropriate line between corporate protections and obligations and those of citizens.

3. *Shaping the elephant: Laws that citizens make through representative bodies set "values boundaries" around the actions of corporations.* In a society soaking in "free market" rhetoric, it's hard to keep in mind that as Chapter Four stressed, corporations operate within values boundaries that we ourselves erect. They can't sell babies or organs from live human beings, at least not legally. Some boundaries are global. In 2003, even as big tobacco corporations kicked and screamed, two hundred citizens' groups, along with the World Health Organization and leaders from forty-six African countries, succeeded in establishing the earth's first public health treaty: the Global Tobacco Treaty. It bars tobacco corporations from advertising or interfering with public policymaking. So far, sixty-four countries have ratified it—but just as with the Kyoto Protocol to limit global warming, the United States isn't among them. Yet the new values boundary around tobacco will save millions of lives.[48]

In 1970, for example, we created the Environmental Protection Agency to set standards corporations must honor. From reducing dangerous pollution in the Great Lakes to getting the harmful pesticide Dursban out of home care products, EPA standards have helped protect our personal and community health. And for two decades, car manufacturers have been required to meet fuel efficiency standards. Here too lies huge potential impact: upping the standard by less than three miles per gallon could eliminate U.S. dependence on Persian Gulf oil![49]

Of course, states and localities also set values boundaries around what corporations can do. Notwithstanding Wal-Mart's successful political maneuver in Contra Costa County, California, other towns—Belfast, Maine, and Hailey, Idaho, for example—have set size limits on Wal-Mart and other superstores, which can be as big as five football fields and run local retailers out of business.[50]

So the question is not *whether* we do or don't set standards that shape corporate behavior but precisely *what* aspect of life we as a people consider too important for our common well-being to be left to private interests alone to decide.

In that light, as I noted in Chapter Four, Nebraskans since 1982 have barred nonfarm corporations from purchasing farmland. Nebraskans are saying, in effect, that the individual farm seller's right to sell to anyone is less important than the right of farm communities and all Nebraskans to enjoy the benefits of family-owned farms.

With similar logic, the town of Arcata, California, in 2002 chose not to allow the number of chain restaurants in town to expand beyond the current nine.[51] The town as a whole will flourish best, it decided, the more locally owned businesses there keep profits close to home, rely on local suppliers, and offer more diverse dining choices.

A sense of the appropriateness of boundaries is dawning in the nick of time, for our particular version of capitalism was born in an era of limitlessness in which we believed there really was an "away"—that place nature offered us of endless, free disposal. So we ended up with an economy in which less than 10 percent of the materials used in production actually end up in products. The rest, more than 90 percent, is "waste," most of it degrading our ecological home.[52]

Our awakening may not yet be evident on any big scale in the United States, but in Europe and Japan, a sea change is well along. The European Union requires carmakers to take back discarded cars and to reuse or recycle 85 percent of the material contained in them. Mercedes brags that it can now dismantle a car for recycling in four hours.[53] The Netherlands boasts an 86 percent recycling rate for cars. Denmark has phased out aluminum cans and replaced them with glass bottles that are reused.[54]

Limits are now visible. We now know that there is no "away," so of course, citizens are saying, a producer must take responsibility for the life of each product it brings into the world.

Starting in 2005, European Union countries require companies to take back used electronic products and recycle or reuse at least half of the materials.[55]

In 1991 Germany took the lead in requiring companies to assume responsibility for their packaging. In an ingenious approach, companies pay a fee to carry the "Green Dot" trademark on their packaging. It means they are cooperating in a collection-for-reuse system in which their fees cover the costs. The less packaging, the lower a company's fees, so the Green Dot system has led to reduced per capita packaging.[56] By 2003, German companies had overshot their initial recycling goals, with 90 percent or more of aluminum, glass, and plastics recycled.[57]

Now licensed in twenty European countries, Green Dot has become the world's most widely used trademark. When will it hit America?

In Japan, a 2001 law mandates that washing machines, TVs, air conditioners, and computers all be recycled by manufacturers. Producers must pick up part of the tab.[58]

Sadly, U.S. corporations have killed hundreds of attempts to introduce producer responsibility: Coca-Cola and Pepsi have vigorously opposed even bottle recycling, which has made it into law in only eleven states. Too bad, for the ten states with long-standing "bottle bills" recycle 80 percent of their beverage containers—adding up to more recycled bottles than in all the forty states without bills combined.[59]

As in campaign reform, Maine is ahead of the pack. Recognizing that mercury pollution regularly makes freshwater fish unsafe to eat in eighteen states, Maine in 1997 passed a landmark "take back" law requiring automobile manufacturers to pay for collecting and recycling mercury switches from old cars.[60] In 2003, automakers fought back, arguing that the law unconstitutionally interfered with interstate commerce and impinged on their Fourteenth Amendment rights.

The carmakers lost.[61]

Since there is no place out of sight and mind into which we can throw things, planetary health may well depend on just how quickly we can redesign our economic life, including the corporation itself, to mimic nature's way. In nature, there are no "emissions" released to no good end; everything, including "waste," is put to good use by another living process.

Today, practical visionaries across disciplines are building on the work of pioneers like E. F. Schumacher, author of the 1973 classic *Small Is Beautiful*, to show the way.[62] They include Amory and Hunter Lovins, founders of the Rocky Mountain Institute, who show how we can thrive using a fraction of our current energy budget; Günter Pauli, who writes convincingly about zero-waste production; economist Herman Daly, who makes the "steady-state" economy real for laypeople; and green architect William McDonough, whose goal is buildings that breathe like trees.[63] They and many others are showing us that what are called zero-waste or zero-emission, closed-loop economies are no pipe dream.

In Chapter Eight, you'll peek at a Milwaukee closed-loop city farm with its own heat source, much of it relying on worms!

Since this lifesaving direction requires investments that may not bring *immediate* returns, however, it requires laws setting new values boundaries around corporate actions. The Far Right, in rejecting the Kyoto Protocol on global warming, for example, argues that all boundary-making and standard-setting undermines our economy—despite evidence that conservation and renewable-energy strategies generate more jobs, not fewer.[64]

At a deeper level, what such a negative casting ignores is the deep human need precisely *for* limits—for what are limits but guidelines, a coherent context for human conduct, for helping us choose?

Seen in this light, a feeling of relief might come over us.

It is unbounded, endless choice that makes people crazy. If little kids need rules to know they're loved and to be happy, perhaps all human beings share some of that need. Limitlessness becomes meaninglessness. Nature's very real, nonarbitrary, and universal laws can offer a sense of boundedness, clarifying our options and imbuing them with meaning. All this sparks creativity—as we see in innovative new technologies bursting forth as the European Union responds to product responsibility laws and the Kyoto Protocol. Recently, even some Fortune 500 companies have begun to defy the Far Right and push for mandatory limits on carbon dioxide emissions.[65]

Letting go of human-made laws of economic dogma in which we've sought relief from choice, we may discover that we do better as we embrace the real laws of the biotic community—using them to help us set boundaries around our own and corporate behavior.

4. *Shaping the elephant: Shareholders' actions influence corporate choices*. Although we call shareholders "owners," most aren't in any usual sense of the word. For the most part, their votes aren't binding, but big shifts in shareholder behavior do have effects. And huge changes are laying the groundwork for shareholders to have greater and more positive influence.

"In 1995, the world changed," Alexandra Lajoux, chief knowledge officer for the National Association of Corporate Directors, told me. That was the first year that more than half of the equity of

U.S. companies was held not by individuals but by institutional investors, mainly pension funds.

And "the trend continues," she notes, "so that in the largest public companies, institutional investors typically own 70 percent of the stock value."

This means that "American capitalism has entered into a fundamental new stage," according to William Greider in *The Soul of Capitalism*. Ordinary citizens have "a source of leverage they have never before possessed in the history of American capitalism."[66] Workers' retirement savings, now $6 trillion, account for the largest pool of investment capital in the United States.[67]

Greider cautions, however, that theirs is still "passive power."[68] But what if it were to spring to life? Pension funds could bring interests and perspectives to counter the short-term narrow view of the individual company. "In fact, as fiduciaries, pension funds are supposed to act *only* in the long-term interests of their future retirees."[69]

Take, for example, investments in research or worker training—not necessarily in the short-term profit interest of a given company but very good for our economy. Pension funds would want to encourage such investment because even if workers trained by one company quit and go to a competitor, their training still serves the pension funds' long-term interests in a healthy economy.

So a huge question for democratizing capitalism is whether pension fund beneficiaries will pressure their funds to consider their real, long-term interests. The next chapter suggests that they are beginning to try.

When billions of dollars in pension funds got wiped out in the collapse of Enron in 2001, "it sent a shock wave through the market," said Tim Smith, senior vice president of Walden Asset Management in Boston. "In the past, if you didn't trust management, you just sold your shares in the company. The trend now is to use your leverage as an active shareowner to *change* the company."[70]

With this in mind, pension fund directors might well ask themselves, Am I fulfilling my legal responsibility if I buy stock in companies that might lose money by or be sued for contributing to global warming—estimated to cost over $300 billion annually in environmental damage by 2050?[71] Should I buy stock in food corporations promoting products known to contribute to skyrocketing obesity and its diseases, such as Type II diabetes, the treatment of which now costs nearly one out of every ten health care dollars?[72]

An answer of no could trigger corporations to rethink their myopic profit seeking.

The potential for positive pension fund influence on corporate behavior hasn't been lost on certain labor leaders.

One is Sean Harrigan, who in 2003 took the helm of the California Public Employees' Retirement System, renowned as the largest and most energetic public pension in exercising its fiduciary responsibility to pensioners. CalPERS has used its shareholder votes to protest over-the-top executive pay, to support antidiscrimination policies, and to pressure companies to bring outsourced jobs back home.[73]

He didn't last long.

Republicans emboldened by George W. Bush's election to a second term ousted Harrigan from CalPERS in 2004. But one of his defenders pointed to an irony: "President Bush talks about transitioning to an ownership society," noted Frederick E. Rowe, chair of the Texas Pension Review Board. "Well, we already have an ownership society, and the people who are owners don't know they're the owners. The owners are the people in America who hope to retire, and who are retired, and who depend upon a stream of income that their deferred investments generate. And they don't have many advocates."[74]

The deposed Harrigan had been one, Rowe argued.

Even if Harrigan is still a relative rarity, Alexandra Lajoux is convinced that the rise of institutional investors, like pension funds, has brought real change. "You now hear the phrase 'long-term shareholder value,'" Alexandra notes. "It's very common. Recent thinking is that the duty of directors is to the corporation as a whole," she added, "not just the stockholders but the creditors, the employees, and even the communities in which they work—in other words, the whole corporation.

That's huge.

But even accepting for a moment capitalism's more narrow premise that corporate directors are responsible to safeguard only the interests of shareholders, one nagging question won't let go:

As a corporate board member, why isn't it the height of fiduciary *irresponsibility* not to get your company pronto into the small but expanding club of socially responsible businesses, since—as the following chapter reports—multiple studies document a positive link between social responsibility and profitability? Or, asked another way: A much-touted fact is that intangibles—corporate governance, environmental risk, employee morale, company reputation—comprise a *huge* part of a company's value. All of them, it seems, relate to long-term concerns, not to the next quarter's profit.[75]

So would not fiduciary responsibility to shareholders require boards to avoid any risk of damaging such intangibles?

Some are getting it, but perhaps the pieces don't yet add up to a coherent direction because capitalism's institutions—corporate statutes, corporate boards, laws governing corporate behavior, and the stock market itself—are living through a schizophrenic era: Wall Street–determined "stockholder value" is still driving companies' short-term, destructive behavior, and New York bankers are still encouraging mergers and buyouts that might buoy stock prices but add no real value to the economy. And at the same time, some companies are taking a *very* different route to success.

It is an era not of rigidity but of ferment.

5. *Shaping the elephant: A culture's norms and expectations shape corporate behavior.* It's true that in our culture—shaped by corporate-owned media, probed in Chapter Nine—corporations help determine

the options we feel we have. But it is also true that what corporations are and do reflects to some extent the attitudes, beliefs, expectations, and actions of citizens, those they have to please to stay in business.

In Sweden, McDonald's serves milk, ice-cream cake, and beef that are strictly organic. It recycles 90 percent of its restaurant waste.[76]

But in the almost fourteen thousand McDonald's in the United States?

Nada organic.

And waste recycling in McDonald's stateside? Impossible even to know.

Why the difference? In the early 1990s, Swedes ranked McDonald's near last among admired companies.[77] Protests and leafleting at McDonald's were reported in a dozen or so Swedish towns and cities. Soon after, McDonald's hooked up with Natural Step, an international research and advisory organization helping businesses take a systemwide approach to sustainability. It went organic and tackled its waste. In no time, McDonald's became one of that country's most admired companies.[78]

The company's about-face didn't happen because Swedes suddenly passed new laws. Rather, McDonald's registered the views of Swedish citizens. In 2002, in the United Kingdom, McDonald's said it was not "looking at" organics because "we don't get any enquiries from customers."[79] Two years later, the company reversed itself.[80] Presumably, inquiries started coming in. And as obesity hit the headlines in the United States, McDonald's suddenly developed a taste for salad.

Some gutsy citizens are also shifting norms using attention-grabbing actions like those of Rainforest Action's in Home Depot stores, described in Chapter Four. In addition, the accompanying box suggests the range of recently emerging efforts—most citizen-initiated—to make corporate practices more transparent and to establish standards to raise the bar. They're gradually shifting expectations and norms.

MONITORING CORPORATE PRACTICES, SETTING STANDARDS, CHANGING NORMS—IT'S A START

- In 1988, the *Exxon Valdez* disaster motivated socially responsible investment firms and public pension funds to ally with leading environmentalists to create the Coalition for Environmentally Responsible Economies (CERES). Its sixty-four member companies, including some giants like Sunoco, General Motors, and Bank of America, all accept its ten principles of environmental accountability.[81]
- Since 1995, Verité, a tax-exempt "social auditing organization" based in western Massachusetts, has conducted thirteen hundred factory audits in over sixty countries and offers companies remediation and training to improve working conditions.[82]
- The New York City–based Social Accountability International in 1996 launched SA8000—a standard for corporate practices based on International Labor Organization and other human rights conventions. Among the twelve signatories are Avon, Dole, and Toys 'R' Us. By early 2005, it had certified over five hundred plants in forty-five countries—including those of Eileen Fisher in New York and Chiquita in Costa Rica.[83]
- The Fair Labor Association, founded in 1998 by members of the White House Apparel Industry task force, includes 191 colleges and universities committed to buying from suppliers meeting its fair labor standards.[84] Fifteen companies are currently certified "FLA-compliant," but companies do most of their own monitoring.

Complaints about working conditions are not investigated by an outside group unless the company agrees to it. The companies on FLA's board can veto any decision.[85] Nonetheless, the association has stirred some movement: even Nike, whose CEO, Phil Knight, once threatened to withdraw his donations from colleges joining the Worker Rights Consortium (discussed later in this box), is following some Natural Step principles and starting to recycle (including soft-drink bottles into garments!) and is phasing out vinyl.[86]

- In 1998, students from thirty colleges and universities gathered to launch United Students Against Sweatshops, which has since spread to 160 campuses.[87] They called on their schools' administrators to assume some responsibility for improving the inhumane working conditions of those who make the schools' licensed sports uniforms and sweatshirts. In 2005, its "Unthinkable Undrinkable" campaign to hold Coca-Cola responsible for violence against labor organizers in Colombia succeeded in getting Oberlin, Bard, and Wake Forest colleges to ban Coke. The group argues that the Fair Labor Association's very existence provides a cop-out for schools not willing to commit to independent monitoring.
- In 1998, the Amsterdam-based Clean Clothes Campaign network finalized its own model code of conduct for apparel makers. It's been signed by large trade union associations and hundreds of citizen organizations as well as some companies. The campaign's goal is a uniform code with workers themselves involved in its monitoring.[88]

- In 1999, Dow Jones climbed on board with its own global "sustainability index," tracking the top 10 percent of environmentally conscientious companies worldwide.[89]
- In 2000, United Students Against Sweatshops launched the Worker Rights Consortium to monitor plants, independent of corporations. With its 135 affiliated colleges and universities, the consortium enforces its codes of conduct and works to empower sweatshop workers to report rights violations.[90]
- Corporate disclosure, some believe, itself has power to affect corporate behavior. Started in 2002, the United Nations' Global Reporting Initiative provides a uniform disclosure policy covering a company's economically, environmentally, and socially sustainable business practices.[91]

Of an estimated sixty-four thousand global corporations today, however, a mere 3 percent release corporate social responsibility reports disclosing their social and environmental performance. One challenge is the sheer number of industrywide codes with few specifications accepted industrywide, laments the United Kingdom's ActionAid.[92] Increasingly, however, companies are adopting the uniform Global Reporting Initiative standards for their reports—a welcome trend, but still barely a start.

Alongside the monitoring efforts such as those described in the box, citizens are using "power shopping"—customer boycotts and "buycotts"—to raise the bar, as Chapter Six explores. Means are thus proliferating to make corporate behavior more transparent and to acknowledge the more ethical players. As they gain ground, citizens reward them with patronage. Citizens can also punish transgressors, just as the Swedes did when they spurned McDonald's.

labor standards ignored by government

But before rushing on, let's stop, back up, and ask, Why are such corporate codes and social audits needed in the first place?

The Fair Labor Association, on its Web site, answers that the "growth of the global economy has outstripped the mechanisms for regulating labor rights."[93]

Wrong.

Mechanisms for standard setting—including International Labor Organization conventions, which most of the world's people would consider basic to human dignity—haven't been "outstripped by growth." They've been *bypassed* by governments, especially ours, answering to global corporations, not to their citizens.

If governments were listening to their citizens and protecting our rights—if democracy were truly alive—the other oversight bodies described in the box wouldn't be needed. That is why a focus of this book is on citizens working toward such genuine democracy.

the power of our expectations

My goal in this chapter, however, is to remind us of the many inseparable forces shaping the corporation. And one of those is the power of the citizens' attitudes. Beyond anything corporate statutes, court-granted protections, or laws can achieve, every society creates a *climate of expectations* to which corporate behavior responds.

Increasingly, for example, Americans view Wal-Mart's approach—putting lowest price above worker, community, and ecological well-being—as an unstoppable tidal wave. It's the only way a corporation can survive in today's cut-throat world of international competition. This expectation itself has power; it's in part why Wal-Mart can go on resisting unions (except for government-controlled ones in China)[94] and, as noted earlier, can pay its workers so little that together they are eligible for an estimated $2.5 *billion* in tax-paid public services, from health care to food stamps to unemployment insurance.[95]

To grasp that Wal-Mart's approach stems not from an iron law of international economics but in large measure from what our expectations "normalize," consider Costco. It pays about $5 an hour more than Wal-Mart, offers a solid health plan, and doesn't send jobs offshore. Twenty percent of its stores are unionized. Yet mainly due to low turnover, its labor costs are only 7 percent of sales, while Wal-Mart's are 12 percent.[96]

Next, consider Europe's Carrefour, the world's second largest retailer. Carrefour has 9,600 stores in thirty countries, but unlike Wal-Mart, Carrefour is committed to eliminating genetically modified food and supporting organic farming. It sells furniture certified by the Forest Stewardship Council, an independent nonprofit organization accrediting companies that use responsible forestry practices.[97] Instead of wiping out local producers, it creates partnerships with local small and medium-sized businesses. (No suggestion here of perfection, of course: in early 2005, Thailand retailers charged the company with unfair practices.)[98] Carrefour also makes its energy use and environmental performance public, and it says it's working on reducing its ecological impacts.[99] Many of its stores are unionized, and Carrefour audits its suppliers in China, India, and Bangladesh to make sure they comply with International Labor Organization codes.[100]

Undoubtedly, some of these policies flow from laws governing European corporations. But not all of them.

To Americans, Wal-Mart's cut-costs-no-matter-what approach explains its success. To Europeans, Carrefour's community responsibility at least in part explains its success—$56 billion in sales in 2004 and a five-year average return on equity of a stunning 19 percent.[101]

In each case, the company is responding to what it believes is expected of it by the communities in which it operates.

THE CORPORATION'S SHAPE IS CHANGING

1. A movement is under way to rewrite corporate statutes to ensure corporate accountability.
2. Corporate rights and protections are being challenged, even in some very unlikely places.
3. In many states and localities, citizens are pushing elected bodies to set additional values boundaries around the actions of corporations.
4. Shareholders are joining together to exert real influence on corporate behavior, as Chapter Six explores.
5. New expectations are emerging that corporations should be accountable for the consequences of their acts, and some are responding.

The corporate form is dangerously disconnected from democracy and therefore from the consequences of its actions. The disconnect continues in part because we think a corporation is a thing we can't change.

It isn't.

A corporation is a set of relationships that determine how we relate to things, relationships that take their shape from at least five directions—corporate statutes, the courts, laws and conventions, shareholders, and the intangible but powerful norms created by our actions, expectations, and verifiable standards that citizens set and monitor. None is fixed or apart from us. Each is evolving.

PART THREE

DEMOCRACY AS A VERB

Democracy. It's not what we have, it's what we do.

BUMPER STICKER OF THE CENTER FOR LIVING DEMOCRACY (1990–2000)

Democracy is a way of living that thrives or withers in the actions of each generation. Living Democracy—the more inclusive and effective stage of democracy now emerging—therefore can't be described as one would an object; it can only be told as one does a story. So Part Three tells stories of democracy makers at work while also striving to frame the larger significance of their efforts.

Chapter Six, "Attention," focuses on the emergence of local living economies where citizens are paying attention to the power that can be theirs in everyday economic choices.

In Chapter Seven, "Action," the spotlight turns to the organized action of citizens. Many ordinary Americans are stepping out for the first time to bring about historic shifts in who makes decisions governing our well-being and happiness—from fair wages to affordable homes to reasonable lending rates.

In Chapter Eight, "Choice," I plough into the myths surrounding the food we eat and explore movements that are multiplying our choices by reconnecting farmers, eaters, and a healthier earth.

Finally, Chapter Nine, "Voice," explores who can speak and who can be heard in America. I tackle the myth that we are to blame for our debased media as I celebrate the new sounds of democracy connecting Americans with each other and with their passion for honest public talk.

6

ATTENTION

economics & everyday life

Business is about relationships. Money is simply a tool.

JUDY WICKS, WHITE DOG CAFÉ, PHILADELPHIA

If there were ever a poster child for humanized economic life, it is platinum blond, gentle-featured Judy Wicks.[1] Only she's not a child. Philadelphia restaurateur extraordinaire, Judy fifty-seven, has an exuberance for living that seems reserved for those who've discovered meaning and beauty by going after what they love—in Judy's case, attending to the real human beings and other creatures affected by her business choices.

Judy's White Dog Café is a downtown hive of activity, relying on renewable wind-powered elegance and local suppliers and linked to a range of community betterment initiatives.[2] It's a tony eatery and a welcoming community learning center, all at the same time.

"When I eat the food from my restaurant," Judy told me, "I think of the farmers out in the fields of Pennsylvania picking the fresh, organic produce they will bring into town that day. I think of the goat herder, Dougie, who says the cheese is better when she kisses her goats' ears! When I drink my morning cup of coffee, I think about the Indians in Chiapas, Mexico, who grew the beans. Business is about relationships. Money is simply a tool."

Judy works to bring forth what she calls local, living economies, believing that a democratic economic life is not only possible but essential to fulfilling deep human needs. Economics, à la Judy, isn't about, or at least isn't only about, distant, anonymous links in supply chains. It is about real human connection.

And Judy's not alone. The Business Alliance for Local Living Economies that Judy co-founded has hundreds of member businesses in nineteen chapters nationwide—from Seattle to Salt Lake City—working to build viable face-to-face economies from the bottom up.[3] I'll discuss its Local First campaigns in a moment.

But "Judy economics," as a friend of hers recently dubbed Judy's vision, doesn't neatly fit our dominant mental categories. In Judy's living economies, whether as shopper, business owner, investor, or worker, we pay attention. And from that attention, we "attend to" the impact of our choices on the community and the earth itself, whether it be the chemicals we use to manufacture a product, the detergent we buy to wash dirt from our clothes, the fund to which we entrust our retirement savings, or the wages we pay an employee.

And the cool thing is, we enjoy it. As we pay attention, our lives grow ever richer in meaning, and all our senses thank us.

That's what Judy Wicks's life seems to be saying.

How different this is from the dominant mental map! Society bombards us with cues that the only thing we should really pay attention to is financial gain.

This narrow focus on self is supposed to make us happy, when actually, research here and abroad tells us it's just not true: those who "strongly value the pursuit of wealth and possessions report lower psychological well-being" than those less preoccupied. The more materialistic among us also report experiencing more depression and ill health.[4]

economics as relationships

But what do we mean by economics in the first place?

It's easy to think economics is about things—some*thing* I own, some*thing* a corporation sells. But I've gradually come to see what

Judy is telling us: that economics is not about things, really. It is about relationships. Money or a corporation is a way of organizing our relationships with each other and only secondarily about things. Even something like the home we own is both a thing and also a set of relationships with everyone from our lender to our neighbor to our town's property tax collector to our heirs.

And those relationships of economic life we take for granted today in America—where just five corporations, for example, control over four out of ten of all grocery purchases and corporate branding covers everything from stadiums to socks—are brand new.[5] They have appeared in a blink of historical time. The question is not whether they will change but how they will change.

These reframing thoughts add up to power: Power for us. For if economic life is truly a web of human relationships ever evolving in response to our choices, *then we are creators*. Each of us participates in—or might someday participate in—at least six economic relationships. Some we experience every day.

SIX ECONOMIC RELATIONSHIPS IN A LIVING DEMOCRACY

Relationship	*Who Participates Now?*	*Who Has a Voice and Is Accountable Now?*	*Who Has a Voice and Is Accountable in a Living Democracy?*
1. Consumer	All of us	All of us, but in proportion to how much money we spend and how deliberately we spend it	As income is more fairly distributed, more people have a voice; as consumers make more deliberate choices, we gain a voice

Cont'd.

Relationship	*Who Participates Now?*	*Who Has a Voice and Is Accountable Now?*	*Who Has a Voice and Is Accountable in a Living Democracy?*
2. Worker/ earner	Most of us	Owners, employers, managers	As worker participation, worker ownership, democratic unions, and self-employment spread, workers have a greater voice
3. Voter influencing economic policy via elected representatives	Only half of us exercise our right to vote; the potential remains for virtually all of us to participate	The makers of the biggest campaign contributions	All voters equally, as candidates gain more equal access to voters and voters gain more equal access to candidates and officials
4. Investor/saver	People with surplus income	People with the most money to invest	As wealth is more evenly spread, more of us will have a voice; those who direct savings in keeping with their values will have a say too
5. Direct shaper of economic policies for government or corporations	Very few of us	People with the most dollars for lobbying and the Federal	More and more citizens with vision, shared public values, and skills in

		Reserve and other government agencies	using the arts of democracy to shape policy
6. Owner/ employer	Few of us	The top 1 percent of American households that own more than the bottom 95 percent combined[6]	More and more of us as worker ownership expands and as wealth becomes more evenly spread

But there's one big problem here. The idea that we can use our economic choices to create vibrant local economies flies directly in the face of corporate "globalization."

If you asked a thousand Americans to define globalization, many, maybe most, might respond with images of interconnectedness—music from Mali, food from India, prayer flags from Tibet.

The economist Joseph Stiglitz in *Globalization and Its Discontents* defines globalization as "the closer integration of the countries and peoples of the world," which sounds wonderfully—dangerously—benign.[7] The Pulitzer-winning columnist Thomas Friedman tells us that the current stage of globalization is "shrinking the world from size small to size tiny."[8] Distances are evaporating, he suggests.

How positive! No wonder many people are baffled by rowdy protesters in exotic spots shouting themselves hoarse about how terrible globalization is and even getting arrested to make themselves heard.

But we might benefit by listening for the essence of their concern.

First, corporate globalization in one sense is not drawing us closer together at all. It is distancing real people from the other real people on whom we are dependent. The lines linking us have become anonymous and virtually impossible to track. As corporations contract and "source" all over the planet, the people who bring us our food, clothing, electronics, and so much more become remote, faceless supply chains. A globalized economy means buying from corporations with tens of thousands of distant plants, many known only to the companies and sometimes not even to them.

A sense of common interest and natural human solidarity is harder to come by. It's easier for many to feel the plight of a sweatshop worker in South Central Los Angeles than one in Thailand, even though she may face an even more horrendous life.

Second, the term *globalization*, by focusing us narrowly on the *scope* of activity, may divert us from asking who is in *control* of that activity and therefore who benefits. It encourages us to jump right over the question of power.

Globalization's defenders swoon over growing interdependence, but *corporate* globalization brings deepening dependence as more and more people are forced to live with the consequences of decisions made by a handful of individuals sitting on the boards of global corporations, as well as by decision makers in the International Monetary Fund and World Trade Organization, dominated by corporate interests.[9]

Consider, for example, farmers in southern India whose livelihood and food sources have been destroyed because Coca-Cola is mining area groundwater for its bottling plants.[10] Or corn farmers in Mexico flattened by imported artificially cheap U.S. corn, subsidized by U.S. taxpayers but mainly benefiting General Mills and other big food processors.[11] Or the "outsourcing" of a projected 3.3 million American jobs over the next decade to economies where workers' rights are denied, pressing down wages here.[12]

Is this healthy *interdependence* or poverty-making *dependence*?

The march of globalization—understood as more communication and sharing across national borders—*is* unstoppable. And I, for one, am happy that it is. But corporate globalization—or what I prefer to call "global corporatism"—is not. We can each participate in challenging it, a centralized, inefficient globalism with ever fewer decision makers. We can cut a better path not from an antiprogress Luddite stance but, says the Italian businessman Lorenzo Becawtini, as a "rigorous reconfiguration of democracy that places power and creativity back into the hands of villagers and townspeople, providing them with as many choices as possible."[13]

In this democratic reconfiguration—Judy Wicks's local, living economies—we each play many vital roles.

power shopping

It took decades for the civil rights movement to convince the American people to think differently about race and to enact laws upholding the rights of blacks. Women worked seventy-two years finally to make it to the voting booth in 1920. But in only three decades, we can chart a radical shift in how millions of Americans think about their purchases. They are discovering that we "vote" when we buy. True, these votes are grossly lopsided—for the more money you have, the more votes you get. Nonetheless, our purchases are power.

Citizens are consciously, positively integrating part of their lives—their purchases—with their values.

Why the change?

Perhaps in the past it wasn't easy to see the consequences of spending choices. Now we're learning to see what's been invisible. We can even go online and readily calculate the environmental impact of our choices at http://www.myfootprint.org.

We are finding satisfaction in discovering that citizen and shopper are no longer a dichotomy. In fact, marketing analysts now dub a third of the U.S. population "LOHAS"—an acronym referring to lifestyles of health and sustainability.[14] Sixty-three million Americans now say they base their purchasing decisions on how products affect the world, and four out of five say they are likely to switch brands to help support a cause when price and quality are equal.[15]

coffee-conscious

Seventy percent of the world's coffee is grown by about fifteen million small family farmers worldwide who sell to intermediaries, often at prices as low as half the going market rate.[16] When prices paid to coffee farmers hit historic lows in recent years, hundreds of thousands of families became "coffee market refugees," losing their land and livelihoods.

Making the price collapse even more devastating, coffee profits had for some time been leaving the coffee-growing countries at an accelerating rate. Roughly a decade ago, a third of the coffee's market value stayed in producing countries; today, it has sunk to less than a tenth.[17] The winners aren't consumers but huge global food companies such as Altria (Philip Morris) that process and distribute coffee.

That was the end of this sad story—before, that is, Fair Trade burst forth. It's a movement launched in Europe in the 1980s to guarantee participating farmers a fair price, now $1.26 per pound and slightly more for organic—still a small fraction of what consumers pay. When the world price rises above this floor, farmers get more.

Fair Trade depends on an impartial third party certifying that farmers are paid the Fair Trade price and work within democratic co-ops where farmers make decisions together. In 1999, the United States began to catch up with Europe when we got our own certifier, TransFair USA, a California-based nonprofit. You can spot its "scales of justice" logo on products it certifies.

In the six years since TransFair USA began certifying coffee, Fair Trade in the United States has seen an average annual growth of 75 percent.[18] Today thirty-five thousand stores sell Fair Trade–certified products.[19] Many supermarket chains carry limited Fair Trade product selections, including Wild Oats, Stop & Shop, Kroger, Safeway, and Whole Foods.[20] Costco has just converted *all* its private label coffee to Fair Trade. Similar efforts are under way to help growers of cocoa, tea, mangoes, pineapples, grapes, and bananas. Across the globe, Fair Trade efforts—still in their infancy—are already benefiting over eight hundred thousand farmers and their families in fifty countries in Latin America, Africa, and Asia.[21]

What is motivating this movement?

People.

Take Lina Musayev. Now twenty-three and a student at George Washington University, Lina moved here with her family from Azerbaijan in 1992.

Ten years later, her life took a big turn. It was July 2002, and Oxfam America selected Lina to be one among the ninety-two students from thirty colleges it brought to Boston for CHANGE, a leadership training with intensive exposure to some of the biggest global challenges.

"Farmers from Guatemala came to talk to us," Lina explained. "They told us what Fair Trade meant to them. We got the real story from the roots. I didn't know anything about the coffee crisis. I didn't know it affected twenty-five million people. So when I heard about Fair Trade, I thought, 'This is incredible. It's working. It's making a difference.'

"The next day, literally, my friend Stephanie, who'd come from Georgetown University, and I founded United Students for Fair Trade.

"She and I are really close. We made a great team.

"First we had to present the idea to the other students in our training. We said, 'You are the students. You are the base for this organization. We had to get them to pledge to go back to their universities and find people to bring Fair Trade coffee to their campuses.

"The response was awesome. Oh, my God, very positive, most followed through.

"Once school started, we took our first steps, defining our goals, who are our allies, whose support is necessary, what do we need to make a presentation and to whom. It was incredible. We had to talk to the president, vice president, head of dining services.

"I decided to start from the bottom with a petition saying students wanted more Fair Trade coffee, and we got two thousand students to sign. That's out of ten thousand. It worked. We sent a letter to Starbucks. We pushed for Fair Trade coffee at every university event, like teachers' meetings."

In only three years, George Washington passed a resolution that calls on all on-campus vending outlets to serve 100 percent Fair Trade coffee, and similar measures have passed at Smith College, Harvard, UCLA, and UC Davis. At least fifteen campuses now serve only Fair Trade coffee.

Putting in long hours on what she calls her "passion," Lina learned to be a persistent negotiator. "We got in touch with Dunkin' Donuts. I was on the phone constantly with both sides—the campus and the company. It was a huge campaign to get Dunkin' Donuts because of its espresso Fair Trade coffee. Java City is also on our campus. They came out with a whole line of Fair Trade. That was a big success!

"We're going to try to get the dining service to offer Fair Trade fruit—bananas and pineapples—and chocolate, too.

"I have an amazing team working with me—ten very active students. Our whole George Washington group is over a hundred, most of them pretty new to political action.

"This year at freshman orientation about three hundred people signed up at our Fair Trade table, a huge difference from our first year.[22]

"When I started, I'd ask people, 'Do you know what Fair Trade is?' and I'd get a lot of blank faces. Now, it's 'Oh, yeah.' So I know it's not going to end when I leave here.

"Ten years ago, my family came to America from a communist country. I'm Jewish, and there my family had to hide our religion. When we got here, the community was so helpful to us.

"So maybe my passion for doing what I'm doing is because I was helped. Also, I know it is not easy to make a living; my own parents work 24/7. And I don't think it is fair for people, like coffee growers, to work so hard to make Americans happy and not get fair pay. Americans don't realize that behind what they are eating and wearing are hardships."

I asked Lina what approach she'd found most effective in reaching students.

"The main thing is getting farmers themselves to come to the campus. Hearing the farmers, I see the students say, 'Oh, my gosh—I didn't know this.' Almost like I was!

"UFT was Steph's and my baby, but now it's completely out of our hands. This is hard, but it's also a good feeling. Right now we have students in Nicaragua, one is staying in a coffee co-op and really learning from the roots. Now with Fair Trade, they see kids can go to school and their families can pay for medicine. They don't have to live worrying day to day."

In only three years, the student Fair Trade movement Lina and Stephanie launched has spread to three hundred campuses.

Lina and Stephanie would probably find it hard ever again to view economics as simply anonymous transactions dealing with objects. They are helping shape an economy that's about people, people relating with each other—fairly.

HOW LINA, STEPHANIE, AND THEIR COLLEAGUES DEFINE THEIR MISSION

Students inspiring citizens and consumers to shape a global economy based on human relationships that are just and that nurture communities both locally and globally.

—United Students for Fair Trade

worker-aware

Power shopping when it comes to food is called Fair Trade; applied to other goods, the term of art is "fair labor" or "antisweatshop." Here, too, a citizens' movement has burgeoned with remarkable speed because of actions of a handful of passionate, gutsy people—like students at the University of Michigan who in 1999 called on their elders to pay attention to the welfare of those who make the garments bearing their institution's logo.

Now, you might think that the schools' administrators would fall over themselves with glee to know their students are acting from conscience to help poor people thousands of miles away. But no. Students all over the country ended up having to stage demonstrations, including University of Arizona students' ten-day sit-in at the chancellor's office, to get, along with other principles, a commitment of full disclosure of who supplies the school.

But thanks to a movement that students ignited, in less than a decade a slew of voluntary corporate monitoring and accreditation initiatives have sprung up—some mentioned in Chapter Five—to make corporate labor practices transparent and to hold corporations to a minimum standard of decency.[23]

At the same time, others have begun to seize the new world of possibilities the Internet offers for shoppers to "vote" their values in the marketplace. Two are Mandi and Eric Odier-Fink in Maine, who met in the labor movement (and even used their wedding to educate and raise funds for their cause!). In 1996, they founded Justice Clothing, where online a power shopper can now order jeans, sneakers, or even winter socks. Mandi and Eric call their creation a "one-stop shop for union-made and sweatshop-free apparel."

No Sweat Apparel.com of Newton, Massachusetts, is a similar effort but also a manufacturer itself, listing its factories on its Website. No Sweat was founded in 2000 by Adam Neiman, a forty-eight-year-old roofing company owner, and writer Jeff Ballinger, fifty-one.[24] The *New York Times* calls No Sweat a "virtual mall where all the vendors sell goods that are made by union workers."[25] Wages in No Sweat's unionized factory in Indonesia are 25 percent above the regional minimum, plus a "rice benefit" and full health insurance.

"Where we stand out," Nieman said, "is by reclaiming the union label as the ultimate standard for sweatshop-free apparel." No Sweat Apparel's sales have grown steadily but jumped over eightfold to three-quarters of a million dollars in 2004, and 2005 looks just as strong.

No Sweat's "labor content disclosure form"—detailing compensation and union rights—comes with every pair of sneakers it sells. "Now you can walk down the street without stepping on the worker who made your shoes," says the form.

Neiman recently challenged Nike to provide its customers with a similar disclosure form.[26] So far Nike hasn't leapt at the suggestion.

Online options also include http://www.unionwear.com.

Another Web-based approach helps shoppers do a new kind of comparison shopping. At IdealsWork.com, one can easily contrast brands and the companies behind them on a number of fairness and environmental criteria. Choose a product category from clothes to computers to insurance, identify values you care about, click, and you see rankings identifying which brands most closely fit your values. Co-op America (http://www.coopamerica.org) is another great resource for power shopping.

savings-savvy

When we stash money away for a rainy day or a college education or our golden years, it probably doesn't sink in for many of us that our money isn't "stashed" at all. It is moving around and around, doing a lot of things, with consequences that might not only be violating our values but even our own material interests.

We can shift, however, from passive to active, from unconscious to conscious.

Today, one of every nine dollars invested is guided by social criteria.[27] Between 1984, the first year anyone studied the question, and the end of 2002, such social investment jumped almost 53-fold, climbing from $40 billion to over $2 trillion. It now equals the combined 2000 gross domestic product of Canada, Mexico, and Italy.[28]

Here is how Americans can assert their savings power today:

- By targeting savings toward companies using ethical criteria, such as opposing tobacco sales or protecting the environment

- By using the ownership of shares, including through a pension fund, to advocate with company management for practices reflecting one's values[29]
- By investing directly in community building, such as affordable homes

a sacrifice?

The world of socially responsible investment—SRI, as it's called—has fought hard to shed the notion that paying attention to what your money is doing means sacrificing the better financial returns you get sticking to the "attentionless" path. It's been an assumption that is surprisingly hard to shake, especially surprising in light of considerable opposing evidence.

Then, in early 2005, the cover of Marjorie Kelly's *Business Ethics* magazine broke out the champagne: "Holy Grail Found. Absolute, positive proof that corporate social responsibility pays off."[30]

Inside, Marjorie leads readers triumphantly to two "meta-studies," research that digests the findings of many others over time. One looked at fifty-two studies over thirty years and found "from highly positive to modestly positive" statistical correlations between "social performance and financial performance." The other, from an environmental angle, looked at sixty studies over six years, finding that 85 percent showed a positive link between "environmental management" and performance.[31]

These studies nail down what many people have noticed for years, that socially responsible mutual funds do well.[32] The Domini 400 Social Index (DSI 400)—considered the gold standard of socially responsible funds—has outperformed the S&P 500 on a total return basis and a risk-adjusted basis each year since its 1990 inception.[33]

No M.B.A. is needed to guess why. Socially responsible companies typically have a more forward-thinking management style, better preparing them for crisis; they are likely to have strong relationships with bankers and investors, and they attract devoted employees. These are some of the explanations offered.

does selective investing make corporations shape up?

Customer boycotts can work to alter corporate behavior, as when twelve thousand students pledged to abstain from Citibank credit cards and tipped the company toward more sustainable practices.[34] But as Marjorie Kelly points out, boycotting a corporation's stocks doesn't have the same impact.[35]

Nevertheless, citizens making ethical choices about which companies' stocks to buy, even at current levels, does "raise public moral standards and awareness," and that can have a big impact—as in ending the apartheid regime in South Africa, notes one study.[36]

For one thing, social screening means that more people are watching. "Just to have investors continually ask questions of companies on social activities can have a real impact," said Simon Billenness, senior policy adviser on corporate engagement for Oxfam America.[37]

Socially responsible investment has not transformed the calculus of capitalism. It's normalized the notion that ethical considerations are a legitimate part of a corporation's mission—something laughed at on Wall Street only fifteen years ago.

U.K. pension funds must now disclose whether their investments line up with socially responsible standards, and this new transparency pressure alone created "a dramatic increase" in socially responsible investing, reports Robert Rubenstein, a leader in the movement. What I call shifting norms, Rubenstein terms creating a "herd." He notes that leading lenders, including Barclays, recently committed publicly that their loans will respect social and environmental safeguards. From that simple act, Rubenstein predicts the "rest of the pack" will follow.[38]

shareholders
making their voices heard

Rainforest Action Network's campaign to change Home Depot's purchases of old-growth wood, described in Chapter Four, succeeded in part because it was joined in a unified effort including "stockholder advocacy." Recently, a stockholder resolution also led PepsiCo to introduce a new lid for cans that will save twenty-five million pounds of aluminum a year.[39]

Such socially responsible shareholder activism is key to a range of corporate advances, according to players at the table. The box highlights several.[40]

SHAREHOLDER ACTIVISM

Goals of Recent Shareholder Resolutions Taken to Corporate Boards	*Corporations Whose Policies Changed as a Result*
Preserving forest and recycling paper	Home Depot, Staples
Eliminating polluting mercury thermometers	Cardinal Health, HCA, J.C. Penney
Ending discrimination based on sexual orientation	Cracker Barrel, MBNA, Fifth-Third Bancorp, Wal-Mart[41]
Reducing greenhouse gases that contribute to climate change	American Electric Power, ChevronTexaco, General Electric, Cinergy
Addressing the HIV/AIDS pandemic	Coca-Cola, ExxonMobil
Addressing poor labor standards in Myanmar (Burma)	Unocal

pension beneficiaries as stewards of their money

Pension fund beneficiaries—eighty million Americans—own their retirement funds—in theory.[42] But can they turn theoretical ownership into real power?

In the 1990s, institutions, including pension funds, surpassed individuals as holders of stocks—a milestone potentially giving beneficiaries clout to shift corporate behavior, as noted in Chapter Five. U.S. workers' pension and other benefit fund plans own over $6 trillion in assets.[43] Of that amount, $400 billion are in union-sponsored pension funds.[44] For perspective, that's nearly ten times the amount of money that changes hands on the New York Stock Exchange each day.[45]

To turn labor's potential pension power into real influence, the AFL-CIO decided that union members needed training in how to stand up to corporate boards. So in 1997, the Center for Working Capital in Washington was born.[46]

The center's Capital Stewardship program trains unionists to "steward" their money, and sometimes this means getting down and dirty: Part of its course called Active Ownership and Corporate Governance includes such topics as "various shark repellents and anti-takeover devices and . . . their effect on corporate governance; . . . executive compensation issues and their potential for abuse"; and the drafting of a "shareholder proposal to deter a specific compensation abuse."

Capital Stewardship brags that in its short life, it has helped double the number of stockholder-initiated resolutions filed by unions to four hundred in the 2002–2003 season of corporate board meetings.

Other Americans are choosing to skirt large corporation stocks altogether and instead to put their savings to work close to home so they know it's doing something they believe in. This community banking movement—the fastest-growing part of social investment—I will take up shortly.

reimagining economic life: local, living economies

Living Democracy, I'm arguing, emerges as more and more of us pay attention, as we enjoy our power to choose—whether it be as "power shoppers" for goods produced by workers whose dignity is respected, or as savers aware that where we put a nest egg influences the health of our community, or as pension fund stewards turning our "passive" power into an active force bending corporate decisions toward long-term planetary health, or as investors in community development banks.

I realize that it is hard to see the impact of these developments. Ford is still producing gas-guzzlers. McDonald's still sells double quarter-pounders with cheese that exceed an entire day's limit of saturated fat and fuel our diabetes epidemic.[47]

So a lot of Americans, not seeing much positive change, throw up their hands, believing that the worldwide spread of corporate capitalism is all there is.

"There is no more mint chocolate chip, there is no more strawberry swirl and there is no more lemon-lime," wrote the *New York Times* columnist Thomas Friedman in *The Lexus and the Olive Tree*. "Today there is only free-market vanilla and North Korea."[48]

And since no one's choosing North Korea, the message is that what we have now is all there is.

But to imagine we've reached history's end is silly. The striking challenges and alternatives to centralized corporate decision making in this book make that clear. Plus, the immediate decades ahead will see the end of the fossil fuel bonanza, and at that point centralized control will begin to look even less viable.

Corporate globalization, by definition, depends on transporting goods vast distances. Between 1948 and 1997, tonnage of merchandise shipped internationally grew tenfold, with much of this increase occurring over the last two decades.[49] This is no small matter: transportation accounts for a fifth of the world's energy consumption and *half* the world's oil consumption.[50]

Though we Americans make up only 5 percent of the world's total population, we consume a quarter of its energy.[51] In the past two decades alone, we've increased oil consumption in the United States by a third.[52] We now import two-thirds of our petroleum.[53] In the process, we worsen air pollution, already causing nearly two hundred deaths a day in the United States, and speed global climate change, already costing billions in damage and death.[54]

"Humanity has already consumed close to half the world's original endowment of sweet, crude 'conventional' oil," estimates the U.K.-based Oil Depletion Analysis Center, drawing on sixty-five studies published over the last fifty years. Today, we consume about six barrels of oil for every new barrel discovered.

This can't go on. By 2010, oil production will go into "terminal decline," says Dr. Colin Campbell, a former exploration geologist and oil company executive, considered "dean" of global oil depletion expertise. Campbell's predicted oil peak is right in line with a dozen recent studies.[55]

Today's centralized, fossil-fuel-dependent agriculture, manufacturing, and retail trade will change dramatically, says James Howard Kunstler, author of *The Geography of Nowhere*. For one thing, he predicts "the demise of Wal-Mart style, big-box, national chains." Companies who make their profits off "merchandise made by factories twelve thousand miles away" won't survive in a world where oil costs $100-plus a barrel.[56]

To be able to create something better, however, we must first be able to imagine it.

Just what are the benefits of an economic life that is not centrally controlled over vast distances? In which decision making is relocalized, brought to a more human scale, and embedded in communities?

LOCAL, LIVING ECONOMIES

Feature	*How It Improves Our Lives*
Proximity, as close as is feasible, between producing something and consuming it, especially for food, energy, and other life essentials	We will use less fossil fuel in transportation, so there's less pollution and greenhouse gases. We will have healthier, tastier food because the time between harvesting and eating is shortened. Security will be enhanced because supply is less vulnerable to natural or hostile disruptions.
Centralized economic bureaucracies—global corporations—no longer able to pit one country's workers against another's	Downward pressure on wages is lifted.
Fewer layers of "middlemen"	More wealth stays in the hands of producers and in communities where it is created.
More direct contact between producers and consumers	Less centralized monitoring to protect health and safety is needed because worker empowerment and face-to-face relationships with consumers help keep producers accountable.

	Community bonding and its pleasures are heightened.
Producer and purchaser focus on values broader than the highest financial return, making it possible to conserve and restore water, soil, and air quality.	Greater dispersion of economic wealth and power in small and medium-sized businesses and farms Entrepreneurship, with its creative expression and enhanced self-determination, increases.
Less "sameness," more cultural variety	Landscapes, self-expression, pride in place, and appreciation of differences all flourish.

Getting from here to there—from a centralized, antidemocratic economy to a more democratic, localized one—seems more doable if we pause to recognize that notwithstanding our oil imports, the United States is already relatively self-reliant.

"Almost 60 percent of our overall GDP is created by place-based business, locally owned and largely selling to local markets," notes Michael Shuman, author of *Going Local: Creating Self-Reliant Communities in a Global Age*. We import 14 percent of our gross domestic product, he points out, "and if we were attentive to the trade deficit, we would import much less."[57]

banking on communities

To create local economies requires access to capital. That need is sparking what's called community investing. It doubled in just two years to $14 billion in 2003.[58] Those billions are spread throughout the country in community development financial institutions: 54 chartered banks and thrifts, 142 credit unions, 499 loan funds, and 21 venture capital funds.[59]

Although interest earned is below market rates, the payback record for loans by these funds is often better than that by regular banks.[60] Investors view any loss in return as a gift to their values, just as they get satisfaction from contributing to causes they are excited about.

Two stories of community banking capture that excitement.

In 1980, the husband-and-wife team of Bonnie Wright and Martin Eakes roamed North Carolina counseling unemployed workers on ways to deal with plant closings. They worked out of their car. When their car caught fire ("There went our office!"), the two set up a "real" office. It became the Center for Community Self-Help.

Bonnie and Martin realized that among the biggest reasons people stay locked in poverty is a lack of capital, plain and simple. So they set out to create a financial institution that would be financially sound and at the same time provide capital to those who usually can't get it.

With $70 in profits from a bake sale, they launched the Self-Help Credit Union and the Self-Help Ventures Fund in 1984.

Self-Help is both a direct lender to the financially underserved and a research and advocacy outfit. Since that fateful car fire, Community Self-Help has loaned $2.6 billion to small businesses, nonprofit organizations, and home buyers in North Carolina and beyond.[61]

"We're not going to solve poverty by making one loan after another," Martin has said, making clear that his real goal can't be measured in numbers. "We're too small. The way we can make a difference is by dispelling the myths. One of the myths that is just the most pernicious is that particular groups of people cannot succeed."[62]

Self-Help is changing the playing field: in 1999, it denounced Citigroup and other big banks for targeting poor people for high-fee loans and helped pass a North Carolina law prohibiting certain predatory lending practices and requiring counseling for borrowers before closing on high-cost home loans.[63] The law will keep five thousand North Carolina families from losing their homes, Martin estimates.[64]

Following Self-Help's lead, twenty-seven states have passed similar bills.[65]

the mother of community banking

A decade before Bonnie and Martin's out-of-their-car loans, four friends in their thirties—Mary Houghton, Ronald Grzywinski, Milton Davis, and James Fletcher—two white, two black—hung out at the Eagle, a quiet bar in the shadow of the University of Chicago. At the time, one sold computers for IBM, another was a civil rights activist, one worked in low-income housing administration, and another had just graduated from Johns Hopkins. Only one had any lending experience. Over beer and hamburgers, they worried together about the decline threatening South Side Chicago, where a third of apartment buildings were tax-delinquent and in danger of abandonment by their landlords.

In 1973, the four friends turned their angst into action, securing the resources to buy a local bank, South Shore National Bank, that had been threatening to pull out, too. They turned it into the country's first community development bank—a financial institution with a calling: to spark a neighborhood turnaround. South Shore began offering home ownership loans and soon began working with local entrepreneurs eager to reclaim run-down apartment buildings. By the 1990s, South Shore loans had helped rehab nearly a third of the housing in the vicinity. Demonstrating that it could be done, and profitably, other Chicago banks began competing to make loans there.

Today, South Shore—now renamed ShoreBank—has helped finance the purchase and renovation of forty-five thousand affordable housing residences across the country.

With the ascendance of the Far Right, federal housing initiatives have taken a big hit. But ShoreBank has not faltered. It's gone on to create community development bank subsidiaries and nonprofits in other cities. It has consulted in thirty countries—helping "microlending" take root among poor women in Bangladesh and community banking take off in Afghanistan and Africa.

"What we're really doing is democratizing credit," founder Ron Grzywinski, sixty-nine, told me.

The potential impact of his approach is vast, considering that 95 percent of the world's people have no access to credit, yet low-income borrowers have proved over and over again to be superior credit risks.

In 1995, ShoreBank added a third purpose, ecological health, to its double bottom line of profitability and community betterment. It partnered with the nonprofit Ecotrust in the Pacific Northwest to support businesses furthering environmental sustainability, and two years later, its subsidiary ShoreBank Pacific became the first development bank in North America whose mission is restoring the ecosystem.

In Cleveland, a ShoreBank loan helped turn an abandoned bank building into a vibrant center for environmental nonprofits and businesses. Renovations used "green" building technologies, such as a solar-paneled roof.[66] ShoreBank is helping "erase the misconception" for low-income borrowers that energy-efficient, sustainable construction is unaffordable, Mary Houghton, president, sixty-four, explained.

The dominant mental map says a capitalist bank must care only about profit to succeed. But ShoreBank proves something else. It rewards its employees, two-thirds of whom are African American, based on a triple bottom line: financial, social, and ecological performance. And watch it grow.

Profitable every year since 1975, ShoreBank has invested almost $2 billion in mainly underserved or disinvested communities. To make it to the first billion, the bank needed twenty-six years; to the second, only four. In 2004, its Chicago bank's return on investment exceeded for a third year running the median for comparably sized institutions.

With Self-Help and ShoreBank and other community development banks, more and more Americans can bank their values—and join in "Judy economics."

"buy local or bye-bye local"

"Buy Local or Bye-Bye Local." "Be a Local Lover." These two bumper stickers you might spot these days in Bellingham, Washington, a city of sixty-seven thousand. And on hundreds of storefronts, T-shirts, flyers, and newspaper pages in this bayside city, you'll also see the slogan "Think Local, Buy Local, Be Local."

All are signs of Sustainable Connections, a coalition of locally owned businesses in northwest Washington that in 2003 launched a "local first" campaign.

"'Are you locally owned?' Since the campaign started, more and more businesses are hearing the question," Michelle Long, thirty-three, executive director of Sustainable Connections, told us.

"Before, the question never came up."

More than 250 participating independent businesses now display a poster and a "buy local" decal in their windows. They give special thank-you cards to loyal customers and offer customers coupon books with discounts at member stores.

To kick off the campaign, Sustainable Connections welcomed citizens to compete to collect the most receipts from local businesses in one month. The grand prize? A month of free meals at locally owned restaurants.[67]

Other cities, including Portland, Oregon, and Grand Rapids, Michigan, have also launched "local first" campaigns.

In Salt Lake City, Utah, a bookstore owner took the lead. Betsy Burton, fifty-seven, has owned the King's English Bookstore there for twenty-seven years. Back in the early 1990s, when the first chain bookstore came to town, she watched sales dip. But even worse, she said, was that "everybody bought their language—that they're the superstores and we're 'mom and pops,' which, as a purveyor of words, I found appalling! We felt so helpless—we had to struggle just to keep our doors open."

Over the years, what really irked Betsy and others like her was not the new competition but the fact that local government favored the chains.

Local officials believed that malls and "big-box" chain stores provide jobs and tax dollars and attract customers. So they gave financial breaks to lure the big players.

They forgot that local businesses not only account for the "character" and "uniqueness" of the community but are its economic lifeblood, Betsy explained. Chain stores outsource their accounting, marketing, and other functions (not to mention sending their deposits back to national headquarters). But local stores hire the town's bookkeepers and contractors and deposit in its banks.

The effect Betsy is describing turns out to be huge.

A dollar spent in a locally owned business can generate three times more local economic activity than a dollar paid to a corporate chain.[68] This alone should make a lot of people who love their hometowns sit up and listen. (In Austin, it's estimated that an additional $14 million would be circulating locally if residents shopped only at locally owned businesses. In Tampa, it's $17.5 million.)[69]

Betsy said, "We knew we were struggling not because they were better but because there wasn't a level playing field. I just was so angry."

Eventually Betsy and several other independent business owners decided to do something about the preferential treatment given chains. Fifty or sixty people came to the first meeting they called.

"The anger was just burning in every business owner that came—outrage at the government's pandering to these national chains. We all felt that not only was it morally wrong, but *economically* it was wrong."

Betsy and her allies knew not only that their businesses provided an air of "quaintness" but also that they were the community's economic powerhouses and anchors of stability. By contrast, chain stores can move to where taxes are lower, leaving empty buildings and jobless people in their wake.

Soon their effort, called Vest Pocket, claimed two hundred Salt Lake businesses, and they shrewdly used the local media.

"We have what I call a 'hit squad'—although that's probably not very good language!" said Betsy, laughing. "Every time the city attacked a local business, we would call a press conference, rush to the site, and let the press know the real facts."

When the elections came around, Vest Pocket hosted a debate between the mayoral candidates.

"We asked the really hard questions, and it became clear that one candidate's stance in terms of locally owned business was far preferable. Our candidate won, and we knew we had helped elect a mayor who was on our side," Betsy said. More successes followed, and gradually, Salt Lake Vest Pocket attained recognition.

The group helped defeat a "sprawl mall" near Salt Lake City's airport and established a local business board with a voice in city government.

"We've gotten to know city councillors and the mayor, and they come to us now," Betsy beamed. "We now feel—not hand in glove with government, because, God knows, they don't agree with us all the time—but like we have a voice, and they listen.

"We don't feel helpless anymore. We're a wonderful argument for the fact that even if it seems like there is no chance at all to change things, try anyway."

local lucre

In about twenty towns and cities—from Tucson, Arizona, to Traverse City, Michigan—residents have figured out that one way to keep money circulating at home is to create their own.[70]

"In the late 1800s and early 1900s, every region in this country had its own local currency," said Susan Witt, executive director of the E. F. Schumacher Society, a nonprofit that works on strategies to create "human-scale" economies.

Since 1991, in Ithaca, New York, citizens have been earning and spending "Ithaca Hours"—with one Hour equal to $10. An estimated $95,000 in Ithaca Hours have been put into circulation, facilitating several million dollars' worth of transactions. The public library and the medical center accept them, and the local credit union offers Hour-denominated accounts. About three hundred fifty businesses and two thousand shoppers participate.[71]

communities that own their own

Why are busloads of tourists making Powell, Wyoming, their destination? Because this town of fifty-five hundred stood up for itself. There, a local, living economy is emerging through community ownership.

In the center of town is the Mercantile, a 10,000-square-foot department store. It's not owned by a multinational based in Arkansas; in fact, most of its owners—all 429 of them—live within a few blocks of "the Merc."[72]

The Merc came into being in 2001, when the town's only general clothing store, owned by an out-of-town chain, closed down. With it gone, even buying a pair of shoes meant driving twenty-three miles to Cody or one hundred miles to Billings, Montana.

Then townspeople heard about Plentywood, a town of two thousand in northeastern Montana that had turned a similar crisis around in 1999 by creating a general store owned by the community.

In 2001, it took the Merc's volunteer committee only a few months to sell eight hundred shares at $500 a pop, enough to get the doors open. In year one, the Merc's gross sales had already topped half a million dollars, shooting well past its board's projections. By early 2004, the store had outgrown its space and expanded into a 2,500-square-foot basement nearby.

The Merc is still booming despite a new 186,000-square-foot Wal-Mart Supercenter only forty-five minutes away. In fact, shareholders should receive sizable dividends in the next few years, says retired pharmacist and president of the Mercantile's board Ken Witzeling.[73]

"The Merc completes our Main Street—it gets people excited about coming downtown," said resident Glen Holm, owner of a hardware store across the street from the Merc. "It's the only place in town where you can get cute teen clothes," gushed Tana Wellner, sixteen, who bought a dress for her school formal at the Merc.[74]

Not surprisingly, other towns are paying attention. Sharon Earhart, head of Powell's chamber of commerce, reports calls from as far away as Maine and North Carolina.[75] The Merc has already spawned at least one copycat in Ely, Nevada, population four thousand.[76]

Community ownership is working for Powell. Worker ownership is also improving the quality of life of Americans.

workers as owners

America's brand of capitalism has long assumed that workers sell their labor to those who own the capital. "The law of master and servant," writes the business analyst Marjorie Kelly, "remains the law in employer-employee relationships today, as a living fossil of the notion of ownership."[77]

Given how few workers experience the rewards of ownership, it should come as no surprise then that only a quarter of American employees say they are engaged—feel "loyal and productive"—at work.[78]

Slowly, however, Kelly's "living fossil" may be passing away, as the line separating the supplier of capital and the supplier of labor begins to dissolve. In some spots in the world, it's already disappeared.

In the Emilia-Romagna region of Italy near Bologna, for example, over sixty-eight thousand people belong to eighteen hundred worker-owned cooperatives. They produce almost half of the region's

GDP. In the Basque region of Spain, one hundred cooperating worker-owned enterprises, known as Mondragon, with combined assets of $8 billion, employ forty thousand. And in Argentina, following the economic collapse in 2002, at least two hundred worker takeovers of companies spawned worker-owned enterprises employing more than ten thousand.[79]

The United States is hardly Emilia-Romagna, but as of 2002, a fifth of private sector employees here reported owning at least some stock in their companies; that's roughly twenty-three million Americans—with a median stock value of $10,000.[80] Much is through employee stock ownership plans (ESOPs), the brainchild of conservative Senator Russell Long in 1974, or rather the brainchild of his brazen young assistant Jeff Gates, who has since become a leading American writer on economic democracy and an enthusiast for worker ownership.[81]

Today roughly ten thousand companies offer ESOPs, and in a quarter of these companies, workers own a majority of the stock.[82] Workers in the United States also own stock through options, stock purchase plans, 401(k) plans, and other means.

Big companies with significant worker ownership include UPS, Publix Supermarkets, and W. L. Gore & Associates (the makers of Gore-Tex).[83] In a novel twist giving workers significant governing power, Google's 2004 stock offering entitled employees to buy stock carrying ten times the voting power of that available to outsiders.[84]

Many people dismiss the significance of ESOPs as no more than retirement plans, having little to do with meaningful ownership. However, their benefit is measurable. Now that the United States has a three-decade track record, results are coming in.

In firms with employee-ownership plans in Washington State, a recent survey found that workers held significantly more retirement wealth than in similar non-ESOP firms. The average value of full retirement benefits for a worker in ESOP companies there was over $32,000—2½ times larger than comparable non-worker-owned companies. And wages were higher, too.[85]

Bi-Mart, a chain of sixty-four general-merchandise stores and pharmacies, is among the largest fully worker-owned transfers in recent years.[86] Fanning out over the Pacific Northwest, it defies the "march of corporate globalization is inexorable" cliché. Owner-employee Don Leber, fifty-two, Bi-Mart's director of advertising, explained the secret to Bi-Mart's success.

"Our biggest incentive isn't our wages or benefits," he told us, "but an accumulation of those things. The majority of our people are full time, working a full forty-hour-a-week job, with full health, dental, and optical benefits, plus a 401(k) program."

Compare the quality of work life at worker-owned Bi-Mart with Wal-Mart, where most employees cannot afford the company-sponsored health insurance. Even the cheapest option can cost up to 45 percent of a Wal-Mart employee's annual wages.[87]

Also, Don stressed, the store extends to its customers the ownership feeling that employees experience: "We're a membership store with a small $5 onetime family fee. It's a nominal amount, but it marries us to people. They're connected to us in a different way than a store that they just walk in and out of."[88]

Worker ownership is not just for the middle class.

Seasonal farmworkers in the United States earn on average $12,500 a year. But in Waterloo, Wisconsin, some are making as much as twenty-some thousand.

The difference?

The century-old McKay Nursery—eighteen hundred acres of trees, shrubs, ground cover, and roses—has been owned by its workers since 1984. Almost half its field workers are seasonal, many originally from Mexico. After only two years, workers can become owners and by retirement accumulate savings in the six figures.

"We are the only 100 percent employee-owned nursery in America," explained sales manager Mike Strey, who then jumped right to one of the key advantages worker ownership offers a nursery.

"The wealth of information, in some companies it just retires. It's gone and has to be replaced with a new generation. That's very difficult. But we've got people here who—rather than having their eyes on retirement, if they're that age—are still looking to coach and teach, to leave their legacy, just like they would if they were the sole owner leaving it to their son or daughter."

Because workers have direct access to managers, "innovation comes from every person," Mike added.

Bernardo Garza, fifty-four, a propagation supervisor, has been with McKay's since his youth. "We have people at McKay Nursery, people who are not management and after twenty years they retire with $300,000 to $400,000 from the ESOP," Bernardo said.[89]

"My family always did work in the fields," he went on, "and to tell the truth, we were not too educated. I was fifteen years old when I quit school. But my three kids all finished high school, and I have a daughter who is a nurse and another daughter who works for the airlines.

"Since this company became self-owned, it's changed a hundred percent. We can share thoughts. If you've got a good idea, you can do something about changing the job for the better," Bernardo stressed.

Imagine how much stronger Waterloo, Wisconsin, is because Bernardo and his colleagues and friends are owners of their livelihoods, not migrants with no stake or standing in the community. "One of our workers is the parent of a local high school football star. They've jumped into our community and are making contributions," reported Griff Mason, president and CEO of McKay.[90]

Now travel to the Bronx.

Here a worker-owned success story in another challenging industry—home health care—has former welfare recipients to thank. Cooperative Home Care Associates, founded in 1985, is a worker cooperative—one of the biggest of the three hundred nationwide, most of them launched in the last two decades.[91]

Co-ops are fully owned by their workers, who also control the company—one person, one vote.

Almost everywhere, home health care workers—on which seven million American households depend—suffer a precarious existence: no benefits, irregular hours, and tough working conditions. But fifteen years ago, Florinda DeLeon explained to me the difference that worker ownership could make. She had just completed a two-year term on Cooperative's board of directors.

"Being worker-owned means that we decide what's best for us," she told me. And "I don't ever have to think about being back on a welfare line." Not only was she earning higher-than-average wages for her industry, but she was receiving health benefits and a paid vacation as well.

In the intervening years, Cooperative has grown from one hundred seventy to almost eight hundred workers, and wages are 20 percent above those offered by other New York home care agencies.

How can Cooperative do it?

In part its low annual staff turnover, about 20 percent—compared to a 60 percent industry average—reduces costs. Every new hire entails a big training expense. Also, said founder Rick Surpin, there's more money for worker owners because profits aren't funneled away to outside stockholders, as in other companies.[92]

"Cooperative has set the industry standard for home care in New York, showing that there's a direct link between high-quality jobs for the aides and high-quality care for their clients," longtime Cooperative board member Jan Saglio told me.

"It makes sense. Because Cooperative's aides are better paid, have full-time work, and feel respected in their workplace community, they are more reliable and caring," she added. "They take pride in their work."

In only two decades, Cooperative has inspired the creation of similar home health care co-ops in four states. The U.S. Department of Agriculture was so struck by Cooperative's success that it recently provided six rural communities with grants to study the feasibility of starting their own—more evidence that you never know who's watching.

Finally, consider the spunk of the thirty-four mostly immigrant 9/11 survivors who worked at the famed Windows on the World restaurant atop one of the World Trade Center towers. Still mourning the seventy-three colleagues killed there, survivors created their own worker-owned restaurant, Colors, in Greenwich Village. Their goal is to create "a sense of place and comfort that has been missing in Lower Manhattan since September 11," said one of the co-op restaurant's founders.[93]

"Thank God, we have some hope now," said Ataur Rahman, forty-nine, an immigrant from Bangladesh. "Good things happen from bad things."[94]

A NEW HYBRID ENGINE—THIS ONE FOR THE COMMUNITY

Along with community and worker ownership as tools for community building, a new hybrid developer—community development corporations—has emerged since the 1960s. These are nonprofits with the goal of profit—profiting the entire community. Thirty-six hundred now operate across the United States—several with multimillion-dollar budgets turning whole neighborhoods around.[95]

- *New Community rises from the ashes*. The New Community Corporation rose like a phoenix from the ruins of Newark's 1967 civil disturbances, which wiped out businesses over whole city blocks. Today New Community enjoys net assets of $300 million and each day touches the lives of fifty thousand local residents—through fifteen hundred jobs, child care centers, job training, and a welfare-to-work program. New Community's health care division employs nine hundred and offers everything from prenatal outreach to residential elder care. Seven thousand people live in its twenty apartment buildings. (Three more are in the works.) New Community owns and operates businesses ranging from an automotive training center to a neighborhood shopping center.[96]

- *An abandoned hospital becomes key to recovery.* In 1989, a hospital due to close on Chicago's West Side looked pretty sad. Then Bethel New Life, Inc., paid over $3 million for its nine acres, and with help from banks and from two federal agencies, it transformed the sad space into a bright, modern complex with one hundred twenty-five apartments for the elderly, an eighty-space child development center, a health clinic, administrative offices, office spaces, adult day care services, and performance spaces. With its $8 million budget and one hundred locals on the payroll, Bethel New Life lives up to its name.[97]
- *A fishing industry collapses, then learns.* Drastic overfishing and other pressures virtually wiped out Maine's fishing economy in the early 1990s. That's when Coastal Enterprises, Inc., stepped in, working with the fishing community to develop new products, open new retail outlets, add local processing, and discover new markets. It involves fishermen in sustainability—working to rebuild their livelihoods while avoiding overfishing.[98]

picking up the torch

For many in my parents' generation, very much alive was a belief that democratic economies—including, for example, a right to work at fair pay with decent working conditions—would follow naturally from the spread of democratically elected governments. They would ally through international bodies to set standards, including those protecting the right to organize unions.

In the mid-twentieth century, over a third of private sector workers belonged to a union bargaining on their behalf and achieving huge gains for them—the five-day week, the eight-hour day, and overtime pay. But unions have been under assault. Twenty thousand U.S. workers are fired or have their wages cut each year by companies because of their organizing efforts. Today in private companies, unions represent only about one in twelve workers.[99]

Not only has the value of the minimum wage fallen, but its enforcement has weakened. Enforcement officers per worker have dropped to a third of what they were in the 1950s.[100]

The year I was born, 1944, saw the birth of the International Labor Organization. Perhaps symbolically, the International Labor Organization chose Philadelphia as the site of its first declaration, in which it warned that "poverty anywhere constitutes a danger to prosperity everywhere." Today, 177 governments are its members.

Decades before "globalization" and "outsourcing" had become buzzwords associated with sinking wages in industrial countries and sweatshops in poor countries, the International Labor Organization's constitution was prescient, declaring that any single nation that fails to adopt humane labor conditions is "an obstacle in the way of other nations."

How much farther along Martin Luther King's "long arc" of justice might we be today if the United States had heeded the warning and picked up the torch for worker protections worldwide, backing the International Labor Organization's position that fair economies are good for all?

Dream on.

Today, 104 countries have signed all eight International Labor Organization core conventions protecting workers against discrimination and forced labor and assuring rights of association. But the United States—whose economic dominance has in practice set the global standard—is not one of them. In fact, except for some tiny island states, only Myanmar (formerly Burma) and Oman have shown more aversion to supporting the labor-protecting conventions as the United States. We've ratified just two of the eight.

Thus it is not surprising that we still live in a world where slavery is alive and thriving, trade unions are shrinking, and the world's biggest corporation, Wal-Mart, is aggressively anti-union.[101]

While Americans are taught to assume that capitalism and democracy are joined at the hip, there is nothing inherently democratic about capitalism. Think of the dozens of autocratic regimes over the last hundred years, from Latin America until quite recently to China and Russia today: plenty of capitalism but precious little democracy, even in the formal sense.

So here we are, sixty years after basic workplace rights were enshrined, still living in a world where those who grow most of the food we eat and make most of the clothes we wear are paid so little that they can barely eat or clothe themselves. Where half of the world's workers are "living" on $2 a day or less.[102]

In this time of "democratic deficit," as the International Labor Organization dubs it, we're called to use all means at hand to pick up the torch for values-grounded economies ourselves.

paying attention

In this chapter you have met many torch bearers. Just over three decades ago in the United States, a nanosecond of historical time, none of their movements even existed here—from worker ownership to Fair Trade shopping, from community development banking to local currencies, from stewarding one's pension fund to "buy local" campaigns. The speed of their takeoff suggests that these movements tap deep yearnings.

Yet many of those who experience local, living economies as exciting and empowering still assume that our main task is persuading: We just have to convince others that economic life *should* respect the dignity of all, including the migrant worker in Wisconsin, the home health worker in the Bronx, and the sneakers maker in Indonesia. That we *should* realize there is no "away" to which we can toss our stuff. That we *should* stop shipping goods senselessly around the globe, worsening pollution and speeding global climate change.

I don't think so.

I'm convinced that few of us need convincing. Judy Wicks's vision of an "intricate global web of small-to-small, win-win relationships" makes intuitive sense to people. Most people want a stronger sense of rootedness to place and neighbor; they want to protect and restore the natural world. They want every worker, including themselves, to be paid fairly and treated with respect.

The problem is that too few believe it possible.

What makes the impossible seem possible?

First, shifting the frame—shifting what we measure and therefore what we pay attention to. What we're attuned to is what we can then imagine more of. For one, this means measuring our society's well-being in more than dollar output.

After eighteen years of study in which he found that our economy's growth had brought "no rise in life satisfaction," Ed Diener, a professor of psychology at the University of Illinois, thinks it's time to broaden our measure of prosperity.[103] The Gallup research and polling group recently asked him to design a national well-being index. His goal is "something that could sit next to the Dow Jones average in the corner of the TV screen," Diener explained.

Imagine the impact of a high-profile index that takes into account the quality of social relationships, enjoyment at work, job stability, the functioning of electoral democracy, and the protection of human rights. That's what Professor Diener is shooting for.

Others have developed similar national indices for broader measures of real health.[104] One, the Genuine Progress Indicator, subtracts, for example, our ecological losses and adds the value of parenting to offer a measure more useful than the GDP.[105]

Second, to make the impossible possible, we can acknowledge the power of our example. Since humans are social mimics, whatever piece of a living-economies web ignites you to act, as important as acting is making your action visible. Chapter Nine is filled with possibilities of using the media for "going public" to create the unknowable ripples.

As we come to appreciate the capacities of regular citizens—like Lina, Bernardo, Florinda, and ourselves—we realize that we don't have to lie down before all-powerful corporations. And we can put to rest the mythical notion of an automatic "law of the market." As we pay attention to our daily economic choices—as purchasers, savers, borrowers, owners, workers—we feel our power growing.

7

ACTION

politics & the inauguration of the citizen

"This is what democracy must feel like." Every time I hear that—and I must have heard it twenty different times in completely different settings—for me it says we can't recognize it because we usually haven't had the experience. But it doesn't feel foreign. It's a need we don't always know we have.

MARTHA MCCOY,
DIRECTOR, STUDY CIRCLES RESOURCE CENTER

September 11, 2001. Nineteen hijackers, with a few thousand terrorists cheering them on. We reeled in horror, astonished by what a relatively few smart, organized, committed, persistent people could do . . . to destroy.

If humans are capable of such coordinated evil, why do we so often doubt what small numbers of people with those qualities can do for the greater good? Consider the impact of just four in the wake of 9/11—four who became widows on that day.

"I'm enormously impressed that laypeople with no powers of subpoena, with no access to insider information of any sort, could put together a very powerful set of questions and set of facts that are a road map for this commission," said Jamie Gorelick, former deputy attorney general of the United States, at the 9/11 Commission hearing.[1]

"It is really quite striking. Now, what's your secret?"

"Eighteen months of doing nothing but grieving and connecting the dots," replied Mindy Kleinberg, one of the four 9/11 widows who had pushed hard for the commission. The commission's findings left huge questions, but at least Americans learned, finally, that we *had* been warned of al-Qaeda's threats and that hijacked planes might be used as weapons. And we got a least a hint of the scope of mind-boggling lapses by aviation authorities that tragic morning.

Without Mindy and her allies, we wouldn't have had a 9/11 Commission, acknowledged the coauthor of the legislation creating it.[2]

Or consider the process of coming up with the design for rebuilding the World Trade Center site: "A turning point of American planning" is how the architecture critic Paul Goldberger characterized it. "Thousands and thousands of people talking seriously about urban design is something I never thought I would see," he added.[3] In the end, the city-hired architects had to scrap their initial designs and pretty much start over with the public's priorities in mind.[4]

So Congress gave way to pressure mounted by four outside-the-Beltway women, among many others, and top professionals gave way to citizens' insights.

It is a paradoxical time. Striking examples of the power of organized citizens' influence are emerging even as channels narrow for citizens' voices in shaping public policies—at least those we'd long thought were ours. Chapter Six highlighted the underappreciated power of choices we make every day in our many economic roles from purchaser to worker. Here we turn to the underrecognized power of organized citizen action.

bottom-up power politics

Forty years ago, political parties, however limited, felt like real forces in communities. My parents knew their party precinct leader. Now, though, many Americans experience both major parties as elite-driven, distant, image-selling machines. The consequences of this historic shift are enormous, but they're hard to see without a contrast.

Try Brazil: in a 2002 landslide, voters elected as president a former shoeshine boy and labor organizer, Luis Inacio Lula da Silva—known simply as "Lula." His top campaign pledge was to end hunger and address poverty. What made this possible? Lula's political party, the Workers' Party, has deep roots among the poorest and biggest classes.

There is no American parallel. Only 4 percent of low-income Americans get involved in political campaigns, one quarter the share of upper income Americans.[5]

Into our apparent political void, many "regular" Americans have been quietly—and not so quietly—walking, as we saw earlier in New York's Working Families Party. They are going far beyond protest, although there's plenty of that. They are innovating.

I realize that this upsurge is hard to see. Much more visible is hand-wringing over the decline of civil society as Robert Putnam, author of *Bowling Alone*, and others tell us that we're all too busy in our private worlds to join sports leagues or choral societies.[6]

Such laments about what we've lost miss a couple of things. First, much of what has atrophied consists of groups like the American Legion or women's clubs that were important social glue, to be sure, but *not* schools for building citizen power. Second, backward gazing might allow us to miss new forms of neighborhood-level citizen empowerment right under our noses.

Regular citizens, many connected through religious congregations and union locals, have jump-started a breakthrough in democracy itself, from campaigns in scores of cities for "living wages," easing the lives of millions of poor families, to "study circles" in Kuna, Idaho, which opened the door for major school improvements, and to a poor people's nationwide campaign that convinced H&R Block to change its policies; from a legally binding pact in Los Angeles requiring a huge airport expansion to benefit the surrounding community to new housing trust funds building affordable dwellings; and more.

These citizen-driven successes are telling us that democracy is not a "thing" we have, something done for us or to us. Democracy is *what we do*—something rewarding because it meets our deep needs and capacities for connection with each other and effectiveness in the larger world. Human beings didn't evolve to be passive spectators, they're saying. We were meant for better things.

Yes, power at the pinnacle of the political world seems tighter than ever. Government secrecy is increasing; listening is decreasing—with less and less compromise across the aisles in Congress.

But at the local and state levels, something else is happening: "Public officials see that top down doesn't work," says Martha McCoy, forty-nine, who's devoted fifteen years to creating forums for citizens to find their voices. "And citizens are starting to give up the negative assumption that government is not going to sit down with them. They are asking, How might we deliberate together from the beginning?

"Officials and citizens are learning," she told me, "that imposed solutions are, by definition, going to omit some critical piece and that people can't own the solution if they weren't part of bringing it to life."[7]

citizen solvers

Much of this still largely invisible upsurge of citizen leadership is only a few decades old. Particularly stunning is the burst of faith-motivated, community-grounded political action. "Religious activism" to most Americans conjures up images of Christian Coalition members advancing laws and constitutional amendments from their own moral stance to, say, allow prayer in schools or abolish the right to abortion.

What these images miss is arguably a larger number of Americans whose faith also calls them to overcome fear, shyness, and busy lives to move into the public sphere—but in a different way. Their faith calls them to listen to the worries and dreams of their neighbors, especially the disenfranchised, and to act on *that* agenda.

For some, their community agitation for justice draws on biblical injunctions. Matthew 25:40 is an example, reminding believers, "Truly, I say to you, as you did it to one of the least of these, my brethren, you did it to me." Jim Wallis, an Evangelical Christian leader, notes that the Bible contains three thousand verses about the poor.[8]

"Our faith calls on us to act on the health of our community," declared the youthful but commanding Elder Eddly Benoit. He was rallying new Haitian immigrants, middle-class Jews, and working-class blacks—all members of Greater Boston Interfaith. "Amen! Amen!" they called back in a large, brightly lit, inner-city church hall in early 2005. Soon another young religious leader, Rabbi Jonah Pesner, took the mike to launch the organization's campaign for affordable health care for Massachusetts.

"This is not a political issue; this is not a moral issue; this is a sacred issue!" he called out. "Every human body is a reflection of God." From this soul-stirring declaration, Rabbi Pesner moved seamlessly to the earthly challenge of collecting forty thousand signatures for the organization's health care ballot initiative.

Nationwide, thirty-five hundred congregations—Catholics, Protestants, Jews, and some Evangelicals and Muslims—are dues-paying members of 133 such religious networks, local federations of congregations with members adding up to as many as three million Americans.[9] By one estimate, their twenty-four thousand local leaders every year turn out one hundred thousand "ordinary citizens" for public actions to further their values-based agenda—affordable housing, better public schools, decent wages, and fairer lending practices.[10]

If there is a birth year for this extraordinary flowering of faith in action, it's probably 1972. That was the year a young Ernie Cortes went back home to San Antonio. Trained in Chicago by

Saul Alinsky, the godfather of community organizing who in 1940 founded the Industrial Areas Foundation (IAF)—an odd name for an organization bent on building the power of poor people—Ernie intuited that something was lacking in the hard-edged organizing style he'd been taught.

He started listening to his neighbors in San Antonio, listening to what moved them and what made them angry. He recognized the power of starting with people already connected with each other and with their values through an ongoing, vital institution—their churches.

"We organize people not just around issues but around their values," Ernie explained. "The issues fade, and people lose interest in them. But what they really care about remains: family, dignity, justice, and hope. We need power to protect what we value."[11]

Ernie personally conducted more than a thousand individual meetings during those initial months, all the while looking for potential leaders to invite to second and third rounds of what the IAF calls "one-on-ones." These folks then agreed to hold house meetings to build membership.

"As it turned out, the leaders in the congregations were also the leaders in the youth organizations, PTAs, and unions," Ernie noted. So they encouraged not only their fellow congregants but also their neighbors and coworkers to get involved."[12]

Ernie proved that "most people need to be directly invited into public engagements, contacted personally by . . . folks they know," as the Harvard sociology and government professor Theda Skocpol has observed.[13]

In only three years, Ernie's approach resulted in a first-of-its-kind faith-based IAF affiliate called COPS—Communities Organized for Public Service—with the clout to wrest enough power from San Antonio's blue-blood Anglos to move more than $1 billion in public improvements—from sewers to clinics and parks—into long-neglected neighborhoods of poor Mexican American families. (Back then some streets, residents told me, had mud at times so deep you could hardly walk.)

This new model of allied churches energized by their values began to take hold. The Industrial Areas network has now grown to fifty-five faith-based organizations like COPS, involving two thousand congregations and other members, including unions. They are rooted in twenty-one states, as well as in Canada, the United Kingdom, and Germany.

In Brooklyn, the IAF affiliate East Brooklyn Congregations gained national recognition for building nearly three thousand affordable homes over the past fifteen years.[14] And it was IAF's Baltimore arm, BUILD—Baltimoreans United in Leadership Development—that took the first step in one of the most significant poverty-alleviating reforms since the New Deal.

In the early 1990s, Reverend Doug Miles in Baltimore began to notice more people lining up at the food pantry of his downtown church. With probusiness Congresses letting the buying power of the minimum wage—now $5.15—sink by 26 percent in twenty-five years, low wages are crushing many of the families in IAF-activated congregations.[15]

Miles might simply have added more pantry shelves, but instead he joined with other pastors to go to the root of the crisis: poverty wages.

BUILD, fifty congregations strong, including union support, pushed through a first-of-its-kind city ordinance requiring companies with city contracts to pay their workers a "living wage." Then just over $6 an hour, it rose to almost $9 in 2004.[16] Four thousand service workers benefit from the law.

At the time, I was the editor of the American News Service, and BUILD's living-wage victory was the first ANS story to appear in print.[17] I recall my elation but also thinking, ah, but it probably won't get beyond Baltimore.

Little did I know.

By 2005, citizen organizing had succeeded in passing living-wage ordinances in 121 cities, with seventy more campaigns in motion. In the Rio Grande valley, Texas, the new living wage has brought a pay increase totaling $10 million for the ten thousand public employees there.[18]

Many of the ordinances apply to companies that may not directly contract with the city but get tax-paid subsidies and special tax breaks.

In the decade since his church's lengthening food pantry lines spurred Reverend Miles's BUILD into action, the movement has also managed in three cities—Santa Fe, San Francisco, and Madison—to broaden the living-wage law to apply to all employers.

Businesses have not sat by idly. They are attacking the rights of citizens to create the "values boundaries" around wages by lobbying state legislatures to deny cities power over wage minimums. It's much the same antidemocracy strategy corporations are using in Pennsylvania and Minnesota, for example, to try to deny townships the right to control the urban sludge applied to their fields or limit huge factory-farming operations in their communities.

On the positive side, though, something else new is going on: unions are discovering a whole new way of serving their members. Unions get slapped with the negative "special interest" label by the Far Right, and their membership has shrunk, but unions, still sixteen *million* Americans strong, are the largest citizen movement in the United States—and they're learning. Moving beyond the workplace into the community, they are walking—sometimes literally—alongside faith-based groups and low-income citizen movements like ACORN, a group I turn to shortly.

A new face of the faith-labor connection has taken off in the past decade. The National Interfaith Coalition for Worker Justice in Chicago links sixty religious congregations nationwide for whom better wages and working conditions are not just economic matters but also faith commitments.

Young people have been key in the rapid takeoff of the faith-labor alliance.

"When I started, I was twenty-one, green, sheltered. I had never been west of Ohio," said Interfaith Coalition co-founder Regina Botterill. "By all accounts, I never should have lasted! What has fed me are the relationships, the victories, the learning from mistakes."[19]

Regina began at Interfaith as a member of the Lutheran Volunteer Corps. Mennonites, Jesuits, and other religious groups also contribute volunteers to workers' causes.

In the coalition's eight new "worker centers" in rural Wisconsin, North Carolina, and Arkansas, workers—mostly immigrants—learn their on-the-job rights, how to organize a union, and how to file a complaint. So far, the centers have helped workers recover $1 million in back wages.[20]

Interfaith is also keen on awakening a passion for connecting faith and action among soon-to-be religious leaders. Its five-year-old Seminary Summer places thirty or so seminarians and rabbinic students—drawn from four hundred schools—in labor union internships. So far, one hundred have gotten a glimpse of the struggles of workers, and the coalition hopes that many graduates are now encouraging their first congregations to align with workers' rights to fair pay and respect at work.

citizens' experience versus the experts

A stumper problem for many communities has long been job training. "Job training has generally shown abysmal results," declared Mark Wilson, a labor analyst at the Heritage Foundation in Washington, D.C.[21] But it turns out that that dim view did not take into account what motivated citizens can come up with.

Jolted by the 1990 closing of a Levi Strauss plant that left one thousand people out of work, two San Antonio church-based groups, Ernie Cortes's Communities Organized for Public Service (COPS)—which now reaches fifty thousand families through twenty-seven parishes—and its sister organization, Metro Alliance, began searching for ways to ease the plight of the unemployed and of poor workers. New, well-paying jobs were being created, but San Antonio's many low-skill job seekers weren't filling them.

The groups could easily have attacked the big companies as racist, since so few Hispanics were being hired. But the citizen groups decided that the real stumbling block was lack of effective training. So in 1991, COPS and Metro Alliance members—homemakers, bus drivers, ministers—formed a committee to come up with a solution themselves. They met almost every Monday for two years and held more than three hundred house meetings listening to their neighbors describe their disappointments with the city's training programs. They studied alternatives as far away as Europe and worked strategically with corporations to design training especially for those occupations with a labor shortage.[22]

The fruit of their labor is QUEST—Quality Employment Through Skills Training—which can now boast almost two thousand graduates, prepared not just for *any* job but for skilled, well-paying ones. QUEST participants receive up to twenty-four months of training, a big contrast to the four months most programs offer. With hard lobbying, the community organizations managed to attract $6.5 million from federal, state, and city coffers that made this higher-investment approach possible.

QUEST volunteers recruit and begin screening candidates in community halls and classroom sites scattered throughout lower-income neighborhoods. Trainees get day care expenses covered and other services if needed to stay in training. If a child gets sick or a car breaks down, volunteers help through crises that in a typical program might force trainees to drop out.

"We keep ownership of QUEST in the community; we're not just an office downtown," said Sister Gabriella Lohan of Metro Alliance in the project's literature.

Graduates placed in jobs in 2003 earned an average of almost $27,000, more than three times their pay before QUEST. Four other cities have replicated the QUEST model and together have trained 5,500 people for better jobs.[23]

QUEST's capacity to prove the "experts" wrong came from the ingenuity and hard work of low-income people closest to the problem. It also reflects a sophisticated approach honed by the Industrial Areas Foundation leaders. For them, community organizing is a profession. Its practitioners receive middle-class salaries. Their job isn't to "mobilize" others to act but to embody and mentor core concepts and practices. (See "Citizen Power 101.")

CITIZEN POWER 101

The Industrial Areas Foundation is a results-getting, faith-motivated network of two thousand congregations, unions, and schools. It is also a philosophy of public life, one now infusing the practices of many citizen movements both here and abroad.[24]

- *Relational power.* Power is our capacity to act, growing from the relationships we build. Power is not just about winning but about building sustained relationships for future victories as well. One builds power by acting; thus IAF's iron rule: "Never do for others what they can do for themselves."
- *Relational self-interest.* Acknowledging their legitimate self-interests and recognizing those of others, members find the intersection for community action.
- *Listening.* Building relationships starts with "one-on-ones" in which members sit with neighbors and really listen. Thousands of such meetings go on *before* a new

IAF organization is formed and continue afterward to build trust and uncover interests. (Note the contrast with using door-to-door canvassing to push your preset cause.)

- *Tapping passion.* Listening allows members to get in touch with the anger and compassion that can propel them out of isolation and beyond their comfort zones.
- *Storytelling* is key to one-on-one listening. In public meetings, members also tell their stories to connect policy debates to real human struggle—tapping others' compassion, anger, and sense of justice to make change possible.
- *Disciplined preparation.* Members research carefully and rehearse before any public encounter.
- *Actions and intentional tension.* Actions are public meetings and demonstrations to build public power, to negotiate, and to further solutions. They necessitate tension. (For example, if an elected official arrives twenty minutes late to a prearranged meeting, the IAFer doesn't smile and says, "We expected you at six o'clock.")[25]
- *Negotiation.* The goal is less "getting your way" than it is negotiating self-interests.
- *Accountability.* Members make themselves accountable for tasks, such as turning out a specified number of people for a meeting. Sometimes at public "accountability sessions," members rate the performance of officials (even on giant, on-stage report cards!) and require yes-or-no answers as to whether the official will back the organization's agenda.

- *Mentoring*. Leaders and staff coach members and each other.
- *Reflection and evaluation*. Following each meeting and action, members reflect on what worked, what didn't, and how power developed. Learning never stops.

"These practices dis-organize our current culture of isolation. They create a new culture of relational power. They enable our people to tap into deep pools of energy and imagination, the sources of new solutions, new ideas, new 'lenses.'"[26]

low-income americans moving multibillion-dollar companies

The Industrial Areas Foundation isn't the only underrecognized congregation-based network breathing life into democracy in American communities. At least three other faith-based democracy-in-action networks reach a total of roughly a million families in nearly two hundred cities and towns.[27]

This IAF-and-friends world shares a deeply felt belief that organizing people through their existing institutions, such as churches and unions, has the greatest potential for building citizen power.

But there are other worlds in community organizing—those that engage low-income people who may not have roots in any institution, and that's the problem. An example is National People's Action, a coalition of 302 grassroots neighborhood groups across the country, founded in Chicago in 1972 by a powerhouse, the late Gale Cincotta, a working-class mother of six. Gale came also to be recognized as the mother of the 1977 Community Reinvestment Act, which has bettered the lives of millions, as you'll see.[28]

The undisputed leader in organizing those outside an institutional base is ACORN, launched in 1970 in Little Rock by forty-one welfare recipients and twenty-one-year-old Wade Rathke. Like me at the time, Wade was an East Coast organizer for the Welfare Rights Organization. But Wade was dispatched to the South.

"Nobody else would go," Wade told me, "so I drove into Little Rock, and there I was, going door to door talking to people with a pit in my stomach the size of a grapefruit."

When Wade pushed the Welfare Rights Organization to reach out to low-income people beyond those on welfare and its director refused, Wade started building ACORN.

"It was hand to mouth. We decided that if the effort has value to people, they'll support it, so we started with membership dues of one dollar a month. It took two or three years before it looked like we might make it."

Thirty years later, 175,000 families make up ACORN's eight hundred fifty neighborhood chapters in eighty cities.

It took fifteen years for ACORN to hit the national marquee. In 1985, it ruffled official feathers in Brooklyn and elsewhere by organizing poor people to "squat" in twenty-five vacant buildings the city had been planning to auction. ACORN's audacity was rewarded when the city allowed the squatters to remain, turning over fifty-eight buildings to it and the Mutual Housing Association of New York. The city also funded the buildings' rehabilitation, but only after ACORN agreed to stop squatting.[29]

Once ACORN was off the front pages, most Americans forgot about it. We shouldn't have.

ACORN members act on the most immediate, everyday injustices they face: poverty wages (ACORN has directly won sixteen city living wage ordinances and helped pass one hundred others, according to Jen Kern, director of ACORN's Living Wage Resource Center) and poor schools (in several cities, ACORN has set up its own schools). ACORN has also tackled unaffordable rents and intransigent landlords, as well as lack of credit or fair credit terms—

things the middle class rarely thinks about but are huge barriers for poor Americans.

ACORN is proud that two-thirds of its staff are people of color and that 80 percent of its budget comes from those monthly members' dues Wade introduced—now $10, a big sum for low-income families.

"It's a major ACORN principle—membership ownership of the budget," said Jen, thirty-five. She started with ACORN right out of college. "I told them, 'I can do six months.' That was twelve years ago."

ACORN has played a key role in the impact of the Community Reinvestment Act. It began in 1973, when a bank denied home loans to two low-income people in Chicago and each complained to a local citizens' organization, the National Training and Information Center.[30] A light bulb went on as the group acknowledged the devastating effect of credit flight on urban neighborhoods. Four years later, after agitation by thousands of regular citizens—including Gale Cincotta's National People's Action, ACORN members, and others—Congress passed the Community Reinvestment Act. It says to banks, if you earn money in a given community, you must also serve its needs for credit.

The result? $1.5 *trillion* invested in poor neighborhoods over three decades that otherwise would not have been.[31]

This law requiring basic banking fairness was not only initiated by ordinary citizens but has been defended by them as well—defended against the banking industry's persistent efforts to gut it. I remember ACORN's James Shearin telling me in the early 1990s of the final hours of one of ACORN's efforts to defend the law: "ACORN members stayed in line all night long to get seats in the hearing room. When the paid representatives from the banking industry got there in the middle of the night, the ACORN people were already ahead of them. The bankers were amazed."

More than a decade later, Jen reported a new ACORN victory. "We just settled a lawsuit against Household Finance, one of the country's biggest mortgage lenders," she told me. Household's borrowers would often end up with effectively higher rates than had been disclosed to them.[32]

"Our members did actions [held demonstrations] at its storefront offices across the country and we did stockholder action. We filed complaints with the regulators. Our members told their stories to regulators. And in an unprecedented $484 million settlement, borrowers got checks back."

Because of ACORN and other groups' actions, Household got branded a predatory lender.[33] "We had a big enough impact [on their stock price] that stock analysts started calling us: 'What's up next? Who will take the next pounding?'" Her smile of satisfaction seemed to come through the phone line.

ACORN members next took on the giant H&R Block, claiming that the company benefited unfairly from its poor clients' urgent need for tax refunds. The company charged exorbitant triple-digit interest rates, argued ACORN, for its "refund anticipation loans."[34]

After almost a year, H&R Block backed down—and more. In early 2005, the company became a partner with ACORN to educate poor families. As many as seven million eligible families, ACORN estimates, don't know they're entitled to the federal Earned Income Tax Credit—adding up to a potential $12 *billion* in missed income for poor families.[35] With H&R Block, ACORN will spread the word.

ACORN is touching on no small matter: home foreclosures have nearly tripled in the past twenty-five years, and in 2004, more families with children filed for bankruptcy—with all its attending pain—than filed for divorce.[36]

In 2004 in Massachusetts, ACORN, along with a broad coalition of local organizations, succeeded in passing a law prohibiting predatory lending.[37] And ACORN has created a nationwide foreclosure avoidance program, already helping thousands of families keep their homes.

ACORN membership is primarily low-income. Its success in engaging members in real and effective political struggle is even more striking when one notes that only 15 percent of low-income Americans even vote.

creating new, democratic norms

Faith-based organizers, as well as ACORN, labor unions, and others, have long couched their living-wage pitch this way: any business benefiting from the public purse—in tax subsidies or city contracts—owes it to taxpayers to pay decent wages. The public shouldn't be forced to subsidize companies dragging the community down.

A similar logic surrounds a new social invention of the citizens' movement: "community benefits initiatives"—not just feel-good promises but legally binding accords with businesses and local governments guaranteeing that when citizens' assets—public lands and tax dollars—are involved, the interests of affected citizens are protected.

In Los Angeles in 2001, the coordinated efforts of twenty-five citizens' groups won the nation's first big community benefits agreement—living-wage jobs, affordable housing, and environmental protections for surrounding residents as part of a $70 million, 4-million-square-foot expansion of the downtown Staples Center.

After that sweet victory, another citizen group set its sights higher: a piece of the $11 billion expansion of the Los Angeles International Airport, around which are "the most densely populated neighborhoods of any airport in the country and among the poorest in LA," Madeline Janis-Aparicio told me. She heads the Los Angeles Alliance for a New Economy, a hybrid research-communications-organizing outfit founded in 1993.

For Madeline, her hybrid adds the missing piece to community empowerment.

"The airport had increasingly horrible consequences for people living there—the worst rates of asthma, and noise so fierce you can't hear yourself speak. So some schools have no windows; they're like fortresses—horrendous.

"When we started, fatalism—'There's nothing we can do'—had set in. It was the 'coalition of the defeated,'" Madeline said. "But groups came together—labor, teachers, parents, neighborhood associations—and we spent a year building trust. People began to feel they could dream, and over ten months, we negotiated among ourselves exactly which seventy priorities we'd ask for. We trained people to be negotiators.

"And we won"—half a billion dollars in community benefits funds.

"It even means moving a whole school," said Madeline, "and millions for job training. It means every single employer that even touches the airport has to go to the community first to fill jobs." The agreement also includes money to reduce airport noise, emissions, and traffic, and it assures ongoing monitoring of the airport's health impact on residents.[38]

"All this came out of the community, some of it from people who'd never taken on anything beyond demanding a stoplight, if that," Madeline told me excitedly.

But she also stressed the importance of the expertise her alliance added to "back community people up" in a "supercomplicated land use issue.

"I'm a trained lawyer, and I don't understand a lot of it," she said. "Land use experts worked with the community negotiating team to develop the 'ask list,' to think through what's reasonable and what's not. We did training for spokespeople to hold community meetings and press conferences."

At least a dozen such community benefit agreements are in the works, Madeline said, and she's convinced they will "reshape the nature of land use and economic development."

With federal support for affordable housing cut in half in the last two decades and the concentration of wealth pushing urban housing prices ever higher, citizens have come up with another way to put a "values boundary" around the market.[39] It's called a "housing trust fund," a dedicated public income stream—often from a tiny tax on property sales—to create affordable housing. The largest so far, $100 million, passed in Los Angeles in 2004 after a broad citizens' campaign won the mayor's support.

Its holiday season "demonstrations" included two caroling sessions at city hall, with lyrics for the occasion: not "We wish you a Merry Christmas / And a Happy New Year!" but "We wish we had a housing trust fund / And more housing next year!" Citizens also told the mayor their personal stories of the disastrous impact of housing prices on their families.

Across the country, citizen actions have prompted cities, counties, and states to create more than 350 such funds—with yearly outflows exceeding $750 million.[40]

citizens partnering with local authorities

Citizens are assuming direct responsibility. They are not just seeking relief or redress from government. They are collaborating.

By 1990, neighborhood councils, most officially recognized by their city governments, had emerged in the majority of U.S. cities larger than one hundred thousand people.[41] Many can be traced to an era before the 1980s' rightward antigovernment swerve—to the 1970s, when federal funds flowed to states and cities precisely to increase citizens' participation.[42]

In a handful of cities—Portland, Oregon; Seattle, Washington; Birmingham, Alabama; Dayton, Ohio; and Saint Paul, Minnesota—these councils now afford citizens direct say over significant public money and priority setting.

In Saint Paul, citizens submit proposals, and citizen-led district councils make the first decisions on how to best use nearly $82 million in public improvement money. The councils play a critical role in planning and in allocating funds for constructing and repairing city buildings, streets, and parks.[43]

Perhaps most "built out" is Seattle's Department of Neighborhoods, created in response to intense citizen pressure in the late 1980s. Its dispersed "little city halls" bring government closer to citizens, and its Neighborhood Matching Fund grants have been a huge hit.[44] Citizens propose ideas—from painting murals to deter graffiti to restoring wetlands to creating an oral history show—and also pledge their own labor and cash. The thirteen district councils, made up of community and business group representatives, get to pick the winners. The city matches what the neighborhoods offer.

Since 1989, two thousand matching grants—including support for one hundred fifty new small parks—have stirred neighbors to contribute seven hundred thousand volunteer hours, reported Jim Diers, the department's first director.

In 2002, the new mayor, Greg Nickels, canned Jim and immediately slashed the department's staff and budget.

The mayor "didn't seem to understand the value of empowered communities," was Jim's quiet verdict. "But the neighborhoods lobbied to maintain most of the programs," he assured me. Over $2 million in city matching grants still went to 169 neighborhood projects in 2004, with volunteers contributing forty-eight thousand hours of their time.[45]

Jim, now at the University of Washington, likes to quote his former boss, Mayor Norm Rice, who had predicted that neighborhood planning would be like the genie: "We have let it out of the bottle, and we'll never get it back in."

Rice was prescient: neighborhood matching funds have spread to at least fifteen Washington cities, with the Latino-majority town of Toppenish kicking off a fund of $100,000—larger per capita than Seattle's, noted Jim. You can find them now across the country and as far away as Port Elizabeth, South Africa, and Kobe, Japan.

In the early 1990s, as Jim's vision was just taking shape, I spoke with Ellen Stewart, who told me that she "was really not a joiner but needed some sense of connection" when she went to Jim's office for help and ended up activating a neighborhood council in her Lake City neighborhood.

I asked Ellen a question that was gnawing at me: "Can a city government genuinely promote independent organizations that are not co-opted by it?"

Ellen was adamant: "We go down and testify at city council, and sometimes we testify against the city. I admire the city for creating little monsters [*she laughs*] because they're helping groups that conflict, or may conflict, with their views. They are putting trust in people . . . walking into the unknown, and I really admire them for that."

Though Ellen has since moved, the organization she built continues. Her Lake City community has launched a food bank and farmers' market, built two new parks, and involved hundreds in coming up with a neighborhood plan with a new civic center.

"The beauty of this approach to community building is that it's broad-based, so it doesn't depend on any one person, whether that is Ellen or me," Jim observed.

Across the country, there's been no blueprint for these efforts. Instead, a lot of back-and-forth experimenting is under way. The first citizen participation coordinator in Saint Paul, Jerry Jenkins, told me years ago what she'd learned in the thick of it: "I used to say apologetically that democracy is messy. Now I've decided that I don't need to apologize for democracy. You just have to wade in. You learn the value of creative conflict. You learn how deeply interdependent we all are."

"whole community" organizing

Effective community organizations, several with networks spanning the country and touching millions, are taking off—as are official public channels for citizen voices in many American cities. Over the same period, a parallel but distinct brand of community problem solving is spreading that began with one man's insight into the power of honest talk and real listening to create change.

I first met the late Paul Aicher, a friendly-faced, avuncular former businessman, in Washington in the late 1980s. I was touched by what I thought of as his "nice" vision of reviving a nineteenth-century American Chataqua movement of thousands of home discussion groups on public concerns.

Sure, it had taken root in Sweden, but here?[46] Fat chance, I thought to myself.

Little could I have guessed that fifteen years later, Paul's baby, the Study Circle Resource Center in Pomfret, Connecticut, would be working in three hundred communities and be responsible for bringing blacks and whites together in places where that had never happened before.

The study circle setup is deceptively simple: a diverse spectrum of people comes together in small, facilitated groups of eight to twelve for two hours a week over four to five weeks. They talk. They listen. The center provides discussion guides to help citizens work through their concerns, whether they be the school achievement gap, police-community relations, or sprawl; each community focuses its study circles on whatever is "up" for that community.

Ideally, a number of study circles take place in a single community at the same time and arrive at suggestions to address a chosen concern. All study circles then come together for an "action forum" to discuss proposals generated by the groups as well as to initiate implementation.

In 1995, study circles went through an acid test in the Los Angeles Day of Dialogue, following the O. J. Simpson verdict.[47]

"The shock of the verdict caused a veneer to slip," said Carolyn Webb de Macias, chief of staff to Los Angeles councilman Mark Ridley-Thomas, who first proposed the Day of Dialogue. The way Americans talk about race has regressed, she said.

What to do?

They turned to the Study Circles Resource Center for help. The result was nearly one hundred interracial gatherings throughout Los Angeles to ease tensions rubbed raw after the high-profile murder trial. Churches, unions, and workplaces took up the call—even the Biltmore Hotel, where managers, housekeepers, and bellhops all got together to talk.

Martha McCoy, director of the center, would have been more surprised if—after the Los Angeles riots in 1992—she hadn't already seen the study circle idea take off in Lima, Ohio, a city of fifty thousand people, a quarter of whom are black.

One whose life has changed through the study circle initiative is the Reverend Lamont Monford, pastor of Lima's Philippian Baptist Church.

"My mother was murdered fourteen years ago," Monford told an ANS reporter in the mid-1990s. "The only thing we know is that she was murdered by a white man. At the time, I was angry because it seemed like the police weren't doing enough. The study circles allowed me to open up and share my feelings. They connected me with white people who care."

His black Baptist church developed a "covenant" with a white Catholic church to work together on several community projects.

Friendships began to grow, and other black-white networks formed "action groups," said Lima's mayor, David Berger. One—comprising a synagogue, a Catholic church, a black Baptist church, and a Methodist church—decided to provide support for a community center, helping with tutoring and recreation for young people.

Thousands of citizens in Lima have participated in study circles ranging in focus from race relations to violence to youth. Results include a new YMCA downtown where it is accessible to the entire community, instead of in the suburbs as originally planned, and a thriving soup kitchen-cum-recreation-and-tutoring program.[48]

Or take Kuna, Idaho, where the pressures of growth—its population doubling in a decade—had strained relations between longtime residents and young people whose school bond measures had been repeatedly rejected. The school's superintendent turned to study circles; and since 1998, they've affected enough hearts in the town to defeat a school board recall, pass a school improvement bond, and spark an intergenerational celebration. High schoolers held a "senior prom" for senior citizens.[49]

Kuna's government now considers study circles part of how it does business.

"For people even to come to the table, they have to know the talk will be connected to action, to real change," Martha McCoy stressed to me.

That means that her center has increasingly become an animator of community organizing. "But it's a *whole community* organizing," said Martha, making sure I grasped the contrast with some other initiatives discussed here. "Our practice brings people on the inside and on the outside together to deliberate," referring to those who have and don't have formal authority.

"In Fayetteville, North Carolina," she continued, "the race relations study circles meeting for years included officials in the fire and police departments, along with regular citizens. These diverse groups decided that more people of color needed a chance to become firefighters. Partly because the fire chief was participating, the idea moved forward quickly. Now a historically black university, Fayetteville State, is about to train women and people of color in firefighting."

It's crossing the usual boundaries that makes solutions possible, Martha said, echoing Ken Galdston's observation in Chapter Three about the power of joining diverse voices. This discovery is at the heart of James Surowiecki's book *The Wisdom of Crowds*, where he observes that "the simple fact of making a group diverse makes it better at problem solving."[50]

Study circles are a cousin of another largely unsung development, the community visioning movement.

up from ugly duckling

In the 1970s, pollution in Chattanooga, Tennessee, was so bad that drivers had to turn on headlights at noon to cut through it. But in the 1990s, this once-charming city—famous for its choo-choo—went from racially divided ugly duckling to swan, winning international awards and the envy of its neighbors. Its rebirth sprang in part from big investments in the city's cultural renewal—including the world's largest freshwater aquarium, attracting over a million visitors a year; a renovated theater involving one thousand volunteers annually; and a new riverfront park.[51]

But all these weren't the city fathers' ideas. They began twenty years ago when fifty spunky, frustrated citizens declared that the old ways of making decisions weren't working and drew their fellow residents—across race and class lines—into a twenty-week series of brainstorming sessions they called "visioning." It was the whole community approach Martha spoke about.

Their goal was hardly modest—to save their city by the end of the century. They called it Vision 2000. They drew up thirty-four goals, formed action groups, sought funding, and rolled up their sleeves.

By 1992, halfway along, the Visioners had already achieved a remarkable 85 percent of their goals. Smog was defeated, tourism was booming thanks to the new aquarium, crime was down, and jobs and low-income housing were on the rise. People stayed downtown after dark, and the refurbished riverside had become an oak-dappled mecca.

Chattanoogans didn't stop there. In 1992, a citywide meeting to shape a school reform agenda drew not the small crowd expected but fifteen hundred people, who generated two thousand suggestions.

By now the approach has seeped its way into the city's culture. In 2002, to plan a big waterfront project, three hundred people participated in a "charrette"—an intensive effort to finish a project by a certain deadline—where teams used rolls of butcher paper to draw what they wanted to see happen.

"Basically, everything we do, any major initiative in Chattanooga, now involves public participation," said Karen Hundt, forty-five, who works for a joint city-county planning agency. "We just had a public unveiling of a new twenty-year plan for our downtown a couple of weeks ago. It was seven o'clock in the morning, it was raining, and we had over five hundred people show up. And that's kind of typical for those sorts of things here."

From Atlanta to West Springfield, Massachusetts, from Bahrain to Zimbabwe, citizens taken by Chattanooga's story are rewriting it to suit their own needs.

Planners who used to tear their hair out trying to sell their plans to citizens now find "'selling' unnecessary," said Tyler Norris of the Boulder-based consulting firm Community Initiatives, "because people feel 'it's my plan,' since they've been involved all along." Across the country, "community visioning has become less a discrete activity than a core part of our community DNA," he added. "It's now difficult to find any community in America that does not sport one or more multisector collaborative initiatives focused on individual, family, and community well-being."[52]

stepping inside politics

Roles played by citizens chronicled here—policy innovator and shaper, for example—are in some electoral democracies possible through the efforts of major political parties. In Brazil, members of the Workers' Party—now one of the country's largest—came up with "participatory budgeting," in which as much as a fifth of a city's budget is determined through multistep, face-to-face neighborhood deliberations.[53] Three hundred Brazilian cities now use the approach, inspiring scores of others around the world to try it, from Durban, South Africa, to Saint-Denis, France.[54]

But this example assumes an electorate that sees political parties as channels through which they can be heard. In the United States are strong clues that not many of us share the feeling.

One is that the proportion of Americans surveyed who identify themselves as independents—not affiliated with any party—jumped from 23 percent in 1952 to 36 in 2002.[55] That Greg Palast's book *The Best Democracy Money Can Buy* stayed on the *New York Times* best-seller list for nearly a year might be another clue. When money speaks loudly inside politics—as Chapter Four suggests—many Americans start to doubt that their political parties belong to them.

The result is a distance between government and us that can feel unbridgeable. I still smile recalling a 1980s *Phil Donahue* show at the time of the $200 billion federal savings and loan industry bailout. An irate guest exclaimed, "The taxpayers shouldn't pay for this; the government should!"

Yet more and more Americans are determined to repossess the electoral process for democracy.

Among those showing the way is the Working Families Party, showcased in Chapter Four. In New York and Connecticut, citizens are creating political parties reflecting the interests of working people with an approach that avoids the risk of wasting votes.

the new era of internet politics

"The era of top-down politics—where campaigns, institutions and journalism were cloistered communities powered by hard-to-amass capital—is over. Something wilder, more engaging and infinitely more satisfying to individual participants is arising alongside the old order," writes Micah Sifry in *The Nation*. He then describes the birth of Internet-enlivened politics.

It's Burlington, Vermont, 4:31 P.M. on April 23, 2003, at the unkempt campaign hub of Howard Dean, Vermont's ex-governor, who was still unknown to most of the nation. Matthew Gross posts a message titled "Ask the Dean Campaign" at SmirkingChimp.com, a popular forum for "dissing" President George W. Bush.

Thirty questions come back in an hour, and Matt's colleague Zephyr Teachout starts answering. Soon a participant on the site responds: "This is too cool, an actual direct line to the Dean campaign committee! Pinch me—I must be dreaming!"

Ultimately, more than four hundred people posted comments on Gross's "thread," as a continuous Web conversation is called. "Never before had the top-down world of presidential campaigning been opened to a bottom-up, laterally networked community of ordinary voters," a frequent user of SmirkingChimp told Sifry.[56]

first time voting, first time running

Another sign that something is stirring in electoral politics is the addition of 7.5 million ballots in the 2004 presidential election, compared to four years earlier.[57] And in several races, razor-thin margins dramatized the importance of every single one.[58]

The 2004 election also saw some newcomers jump into the race themselves. Howard Dean's supercharged primary bid may have imploded, but his direct style, combined with the campaign's youthful energy and innovative uses of the Internet, inspired about one hundred people to run for office, half of them for the first time.

With Dean's blessing and help from his supporters, one-third of them won—including the mayor of Salt Lake and governors of Montana and New Hampshire.[59]

Scott Merrick in New Hampshire was one of the Dean-motivated. He won a seat in his state's assembly in the first election in which this nineteen-year-old college sophomore was even eligible to vote!

"There were definitely people who thought I was joking when I first came to their door, but when they realized what I was doing and that I actually knew what I was talking about, they did a 180," Scott told us.

As a recent New Hampshire public school grad, Scott had some built-in credibility when he told voters of his concern that federal mandates are forcing teachers to narrow their teaching to standardized tests, sacrificing time for honing students' critical-thinking skills. Meeting voters face to face—something his opponents did not do—was crucial, he said. "A huge message that I got from a lot of people was that they would vote for me because I was actually taking the time to go to them.

"I would go and knock on someone's door and have a half-hour, forty-five minute exchange. . . . If you can go to one person, have a conversation, and get them to even consider other views, then you're making a difference."

In Georgia, Alisha Thomas Morgan's journey also suggests that electoral politics isn't as stuck as it appears.

In 2002, Alisha, a twenty-two-year-old Democrat, became the first black and the youngest of any race elected to the Georgia house of representatives. And she was elected in mostly white, well-off Cobb County—the former stomping ground north of Atlanta of Republican firebrand Newt Gingrich.

"I was twenty-one or twenty-two, walking into a meeting saying I was running for state representative," she told Billy Wimsatt, founder of the League of Independent Voters. "I know in the back of their heads, people were probably thinking 'that's cute.'"[60]

But Alisha won. In office, she focused on education, health care, and prison reform for juveniles.

In the 2002 election Alisha and her volunteers went door to door, like Scott did, introducing the candidate and handing out sixty thousand leaflets.

"My home phone or my cell phone number is on everything I send out," she told Billy. "When I was running, I got anywhere from twenty to thirty calls a day. And I returned all those calls."[61] Her personal approach worked both in 2002 and two years later in her landslide 66 percent reelection victory.[62]

"When I come to people's doors and listen to them, people see that I'm someone they can talk to," she said, as a way of explaining her success.[63]

The clear line between organized citizen initiatives and electoral politics is also blurring.

"We're getting increasingly involved in electoral politics," Jen Kern of ACORN told me. "In 2000 in Chicago, we got out our members and we elected one of our own, former postal worker Ted Thomas, as alderman in the fifteenth ward." (And this despite an election day barrage against him by four hundred well-paid patronage workers.)[64]

With victory upon them, ACORN members did not just sit back. They think an alderman should be a "community mobilizer" who lets the community "figure out the decision-making process," wrote two longtime ACORN leaders.

In Chicago, it's every alderman's job to come up with a list of streets for resurfacing, they note, but instead of making those choices himself, Thomas invited residents to join him on a bus tour. "As the bus bounced over the potholes on the nominated streets, the riders voted on which streets would get the funding," reported the ACORN longtimers. And when "Ted discovered a pot of $1 million for community development in his ward, he called a community meeting to ask for proposals for spending."[65]

Though the old power brokers ran a well-known ex-pro football player against him in the next election, the voters returned Ted to office.

"In Knoxville, Tennessee, and San Jose, California, we're electing our own living-wage activists," Jen said. In 2005, ACORN stalwart James Garner was elected mayor of Hempstead, New York, on the Working Families Party ticket. A son of Jamaican immigrants, he defeated a sixteen-year incumbent.

at the table

From Chattanooga to Kuna, from Los Angeles to Little Rock, citizens are creating new, more participatory, fairer ways of doing the public's business. They are moving beyond protest to a seat at the problem-solving table.

Living wages, fairer access to credit, and affordable homes—in these and more ways, they are making real the opportunity that is the heart of freedom itself. The contrast with Washington—gripped by right-wing dogma—is striking. Masked in language of opportunity, the Bush administration continues the Right's multidecade attack on federal programs that protect opportunities to decent work, housing, and education.[66]

Today local and federal seem planets apart, but it's worth remembering that in the past, local innovations, such as those this chapter highlights, have risen to become federal policy. What became the New Deal, one scholar stressed, was not all "seat-of-the-pants improvisations. Some had been germinating for generations in city soil. Some had already been battle tested, first in neighborhoods, then at city and state levels."[67]

It can happen again.

The stories here suggest that our society's habits of heart are evolving.

"Within local government, the notion that people have to have a say, that they *want* to shape their own version of civic life, to create their own democracy, has been 'normed' to an incredible degree," said Chris Gates, head of the century-old National Civic League. (Now I see that *norm* has become a verb . . . and I like it!)

"The convincing-them work is largely done," he went on. "Now people want to know how to make it real."

And Martha McCoy, longtime director of the Study Circles Resource Center, echoed Chris's thought: "What's changed for me is, I realized I'd underestimated now how much people really want to be involved. If people know their voice will be heard, they will be there. This was my 'aha' moment."

The art of citizen problem solving is advancing—just look back at "Citizen Power 101"—enabling more and more of us to experience the possibility Martha is talking about. It's what Jean True in Kentucky described to me in the 1990s as the great time she was having "going toe to toe and head to head with state legislators."

No longer stuck in reactive protest, citizen engagement in politics is becoming proactive, reflective, and inclusive. That's why Michael Gecan, a national leader with the Industrial Areas Foundation, refuses to label his a "citizen organization"; it is, he says, a "power organization."[68]

With all this ferment, Martha poses the next pointed question to all Americans: "None of us had to wake up today and say, 'I have to remember to be a consumer, to go to the mall.' No one! The opportunities are all around us, and they're alluring; the structures are in place, and all we have to do is use them. Yet when we talk about being a citizen, it feels onerous; it's like taking your medicine. But once people engage, it builds out.

"So how do we create ways for democracy as welcoming as the market? The feeling that opportunities abound for me to make a difference?"

8

CHOICE

the myth of choice & the taste of democracy

A power over a man's subsistence amounts to a power over his will.

ALEXANDER HAMILTON, 1787[1]

At age twenty-six, I had a hunch about food.

I figured that maybe food—essential to life and at the center of human culture—could be the thread I might pull to unravel the complexities of the economic and political order. Since feeding oneself and one's offspring is the first instinct of all living creatures, how could it be that we, the brainiest species, hadn't yet figured out a way for everyone to have enough to eat?

What question could be more basic?

Hamilton had it just right, I intuited. Without power over our food, any notion of freedom or democracy is empty.

That's where I began, and this hunch has taken me far and wide, from my first job in the ghettoes of Philadelphia in 1968 to teaching at a sustainable-farming center in India's Himalayan foothills in 2003—from witnessing the gut-wrenching devastation of hunger to glimpsing real solutions.

The precursor to this book, *The Quickening of America*, published in 1994, had no chapter on food: then I couldn't see enough

---

This chapter was written with Anna Lappé.

signs of democracy coming to life in our food economy to warrant it. What a difference today!

Americans are reknitting ties to the earth and rediscovering the love of healthy food. They are re-creating local food economies and reducing energy use by cutting transport distances. Farmers are rethinking blind adherence to the chemical path and embracing ecological practices. With their allies, they are igniting public concern about an agribusiness subsidy system gone terribly awry and bonding together to sell and process their own crops.

At the same time, urban communities are creating their own gardens and linking consumers and farmers. Farm-to-school programs are flourishing, with schools adding their own gardens for hands-on learning. Confronting the obesity epidemic, they're making healthy food an attractive and practical option and restoring mealtime to its place at the center of a satisfying social life.

All this adds up to a radical redirection of our food system, with Living Democracy emerging as much more than a metaphor.

It also adds up to common sense.

Yet many Americans would dismiss it all—organic apples and freshly picked kale as common as Cheetos and Coke? Urban neighborhoods increasingly becoming self-provisioning communities?

Nice, yes, but plainly naïve.

After all, aren't Americans choosing the opposite? Aren't we choosing an efficient "modern," delocalized, supersized food system with megafarms, feedlots, and food processors, selling through mega–chain stores filled with processed "food products" that have traveled megadistances?

Since choice is key to almost any definition of democracy and freedom, let's look at this premise with fresh eyes. For the big picture, I'll suggest we step back—well, up. Way up. Imagine we are landing here from Mars. (OK, it's a trite device, but it works!) We're surveying this strange little planet called Earth.

We look with wonder at how all the animals live, taking in this amazing dance that sustains life. We see species eat other species but rarely kill their own and *never* choose to kill themselves. They know exactly what their bodies need to thrive, and they go for that.

But wait. Look at those "human being" creatures. What a strange anomaly they are. They have no natural predators to fear, but they kill each other—more than one hundred million in the past century, most of that toll being civilian deaths in war. Not only that, but these humans are killing *themselves*—suicides take the lives of almost 60 percent more of them than homicides do.[2] Now look a little deeper. Notice another way they are killing themselves. In addition to suicide, you find the oddest practice: while other species eat what is ideally suited to them, humans are killing themselves with what they eat.

Their predicament seems unique in all animal life. And it must be a recent aberration, or else the species would have vanished long ago.

Food for these creatures seems to be a threat both to those who have too much and those who don't have enough.

On the "not enough" side: over eight hundred million humans experience day-in-and-day-out hunger. Here in the United States, where farmers' biggest headache is oversupply, nearly thirty-five million Americans live in families that are food-insecure—meaning they often don't know where their next meal is coming from.[3]

On the "too much" side: we see an obesity epidemic that's become a disease epidemic. Contributing to cancer, heart disease, and Type II diabetes, obesity causes well over one hundred thousand additional deaths each year, with some authorities placing the toll several times higher; and it eats up more than one in nine private health care dollars—now rivaling the cost of tobacco-related illnesses.[4]

the illusion of choice

And how did we get into such a predicament?

In the dominant mental map laid out in Part One, we human beings see ourselves as little more than selfish accumulators, egocentered materialists. With that view of ourselves, we can do no better than to turn over our fate to the market; we're too selfish to come together to deliberate over a desirable future.

So where does this shrunken view of human nature leave us?

Well, we tell ourselves, even if our choices feel limited in the political realm, at least in the marketplace we have *choice*—an abundance of it. We choose independently according to our unique desires.

Now let this sink in. If we really were *choosing*, we humans would be an evolutionary first, the first species to choose to kill itself by the food it eats. This seems highly unlikely. More likely we're being robbed of choice in ways that we're only beginning to grasp.

FIVE WAYS WE'RE ROBBED OF CHOICE

1. Fewer and fewer people decide what foods are marketed to us, based on a narrow calculus of highest return to their corporations' stockholders. So our options narrow—at our great peril.
2. As public airwaves are reduced to private commodities for selling other commodities—especially "food products"—our tastes are manipulated.
3. Concentrated power enables food corporations to purvey false messages and to influence government policies so we're kept in the dark—making smart choices harder.
4. Their enormous wealth gives agribusiness corporations the muscle to intimidate truth tellers, further denying us information and reducing our choice.
5. As agribusiness control tightens, farmers have less and less bargaining clout. Increasingly, they lose the choice to farm independently or even to farm at all.

Let's look at each one.

1. *Fewer and fewer people decide what foods are marketed to us, based on a narrow calculus of highest return to their corporations' stockholders.* Thirty-five thousand food items line a typical supermarket's shelves, *and I'm saying that our choices are limited?*

On the surface, it does seem implausible, but a narrowing of choice is built into a food industry in which just ten corporations now control roughly half of all U.S. food and drink sales. This means that in 2000, just 138 people, the boards of these ten corporations, made decisions affecting the health and welfare of hundreds of millions of people—not only here at home but, as food companies go global, around the world too.[5]

It's no coincidence that as control in the food industry has gotten narrower and narrower, we Americans have grown wider and wider. Now two-thirds of us are overweight, and one in every six children is obese, a rate that has tripled in thirty years.[6]

My favorite chapter in *Diet for a Small Planet* is called "Who Asked for Froot Loops?" in which I ask readers to imagine themselves as the chief executive of Food Conglomerate, Inc. Every decision aimed at fattening the bottom line—more processing, additives, sugar, salt, and fat—ends up degrading our food or making us fat.

The more processed, the more profit. Farmers sell corn for 4 cents a pound. But Kellogg's sells us cornflakes for $3.33 a pound.[7] (Kellogg's profits surged nearly ninefold in the 1990s.)[8] Buying Pringles at $1.50 per canister, we are paying $4.00 per pound for potatoes plus additives, when organic potatoes cost less than $1 per pound.

Processing is more than a pocketbook problem. It's a health problem.

Companies now add cheap high-fructose corn syrup to everything from yogurt to crackers—it even shows up in a Starbuck's egg salad sandwich! It is virtually the sole caloric sweetener in U.S. soft drinks. But high-fructose corn syrup doesn't work in our bodies like sucrose (white sugar) does. Fructose doesn't automatically stimulate insulin or leptin, which we depend on to signal our brains that we're full.[9]

Many nutritionists believe it's no coincidence that over the past thirty years, as high-fructose corn syrup intake leapt over 1,000 percent, obesity hit crisis levels. Plus, high-fructose corn syrup is implicated in elevating triglycerides in the blood, worsening our risk of heart disease.[10]

Manufacturers of processed food also love cheap "trans fats," but as many as one hundred thousand cardiac deaths could be avoided each year if we didn't eat them.[11]

Finally, to make crackers, breakfast cereals, chips, and cookies, most companies process the heck out of grain, lengthening their products' shelf life but removing a quarter of the protein and more than a dozen key nutrients. Processing robs us of whole grain's power to reduce the risk of heart disease and to maintain a healthy weight. Yet 40 percent of Americans now eat no whole-grain food at all.[12]

And where is our choice to use our purchases to support diverse, competitive business ownership?

Coca-Cola, for example, sells nearly *four hundred* brands, creating an illusion of diversity that undercuts a consumer's choice for real diversity.[13] When we buy Maxwell House coffee, Altoids mints, Baker's chocolate, Philadelphia cream cheese, or Oscar Mayer wieners, how many of us know we're giving our dollars to a single company, Kraft? Or that Kraft is a division of Altria, formerly Philip Morris?

The choice of consumers to buy the products of local, smaller food companies and the choice of new companies to break into a market are both constricted by the concentrated power of the supermarket giants. As of 2003, five supermarkets controlled 46 percent of retail sales, almost *double* their market share six years earlier.[14] In just sixteen years, Wal-Mart has become the country's largest grocer—predicted, by 2007, to command more than one of every three dollars spent in the United States for supermarket food.[15]

These big chains (except for Wal-Mart, which uses other strategies) charge substantial "slotting allowances"—onetime payments by food manufacturers to get a spot on the retailer's shelves or to get initial access to its warehouse.[16] Only the biggest manufacturers can afford them.

Monopoly power also limits choice when it brings higher prices. The price of bacon, for example—where only four companies control over 60 percent of the pork-processing industry—rose almost twice as fast as the overall Consumer Price Index between 1994 and 2004.[17] And the poor pay the most. Reflecting a widespread pattern, grocery stores in San Francisco's low-income communities charge as much as 60 percent more for the same products as in wealthier neighborhoods.[18]

Also galling, food companies demand that we pay a premium to get the healthier product. Froot Loops with less sugar costs 20 percent more than a regular box!

True, as many as ten thousand new product "choices" hit the market every year—have you tried chocolate-covered French fries or green ketchup?[19] But the choice most Americans still do *not* have is that of fresh, pesticide-free, whole foods at attractive prices in conveniently located stores.

2. *As public airwaves are reduced to private commodities for selling other commodities—especially "food products"—our tastes are manipulated.* Huge advertising budgets enable big companies to hire top marketers and psychologists who cook up new ways to play on our "weak satiation mechanism" for fat and sugar. (That's a fancy term for not being able to stop!) They turn what was an evolutionary advantage when we were hunters and gatherers—that is, our reflex to binge when we found the beehive (sweets) or made the kill (fat)—into a threat to our survival. Fat and sugar now comprise *half* the calories Americans consume.

I chuckled when a young mother I met recently told me how her five-year-old had already seen through the advertisers' ploy. Reacting to a junk-food commercial on television, her daughter exclaimed, "Mommy, they're trying to boss me!"

Worldwide, dollars spent to incite us to buy are predicted to pass the half-*trillion* mark in 2005.[20] That's roughly equivalent to the entire annual income of nearly seven hundred million of the world's poorest people.[21] Food processors are second only to automakers among the top advertisers.[22] They bombard children with tens of thousands of TV ads a year, the vast majority of which are for candy, sugary cereals, salty and fatty snacks, and other junk food. McDonald's alone spends over $1 billion every year on ads.[23]

By contrast, the entire government nutrition education budget now amounts to just one-fifth of the advertising budget for Altoids mints.[24] (When did you last see a TV commercial for broccoli?)

Ads don't limit our choices, we're told, they inform our decision-making.

But some neuroscientists aren't so sure. One, Read Montague, recently conducted taste tests pitting Coke against Pepsi. In the blind test, Pepsi excited more activity in the area of the brain that processes feelings of reward. But once brand names were revealed, subjects experienced taste differently. Part of the brain associated with cognitive powers such as memory of prior impressions kicked in and almost all the subjects now preferred Coke. Brand conditioning, it turns out, can override taste buds![25]

Having shriveled from a public communication tool—necessary to democracy—into products themselves, media outlets have become advertisers' tools shaping our tastes, even remaking our desires, often to the detriment of our health.

3. *Concentrated power enables food corporations to purvey false messages and to influence government policies so we're kept in the dark—making smart choices harder.* Our Department of Agriculture

is supposed to offer impartial guidance to what's good for us. But can it?

Of thirteen members of the Department of Agriculture's Dietary Guidelines Advisory Committee in 2001, seven had current or past financial ties to the meat, dairy, or egg industry. Medical professionals and others, troubled that the public was being misled by "experts" with vested interests, sued. After a yearlong effort, they won, yet little has changed.[26]

Industry influence can have deadly consequences, stresses Dr. Marion Nestle, esteemed nutrition professor at New York University. In a 1993 example, she notes, the Agriculture Department sought to require meat and poultry to carry labels with safe handling and cooking instructions. But the American Meat Institute—the oldest and largest meat and poultry trade association—resisted. The industry group even took the department to court, claiming that the labels would unnecessarily scare us.

The court ruled in industry's favor. Less than a week later, three children in Texas died from eating meat contaminated with a deadly strain of *E. coli*, bacteria that are killed when meat is properly cooked.[27]

Most successful in keeping us in the dark about our food and limiting effective choice is the biotech food industry, led by Monsanto, which controls over 90 percent of genetically modified seed.[28] In less than a decade, it managed to infuse genetically modified organisms (GMOs) throughout our food system with virtually no awareness, much less public debate weighing the potential benefits and risks: today, most soybeans, cotton, and canola, as well as 38 percent of corn grown in the United States is from genetically engineered seed.[29] Yet a 2004 public opinion survey found that 70 percent of Americans thought they'd never eaten GMOs.[30]

Without labeling products containing GMOs, we can't choose whether to eat them or not. Yet the federal government has refused to require GMO food labeling despite the fact that 93 percent of

Americans favor it.[31] In 2002, worried Oregonians stopped waiting for the federal government and placed a measure on the ballot to require the labeling of foods containing GMOs sold in their state. Theirs was hardly a radical demand—forty countries require GMO labeling, even China!

Quickly, dozens of companies, including Monsanto, H. J. Heinz, and General Mills, went to work, pouring $5.4 million into a campaign against the measure. Spending roughly thirty-three times more than the initiative's backers, industry frightened voters by telling them that labeling would burden taxpayers and disadvantage farmers selling products out of state.[32]

Denied a fair debate on labeling, Oregonians defeated the initiative.

Three years later, Monsanto's own thousand-plus-page study reported that lab rats fed one of the company's genetically modified strains of corn developed kidney and blood abnormalities.[33] This, after years of ridiculing anyone who dared to suggest that GMOs may not be nutritionally identical to other foods.

This shock may give new life to those seeking to block GMOs' spread. Less than a year before this report, Mendocino County, California, became the first political entity in the United States to bar them. Oregonians may soon have second thoughts.

To argue that some agribusiness companies help disseminate lies about their products—further undermining our capacity to choose wisely—is a heavy charge.

Consider the antiorganics campaigner Dennis Avery. Since the late 1990s, he has publicly claimed that organic foods are dangerous, more likely than pesticide-sprayed foods to carry a deadly strain of *E. coli* bacteria. The Centers for Disease Control and Prevention refuted his claims, and the actual CDC data on which these claims are based do not implicate organic foods. But that hasn't stopped Avery's charges from echoing around the globe, from conferences in Australia to congressional testimony in the United States to mainstream news programs like *20/20*.[34]

And who pays Dennis Avery's salary?

The academic-sounding Hudson Institute, funded in part by agribusiness giants including Archer Daniels Midland, Syngenta, Dow, and their industry associations.[35]

4. *Their enormous wealth gives agribusiness corporations the muscle to intimidate truth tellers, further denying us information and reducing our choice*. Fear works, as we saw in the Oregon vote on GMO labeling. It can certainly shut people up. And one way to manufacture fear is to sue public figures who are gutsy enough to speak out. In 1996, a rancher and food activist named Howard Lyman appeared on the Oprah Winfrey show, where he described the common practice of feeding "rendered" (a nice word for ground-up) cows to live cows.

To which Oprah exclaimed, "It has just stopped me cold from eating another burger!" Texas cattle ranchers then hit Winfrey and Lyman with a $10 million lawsuit for disparaging beef on national television. Laws against food disparagement or libel are on the books in thirteen states.[36]

Winfrey and Lyman eventually won, but as soon as the first lawsuit was over, more than one hundred livestock owners came after Winfrey again with a federal suit. It was dismissed in 2002, but only after another four years.[37]

Big bucks, it seems, can turn people into bullies.

Not only does giant Monsanto sue small family farmers for patent infringement, but it intimidates its critics. My former husband, the late scientist Marc Lappé, wrote one of the earliest examinations of GMOs, *Against the Grain*. As the book was going to press, his publisher received an intimidating letter from Monsanto and canceled publication. Marc had to find a more courageous publisher.

Then, in the mid-1990s, Monsanto lawyers threatened producers of a Fox News–owned and –operated station in Florida, pressuring the station with "dire consequences" if it aired a story about the controversial Monsanto growth hormone rBGH commonly fed to dairy cows. The two award-winning journalists who'd reported the series, Jane Akre and Steve Wilson, refused to kill it but tried (with eighty-three revisions!) to accommodate Monsanto's reservations.

Eventually the TV station did kill the story and fired Akre and Wilson. Using whistleblower protection laws, the husband-and-wife team took Fox to court in 1996. After a five-week trial costing the couple hundreds of thousands of dollars, the jury decided that the story Akre and Wilson had been required to sign off on had indeed been slanted and distorted. It awarded Akre $425,000.

But here's the kicker. The verdict was overturned in a decision that brought to light a disturbing fact: no law, rule, or regulation, the Florida appellate judges decided, prohibits the media from distorting news. That's right—since the media may legally distort news, Akre and Wilson didn't qualify for whistleblower protection!

Today rBGH is still widely used. Yet before consuming it, few Americans have had the choice to weigh the kinds of concerns Akre and Wilson tried to bring us.[38]

In all these ways, American consumers are drowning in products but robbed of choice.

Do I sound a bit melodramatic?

Or maybe not dramatic enough, if by choice we mean access, based on impartial information, to healthy food, readily available—as well as the choice of locally produced food from diverse companies. But Americans are discovering how to reclaim choice. It's a stunning story of innovation to which we soon turn. But before turning to emerging solutions, consider a fifth thief of choice in our food system, this one constricting farmers.

5. *As agribusiness control tightens, farmers have less and less bargaining clout. Increasingly, they lose the choice to farm independently or even to farm at all.* As mentioned earlier, economists tell us that when four (or fewer) companies control at least 40 percent of a market, we can say good-bye to effective competition.[39] Keep that fig-

ure in mind when you ponder what farmers are up against as they try to sell their products: today four beef processors control 84 percent of the market; with pork, it's 64 percent; with chicken, 56 percent. In selling their crops, farmers' options are no wider. Four companies process 63 percent of flour and 80 percent of soybeans; the largest three export 81 percent of all U.S. corn.[40]

"There isn't one grain of anything in the world that is sold in a free market. Not one! The only place you see a free market is in the speeches of politicians."[41]

So said not an irate farmer but the CEO of the agribusiness giant Archer Daniels Midland. He should know: 85 percent of recent fines on price-fixing cartels were paid by agribusinesses. Archer Daniels Midland, along with others including Cargill and Tate & Lyle, have paid over $1 billion to settle price-fixing lawsuits brought against them.[42]

On the front end, too, when buying chemical inputs, farmers also have little choice. Six companies share 75 percent of the market. GMO technology is even more tightly held, as noted earlier, with just one company, Monsanto, now controlling over 90 percent of the global genetically modified seed market.[43]

With so little bargaining power, farmers have watched agricultural export prices, adjusted for inflation, sink to only 42 percent of what they were in 1975.[44]

"The marketplace is to us what the Constitution is to a lawyer: It's a foundation," Keith Bolin, a farmer in Northwestern Iowa, told us. "And when we lose our foundation—an open, transparent market—we've lost our freedom."

So processors and marketers—not farmers—capture an ever-bigger slice of the profit from food sales.

For every dollar we spend on food, the farmer gets 19 cents, down from roughly 27 cents just two decades ago.[45] With that thin slice, the farmer must pay the mortgage and purchase machinery, seeds, fuel, fertilizers—and on chemically dependent farms, buy pesticides, and antibiotics, too.

Squeezed tighter and tighter, farmers are forced off the land at the rate of fifteen thousand farms a year.[46] Today the biggest 8 percent of farms account for nearly three-quarters of all production.[47] The human toll in farm communities can be measured in youth drug abuse rates worse than in cities and farmer suicide rates as much as three times the national average.[48]

Keith, forty-three, helped us understand what it's like in the eye of the storm.

His family, with four kids, gets by raising hogs for Niman Ranch using humane and sustainable methods. But most of his neighbors have gone out of business, and 43 percent of students at the local school are now so poor that they qualify for subsidized lunches.

Most of the holdouts have turned to contract farming: they sign up with nonfarm corporations to produce under exact specifications for a fixed amount. It's the only "choice" many feel they have. "They love farming, and it's often the only way to stay on the farm and not take a job at Wal-Mart," Keith explained.

Overall, contract farmers now supply 36 percent of the value of crops and livestock sold in the United States.[49] But nearly all poultry and egg producers are under contracts in which companies such as Tyson own the flocks and supply the feed while the farmer provides the labor, chicken houses, water, and utilities.

The arrangement puts the corporation in charge, but farmers still shoulder the risk. "Contract poultry producers often have to take on as much as a million dollars in debt to build facilities before they even begin," explained Auburn University professor Robert Taylor. Contracting farmers are in theory guaranteed a price for what they produce, but companies like Tyson have been known to stop honoring contracts without reimbursing farmers, even if there are months or years left on them.[50]

"Basically the [company] controls everything," said Taylor, an expert in contract farming. "This is why poultry growers are sometimes called 'serfs with a mortgage.'" A far cry from the independent family farms proven to be the most efficient in the world and the lifeblood of rural communities.

Contracting undermines community solidarity, too, because most contracts require farmers to sign nondisclosure agreements. They're forbidden to reveal the terms of their contracts to anyone—not their banker, not their priest, *not even their spouse*.

"It's a way to keep everybody in the dark. If you don't know what your neighbor is getting, how do you know if you got a good contract or a bad one?" Keith asked. Some states have outlawed nondisclosure policies, including Keith's state of Illinois, thanks to efforts by farmers like him.

Contract farming also "robs wealth out of local economies," Keith explained. "You could make the case that it's not a lot different than the Wal-Martization of downtown's Main Street."

Huge factory farm operations associated with the contracting system combined with concentration among packers and processors squeeze out family farms without benefiting consumers—remember the rising price of bacon?

Compare the scale of the average Minnesota family hog farm with thirty to eighty sows in all stages of growth—breeding, farrowing, and finishing—with a contract factory hog-finishing operation with five thousand hogs. The huge scale, the off-site control, and the narrow bottom-line interests of factory farms degrade rural life—bringing inhumane treatment of farm animals along with the blight and health hazards of odor and manure pollution.

Ronald Reagan, Keith reminded us, used to criticize Russia's agriculture for being centralized in the state's hands. So people's choices and freedoms were limited, and they were unable to feed themselves. "Corporations are doing the same thing here," he said. "The only difference is they had a hammer and sickle over the doorway rather than a Cargill or Smithfield flag. And to be honest with you, I fear the Cargill and Smithfield flag just as much as the hammer and sickle."

ARE WE "CHOOSING" THIS?

- *Taxpayers subsidize the narrowing of choice.* Federal farm subsidies amount to an average of $19 billion every year—totaling $75 billion from 2000 to 2003.[51] Their primary effect is to reduce costs for giant food processing companies, not to help struggling family farmers. Since 1995, three-quarters of the funds have gone to the largest 10 percent of farms. Two-thirds of our family farmers get no subsidies at all.[52]
- *Illness.* Each year, seventy-six million Americans—one in four of us—suffer foodborne illnesses, accounting for 325,000 hospitalizations and roughly five thousand deaths.[53] Mostly because of worsening obesity, an American child now has nearly a *one in three* chance of developing diabetes.[54]
- *Paying for illness.* Overall, one of every eleven health dollars goes to treat obesity-related conditions.[55]
- *Pesticide harm.* Pesticides poison between ten and twenty thousand farmworkers a year (and those are only the reported cases).[56] The average American carries residues of at least thirteen pesticides, concludes a Centers for Disease Control study. One insecticide, Dursban (Dow Chemical), was found on average at levels three to almost five times above what the government deems "acceptable."[57] In another study, preschoolers fed standard fare carried in their bodies six times the by-products of dangerous pesticides—those implicated in mental and physical impairment—compared to children eating organic food.[58]

- *Waste of resources*. The production of just one pound of U.S. feedlot beef uses sixteen pounds of grain and soy and between two and twelve thousand gallons of water, in part because more and more cattle are fed on crops from irrigated land.[59] (Twelve thousand gallons is as much water as an average American uses for all purposes in four months.)[60]
- *Soil loss*. Our extractive farming practices mean that for every pound of food eaten in the United States, we lose six pounds of farmable soil.[61]
- *Animal waste pollution*. Huge hog, cattle, poultry, and sheep operations release 1.5 billion tons of animal waste every year.[62] That's roughly 130 times the amount of waste produced by all humans in the United States.[63]
- *Water pollution*. Nitrogen and phosphorus in fertilizer runoff flows down the Mississippi River to the Gulf of Mexico where it kills aquatic life, creating a dead zone the size of New Jersey.[64] Nitrate from fertilizer has made a quarter of U.S. drinking-water wells unsafe to use.[65]
- *Worsening global warming*. U.S. food production accounts for 17 percent of our total fossil fuel use and 10 percent of our greenhouse gases contributing to global warming.[66] Agriculture's greenhouse gas emissions caused over $450 million worth of damage in 2001 alone.[67]
- *Overall negative impacts of agriculture in the United States*. The damage—from pollution, pesticide harm, and more—is estimated at $5.7 billion to $16.9 billion annually.[68]

tasting democracy

Our food system's rapid refiguring over the past century—from decentralized family farms producing for local and national markets to a centralized, corporate-controlled system geared to global markets—was not inevitable. It flowed from economic and political assumptions outlined in Part Two.

But a blaring alarm is awakening Americans to what's been lost. For what could be a louder wake-up call than the realization that our diet is becoming one of our worst health hazards? Or that food production is becoming one of the biggest assaults on the environment? Or that our rural communities are turning into ghost towns as family farms give way to contracted operations?

Americans are digging to the root of the problem and creating new, fairer, more democratic, and more satisfying economic relationships—and with them, more choices.

power in participation and vision

Cooperatives owned and directed by members, as Chapter Six describes, bring democracy to the workplace. In the rural workplace—the farm—Organic Valley is taking the lead. You may have seen its milk or yogurt in the dairy case. It's the country's largest organic cooperative, cooked up by a handful of farmers in southwestern Wisconsin in the late 1980s.

The Organic Valley idea is simple: farmer members sell collectively, strengthening the marketing power of each individual. From its shoestring beginning, Organic Valley has taken off—now providing solid livelihoods for seven hundred family farm members and over three hundred employees.

It's the active participation of its farmer members that explains the company's rise, says George Siemon, a founder and CEO of Organic Valley. From monthly phone calls with elected regional representatives to farmer involvement in marketing, members have a real voice, George told us.

And Organic Valley offers its member farmers another benefit: it shields them from the wildly fluctuating market price for milk, which became even more erratic after the government lowered its price support safety net in the late 1980s. In 2002, prices for "conventional" milk (produced with pesticides, antibiotics, and genetically engineered growth hormones) were the lowest since the 1970s, increasing only slightly since.[69] Month to month, they can drop 60 percent or more. (Imagine running a drugstore or car dealership in which prices for all your products could fall 60 percent in one month!) By contrast, co-op members are guaranteed a fair price.

Organic Valley remains independent and democratically run while many organic businesses have succumbed to the forces sketched out in Chapters Four and Five. Cascadian Farm, founded in 1972, is now a division of General Mills. Odwalla juice, founded in 1980, is now a piece of Minute Maid, a division of Coca-Cola. (Remember those four hundred brands?)[70] Monopoly power is infecting organic dairy markets, too, where Horizon dominates supermarket sales of organic milk with 70 percent of the market.[71]

"Organic Valley also could have sold the business, and the first one hundred farmers would have been millionaires," George said, "but we've steered away from that. You can only serve one master, and that's your owners." Organic Valley's owners are its family farmers.

Throughout the Midwest, scores of farmer co-ops—sadly, though, mostly not organic—have been popping up in the past fifteen years to keep more wealth and real choice back on the farm.

"Basic commodity prices are so low, farmers have to figure out a way of capturing more of the consumer dollar," longtime Minnesota chronicler of farming trends Lee Egerstrom, sixty-one, told me.[72] "And co-ops are the way to do it."

In the mid-1990s, the American News Service interviewed Barb Frank, a third-generation farmer in Renville, Minnesota, and a friend of Lee's. Barb's family farm was teetering on the edge. "We had to change or lose everything," she said then. So Barb took the plunge to invest in becoming a member of a new egg cooperative nearby—Golden Oval Eggs, controlled by its members, who commit to selling only through it.

In just a few years, the Frank family income shot up. Today Barb's daughter and soon-to-be son-in-law are farming with her. "It's amazing. I never thought I'd come back here to make a living, and now we've built two new barns," her daughter Becky Frank told me recently.

Sugar beet co-ops in Minnesota are also freeing farmers from the agribusiness squeeze. Co-op members effectively make twice as much as they used to, Lee explained to me, because they get paid once for their crop and again in the return on their member equity in the co-op.

"Don't get the wrong idea. We're not visionaries," he chuckled. "We're just catching up with our cousins in northern Europe. In the Netherlands and Denmark, about two-thirds of what comes out of the ground is controlled by farmer co-ops." That's why their family farms are surviving, Lee believes.

choosing organic

It seems to have happened almost overnight. Nearly three-quarters of all grocery stores now carry organic products. Some experts estimate that by 2007, the U.S. organics industry will bring in $31 billion, equivalent to the annual revenue of Archer Daniels Midland, the world's fifth-largest agribusiness corporation.[73]

The growth in demand for organic products reflects an increasing number of consumers who want to know that when they're biting into their apple, carrot, or collard greens they are not endangering their health. They want to know that neither land nor laborers were hurt to grow their food. As these consumers awaken, they make viable a new breed of farmers.

Farmers making the effort to go organic is a gift to us all.

Using no synthetic chemicals, organic farming reduces overall emissions of nitrous oxide, produced when soils and chemical fertilizers interact.[74] A greenhouse gas nightmare, nitrous oxide has 310 times the heat-trapping power of carbon dioxide.[75] Soils farmed organically also absorb carbon dioxide from the air and lock it into the soil as fertile humus, making organic farmland a sink, not a source, of carbon dioxide.[76] Neither do organic farms use antibiotics on livestock, helping reverse the growing crisis of antibiotic resistant strains of bacteria threatening human health.

Organic farming typically uses less energy than chemically dependent farming methods—half as much, according to one study.[77]

Finally, growing organic protects farmworkers and consumers from harm and also yields a premium price for farmers.

Hearing the term *organic*, it's easy to think only of the absence of something, that is, pesticides, hormones, antibiotics—the works.

But organic farming today doesn't mean going backward to the era before the chemical onslaught in the mid-twentieth century. It's part of a scientific revolution based on deepening understanding of ecology: Farmers enhance nutritional quality and productivity—enjoying yields comparable to those of farmers using chemicals—by using improved tilling practices and working with the interactions of plant varieties, insects, soil microorganisms, composts, and other natural processes.[78] It's more accurately called ecological farming: instead of chemically dependent and soil-eroding, ecological farming is knowledge-intensive and soil-enhancing.

a new kind of shareholder

"There was no other way to get into farming," says Wisconsin farmer David Perkins about his family's decision to join a related movement known as community supported agriculture, in which participating farms are called CSAs.

In this brand-new business model, consumers and farmers become partners: consumers buy a "share" of the future harvest so the farmer has capital for planting without the burden of a bank loan. Each week of the growing season, members can count on prepaid fresh produce delivered to them or to convenient pickup sites. On "U-pick" days, members can take part in the harvest themselves.

Members of Barb and David Perkins's Vermont Valley Community Farm pay $420—in four installments if they so choose—and get organic produce delivered all summer and early fall at roughly 80 percent of the retail price.

A few years ago, my daughter Anna and I visited the Perkins's place outside Madison. Both now forty-eight, Barb and David sold their house in the city in 1994 to try their hand at farming CSA-style.

At dusk, we sat in their yard looking out on about sixty acres of land in a long valley nestled between deep green hills while Barb and David filled us in.

They told us that when they started the CSA ten years earlier, they and their children set a five-year goal of five hundred members. With that base, they figured they could make it financially. They hit that target right on the nose, and have since grown to eight hundred members.

A lot of the work at Vermont Valley is done by "worker-shares"—members who pay for their produce by contributing several hours a week of their labor. When we asked who usually chooses to work, Barb says there is no "usually."

"All kinds of people"—Barb counted off on her fingers—"ministers, teachers, students, a massage therapist, a painter, an insurance adjuster. You name it.

"We do it because it's a way to get people involved with the farm. It's important for people to have that deep connection." Last season, fifty-five worker-shares helped out.

When we connected with the Perkinses recently, David reported that growth has been steady, just through word of mouth. "We're not marketing geniuses," he said; "we're just offering people something that's important to them, and they really like being part of it."

As we sat in the grass with the Perkinses that early fall evening, Barb shared a story that Anna and I have retold many times.

"Every now and then, I have a moment that makes all the hard work, all the long hours, all the sweat we've put into this place worthwhile," Barb said, smiling. "Yesterday I was at a restaurant in town, and I saw this little kid, wide-eyed, grab his mom's arm and point at me.

"He said, 'Mommy, Mommy, look. There's our farmer!'"

A thousand CSAs are now spread out across the country, with sixteen in the Madison area alone serving eight thousand people—that's eight times the number just over a decade ago.[79] You can find CSAs, farmers' markets, and community gardens near you at http://www.localharvest.org.

"For us it's the only approach to farming that makes sense," David said.

Farmer cooperatives, community-supported agriculture, farmers' markets—all are part of a new food economy based not on highest return to shareholders but on highest return to the land, its stewards, and those who depend on its harvests.

Also enjoying new energy are consumer food cooperatives. After 9/11, grieving and angry citizens in Northfield, Minnesota, began a weekly downtown vigil, Phil Stoltzfus, professor of religion at Saint Olaf College, told me.

"We got to know each other, and from our group came Just Food—the nation's newest food co-op. We opened in 2004 with 750 household members; now we have one thousand. And that's in a town of only twelve thousand people," Phil beamed. "We specialize in food produced locally. The co-op transformed our town. The state representative, the mayor, everybody is joining."

Nationwide, there are roughly five hundred food cooperatives, stores owned by their members, focusing on whole, organic, local food.[80]

FREEING OURSELVES FROM THE "I CAN'T AFFORD IT" MYTH GIVES US CHOICE

For roughly forty million underpaid and otherwise limited-income Americans, every purchase is a stretch. But many Americans do have financial wiggle room. On average, we spend only a tenth of our disposable income on food, and food expenses take an ever-shrinking bite out of our pocketbooks—15 percent smaller than thirty years ago.[81]

Since healthy eating lowers the risk of disease, any additional cost we might think of as buying health insurance—only much tastier. Actually, though, healthy eating can be a terrific bargain.

Nutritionists agree that healthy eating requires a shift toward plant foods and away from animal-derived foods. My first book, *Diet for a Small Planet,* provides plenty of reasons why vegetarian eating makes sense. Recently, the Mediterranean diet—big on fresh veggies, fruits, whole grains, and olive oil but light on meat—proved in a ten-year study to reduce by 23 percent the risk of death from all causes among older people.[82] Think of the savings: grains, beans, peas, lentils, nuts, seeds, potatoes, and other root crops—all typically cost less than meat. And popping a big myth, a Department of Agriculture study says that fresh produce actually costs less than processed. The recommended three servings of fruit and four servings of vegetables a day costs a mere 64 cents.[83]

Shifting toward unprocessed foods we cook at home is also a big money saver, even when those foods are organic. Froot Loops cost roughly $3.72 a pound—35 cents per serving. Compare that to the enjoyment of hot, whole-grain organic oatmeal for just 13 cents per serving.[84]

So enjoy, be healthy, and save!

To get started, look for *Grub: Ideas for an Urban Organic Kitchen* by Anna Lappé and Bryant Terry (New York: Tarcher/Penguin, 2006); http://www.eatgrub.org.

concrete, compost, and change

It's an overcast day on Chicago's South Side, and Erika Allen, thirty-three, wants to show off her worms. Determined, she digs into a wooden box filled with several feet of dirt as black and moist as chocolate cake. Surrounding her are seedlings and garden hoses, shovels and rain boots; the greenhouse air is thick with life. From next door comes the laughter of kids in the First Presbyterian Head Start program.

"I'm carrying on a family legacy," said Erika, the exuberant coordinator of Growing Power, as she digs deeper for the worms. "I grew up doing organic farming, taking food into food-insecure communities, selling produce in inner-city markets. That was just what we did."

Her father, Will Allen, a retired, six-foot-seven pro basketball player, founded Farm City Link in Milwaukee in 1995, which eventually evolved into Growing Power a few years later.[85] Today they operate in both Chicago and Milwaukee. In Milwaukee are six greenhouses, a food retail outlet, and a commercial kitchen, plus livestock and beekeeping. Nineteen young people, most of them from disadvantaged backgrounds, work there alongside a hundred or so volunteers.

"We're not just growing food; we're growing communities," Will said.

Their compost is a big moneymaker, thanks to the worms. Each day, eight thousand pounds of mash from a local organic brewery, a thousand pounds of coffee grounds from nearby restaurants, and another ten thousand pounds of too-old-to-eat produce from food banks are combined—creating compost to feed tens of thousands of worms, which in turn break down the food scraps. Their castings create top-grade fertilizer that sells for $36,000 a bin. "It would take a rancher three hundred steer to equal the value of my worm livestock," Will told Toronto's *Now* magazine.[86]

In another greenhouse, four thousand tilapia—a tasty little fish that evolved in Africa, the Middle East, and Asia to live in shallow still water—fill a 4,400-gallon fishing hole. The water with fish manure circulates into canals and trays that feed the growth of five thousand pots of herbs and greens, including watercress, cilantro, basil, eddo, and baby bok choy. Local restaurateurs pay $50 a month for the herbs.

Where others see depressing vacant lots, Erika and her father see farms. Theirs is a vision of urban and rural communities, here and across the globe, creating their own food systems—making compost with worms, planting and harvesting in community gardens, and providing their own healthy food.

Erika picked up many of these threads.

"When you create something that's community-operated, wealth stays in the community, as opposed to going to some big chain that may not be even located in this country. That means people looking at investing in their own companies, their own food buying clubs, their own co-ops."

And it means teaching people how to grow their own food.

Filling raised garden beds with top-quality soil, Growing Power makes gardening possible even where soil is contaminated with heavy metals. With the support of Heifer International, they're creating assembly "kits" of their biological raised-bed growing system to disseminate across the country and abroad.

Erika is eager to bring the tilapia fish farming that's been so successful in Milwaukee to inner-city Chicago.

"You can get a group of women who have never used a power tool, and they can build this fish system," Erika said. "It's simple *and* sustainable." It's a scaled-down version of the Milwaukee setup: the worms fertilize soil above the tanks and release waste into the water; the fish, in turn, release ammonia, taken up by the plants growing in the soil above the fish. "It's a complete, closed cycle," Erika noted.

Touring with Erika through the greenhouse and abandoned lots surrounding the church that Growing Power–Chicago calls home, one has to squint hard to see thriving farms. But Erika's enthusiasm helps. She envisions families here eventually composting, using the soil to grow their own food, and sharing the harvest with the community.

With nearly nine thousand city-owned vacant lots, there's no shortage of ground in which her vision could take root.[87]

Urban people around the world are doing it. In Singapore, ten thousand urban farms produce 80 percent of the poultry and 25 percent of the vegetables consumed. In London and Vancouver, 14 percent and 44 percent of residents, respectively, grow food in home gardens.[88]

Like the Perkins's CSA, Erika is connecting urban consumers with local farmers. Her Rainbow Farmers Co-Op delivers an affordable basket of fruits and vegetables to about three hundred families every week of the growing season.

Integral to their work, Erika and her father stress, is getting young people onto the land. "When everything around them is not positive or nurturing," Erika noted, "they can be part of something that *is* positive; they can see that their work makes things grow. It's that idea of 'growing power.'"

Erika and Will are not alone.

The Food Project grows food both in Dorchester, one of Boston's poorest neighborhoods, and in upscale Lincoln, fifteen miles west of Boston, creating "a community that bridges race and class and the boundaries of geography," the project's associate director, Anim Steel, said. "That personally gives me hope."

Steel's hope is in the six hundred teenagers who've worked with the Food Project since its founding. It's in the crunch of the 250,000 pounds of vegetables the youth help grow on their thirty-acre organic farm in Lincoln, in the seventeen hundred volunteers who work with the project every year, and in the 250 members of the CSA and the thousands who shop at the Food Project's farmers market, use its catering services, or buy its own value-added products (like its sought-after salsa).

What difference has the Food Project made in the community?

"One of the biggest differences is that the citizens of Boston—from the very poor to the very rich—are able to eat good, healthy food. Half of our food goes to shelters or to low-income farmers' markets. That's a concrete difference."

Then there's the less concrete, "like the young people who discover their gifts," Anim said. "This one kid—he was so shy. He's from Cape Verde and came to America speaking no English. When he had to do his first presentation at the project, he actually wept he was so shy. Last year, we went to his high school graduation. He was a valedictorian speaker, and he told us he'd gained a lot of his confidence through the project."

In the past five years, more than two hundred community organizations like the Food Project—mixing teenagers, food, and farming—have taken off.

classrooms, collards, and growing democracy in schools

With the attack on all things public, funding cuts have made many public school districts desperate. Some are resorting to bake sales and bingo, even blood plasma drives, to buy books.

Enter the junk-food and fast-food industries, which encourage schools to sign exclusive "pouring rights" contracts with soft drinks companies in exchange for money for the school.

To save money, schools now use fast food to replace lunchroom costs. Candy, chips, and "sweet baked goods" account for 85 percent of snacks sold in school, and drinks of "poor nutritional value," such as sugary sodas and juice drinks, make up 75 percent of beverages, says a recent survey by the Center for Science in the Public Interest.[89] More than half of the 932 school districts that responded in a recent Texas study had signed exclusive vending-machine contracts.[90]

Now in over a thousand schools each year, teachers and administrators don McDonald's uniforms and serve up Big Macs and French fries for "McTeacher's Nights." A share of the proceeds returns to their school.[91]

Defending her school's decision to participate, a principal of a San Francisco school said, "We teach about nutrition at this school, but honestly we can't tell people to stop going to fast-food restaurants. It's their choice."[92]

There is that word again—*choice*.

And what are the choices of school administrators?

With public funding shrinking and school lunch contracting options increasingly limited, many feel they don't have much choice. They must raise money any way they can.

And students? If junk food or low-nutritional-quality food is students' only at-hand option, are they able to choose?

But school districts from Chicago to New York have begun to say, Wait! We *do* have a choice, and it's high time we claimed it. With American children now having a one in three chance of developing diabetes, our children's lives are at stake.

Alarm over the health consequences of our fast-food diet spurred citizens in Los Angeles—the country's second largest school district, with nearly 750,000 students—to act. In 2002, parents and administrators said no to pouring-rights contracts and successfully pushed state senate bills that phase in bans on soda and junk-food sales in the district's elementary, middle, junior, and high schools.[93]

The greatest resistance came from the schools' financial directors, said Andrew Glazier, the chief of staff for the board member spearheading the measures. A big high school can make $80,000 from selling soda.

"We could make money selling cigarettes on campus, too, but we don't do that," Andrew quipped. "And by all accounts, obesity is the new tobacco. Forty percent of our students are overweight or obese—that's scary. This is the first generation that is going to live less long than their parents, and a lot of it has to do with diet."

An interesting twist in the story, Andrew said, is that companies are now coming to them asking for advice about how to make their products "LA-Unified-certified." "We're a large enough consumer that we can influence supply," he explained.

Since its big win, the district has gotten calls seeking advice from school districts as far away as Maine and Canada. "A lot of people are saying if LA Unified can do it, anyone can," Andrew said.

In mid-2005, New Jersey jumped into the lead, becoming the first state to ban junk food in schools.

These pioneers are helping a new generation learn the connection between food and health—that broccoli doesn't grow on aisle 3 but in well-tended earth.

They are also giving birth to a school garden movement.

In California, the state has declared the goal of a garden in *every school*. "People are tired of seeing schoolyards that look like prisons," one expert in what are called "edible schoolyards" explained. Describing the manifold motivations for school gardens, she said, "In designing, building, and transforming an asphalt desert into a vibrant ecosystem, kids learn that they have the power to make change. It's a powerful lesson."

It is a lesson in choice: from cement schoolyard plots and abandoned city lots to lush gardens.

cheating for taste

At college, too, healthy and even local food is finding a way through the centralized corporate food service.

I know that teens falsify IDs all the time to buy beer—but to eat local organic food?

Apparently the temptation got the best of Yale University students in 2004 when word got out that food served in the dining hall of one of Yale's residential colleges "rocked." Eight students from another residential hall tried sneaking in with forged IDs. They got caught succumbing to the lure of the sustainable dining program, inspired and guided by famed California restaurateur Alice Waters and her Yale-student daughter Fannie. It offers local, seasonal, and sustainably grown food.

Yale's Berkeley College gets half its produce from local suppliers, compared to only a fifth in the other dining halls. Joshua L. Viertel, the Yale program's associate director, noted that the $6.5 million that the university spends each year on food for students could help keep more local Connecticut farms from going out of business as more than eight thousand acres worth of farms do each year in that state alone. "We cast our vote three times a day," he said.

"So many environmental movements are based on self-denial," Viertel told *E Magazine*. "This takes a hedonistic pleasure in doing the right thing."

Yale reports that the cost of the healthier food runs about 50 percent higher than what it had been spending. An anonymous donor covered the gap the first year, and Yale's Sustainable Food Project is now working to have the school take on the additional cost.

From the College of the Atlantic on the Maine coast to Oberlin College in Ohio, cafeterias are starting to look to the local. A few are even getting some of their food from student-run organic gardens.

In 1990, 650 co-op housing students who run their own kitchens at Oberlin College in northeastern Ohio started buying more local food. In a little more than a decade, these co-ops and the college dining service together were spending about a tenth of the school's food budget locally.

"We felt like we actually [helped] the local economy and reduced the fossil fuel involved in hauling all that food from 1,300 miles away," 1993 grad Brad Masi told *E Magazine*. Plus, Oberlin's food waste enriches soil in a three-acre organic garden that is part of the school's seventy-acre George Jones Farm, which Masi now manages. Kitchen grease is converted into biodiesel fuel using a bike-powered processor that Oberlin junior Sam Merrett designed and built. Using biodiesel in the farm's tractor is part of the vision.

Masi said he felt encouraged. "When I was a student taking environmental courses, I started to get a sense that humans were parasites spreading over the earth, depleting and polluting." He's now working in a farm office built of local clay, straw, and timber.[94]

Rethinking school cafeteria fare—bringing in local, fresh foods—is occurring throughout the education system, from colleges to preschools. In the mid-1990s, just ten U.S. school districts had farm-to-school projects; by 2005, there were more than four hundred buying some food from local farmers, according to the Community Food Security Coalition. That's a fortyfold increase in a decade.

globalized, highly centralized food—is it viable?

As Chapter Six acknowledges, corporate globalization can feel inevitable. And it flies in the face of everything the Perkinses in Wisconsin, George at Organic Valley, and Brad at Oberlin are creating. If farmers in China can grow apples cheaper than Oregon farmers, then let's *import them apples!* And kiwis from New Zealand, and flowers from Central America.

From the early 1960s to the early 1990s, worldwide agricultural trade increased five times faster than both agricultural output and population growth.[95]

We now export tomatoes and breakfast cereal, and we import them too. We export 2.5 billion pounds of beef (about 10 percent of our total production) but then turn around and *import* even more of it. It's predicted that in 2005, notwithstanding our virtually unparalleled agricultural endowment, the U.S. will import in farm products about as much as we export, roughly $50 billion.

We import Danish butter cookies and export our cookies to Denmark. Wouldn't it be a lot simpler to just exchange recipes? wonders economist Herman Daly.

About 17 percent of total U.S. energy is used in the food system, reports Cornell professor David Pimentel.[96] In the 1940s, we got back about 2.3 calories of food energy for each fossil energy calorie we used, says author Richard Manning. But by the last accounting, way back in 1974, it was already one for one.[97]

How secure is a future built on a globalized food system dependent on petroleum-based inputs and fossil-fueled transport when experts warn that we're already using fossil fuel far more quickly than we are discovering new reserves?[98]

With transport and chemically dependent farming built on an energy source causing deadly pollution and destructive climate change—and whose price is rising—local, sustainable production may soon start to look not quaint but logical.

In addition to the vulnerability of our food system, consider this: How protected is our health when deadly bacteria at just one processing site can spread to millions of people before anyone is even aware? That's inevitable in our highly centralized system, with supply chains radiating across the entire country. And it's just what happened in 2002 when giant poultry processor Pilgrim's Pride recalled 27.4 million pounds of meat, or enough servings for about a third of the U.S. population![99]

Note that because of the strong arm of the food industry, our government does not have the authority to order food recalls; it can only request them. Yet thousands of Americans die each year from foodborne illness.

"It is truly not sustainable" said Mark Shultz, policy director at the Land Stewardship Project, referring to "the energy and financial and human costs" of the centralized factory farm system. Yes, he told me, in Minnesota factory farms produce most of the hogs, but most hog *farmers* are still family farmers, and more and more of them are "using humane and environmentally sound practices.

"In the southeastern county of Ripley (which has 115 registered voters), farmers recently held out against a New Jersey investor and a lot of intimidation," Mark said. They blocked a 2,100-cow factory farm.

"This is about a township protecting its people," local supervisor Kerry Shroder explained in a *Minneapolis Tribune* article Mark sent me.[100] "It's about democracy."

"I don't think factory farming will last forever," said Mark.

conscious choice and living democracy

After we'd talked awhile with George Siemon from Organic Valley in Wisconsin, he jumped to this insight: "So," he said, "Living Democracy is about *conscious* choice."

Exactly.

While we're told we're choosing this world gone awry, with hunger amid plenty, with food-related illnesses killing thousands every year, with farmers depleting our soils to eke out a shaky livelihood—and even then increasingly unable to make it—many don't feel like they've had any choice at all. It seems to be "just happening."

Creating healthy food economies means reclaiming our power; saying yes, we do have a conscious choice, as George declared. Nothing is more basic, more intimate, and yet more universal than food. Perhaps that's why as a young woman I began here. If we could realign our daily relationship with the earth and its bounty, I became convinced, other pieces of our broken economic and political order would settle into place.

Maybe George is telling me my youthful hunch was correct.

What his life and those of Erika and Will Allen, as well as communities from Los Angeles to Oberlin, show us is that we *do* have choice. We choose every time we lift our fork, every time we cast a ballot, every time we speak out at a school board meeting, and every time we step up as citizens to create new, fairer economies.

If you think the stories we've chosen here sound a bit too "idealistic" to affect the big, sorry picture, note as you walk up to your local supermarket's organic produce section that just one short decade ago, you would not have found it in a single major chain. Note as you visit your neighborhood farmers' market that just ten years ago, only a third as many dotted the country. And as you admire or lend a hand at a nearby community garden, note that today between fifteen thousand and eighteen thousand community gardens can be found across the country, almost double the number a decade ago.[101] In these economic relationships, trust and mutuality replace the manipulation and fear governing so much of our food economy.

And the squeezed-out farmer? Well, in Minnesota, and perhaps in other states, citizen efforts are bucking the trends. The number of family farms there has actually increased in recent years.[102]

"When I see farmers staying on the land, creating their own marketing cooperatives," said farming analyst, Minnesota farm-raised Lee Egerstrom, "I think, hey, we're making capitalism far more democratic than Karl Marx or John D. Rockefeller ever dreamed of!"

Idealistic? Absolutely. But also fundamentally practical—for a democratic food system is the essential soil for growing a healthy society. Maybe that explains why more and more Americans are beginning to acquire a taste for democracy.

9

VOICE

the debasement of the media & the sound of democracy

Servitude cannot be complete if the press is free: the press is the chief democratic instrument of freedom.

ALEXIS DE TOCQUEVILLE, 1835[1]

Press freedom—it's enshrined in the American way of life. After all, the very first amendment to our Constitution protects it, and Thomas Jefferson felt so strongly that if forced to choose, he once said, he'd sooner forfeit elected government than give up the free press.[2]

So now the question: If our news is so free, why isn't every revelation in this book already old news? None of these stories are arcane, relevant only to a narrow slice of America; they touch on the most critical questions of our time. Why *are* so few of us aware of the alarming measures of decline and the promising breakthroughs—all key pieces of the big picture we need in our "pursuit of happiness"?

That's the $64,000 question, or more apt for media today, it's the $70 billion question, as you'll soon see.

Here's my stab at an answer.

This chapter was written with Anna Lappé.

We assume freedom of the press to be among the most deeply embedded of American values, and maybe this is part of our problem: that too many of us do *assume* press freedom—which is hardly the same as deeply valuing it. In fact, in a 2004 survey, a third of high school students said newspapers should have to get government approval before publishing stories.[3] And the United States now comes in a sad twenty-fourth in a ranking of press freedom throughout the world.[4]

We've been encouraged to believe that being muzzled by government is the only real threat to a free press—or what today we call "the media," shorthand for "media of communication." And many of us don't seem to take that threat very seriously either.

We sigh with relief, knowing that our journalists don't face threats like those in China, Burma, or Iran, where reporters have been jailed for their writing even in recent years. Or face fear of death as Azerbaijani journalists must after a colleague was killed in 2005 after criticizing his government.[5]

Not here, no way, we're safe. We have media fit for democracy.

But here is the snag: while we've been watching our backs against government censorship, a threat to the open exchange of ideas and information—essential to democracy—marched in through the front door. The Founders, like most of the rest of us, never imagined a challenge to the principle of press freedom from the mundane, everyday workings of capitalism and its relentless pressure toward consolidation.

The threat began when "the press" got demoted.

In prior eras, and certainly in the eyes of our Founders, it was an "instrument of freedom," to use de Tocqueville's words. In "old Europe"—France in the eighteenth century—journalism constituted the "Fourth Estate," a pillar of society equal to government. But by the late twentieth century, the media had become a "product," an expensive product whose purpose is selling other products.

"We're not in the business of providing news and information," explained Lowry Mays, CEO of Clear Channel, owner of more than twelve hundred radio stations, to *Fortune* magazine in 2003. "We're not in the business of providing well-researched music. We're simply in the business of selling our customers products."[6]

Or even more starkly: "Television is just another appliance. It's a toaster with pictures," quipped Mark Fowler, the chair of the Federal Communications Commission during the Reagan presidency.[7]

Demoted to "another appliance," the media are now a multibillion-dollar industry in which a frenzy of mergers over the past twenty years has wiped out hundreds of competitors. Creating a company worth an estimated $350 billion, the AOL–Time Warner merger in 2000 broke all previous records.[8] By the turn of the millennium, only six companies were left standing—all preoccupied with their shareholders' financial health, not our society's health.

The result is a downward spiral of programming: news sound bites shrink to a seven-second average—one-sixth the length of a typical commercial.[9] Entertainment replaces news. Election coverage gives way to candidate ads. Crudeness becomes commonplace. And despite an increasingly interconnected world, foreign coverage withers; local coverage geared to communities' distinct concerns does too.

A NATION TUNED IN

The average U.S. household has 2.4 televisions and 5.6 radios.[10] Three out of four Americans have Internet access.[11] On average, each American "consumes" daily 4.5 hours of television, 2.9 hours of radio, and 1.6 hours of Internet surfing.[12]

I admit to feeling the sting of media's retrenchment rather personally. Two decades ago, I was invited twice to appear on the *Today Show,* and from Pittsburgh to Chicago to San Francisco, other TV news shows wanted my views. In recent years, though, a publicist told me it's much harder: "They say your work is too political."

Too political? That's probably not what was really meant. Fox News is political every moment of every day—it's just political of a certain stripe.

Conceiving of the media like another business and permitting extreme ownership concentration hold especially big dangers for democracy.

AS EVER-FEWER PEOPLE DECIDE WHAT'S NEWS . . .

- Just ten corporations—AOL–Time Warner, Disney, General Electric, News Corporation, Viacom, Vivendi, Sony, Bertelsmann, AT&T, and Liberty Media—control most of what we see, hear, and read.[13]
- Four companies sell 90 percent of music.[14] Six film studios generate 90 percent of U.S. theater revenue.[15]
- On the Internet, most traffic is driven by the biggest, corporate-owned Web sites. Of AOL's 31.3 million subscribers, 80 percent never leave AOL-linked sites.[16]
- Since 1975, the proportion of daily newspapers that are family-owned has plummeted from 75 percent to less than 2 percent, bought out by Gannet, Knight-Ridder, Hearst, and Tribune Company.[17]
- Just three companies control one-quarter of all daily newspapers circulated in the United States.[18]
- Clear Channel now owns more than twelve hundred radio stations, reaching one hundred million listeners in all fifty states.[19] It also owns forty-one TV stations and 179,000 outdoor advertising displays—billboards, "street furniture," and "transit panels"—plus 220 radio stations and thirty-one entertainment venues in dozens

of other countries.[20] Clear Channel is one of the biggest concert promoters in the United States, reaching sixty-nine million people at more than thirty-two thousand events every year.[21]

. . . DEMOCRACY LOSES

- The fifty largest media companies and four of their trade associations spent $111 million on lobbying between 1996 and 2000. Today nearly 300 media-related lobbyists roam Capitol Hill—that's three per senator![22]
- The average televised sound bite hovers around seven seconds, down from forty-two seconds in the 1960s.[23]
- Entertainment "news" stories now make up one in fourteen news items; twenty years ago it was one in fifty.[24]
- Stories about foreign affairs have dropped 25 percent since the late 1970s to just one in every six in recent years.[25]
- Product placement woven into TV or film is commonplace. Now some TV and film characters are hired by specific brands to tout their wares as part of the script.[26]
- Corporate media turn increasingly to industry and government press releases, news briefs, and video news releases.[27] More than half of "news" has been massaged by public relations professionals, who now outnumber working journalists.[28]
- In 2004, candidates and their allies paid media $1.6 billion to run political ads—double the amount four

years earlier[29]—providing a good chunk of broadcasters' income. Here is a clear conflict of interest, since media coverage of campaign finance reform could affect these lucrative ads.[30]

- Channel One broadcasts into twelve thousand middle, junior, and high schools, where eight million kids sit daily through its twelve minutes of news and commercials.[31] In one study, many junior high schoolers couldn't distinguish between the news and the ads.[32]

For much of this material and more, see Robert McChesney, *Rich Media, Poor Democracy* (New York: New Press, 2000).

Network news anchors become media stars, not risk-taking truth seekers, and reporters fail to challenge misinformation deliberately spread by government.

For example, during the run-up to the war against Iraq in mid-2002, report Sheldon Rampton and John Stauber in *Weapons of Mass Deception*, two-thirds of Americans polled believed—because the administration repeatedly linked them—that Saddam Hussein was connected to al-Qaeda and 9/11. Seventy-nine percent believed that Iraq already possessed or was close to possessing nuclear weapons.[33] Both were false. So the majority of Americans supported a costly war based in part on false perceptions unchallenged by corporate media.

What could be more threatening to our democracy?

And even after both notions had been thoroughly debunked, over two years later the majority of Americans *still* believe these false notions.[34]

What does the transformation of the media mean for the voices, the stories, and the lessons—and even the ads!—we're *not* getting?

In 1996, consumer reporter David Horowitz was fired from KCBS-TV in Los Angeles after auto manufacturers complained about his reports on car safety. Management at the station told Horowitz they were concerned about his investigating, "not because it's right or wrong, but because it may cost us advertising." Indeed, in a survey of television newsrooms by Marquette University's Lawrence Soley, three-quarters of respondents said that advertisers had tried to influence the content of news at their stations.[35]

In the two weeks before bombs fell in Iraq in 2003, among on-air pundits interviewed on the three major networks' evening news programs and on PBS's *NewsHour with Jim Lehrer,* only 3 out of 393 were antiwar voices, reports Fairness and Accuracy in Reporting. But 34 percent of Americans opposed the war—ten times their representation in the media.[36]

In media as big business, it turns out that even having money doesn't guarantee access. Selling ads, even public interest ads, isn't always in the media's interests—that's what the Sierra Club found out in 2003 when neither Clear Channel nor Viacom would allow it to buy billboard space for its campaign to save Zuni Salt Lake, sacred to several Native American tribes.[37] The Sierra Club concluded that the media companies refused its cash because they didn't want to jeopardize the more lucrative business they had going with the company threatening the lake.[38]

public interest—what's that?

With the rise of rigid marketism, described in Part One, the concept of a public whose interests need attention has gotten lost. So what's an agency that was created to protect the public interest and free speech to do?[39]

Established in 1934, the Federal Communications Commission (FCC), whose commissioners are appointed by the president, began in the 1980s to chip away at this bedrock mandate.

In 1984, it eliminated the requirement that cable operators provide local programming in exchange for access to markets.[40]

Next came the demise of the Fairness Doctrine, which had governed TV and radio for most of the twentieth century.[41] In the Red Lion case in 1969, the U.S. Supreme Court had, for example, unanimously upheld the doctrine, confirming that it is "the right of the viewers and listeners, not the right of broadcasters, which is paramount."[42] In the 1960s, media carrying ads for gas-guzzling cars had to pay for rebuttal airtime by public interest groups.[43]

Then, in 1987, the FCC struck down the Fairness Doctrine. The turning-point case came from Syracuse, New York, where an antinuke group complained that the local TV station had refused it airtime while broadcasting nine paid editorials in support of building a nuclear plant. Reagan appointees sided with the TV station. When Congress tried to fight back a year later with laws to protect the Fairness Doctrine, Reagan vetoed the bills.[44]

Then came 1996, the big year. Heavy media industry lobbying succeeded in convincing Congress to give digital frequencies to existing TV stations—*free of charge*, a gift valued at $70 billion.[45]

"Beachfront property on the cybersea" is what the FCC chairman at the time, Reed Hundt, called the giveaway.[46]

The same law, the 1996 Telecommunications Act, also opened the door to greater concentration of ownership. Before it passed, one corporation could own no more than two radio stations per market and a maximum of forty nationwide. The act upped the limit to eight in one market (and oversight is lax even on this high ceiling) with virtually no limit in multiple markets. It also lowered limits on cross-ownership of media—that is, for example, owning the newspaper, radio, and television stations in a given market.

Immediately, diversity of ownership collapsed to the extreme concentration documented in the "As Ever-Fewer People Decide" box.

"In exchange for free use of a public resource," said Gigi Sohn of the Media Access Project, "broadcasters must serve as trustees for the public by providing programming that meets community needs."[47]

Only they don't, and the FCC doesn't require it.

On assuming chairmanship of the Federal Communications Commission in 1998, Michael Powell (son of General Colin Powell) baldly remarked that the "'public interest' is about as empty a vessel as you can accord a regulatory agency and ask it to make meaningful judgments."[48] A few months after taking office, he joked with the American Bar Association, "The night after I was sworn in, I waited for a visit from the angel of the public interest. I waited all night, but she did not come. And in fact, five months into this job, I still have had no divine awakening and no one has issued me my public interest crystal ball."[49]

Upon Powell's resignation in 2005, President Bush appointed as FCC's chair Kevin Martin, a lawyer in his first campaign. Whether Martin can see what Powell couldn't remains an open question. We do know that he faces a growing citizens' movement demanding that the FCC protect diversity of media ownership and reinstate the Fairness Doctrine.

I'll save its heartening impact for the end of the chapter.

the media we deserve

Trapped in the myth of an impartial market fueled by consumer "demand," we're told that the degradation of programming is our own doing. We read it, we watch it. Media corporations simply respond to us.

It's our fault.

The argument is familiar. Sounds like the junk-food one: Americans eat the high-fat, high-sugar, low-nutrition stuff, so we deserve the consequences, even if that means disease and early death. Missing in this self-flagellation—or more often, the blaming of our neighbor—is that the food industry knows exactly what it's doing, as Chapter Eight suggests. Humans are hardwired to have a "weak satiation mechanism" for fat and sugar, meaning that once we have become habituated, it's hard to stop eating foods that are bad for us.

And the food industry knows that advertising works, especially on young people. It literally whets our appetites. It even alters how our brains judge taste.

In a loose parallel, media corporations are aware that of course we humans can be drawn to the lurid or the bizarre or simply to voyeuristic titillation. People once flocked to beheadings, burnings at the stake, and gladiatorial matches. Media moguls know they can make money on the sex lives of movie stars (or presidents) and sensationalized celebrity nuptials and trials. That's not a question.

What's missing is the prior question: Is the current selection of programs what most of us would *choose* if we had a say?

Probably not.[50] Even if some viewers do find reality shows' jacked-up drama hard to resist, many would *also* like to see a spectrum of media now missing. And many might well choose to forgo their indulgence in the most debased programming if they knew that meant also protecting their children from it. Just as one might shop in a liquor store next to a school but never approve zoning to permit it in the first place—if there were a choice.

Second, the "we asked for it because we watch it" argument ignores the fact that those asking, so to speak, are a decreasing segment of us. As programming becomes more degraded and less diverse, many Americans tune out altogether or tune in begrudgingly. Fifty-eight percent of Americans now agree that "the media get in the way of society solving its problems."[51]

The "we're giving them what they want" circle becomes self-reinforcing. That leaves many Americans with only the LOP buttons on the remote—the "least objectionable programs," not what they feel they are choosing.

democracy isn't cheap

Media companies, like any business, keep their eyes fixed on the highest return to shareholders. "Highest" is especially apt when considering the media: today newspapers average a 23 percent profit margin while local TV news shows boast a 45 to 50 percent profit margin.[52] Compare that to the rate of return of Standard & Poor's index of 500 representative companies traded on the stock market: it was 11 percent in 2004.[53]

But even without exceptionally high profit demands, if we leave the core function of democracy—communication about the most important matters of our common life—to the profit pressure marketplace alone, we're in trouble. It's cheaper for a news outlet to cover the school shooting than to probe the school reform initiative that might reduce the triggers to violence. It costs less to pick up a press release from a public relations firm or a government agency than to assign a reporter to dig for the real story.

And no-contest, it is certainly more profitable to sell airtime to candidates for ads than to cover their campaigns. In 2004 in swing states, half-hour local news shows averaged three minutes of campaign news but double that amount, six minutes, of campaign ads.[54]

Cost-cutting also opens the door to the media's becoming a conduit for propaganda.

In early 2005, many Americans were shocked to learn that the Bush administration was spending $254 million annually, twice what the Clinton administration spent, on public relations contracts to produce and distribute hundreds of ready-to-serve news segments broadcast on local and network stations. They are "designed and executed," said the Government Accountability Office, "to be indistinguishable from news stories produced by private sector television news organizations."[55]

Thus taxpayers are footing the bill for "news" segments promoting government policies, such as the war on Iraq and privatizing Social Security.

Ninety percent of TV newsrooms now rely on video "news" releases produced by government and corporations, according to one video release company. TV stations often do not know the source of the segments and sometimes deliberately delete any reference to their source.[56]

"Wouldn't it be great if citizen reporting could go into exposing the use of video news releases and other fakery behind the staging of your local and national nightly news?" writes Sheldon Rampton, coauthor of *Weapons of Mass Deception*. "The technology is available now to make this possible. . . . All it will take is for some people to get organized and start doing it."[57]

And there is another challenge that profit-only media can't meet: news that matters most to our well-being, from global warming to homelessness, often is not "breaking news" captured in a few shocking photos or summed up by a quick body count. It is slow-boiling. It doesn't fit well into seven seconds.

My own experience as founding editor of the American News Service—covering "America's search for solutions"—taught me these painful lessons. Over five years, we distributed sixteen hundred stories, and most were published. Nearly three hundred newspapers, including almost half of America's largest, carried them. Our goal was to stimulate bottom-up democracy by allowing Americans to see others like themselves engaged in public problem solving—from gang peacemaking to living-wage initiatives. And it worked . . . as long, that is, as we gave our material away. Editors realized the unique value and appeal of ANS stories. But when we began to charge for them, even a modest fee, the newspaper's business side overrode its editorial side. You can't prove that these stories contribute to our profit, most said. So we're not paying you a dime.

a right to hear and be heard?

The understanding of press freedom in which our culture is steeped is a *negative* one: we equate press freedom with not being stopped from doing something. We don't expect a *positive* right to hear, see, or read what we need to become powerful. Neither do we imagine enjoying a positive right to be heard.

In earlier times, when being heard meant having enough gumption to stand on a soapbox and shout out your message in the town square or, as Tom Paine did in the late eighteenth century, publish and distribute flyers or booklets, perhaps this negative right—the right not to be gagged by government—was enough. But today, having a soapbox doesn't get us far.

Notwithstanding the enormously wider views on the Internet, as I'll explore shortly, most Americans get most of their news from corporate media. About half of us get our news from "local" TV. Next are "local" newspapers, followed by cable TV news and then by network news.[58] I put "local" in quotation marks because control is mostly *not* local. And the concentration of control over these media effectively bars most Americans from hearing the diverse views essential to wise public action and from hearing and seeing themselves, or others like them, in the media.

Of nearly fifteen thousand sources analyzed by Media Tenor's Ina Howard on the three evening network news shows over three months in 2001, nearly three-quarters of those with identifiable partisan affiliation were Republicans and one-quarter were Democrats. Yet the American population at large is fairly equally divided.[59] Women made up just 9 percent of political and professional voices, and 8 percent of the presenters were people of color.[60]

Millions of Americans are, however, stirring up this mix. They're bringing up to date our understanding of press freedom and freedom of speech. They are claiming their positive democratic rights for access to diverse views and to be heard themselves.

Media democracy movements are bringing out the young and the old, the hip MTV audience and the sober PBSers, the breaking-news Internet bloggers and the hometown low-power radio broadcasters. Soapboxes may be useless, but these Americans are showing us that even in this era of corporate consolidation, we can become media makers ourselves.

They are also challenging federal rules permitting a tiny minority to control and degrade the conversation of democracy. They're insisting that the time-tested Fairness Doctrine to abet diversity be updated and reinstated.

These media-democracy doers argue that the media are not like a toaster at all. The media are what Jefferson treasured as the essence of the democratic promise. So they need their own rules, not toaster rules. They need rules that keep conversation open and keep it accountable—not just to our basest tastes in raunchy entertainment but to our highest desires for communities that work.

Let's look at some of the chords these positive agitators are sounding.

real news for less

Real news costs more, I've said, but new technology is altering the equation, allowing those to get in the door whose motives are not a 20-percent-plus profit margin. I'll start with my own family.

Just as my American News Service was folding five years ago, my son Anthony Lappé joined colleagues who'd launched another one—an online news service using a very different model. In 1999, two young men, Canadian independent TV producers Josh Shore and Stephen Marshall, founded Guerrilla News Network, and shortly after that, Anthony and Wharton School graduate Ian Inaba joined them to build GNN.tv.

The four had watched their peers and even younger people become increasingly alienated from packaged, uniform corporate news programs. So they designed a new news genre to reach them—a gritty, no-nonsense Web design with daily news features as well as MTV-style short videos featuring hard political content.

Having started with just a few thousand dollars in cash, by 2005 GNN's videos had aired all over the world and won awards at the Sundance Film Festival. Penguin had published Anthony and Stephen's book, *True Lies*, and their Web site was attracting an average of twenty thousand unique visitors a day.[61]

The group also produced the Eminem video *Mosh*, which *New York* magazine called "one of the most important pieces of mainstream dissent since the 1960s," and their film *Battleground: 21 Days on the Empire's Edge*, an on-the-ground investigation of unreported stories in Iraq—including the U.S. military's use of depleted uranium. It aired in May 2005 on Showtime, which is, ironically, owned by media giant Viacom, whose chairman, Sumner Redstone, announced that a Bush victory in the 2004 election would be best for his company's bottom line.[62]

"After spending much of the 1990s trying, and failing, to convince the major television networks to give us a show, we realized we had all the tools we needed to make our own 'news network,'" Anthony told me. "Thanks to the Web and low-cost, high-quality digital video technology, you don't need much money to compete with the big boys anymore—you just need passion and some good ideas."

The GNN Web site's unique design illustrates the Internet's possibilities for more democratic dialogue, or "multilogue" rather than one-way talk. GNN.tv welcomes its users to create their own blogs and to rank each other's work. In the first year, more than three thousand people from as far away as New Zealand and Hong Kong were writing blogs on the site.

OK, I know this sounds like a mom's brag, but my point is that GNN is possible only because millions of Americans of all ages who hunger for real news turn—increasingly—to outlets like my son's.

Other news sites not driven by profit return but by a passion for democracy include Tompaine.com, Truthout.org, Commondreams.org, Americanprogress.org, and Alternet.org.

More Americans also turn to bloggers—individuals creating online journals of commentary and sometimes breaking news. In a page-one example, in early 2005, bloggers from the Daily Kos exposed the real identity of "Jeff Gannon," who had been admitted to Bush press briefings and was paid by an obscure Republican Internet group called GOPUSA. His assignment was to throw softball questions at the president.

In fact, Gannon was James Guckert, a right-wing political hack. But it took corporate media more than a week to catch up.[63]

A powerful example of the reach of not-profit-motivated media is Democracy Now!—created first on Pacifica network radio by award-winning journalist Amy Goodman.

Amy is among those who've discovered that radio can morph into television. It's not cheap or easy, but it's possible on a low budget because the Internet enables Amy and her team to take advantage of the collaborative support of thousands—from volunteers who daily transcribe her shows to video makers around the world who send free footage.

Commercial broadcast networks spend hundreds of thousands of dollars on software enabling high-speed, real-time editing between cameras, audio, and video, but for an independent like Democracy Now! the price is out of the question. So, "Open Flows, a collective technology company, worked with Democracy Now! to lay the foundation for an 'open source' version of the software," Ana Nogueira, a Democracy Now! television producer, explained. "Now, any community media outlet can use this, whereas before it was priced out of reach."

Thanks to participatory media, Democracy Now! broadcasts on more than 170 radio stations. Anyone, anywhere in the world, can hear or view Democracy Now! through what's called "streaming" video and audio on the Internet at Democracynow.org. The nonprofit Free Speech TV channel on the DISH Network, which reaches over eleven million households, also carries the show.[64]

The reach of both GNN and Democracy Now! "demonstrate the importance building grassroots support," said Joshua Breitbart, a founder of Rooftop Films. "Many radio stations are carrying Democracy Now! because of local campaigns pushing for it."

The rapid growth of Internet news and its instantaneous spread through e-mail mean that now even government officials and corporate media sometimes feel compelled to respond—as in the case of President Bush's use of the fake reporter planted in press briefings.

Amy Goodman calls this pressure "trickle-up journalism."

so you want to make movies?

Any Friday night in New York City in the summer, rooftops throughout the city are turned into open-air theaters with hundreds of people watching cutting-edge documentary shorts and videos from around the world.

Rooftop Films is the New York City take on an international phenomenon called "microcinemas," public spaces turned into makeshift movie theaters and conversation hubs.

A TV-quality documentary or short feature film that would have cost a million dollars a decade ago can be made today for one-tenth that—and a shorter documentary for a fraction of *that*. The effect is just beginning to be felt, from New York City rooftops to video cameras in the hands of human rights activists and guerrilla video makers from the foothills of the Himalayas to the streets of Oakland, California.

The films shown are typically those that "would NEVER get seen by ANY audience of ANY size ANYWHERE," reads an e-mail from Joel Bachar of Microcinema International. Joel's all-caps enthusiasm makes more sense when one appreciates, as noted earlier, that since the 1930s, six production companies have controlled roughly 90 percent of the film industry.[65]

"People actually talk to each other at these [microcinema] events," he emphasized. "They come early and stay late, as opposed to the way people shuffle in and out of the Cineplex."

"We're not just trying to make smarter individuals by giving folks *more* information," concurred Rooftop Films founder Joshua Breitbart. "We're trying to make stronger communities."

"We are social beings," Joel added. "People want to return to the campfire. So much of society isn't about connection, it's about distraction. Intimate and meaningful events such as these screenings are places where social change begins."

In addition to creating "stronger communities," in Joshua's words, independent films are connecting with real-world social change campaigns, with real results.

Filmmaker Judith Helfand, forty-one, uses a grassroots approach to distribute her documentary, *Blue Vinyl*—and its message. An exposé of the vinyl industry and the dangers of polyvinylchloride plastics, *Blue Vinyl* traces Judith's steps to an alternative to vinyl siding for her Long Island childhood home.

From the beginning, Judith wanted her film to ignite action to confront a notoriously toxic industry. Quite a goal, considering what she's up against: the plastics industry spends millions to get the public to believe its products are safe, from the $50 million it spent in the past ten years alone on lobbying government officials to producing *Hands On Plastics* and *Hands On Plastics Jr.*, free educational kits extolling the benefits and safe uses of plastics for teachers.[66]

Touring the film, Judith coordinated showings with Health Care Without Harm—medical industry professionals working to get unsafe plastics out of hospitals—and Building in Good Faith, a consortium of religious groups fighting for nontoxic building materials for low-income housing. She then co-founded Working Films to help other filmmakers spark community activism.

When HBO aired *Blue Vinyl* in 2004, dozens of e-mails flooded Judith's inbox: "The *Blue Vinyl* story was an awakening. Thank you." And from a high school teacher in Elgin, Illinois: "I want to use your film as a culminating activity for my Air Pollution Unit. I can't wait!"

"Most media we see are the opposite of democracy; they make you feel like you can't do anything. We create an antidote to that," said MediaRights executive director Nicole Betancourt. MediaRights is on the forefront of Judith-style filmmaking: promoting films as part of real-world-solutions campaigns that connect filmmakers with "citizen solvers."

Who could have imagined even five years ago that a documentary would break box office records? That's what Michael Moore's *Fahrenheit 9/11* did in 2004. Then came *Super Size Me!*—a graphic exposé of the health impact of a thirty-day McDonald's binge. It's been shown not only on thousands of movie screens but also in school districts and even on Capitol Hill, fueling the national conversation about the health hazards of fast food. And it might well be a reason McDonald's committed to phasing out supersizing, though of course the company would never say so.

The power of film goes beyond the big screen. It's making itself felt on the little screen, too: on our computers.

The Meatrix, a flash-animated video, reveals the factory-farmed truth under the veneer of happy pigs. More than six million people have viewed it in Polish, Spanish, French, German, and Portuguese, as well as English.[67]

"One viewer said her five-year-old son was so affected that the entire family changed the way they were eating," said Diane Hatz, of the Global Resource Action Center for the Environment (GRACE).

Even the media granddaddy, radio, has a new face.

going local

Imagine this: city officials in your town are jumping up and down about a proposed new mall. Local media hail the plan's benefits too. The mall is approved, but almost as soon as it opens, it hits financial problems, and Wall Street docks your city's credit rating. Only then do you learn that the city had used federal housing money as collateral for the loan to build the mall, and now it risks losing these funds—money needed to subsidize home improvements for the poorest residents.[68]

You then discover that the family who owns almost all local media had direct business interests in the failing mall.[69]

For the residents of Spokane, Washington, no imagination is required. This is exactly what happened several years ago in that city of almost two hundred thousand people. As in many cities across the country, newspapers, television stations, and radio stations are owned by one family or company, potentially putting citizens in the same spot—denied information to make good choices because of conflicts of interest.

Fortunately, there's a postscript to the Spokane story.

A year after the debacle, local citizens launched the area's first noncorporate, people-powered, low-power FM station, Thin Air Radio. Low-power stations broadcast at one hundred watts—enough, depending on terrain, to reach ten to fifteen miles. Today, Thin Air Radio of Spokane broadcasts diverse perspectives and music seven days a week.[70]

Low power is, by definition, local. Very local. And the mission of those involved is to carry the news about their communities, in striking contrast to corporate media. A 2003 survey of six so-called local stations in six media markets found that "less than one-half of one percent of the [television] programming went toward covering local public affairs."[71]

Yet locally is where Americans engage. To do so, we need stories of regular citizens addressing problems and finding solutions—stories evoking the "Hey, we could try that" response.

Local news makes local connections. Todd Wickstrom in Ann Arbor, Michigan, told us that after his local paper, the *Ann Arbor News*, carried a story about his school garden project, a local foundation called offering seed money. Or, remember Charlie Johnson in Chapter Four? It was because his local paper in Heron, South Dakota, ran a column about the petition drive against corporate farming, which then got picked up elsewhere, that the whole campaign took off.

The downsides of losing localism may be hard to quantify, but some are dramatic—even fatal.

"It's like something out of a nightmare," wrote Eli Pariser in an early 2002 e-mail to Moveon.org's two million members. Eli, then campaigns director, told about the impact of media consolidation on Minot, North Dakota.

On January 18, 2002, thousands of gallons of toxic ammonia leaked out of a derailed train near the town. Minot officials tried to use their emergency system to alert the community, but it didn't work. Desperate, they called the local radio stations. No one answered—for an hour and a half. In the meantime, hundreds became sick and were hospitalized, some even partially blinded. Pets and livestock died.

"Where were Minot's DJs? Where was the late-night station crew?" Eli asked.

At six of the seven local radio stations, the answer was clear: local staff had been cut when Clear Channel bought out the stations.

"It's harder and harder," Eli notes, "for Americans to find out what's going on in their own backyards."

transforming ownership: low power to the people

For years, the Federal Communications Commission was at war with low-power "pirates" operating without licenses. It bragged in 1998 that it had shut down over two hundred pirate stations.[72] But citizen groups pressed for a legal low-power status, and in 2000, the FCC got on board, at least partially. A total of six hundred licenses have so far been granted; half are religious stations.[73] Three hundred low-power stations are currently on the air, and four hundred applications for low-power FM frequencies are pending.

The Philadelphia-based Prometheus Radio Project, originally part of pirate radio itself, helps communities take advantage of now legalized low power. Its name comes from a Greek myth in which Prometheus, a Titan, steals knowledge of how to make fire from the heavens and teaches mortals how to use it. In its real-world twist, Prometheus teaches people how to light the fire of radio in their communities.

Prometheus hosts modern-day barn raisings. Each year, Prometheus chooses two or three among applicants for a low-power frequency and gathers people from far and wide, those with technical skills along with those who just want to lend a hand.

In each community, "we build the station from the ground up, from the microphones to the antenna," Hannah Sassaman explained, speaking from Prometheus's Philadelphia office.[74] "We think of a small community radio station like a public library or a public school or a town hall. It is something that every town needs to have in order to have a full democracy."

Prometheus advocates on Capitol Hill and participates in key legal battles—like the one culminating in a court decision we will take up shortly that defeated the FCC's 2003 attempt to weaken media ownership rules even further.

What difference can having a community station make?

Just ask the folks of Opelousas. Prometheus went to this town of twenty thousand in southwestern Louisiana to help a civil rights group launch a community station. Part of the group's motivation, it told Hannah, was that there, in the cradle of zydeco music, you could no longer find it on the dial.

Thanks to low-power KOCZ, "you can now hear zydeco in the place it was born," Hannah said proudly.

The station recently brought high school students on the air to talk about teen pregnancy. "This is not some boutique, niche activism," Hannah said. "It's something everyone cares about."

Or ask the Coalition of Immokalee Workers, with twenty-five hundred immigrant farmworker members throughout Florida. Prometheus traveled to Immokalee in 2003 for one of its "station raisings." The workers, mostly Latino, Haitian, and Mayan Indian immigrants, receive the same wages as they did in 1970. For over a decade the union has been fighting, but effective organizing is difficult with members spread over many miles.

Thanks to Prometheus, the union now has its own low-power station broadcasting in Spanish so it can communicate instantly with members. When a local company failed to pay several hundred members for their work on hurricane relief reconstruction, Radio Conciencia, as it's called, spread the news on the air and invited community members to union headquarters for a public discussion. They expected a few dozen. "Two hours later, nearly three hundred workers had arrived," said Hannah.

Boosted by their radio's reach, the union finally triumphed in 2005 in its four-year boycott of Taco Bell. Taco Bell's parent company Yum! committed to pay a penny-a-pound surcharge on tomatoes and to buy only from growers who pass the entire raise on to farmworkers. The sum sounds tiny, but it almost doubles the price tomato farms pay for each 32-pound bucket. Yum! also agreed to work with the union to improve working conditions.

Success resulted in part from the effective coupling of grassroots action, including student support from three hundred universities nationwide, and a 2003 Yum! shareholder resolution receiving 33 percent of the votes—a minority, yes, but clearly what it took to wake up company directors.[75]

Or ask Marianne Knorzer, forty-three, her father, Erv Knorzer, seventy-three, and the community of Oroville, California, about three hours northeast of San Francisco.

When we called Marianne, station manager at low-power KRBS, she whispered hello before changing phones. She didn't want to disrupt the twenty-four-hour Dr. Seuss marathon manned by dozens of teacher and parent volunteers. "It's the greatest thing when kids hear their teacher on their radio reading to them!" Marianne beamed across the phone lines.

KRBS was built Prometheus-style, too, with seventy-five people arriving from all over the West Coast. The daughter-father team started the station after Clear Channel bought the only two local radio stations and the newspaper in neighboring Chico bought the local paper, putting all three of the region's dailies in the same company's hands.

In a region of sixty thousand people, "trying to get the word out about anything going on locally was hard," Marianne said.

"With over fifty volunteer programmers, we're creating a voice for Oroville," she said. In a town without a physical gathering place, the station has become a community center of the airwaves.

From Temperance, Michigan, to Moncks Corner, South Carolina, low-power stations are taking off. Many more would be under way already were it not for the National Association of Broadcasters, which convinced the FCC that these stations would interfere with commercial ones. The broadcasters succeeded in blocking low power from top markets.

With that, "we lost about 70 percent of possible stations," Hannah said, "and they ironically called it the Radio Preservation Act 2000."

Then in 2004, the FCC's own study found that the broadcasters' objections were bogus. But it will now take organized pressure from citizen groups like Prometheus to get those stations back. "It's going to take another act of Congress," Hannah told us. The muscle of this burgeoning citizens' movement could make that happen.

uniting communities wirelessly

Lamenting the "digital divide" separating races and classes, some communities now see Internet access the way our forebears saw literacy, as essential to participating in democratic community life.[76] They are dead set on closing the digital gap, and wireless networks covering a whole municipality offer the way.[77] Philadelphia will soon be the first major U.S. city where anyone, anyplace, can jump online.

Not surprisingly, large telecommunications companies aren't happy. They are lobbying furiously to block public community wireless networks and have succeeded in over a dozen states.[78] In 2004, Verizon and Comcast lobbying in Pennsylvania resulted in a law denying, as of 2006, local governments the right to create community networks without first giving the primary local phone company the chance to provide it. Because the law isn't retroactive, Philadelphia and a few others will be allowed to proceed.[79]

One is Kutztown, Pennsylvania, where residents have been enjoying publicly provided high-speed wireless Internet access since 2000 for only $15 a month. Frank Caruso, the town's director of information technology, said he feels sorry for communities that will not be able to get wireless networks before the 2006 deadline and thus will be forced to deal with Verizon first.

"They don't realize that their throats have just been cut," Caruso said. "It's almost like Verizon is Big Brother." Caruso noted that once his town started offering cable television service with its wireless service, the private provider dropped its prices by 40 percent to compete.[80]

That's the competition just wiped out by Pennsylvania's Verizon-led law.

democratic software

In 2004, a new Internet search engine spread like wildfire. Aptly named Firefox, it was created by a Florida teenager, Blake Ross, now a Stanford junior. The superiority of Firefox comes from its democratic, participatory nature. An urgent security hole or bug that might take Microsoft months to correct can be patched up in as little as thirty-six hours by Firefox's army of volunteer programmers.

Firefox is freely downloadable on the Internet from Mozilla (http://www.mozilla.org) and is "open source," meaning it's a work in progress, constantly being tweaked by thousands of volunteer programmers worldwide. In its first few months, twenty-five million people worldwide downloaded the Web browser, taking nearly 5 percent of Microsoft's share of the browser market. Says *Wired* magazine, "Watch your back, Bill Gates."[81]

AMPLIFYING THE SOUND OF DEMOCRACY

- *Producing community-content media:* Every week, one million volunteers at community media centers across the United States produce twenty thousand hours of TV programming, more than the combined programming produced by NBC, CBS, ABC, Fox, and PBS!

Technically they're called public, educational, and governmental (PEG) access channels.[82]

- *Democratizing policy:* To keep the public's interest front and center in the law and in FCC standard setting, the Media Access Project, the Center for Digital Democracy, and dozens of other nonprofits educate the public, pursue critical court cases, and promote the public interest in various forums behind the scenes.[83]
- *Connecting media-democracy reformers:* Advocates, organizers, researchers, and funders are connecting through the grassroots-driven Allied Media Project conferences in Ohio and the Free Press's media reform national conventions, which attracted two thousand people the first year, 2003.[84]
- *Making media to inform citizens:* MediaRights, Working Films, and other organizations help maximize the positive impact of film and other media on issues from global warming to prison violence.[85]
- *Getting youth to the mike:* Exploding across the country are youth-driven media projects, from youth-run radio and television stations to newspapers and magazines. *In the Mix* is a national weekly series produced and hosted by young adults, broadcast on over one hundred PBS stations as well as the Armed Forces Network and instructional TV networks in schools.[86]
- *Becoming a media maker:* Born on the streets of Seattle during the 1999 protests of the World Trade Organization, the online Independent Media Center had 1.5 million viewers in its first week, eclipsing visits to CNN. Using open-source software allowing anyone to publish, the center's sites—all known as "indymedia"—

> have spread to more than a dozen countries. Its hub gets as many as one hundred thousand hits a day.[87]
>
> ---
>
> Find many more examples of ways of democratizing media in "Transforming Media, Inc." by Anna Lappé, available through http://www.smallplanetinstitute.org.

citizens' voices shaping the rules

"Once people understand that the media are government-created systems, they see that regular citizens can actually have influence. Then the sky opens," said Josh Silver, managing director of Free Press. His national organization was created in 2002 to multiply the impact of the hundreds of organizations working to democratize the media.

That sky has opened for Jenny Toomey, thirty-seven. Now it's even hard to get her on the phone. Singer, guitar player, and cofounder of the Simple Machines record label, she's also the executive director of the Future of Music Coalition, a somewhat unlikely coalition of musicians, policymakers, and media users with the modest goal of reshaping media rules in the public interest.

To Toomey, the impact of the 1996 Telecommunications Act on radio is a cautionary tale about what happens when Americans aren't paying attention. As noted earlier, the act turned over the digital frequencies to existing TV stations free of charge, with virtually no requirement for public interest programming. This gift to corporate America is valued at $70 billion.[88]

It also weakened the federal standards protecting against the concentration of media ownership. The result?

"We lost one-third of independent radio owners in the first four years" after the act, Toomey noted. And just two companies, Clear

Channel and Viacom's Infinity, control nearly one-quarter of the entire national radio market. The effect on music is radical: in the most popular commercial formats, 80 to 100 percent of the music played consists of songs owned by five major record labels or majors working with so-called independents, according to a survey by the Future of Music Coalition.[89]

The shock of the 1996 rule change—particularly for radio—awakened many Americans, with Toomey and a broad coalition helping sound the alarm. So by the fall of 2002, when the FCC launched that agency's most comprehensive reexamination of media ownership rules, a groundswell brought together the National Rifle Association and grassroots groups like Reclaim the Media in Seattle.

By the time the agency sat down again to vote on limits on media concentration in 2003, nearly 250 groups, representing hundreds of thousands of Americans, had taken a stand against further watering down rules protecting diversity of ownership. A record *three million* Americans had contacted Congress and the FCC, most opposing further weakening of diversity standards.

How did the issue move from invisibility in 1996 to become so hot only seven years later?

Millions of Americans began to see their connected fate and the media as a critical link to their public world—one with the potential to either expand or deny their power.

In 2002, the FCC announced its policy review, counting on a single official public hearing in Richmond, Virginia.

The commissioners were in for a surprise.

Citizens pressed, and more than a dozen hearings were held. "We had four weeks' notice and about $3,000," said Susan Gleason of Reclaim the Media-Seattle. But she and her allies brought together four hundred people for more than three hours of testimony before the FCC commissioners. At the end of the day, nearly one thousand people turned out to see Public Enemy's Chuck D in a concert laced with media democracy speeches. From computer stations in the lobby, many sent on-the-spot feedback to the FCC.

Thanks to people like Susan, other hearings across the country were standing room only as consumer advocate groups, filmmakers' associations, and media workers' unions all urged members to speak out. Others took to the streets, demonstrating in front of the FCC offices.

Despite this unprecedented outcry, the commission voted 3–2 along party lines to further lower the ownership diversity standards.

But citizens didn't give up. A public interest coalition, led by the Prometheus Radio Project and the Media Access Project, arguing for citizens' right to hear and be heard succeeded in convincing a court to stay implementation.

Then, in June 2004, the citizen groups won a stunning victory:

The court ruled effectively to send the FCC back to the drawing board to rewrite the laws. Although the decision doesn't alter the concentration-enabling framework already on the books, "this is a big, big win for diversity in the media," said Jay Schwartzman, president and CEO of the Media Access Project.

In the 1980s under the Reagan administration, the mandate of the Federal Communication Commission shifted from "protecting the public interest" to letting "the market" run its course. In reality, by allowing concentration to go unchecked, the FCC decisions created a new form of private regulation—one benefiting big business.

Media regulation FCC-style "is like creating highways that only allow Hummers," said Jenny Toomey of the Future of Music Coalition.

Media based narrowly on the highest return to shareholders erode the dialogue of democracy. Since the functioning of capitalism as we know it returns wealth to existing wealth holders, inevitably the big get bigger and bigger until competition collapses. Free markets are not born and don't live on their own; they are created and sustained by democratic politics setting the ground rules on behalf of citizens—the public that Michael Powell just could not see.

Democracy rests on the concept of a public—and therefore a public interest—real to all of us, not a vague throwaway line. As noted at the start of this book, democracy is in essence about voice:

it is not only about who can speak but also about who gets heard and about our right and need to hear many diverse voices.

Today's crisis of voice is not just about the tightening of media ownership. It runs deeper: it is the shift to viewing the media of communication as mere commodities in the first place. From that narrow frame, citizens lose their voices along with the rich mix of views that is the conversation of democracy.

But not all Americans, by any means, have given up on their core commitment to the media as a public good. And new media technology is cracking open the conversation. It's enabling citizens to bypass debased media and connect directly with each other. It's arming citizens with tools to better hold authorities accountable, and it's allowing more people to create media themselves.

All this is the sound of democracy.

PART FOUR

DEMOCRACY IN OUR BONES

I wonder whether Americans still believe liberty has to be learned and that its skills are worth learning. Or have they been deluded by two centuries of rhetoric into thinking that freedom is "natural" and can be taken for granted?

BENJAMIN BARBER[1]

Human beings skilled in "doing democracy" aren't born that way. Yes, we humans arrive in this world as innately social creatures. In fact, scientists tell us that if we aren't nurtured by intimates from infancy, we shrivel up and even die.[2] Neuroscientists are also learning that we're hardwired to enjoy cooperation and also that our brains house "mirror neurons," which beneath our conscious awareness mimic what we observe in others.[3]

Yet despite our social wiring, effective democracy-making is an art that must be learned, just as one would learn to play the piano, dribble a basketball, or read. To create societies that foster life, we can build a democratic culture, one that instills certain habits of heart and mind as well as specific skills. On our Web site, we include an introductory guide to ten such "arts of democracy."[4] All this suggests that democracy be consciously taught in schools, not as a nice "add-on" for high-achieving kids, but as the key to transforming America's failing educational system.

Democracy also calls us to rethink the meaning of security. We reactively reach out for a protector, but in reality the surest protection from fear and harm is what we together create by reaching out to each other.

The lives of people in Part Four suggest that learning to "do democracy" turns out to be not the "spinach" we must eat to move on to the dessert of personal freedom. Rather, it is the unending personal growth that makes life worth living.

10

LEARNING

sharing power & apprenticing democracy

As the fitting apprenticeship for despotism consists in being trained to despotism, so the fitting apprenticeship for self-government consists in being trained to self-government.

HORACE MANN[1]

I plodded through school, striving to please my teachers but never feeling I had much to offer. Anxiety surrounding education didn't lift for me until leaving graduate school at twenty-six. Within months, anxiety was replaced by excitement as I discovered questions inside that drew me to libraries, lectures, and spirited conversations. My life became an exploration of the next question . . . and the next.

Only many years later did I begin to connect my experience to democracy. Gradually I realized that the love of learning, though coming belatedly to me, lies at the heart of a democratic culture. To be equipped to come together to address the complex problems of today's world—to be democracy makers—young people need the opportunity to learn in the classroom what I discovered only after leaving.

Zawadi Powell is one of a new generation showing us the difference it makes to learn the arts of democracy at a young age.

Over a decade ago, I spoke with Zawadi, then a high school senior at Central Park East Secondary School in Harlem.

"When I came to this school, it was hands-on, . . . more active," she told me. "Everything just made sense to me. It was fun to come here. At my old school, we just listened to the teacher talk all day. Here we work in groups. We learn through writing plays and doing projects. It's a whole different experience."

She and her classmates—mainly from lower-income African American families—shattered stereotypes and statistical trends. Zawadi graduated, just like over 90 percent of her school's incoming ninth-graders. And like 95 percent of her fellow grads, she went on to a four-year college. Compare this to just under 40 percent of all New York public high school graduates.[2]

Zawadi attended Brown University, and since graduating, she's studied in Ghana, taught school, and helped launch two nonprofits. Soon she will begin graduate school in North Carolina, she told me when I caught up with her in 2005.

Zawadi explained to me how her high school shaped who she is today. "I can draw my own conclusions. I'm not a follower," she says, laughing. "I don't take things at face value or fit into someone else's model. I've learned to live through exploration, realizing that every experience is a lesson."

I think it's safe to say Zawadi is every educator's dream. And the high school that "just made sense" to her also has made sense to a lot of others struggling to understand how to turn around the crisis captured in the following box.

OUR SCHOOLS AREN'T WORKING

- *U.S. schools are lagging internationally*. The United States ranks eighteenth in overall educational achievement among twenty-four industrial nations, lagging behind, for example, the Czech Republic, Ireland, and Hungary.[3] And among high-income countries, we rank twelfth in literacy scores among adults.[4]

- *Graduation rates are low.* In our thirty-five largest cities, nearly half the high schools graduate less than 50 percent of entering freshmen.[5] We rank tenth among other industrial nations in the share of our twenty-five to thirty-four-year-olds with a high school diploma.[6]
- *Spending is high and unfairly distributed.* The United States spends more per person on public education than nearly all other high-income countries.[7] But our wealthier school districts spend three or four times more per pupil than our poorer ones, even within the same state.[8]
- *Ethics are eroding.* Seventy-four percent of students admit to "serious" cheating at least once during the past school year.[9]
- *Our children are not safe at school.* Seventy-one percent of public schools experienced one or more violent incidents in the 1999–2000 school year.[10]
- *Buildings are decrepit.* School buildings are in such disrepair that $112 billion is needed just to bring them up to par.[11]

Zawadi's Central Park East Secondary School was founded in 1985 in what was widely perceived as New York's *least* successful district, and until the last decade, it remained a lonely beacon of possibility in the world of public education. But word of its effectiveness spread so that by 2000, a whole movement of small schools had sprung up in New York and beyond. Its record so impressed Boston school authorities that they suspended some rules and regulations to allow nineteen similar pilot schools to form, spearheaded by the same education visionary, Deborah Meier, who launched Central Park East elementary and secondary schools.

When Deborah Meier bucked conventional wisdom to create the elementary school in Harlem that made possible Zawadi's positive high school experience, what exactly did she and her colleagues do differently? What approaches do the islands of success share?

Deborah would be the first to argue that there is no formula. But in broad strokes, the discoveries made through taking risks and involving teachers, parents, students, administrators, and community members build on a largely unrecognized tradition of democratic schooling. By "democratic schooling" I mean nothing too esoteric. I mean education that engenders the attitudes and capacities in citizens that democracy must enjoy in order to thrive.

These trailblazers are showing us that democratic education and good education are in fact the very same thing: developing the capacity to be responsible for oneself, to know oneself well enough to discover one's own passions and how to feed them through a lifetime of learning and satisfying work, to be able to collaborate in creating communities that work for all, and to have the courage to stand up for what's right even when it's unpopular—that pretty much sums up what most of us dream "education" could be for ourselves and our children.

These educators at "democracy's edge" show us that our dream is not only possible. It is happening.

As Deborah Meier's work began to pay off, others were experimenting with similar approaches. Theodore Sizer, a Brown University professor of education, launched what became the Coalition of Essential Schools. Since the 1980s, its core lessons about "what works" have quietly—perhaps too quietly—spread.

Conventional wisdom has it that only private or charter schools (public schools organized outside the school system) are free to experiment with radical change. Not so. Successful innovation is under way through at least a half dozen networks in the world of public schools, remaking more than six hundred nationwide.[12] These democratic school movements have caught the eye of the Bill and Melinda Gates Foundation, whose significant support is stoking these fires.[13]

the antidemocracy current

Unfortunately—although these schools are proving that kids, even from disadvantaged communities, can excel brilliantly—you've probably not heard of them.

What you probably *have* heard is something quite different: that America's schools are in crisis and therefore we must scramble. Quick! More testing, tighter security, wider use of voucher systems to enhance competition. Behind all of these moves is one mind-set: How can we get *tougher*? And what could be tougher than the Bush administration's No Child Left Behind Act? It mandates punishing schools by allowing students to leave (and take their funding with them) if test scores don't reflect adequate yearly progress, and it threatens firing all or most of a school's staff or turning the school over to a private management company if test scores fail to meet state requirements five years in a row.[14]

We hear calls for our schools to do the same old things they've always done, only *better*. But if our educational system stays on this track, we're doomed. More, or even better, is not enough. The world has changed radically since our industrial assembly-line model of schooling took hold more than a century ago.

WHY "MORE" OR "BETTER" ISN'T ENOUGH

The world is changing, but our schools are not meeting the needs that flow from these changes.

Changes Under Way in Our World	*Consequent Needs for Democratic Schooling*	*What Our Schools Do Instead*
Fast-expanding information: Knowledge growth across all fields, including technological developments	Knowing how to learn, discovering the joy of teaching oneself	Emphasize routine tasks, repetition, and retention of facts and figures (to pass tests)

Cont'd.

Changes Under Way in Our World	*Consequent Needs for Democratic Schooling*	*What Our Schools Do Instead*
Greater diversity: More cultures interacting, leading to heightened interdependence	Appreciating diversity and recognizing how our interests are linked to others; learning interaction skills	Offer little training in teamwork and conflict resolution and seldom reward collaboration; segregate by class, race, and aptitude
Deepening problems: Growing magnitude and severity of problems	Developing the skills to negotiate interests, hold others accountable, and solve problems	Provide meager training in problem solving
Spreading alienation: Growth of huge, distant, impersonal institutions	Opportunities for meaningful face-to-face relationships	Are large-scale and hierarchical; separate, atomize, and isolate
Loosening of bonds: Decline of family life and community institutions	Schools as centers of community life	Isolate students from one another and from community life

a culture of connection

Educating for democracy starts with creating a culture of connection—that's what the successful schools are showing us. A democratic school culture is the antithesis of nameless kids shuffling from one unrelated class to the next every forty-five minutes to face down a distant teacher who's too pressured even to notice how disconnected it all is.

"At my school, it feels like we're lost in classrooms," wrote one Rhode Island student about why her school didn't meet her needs.[15]

My longtime friend George Wood left a tenured education position at Ohio University thirteen years ago to walk his democratic-education talk. Now, as a high school principal, he cuts to the quick: "The issue is not test scores or dress codes—the issue is connection."

His rural high school, Federal Hocking in Stewart, Ohio, is one of the two poorest districts in his state's poorest county, yet his school's dropout rate is only about 10 percent, and nearly 70 percent of Fed Hock students go on to college, up from about 20 percent before George began.

By "connection," George means both in and outside of school. He means kids connecting to what they are learning and seeing the connections among the subjects they study, and he means connecting all that with real-world change. He means relationships among students and between students and teachers.

Of course, he's not referring to just any kind of connection. The word *respect* pops up a lot when talking with George Wood. Relationships of mutual respect, George believes, form the basis of effective learning communities and of democracies. Yet most of our schools are organized to "ignore, if not exclude, such relationships," as Deborah Meier writes.[16]

creating a culture of connection

Relationships of mutual respect—of trust—don't arise out of thin air, though, or even by bringing everyone together to hammer out a "mission statement" about respect. At least six big breaks with today's typical schools are proving necessary to make genuine connection possible:

SIX LESSONS FROM EFFECTIVE SCHOOLS

1. Scale matters. Keep it small.
2. Make time for each other and for in-depth study.
3. Pursue meaningful questions.
4. Encourage student-initiated, hands-on projects and demonstrations.
5. Foster self-assessment, charting one's own development.
6. Share authority and teach democracy by practicing its arts.

1. *Scale matters. Keep it small.* The average American high school has almost eight hundred students, and many have over a thousand, but educators are learning what anthropologists have known for some time: that we humans can't relate to more than a few hundred people without feeling lost. It should not surprise us that hard evidence now shows that small schools tend to generate higher achievement than large ones. This is especially true for poor kids.[17] In fact, one study suggests that small schools can overcome up to 70 percent of poverty's negative impact on academic performance.[18]

In larger districts, educators are learning that even large student bodies can be made "small." They cluster students in "schools within schools," often based on core learning themes. Such schools often have smaller class sizes, too—usually not due to bigger budgets but because the schools' priorities have shifted dollars to teachers.

2. *Make time for each other and for in-depth study.* Making deep human connections also takes time—sustained time. In George's school, students start each day in a small group led by the same teacher throughout their high school years. So there is enough time really to get to know each other. These "advisories" or "family groups" become a student's anchor.

In Ithaca, New York, at Lehman Alternative Community School, students are in charge of the school's Web site, and here's how they define family groups: "Consider them a combination of homeroom, support group, guidance office, and fundraiser. Each family group is like a little family of 8–14 students, plus a teacher. They meet twice a week to check in about what's up, help each other out, hear announcements, keep track of schedules and graduation requirements, bond, and make plans for raising the hundred dollars each family group puts towards Spring Trips."[19]

When teachers share with counselors this emotional support work as well as individual advising, students get "one-on-one attention from a caring adult, and the whole faculty . . . is invested in the students' success," says the Institute for Student Achievement.[20]

At Boston's Fenway High School in downtown Boston, one of nineteen area pilot schools sparked by Deborah Meier, students are grouped into three learning communities of eighty students, each with its own faculty and student support staff who stay with the same pupils from ninth through eleventh grades.[21] "We are a community," one student writes. "Fenway is a school for everybody. . . . We are all getting what we need, but we have different needs."[22]

In its twentieth year, Fenway was designated by the National Association of Secondary School Principals a "breakthrough school"—meaning that at least 50 percent of students are minorities, at least half qualify for subsidized lunches, and still 90 percent graduate and 90 percent go on to college. (It's called a 50-50-90-90 school.)[23]

Literature assessing effective schools uses all sorts of words to stress the same thing: trust building, connection, and mutual respect make all else possible.

What does respect for students look like? Here's one example that could happen anywhere.

At Fenway, librarians invited students to recommend their favorite book. About fifty did, and they became the library's first "Power Readers." Each wrote a paragraph about his or her book and provided a published review. The library then bought five copies of each book, along with new display shelves for photos of students with their books. Books were labeled with the names of the recommending students.

Students flock to the Power Readers' display, reports the library staff, who also say that more than ever before, they are enjoying conversations about books with students and teachers.[24]

Connecting to new curriculum content takes time and concentration too. But today's typical seven high school periods, just forty-five minutes long, scatter rather than focus attention. That's why Central Park East Secondary School and Federal Hocking, along with hundreds of other breakaway schools nationwide, are reorganizing the school day. Every semester, many offer four classes, each eighty or ninety minutes long. Teachers might carry three classes at a time. But there's flexibility—at Federal Hocking, some courses last all year.

With the students' energetic pushing, Fed Hock also introduced two-week immersion courses on the heels of Christmas break. This "intersession" has become another opportunity for deep focus as teachers offer minicourses in everything from outdoor survival skills to oceanography to welding. The school superintendent teaches swing lessons he calls "Not Dirty Dancing."

3. *Pursue meaningful questions*. These bigger time blocks make it possible to move from covering everything thinly to probing a few things deeply. Ted Sizer's network of "essential schools" sums it up with a neat phrase: "Less is more."

Behind the approach is an assumption that once one gets the taste for learning—which can only come by exploring real questions deeply enough to experience the joy of mastery—that taste will become an appetite. And that appetite will drive us to ask the next question and the one after that. Any loss in knowledge of, say, the world's capital cities is more than made up for by an irrepressible habit of digging for knowledge that sticks with us precisely because it has meaning.

When I asked Zawadi what aspect of her high school experience she's most aware of carrying forward, she did not hesitate for a second. "The 'habits of mind' are haunting me," she said, laughing. "Like, what's your evidence? What difference does it make? How does that connect? My thought process has a lot to do with embracing these questions."

At Zawadi's school, David Smith described to me the two-year combined seventh- and eighth-grade humanities class he taught before becoming principal. It met in two-hour sessions, and behind the lesson plan was this core question: What is power through the focus of American history?

"We designed questions that are open-ended, with no right answer, so the students returned to the questions over a long period of time," David explained.

"The class reads about the American Revolution and the Civil War, focusing on the Americans who were originally left out of the Constitution and how they pushed themselves back in."

Throughout their work, students of Central Park East are encouraged to approach learning through five "essential questions" that the school hopes will become "habits of mind"—the five "essential questions" that still "haunt" Zawadi.

CENTRAL PARK EAST'S FIVE ESSENTIAL QUESTIONS

Connections	How is this event or work connected to others?
Perspective	From whose viewpoint is this being presented?
Evidence	How do you know what you know?
Supposition	What if things were different?
Significance	Why is this important?

Needless to say, the approach flies in the face of today's obsession with high-stakes, multiple-choice tests that most reward memorization of disconnected bits of information.

4. *Encourage student-initiated, hands-on projects and demonstrations*. Call it project learning, portfolio preparation, or mastery through creating exhibitions. The idea is simple. Most of us learn best when we exercise choice, when we pick topics that matter to us and express what we've learned by interpreting the information

in our own way and then demonstrate our understanding by putting our new learning together so that it makes sense to others.

At Central Park East, this is no small matter. "The school's 330 students begin collecting exemplary work in their major subjects as early as the ninth grade," Deborah Meier explained. That work constitutes their portfolios. To graduate, students must complete fourteen portfolios and give presentations in four major subjects, plus one of their choosing. By the time they present before their graduation committee—which includes fellow students—they've produced multiple drafts and carefully tested their theses.[25]

For Zawadi, theater was a passion, and her portfolio included her own plays—pieces that continued to be performed at her alma mater years after she graduated.

Zawadi reflected with me about the impact on her life of this approach to learning: "There are so many things I learn that people don't really teach me. I'm just able to figure them out. It's understanding how to question. It's being able to draw my own conclusions."

As Zawadi talked, I flashed back to the 1960s when I discovered for the first time the question about the roots of hunger that sparked a lifelong quest.

5. *Foster self-assessment, charting one's own development*. The shift from stuffing ourselves with information so that we can prove to authorities that we "know" it, on the one hand, toward taking responsibility for our own growth because we ourselves have goals to meet, on the other hand—this is huge. But the shift is also subtle, so subtle that it is often skipped over as a hallmark of effective education.

A high school athlete has no trouble telling you how much she's cut her time in the one-mile run since last season, notes George Wood, but typically schools don't encourage students to take responsibility for monitoring and assessing their own learning. Instead, everyone counts credits.

Developing portfolios of one's best work, however, helps shift consciousness toward self-monitoring and instill it as a habit. Students create and refine their portfolios over time—oh, so different from my own memories of handing in an "assignment" that I expected only to toss aside once a letter grade was scribbled at the top.

At Federal Hocking, among the fourteen portfolios required to graduate is an autobiography in which students reflect on their development and goals. Another exemplary public school in Providence, Rhode Island, also requires students to write an autobiography, asking for seventy-five pages.[26] (And this in a school for youngsters marked as underachievers before they arrive!) At Federal Hocking, in the works is an "owner's manual," a single personalized workbook in which each student keeps track of milestones across three dimensions of his or her school experience—academics, career, and citizenship.

The habit of mind of setting goals and reflecting on one's own development is instilled in other ways as well. At Fenway in Boston, students complete a "senior reflection" questionnaire on which they assess their school experience as it relates to their life aspirations. The school also models self-monitoring. Fenway surveys its graduates two and three years after they leave and shares the feedback with staff.

6. *Share authority and teach democracy by practicing its arts*. "One of the things we really do well here," George told me, "is we share authority with kids. They make real decisions. It creates relationships that show respect." Among the far-flung fraternity of breakthrough schools, the necessity of creating a culture of mutual respect is a common theme.

It didn't happen overnight at Federal Hocking. Adults' respect grew as young people proved themselves eager and able to shoulder responsibility.

"It began with my being able to see what I could delegate, and then I watched as the students handled it successfully. First I realized the students could take charge of approving fundraisers—what could be sold in the school and when. And they do a great job. The students decided, for example, that you can't sell candy in our school. 'That's not what we do here,' they said. Then I handed over responsibility for scheduling school events, like club meetings. That works well too.

"But the big shift came a few years after I arrived when the staff began to debate reorganizing the schedule—moving to longer periods and the semester system. Students got involved and studied scheduling in other schools, even visited some. They wrote reports on what they learned. When the time came to make the decision, I'll never forget the meeting.

"In the inner circle were thirty teachers debating all the issues. Around them were even more students—fifty! They weren't allowed to speak, but the teachers saw how carefully the students had prepared and observed. The teachers were impressed."

From there, George could feel teachers opening up to truly sharing authority with students, and today students help hire new teachers and serve on the site-based committee that governs most aspects of school life.

Together, a team of students and a team of teachers do most of the hiring at Federal Hocking. "I don't do much more than collect résumés and call references," George confided.

"The students seem to take hiring much more seriously than anyone. They have their questions ready. They sit in on the candidate's sample class.

"And it works. I remember one math position. The teachers wanted the female candidate; the students, the male. Both dug in their heels. At our school, finalists spend a whole day here. They teach a class, have lunch with students, and meet with the hiring teams.

"After all that usually views are pretty close. But this time there was a big difference. So they asked me to break the deadlock. I refused. 'This isn't my decision—it's yours,' I told them.

"At the end of the visit, we ask candidates to write down their impressions and questions. The person the students favored said in his exit slip that his interview with the students was the toughest he'd ever been through and that he hoped he'd done well. His respect for them was evident. It was this exit slip that brought the teachers around to the students' view.

"He worked out great," George added.

Then George paused.

"Of course, I've had teachers apply who refused to come here when they found out they would be interviewed by students."

At that I laughed and said that such reactions probably save him a lot of grief from inadvertently hiring the wrong person.

Sharing authority with students means they make decisions with huge consequences for their school. At the Lehman Alternative Community School in Ithaca, students also help hire and serve on a whole range of committees, including the Agenda Committee, which plans weekly all-school meetings where basic policies are set. On the Alternative Community Court, students determine the consequences for student infractions.

"When you make decisions, you feel you are more responsible for making them work," George told me. "That's why kids then come to us if there's a problem. 'Hey, so-and-so brought drugs to school. He needs help.' Or whatever it is. It's their school now."

George's comments draw me back to a thread running through these pages: democracy is a culture of *mutual* responsibility that emerges only as all feel like "owners," not victims or spectators. These six lessons being lived in schools across the country show us the way.

mastering the arts of democracy

Sharing authority is certainly part of "doing democracy," but doing it well takes more. It means mastering specific skills, what I like calling the "arts of democracy"—especially the art of creative conflict.

Democracy isn't a static condition. It is, by definition, change, and all change involves conflict. When somebody thinks it's possible to improve on the status quo, it's no big shock that somebody *else* feels criticized. So learning to use conflict creatively is a primary art we must master for effective democracy.

Although conflict in schools that spirals into ugly violence grabs national attention, thousands of schools are learning to deter violence and turn conflict into strength. Many schools are training both students and teachers to mediate differences among their peers, in a movement unheard of only twenty years ago.

It works this way: students volunteer for mediation training—typically fifteen hours covering active listening, paraphrasing, reframing, and role playing. The new mediators promote their services and encourage their peers to bring unresolved disputes to them. Once mediation programs are under way, schools often find many more students volunteering than they can use.

"One teacher typically becomes the point person," Richard Cohen, a founder of the movement, explained to me.[27] "When a conflict arises, this person chooses two students who might be right for those two parties. Some schools handle three hundred to four hundred cases a year, and a mature program reaches 10 percent of the student body each year."

In the past decade, the number of participating schools has jumped from five thousand to between ten and fifteen thousand.[28]

"In a new high school in Lincoln-Sudbury, Massachusetts, they even built into the plans a suite of rooms specifically for mediation," Richard said. "That's how far we've come.

"What I love about mediation training is that it puts students themselves in charge of an aspect of school that is so important to them—their relationships. And all types, not just the honor roll students, are involved.

"We often train adults and students simultaneously. Students come to see teachers as people. They use first names. And the adults come to appreciate how earnest and capable their students are. It's not unusual to find that the average student is a better mediator than the adult. Effectiveness depends on being good at reading people, making them comfortable. You can get a seventeen-year-old with a ton of that kind of interpersonal intelligence.

"We teach kids that conflict is normal, that there's no way to avoid it, and that it can be positive," Richard told me. "We ask kids whether they've ever felt closer to someone *after* going through a conflict. And a lot of hands go up. They get it. We also teach that conflict can be resolved cooperatively, not always competitively."

As with many breakthroughs toward a culture of Living Democracy, school mediation now has a long enough track record to measure its success. Summarizing twenty-three studies, a 2003 report shows that in more than nine of every ten cases, school mediation achieves a resolution, and disputants express satisfaction at almost as high a rate.[29]

learning as community problem solving

As the godfather of democratic education, John Dewey, observed a century ago, education is "a process of living and not a preparation for future living."[30] But for most kids, education is just the opposite: it feels "made up." At best, it's about "practicing" for some unknown future.

How disempowering is that?

By contrast, when young people engage in learning through projects in the community of their school or their neighborhoods or even the wider world, their work doesn't feel made up. It makes sense.

At Federal Hocking, for example, almost all seniors receive course credit for apprenticeships in local businesses and organizations. These internships range from mastering surgical skills for neutering pets at the vet's office to getting up at dawn to learn how to bake bread at the local specialty bakery.

At Federal Hocking, internships teach something that "schoolwork" alone often can't. "If I don't show up at school, it goes on anyway," one student told George, "but if I don't show up at my internship, the work doesn't get done."

"One of our students, Summer Williamson, was a nursing intern," George reminisced, "and that winter we had a bad snowstorm that trapped nurses at home. Summer said she'd stay at her internship as long as they needed her; she and one other nurse kept the unit going for two days. She hung in there. That's how responsible our students feel. Now she's a registered nurse."

For many, the vision of students out in the community brings to mind "community service"—youngsters brightening the days of elders in nursing homes or lending a hand in neighborhood cleanups. Today, in 64 percent of public schools, including 83 percent of high schools, students participate in school-organized or school-recognized community service.[31]

In 1992, Maryland became the first state to require community service; today, a tenth of all public high schools and four in ten private high schools require community service to graduate.[32] Interestingly, though, more than half of young people oppose the requirement.[33]

Service connotes charity—"doing for" those less fortunate; so perhaps the students who oppose a requirement speak to a real contradiction: Can one effectively *coerce* altruism? In Bethlehem, Pennsylvania, in the early 1990s, parents sued the school board to halt mandated community service. They lost.[34]

In part because of such questioning, community service is giving way to "service learning"—with the emphasis on learning. In a third of public schools, service learning has been integrated into the curriculum; at the high school level, it's almost half.[35]

But the term doesn't capture what my hero of this movement, Marvin Rosenblum, is proving—the power of what he calls "apprentice citizenship." Marvin, founder in 1988 of Kids as Planners, later renamed KIDS Consortium, in Lewiston, Maine, argues that young people come to value themselves and their capacities by tackling real problems important to them. He notes that "very few subjects cannot be appropriately learned in the community itself—history, geography, social studies, architecture, the arts, the sciences."[36]

When I first met Marvin, now seventy-five, in the early 1990s, apprentice citizenship was barely more than a twinkle in his eye. Twelve years later, his approach had reached fifty thousand students and thousands of teachers in New England, and big expansions were in the works.

In KIDS Consortium, students tackle real-life problems and make lasting contributions to their communities: one class studied traffic speeds downtown using a speed gun lent by the local police and then used its findings to convince officials to install a traffic light to reduce speeding and save lives.

Five years ago, Trisha Smith at Holbrook School in H[illegible]n, Maine, now thirty, attended a workshop for teachers [illegible] got her first whiff of the KIDS approach. Her voice bu[illegible] with enthusiasm as she recollected, "I didn't know a[illegible]ferent because I was just starting. And maybe it appeal[illegible] me because I was an unconventional learner myself." F[illegible]er that term means kids "who don't necessarily like to sit [illegible]eir desks and do what they are told."

Trisha's first chance to try KIDS out came when the state decided to straighten a roadway near her school, seriously disrupting the landscape. Her fifth-grade class helped build erosion controls, protecting water they knew they would ultimately drink.

"I learned a lot, too, so they could see the teacher doesn't have all the answers. This strengthened the student-teacher bond. It shifted the power," Trisha reflected.

Then came another unexpected chance for her students to make a dent. Lifeflight of Maine, a health emergency service that also educates about public safety, sent Tom Judge to Trisha's school to speak. Lifeflight personnel witness up close the high accident rate among seventeen-to-twenty-five-year-olds. They figured that if they could teach students the importance of using seat belts and helmets before they reach those most dangerous years, they could save lives.

"Turning off the faucet is a better alternative than mopping up the mess. Kids understand this analogy," Tom told Trisha.

At the first presentation, Tom invited Trisha's students to become "agents of change" under the theme "Mission Possible."

"Their eyes were the size of saucers," Trisha remembered, laughing. "From there, the choices were theirs throughout. They wrote letters, invited other speakers, and created their own PowerPoint presentation. They carried out a schoolwide survey and collected data from five communities, analyzing the results and graphing each question on a poster. Students used photos, student quotes, and sample student work to present their work on the computer. Now that's an in-depth skill for a fifth-grader!" she added, with evident pride.

"It was a wicked cool PowerPoint," student Kevin Paine told me.

Before it was all over, the students had given numerous presentations of their findings and Maine's governor had visited the class, complimenting the students on their "very good data."

As Trisha talked excitedly about the effectiveness of apprentice citizenship, she kept returning to Kevin to make a special point. He, like Trisha herself, "is a nontraditional learner. He doesn't like to just sit down and read and write because he's told to," she told me. "But he's got a heart of gold and he'll do anything to help out on something real. Getting Kevin to write two paragraphs for an assignment is tough, but he sat down and wrote a two-and-one-half-page thank-you letter to Tom."

"What was the hardest part?" I asked Kevin, who's now thirteen.

"Letting go of the project and moving on to the next grade," he told me. "I was upset we had to stop."

"As a sixth-grader, Kevin heard that fifth-graders were joking on the school bus about speeding without helmets," Trisha explained. "Kevin had such ownership of the project, he felt it was his responsibility to carry it on. So he presented the idea of picking up the ball to the new fifth-graders, and they leapt at it. They ended up making safety presentations at the summer Red Cross camp and were even interviewed on our local TV news."

"In the beginning," Kevin told me, "I didn't think I was going to help anyone. Later on, I realized I was saving lives. Now that's the shocking part."

Parents are supporting her approach, Trisha reports. They see "this is not fluff. Their children are learning skills by applying them to something real. In school usually everything is isolated; but in life it's all integrated. Here it all connects. It all makes sense."

A new study confirms what these educators have found through their risk taking—that children learn best when they can explore the world and interact with adults through "guided discovery."[37]

KIDS Consortium, too, has now been around long enough to be able to boast an impressive track record. Seventy percent of participating students and teachers report improved student problem-solving skills, social competence, pride in work, and positive attitudes, says another recent study.[38]

There is a final facet to the theme of school-community integration.

Not only can kids step out into the community, but the community can be invited in as well. It's happening in a movement called Lighted Schools, in which Waco, Texas, has become the exemplar. There, twelve schools are abuzz with activities from three to six o'clock in the afternoon, not coincidentally the period when youth crime is most likely to occur.[39] In Waco, grades, attendance, and behavior have improved.[40] And there's evidence of crime going down, too.[41] Lighted Schools in Waco has been so positive for kids that the program expanded to family nights offering classes in GED preparation, English as a second language, computer basics, financial literacy, and parenting.

Several thousand Lighted Schools now dot the country, though budget crises triggered by the Bush administration's tax cuts have stymied their spread.[42]

school lessons

Astonishingly, in less than two decades, these gutsy school changemakers have solid evidence of positive impacts of their approaches. George's school, for example, participates in the nationwide reform movement called the Coalition of Essential Schools, mentioned earlier. A 2001 survey of forty-one of its mostly public affiliate schools in eighteen states revealed the following results:[43]

- *Rigorous course work:* 39 percent of eighth-grade Coalition students take algebra, compared to only a quarter of eighth-graders nationally.
- *More college-bound students:* 84 percent of Coalition high school grads enter college, whereas the national average is only 63 percent.
- *Safer children:* Coalition schools report 3.2 instances of crime per thousand students each year; nationally, the average is 10.

The personalized environment of smaller schools might be expected to cost more, but here's what one study in New York concluded: "Though these smaller schools have somewhat higher costs per student, their much higher graduation rates and lower dropout rates produce among the lowest costs per graduate in the entire New York City system."[44]

Note that George's school operates with a per-student budget that's roughly 40 percent of what a typical, wealthy suburban school in Ohio enjoys.

Now take a moment to flip back to "Our Schools Aren't Working." Pause to register the misery and waste reflected in these cold measures of failure. Then think about the richness in the lives of students Zawadi and Kevin, teacher Trisha, or principal George. Zawadi told me that even today, she loves walking into a school, *any* school—her memories are that positive.

The contrast is deeply disquieting. And it is energizing. We know what works. The cover of a recent report on results from a leading school reform network boils much of what we know down to seven words: "Teachers and students know each other well." In other words, the key is connection.

As the cliché has it, this is not rocket science.

But then, transforming schools requires trusting our common sense and finding the courage to change when the dominant message and reward system—as embodied, for example, in the Bush administration's No Child Left Behind Act—tells us to do the opposite: *don't* trust yourself or your students; judge by a standardized measure that excludes many of the very qualities we most value and that children need most to succeed.

Might this be harder than rocket science?

All this is not to imply that standardized tests have no place. They can expose the tragedy of children being passed on through schools to graduate without even the basics. In theory, testing for basic skills could help us hold schools accountable for adopting the proven strategies described in this chapter, methods that engage students in communities of active learning instead of letting them slip through the cracks.

But the standardized testing system, as it currently operates, stifles experimentation toward these proven pathways. Many critics of the federally mandated punitive one-test-fits-all approach charge that Republican rhetoric is actually a clever ruse. While the Bush administration claims that high-stakes testing will enhance school accountability, critics say their real agenda is to prove that public schools can't succeed, providing justification for defunding them. Their target, say the critics, is not poor education but public education itself.[45]

The suspicion was compounded when the Bush administration's No Child Left Behind Act heaped demands on schools while seriously underfunding programs needed to carry out the reforms. In 2004, we learned that the administration also surreptitiously paid the prominent African American commentator Armstrong Williams almost a quarter of a million dollars to use his media access to build support for No Child Left Behind among black families.[46]

Whatever the motive for building them, barriers to democratic education are rising. As in other dimensions of American life, here too we are living in a schizophrenic era, moving simultaneously in two opposing directions.

In such a time, the trick is to keep one's eyes on the prize.

Take George Wood. He's among the harshest critics of the current fixation on testing, but he hasn't let external regulations derail his staff from building a democratic community of learners. Students at Federal Hocking do fine on standardized tests, George says, because the school provides breadth of learning along with a focus on reading all the way through high school—including thirty-five minutes each Friday morning when *everyone* in the school stops and just reads. The school also coaches all students in test-taking techniques—help that typically only children of wealthy parents get.

While we keep our eyes on the prize—the prize of meaningful reform turning schools into learning communities—we must also counteract attitudes deeply embedded in our culture.

For one, most of us assume that progress moves in a straight line, not in zigzags. But real change, democratic change, is anything but even. To pick only one example, even as Central Park East Secondary School—the one that changed Zawadi Powell forever—has inspired hundreds of other effective schools, it may itself have faltered. Some worried observers whisper that its special approach has given way under pressures from state and federal mandates. (I tried without success to interview the current principal, who, as a teacher, I'd quoted positively in *The Quickening of America*.)

Democracy isn't a straight line.

Neither is it ever complete. In the spring of 2004, I recall pulling into the parking lot of Hudson High School in the middle of Massachusetts. It was the school's first semester in a spanking new building, the only school building I'd ever heard of specifically designed to facilitate a democratic culture. Huge piles of dirt and yet-to-be-landscaped grounds proclaimed that this experiment was still unfinished.

Inside the school, I huddled in an activity room with four students and a teacher who've been creating a student-engaged democracy at Hudson. One is ninth-grader Kyle Knobloch. At the time, he sat on the school's Community Council, "which makes just about all the decisions that state law doesn't give to someone else," he explained.

He first got involved in the eighth grade, when he volunteered to help facilitate sessions for kids to offer ideas for making the school better. "What do you guys think?" he told me he'd asked. "But I'd get a room full of blank stares."

"Or they would complain but shrink away from doing anything," Katie Green chimed in.

"But I've stayed involved because I see possibility," said Kim Banks. People have to get used to democracy, and this is all new, the students stressed. "Once the eighth- and ninth-graders get to the higher grades, there will be less apathy," Rita Paulino assured me. "The longer you are involved, the more you see the big picture, you see the changes. The whole experience makes me see the potential of democracy," she added.

I thought to myself that perhaps Shelley Berman, the visionary superintendent who took such risks for over a decade to get this far, might do well to leave signs of construction alone, like that dirt mound outside—and maybe even add a few stacks of bricks. Perhaps we *all* need regular reminders of what Kim and Rita seem to understand so well: that democracy is "becoming, rather than being." It can "easily be lost but is never fully won," as Judge William Hastie reminded us.[47]

the company we keep

Visionary schools are showing that learning thrives in a democratic culture, and democracy is all about change. And change, even positive change, means conflict.

George knows well. He was fired in his fifth year at Federal Hocking. It took a student sit-in and parent protests to save his job. Yet schools are known for being both conflict-ridden and conflict-avoiding. Cowed by higher-ups, teachers often refrain from expressing criticism of, say, the current testing mania because they fear losing their jobs, Deborah Meier notes. Then she points to the obvious: schools cannot teach "collaboration, solidarity, and community . . . when adults are mostly busy complying."[48]

Yet here, too, lies possibility as schools begin to view mediation training programs not just as tools for their students but as opportunities to learn how to use conflict in creative, schoolwide transformation.[49]

Because it was Deborah Meier who first awakened me not to the dream but to the real-life practice of democratic schooling, it is only appropriate that I close this chapter with her voice. After forty years at it, Deborah is forthright about the enormous challenges of really doing democracy. "What staves off discouragement," she says, ". . . is the pleasure we get from the company we keep—colleagues, kids, families."[50]

And the pleasure of which Deborah speaks is possible only as we take risks together, as we share in the struggle to live out the democratic principles we feel in our bones to be true.

11

SECURITY

the exclusion illusion & the power of connection

It is inclusivity that brings security—belonging, not belongings.

JEREMY RIFKIN[1]

In the novel *The Samurai's Garden*, Sachi is a beautiful Japanese girl who contracts leprosy and believes that her disease has dishonored her family. Sachi's parents let her know that she could absolve the family's shame by committing suicide. But Sachi, cursing her own cowardice, runs away to a remote mountain leper colony. There redemption comes only through her relationship with Matsu, the one friend from Sachi's youth who never severs touch with her.[2]

Like me, most readers are probably appalled at the thought of disease being treated as dishonoring or shameful and dismayed that these feelings persist in AIDS prejudice today. Sachi's story grabs us in part because it feels quaint.

Yet the more I explore the great blight on our lives that violence is in America today, the less quaint the novel's storyline feels. Sachi stays with me in part because I realize that as a society, America has come to view violence through a lens not unlike Sachi's parents': to save ourselves and cleanse our society we believe we must banish, punish, and destroy offenders. Too often we view them not as human beings like ourselves with the capacity to do right as well as wrong but as pariahs to be purged.

Yet the "toss 'em out, lock 'em up" approach toward transgressors that flows from this framing is failing to give us the security we long for.

Imprisonment, tearing families apart and leaving children without parents, has hit an all-time high.[3] The number of Americans behind bars quadrupled in a little over two decades and continues to increase.[4] We isolate mostly young men in the prime of their lives in degrading and violent prisons—particularly young African American men, one in three of whom is in prison, on probation, or on parole. In big cities, it's one in two.[5] Half of the imprisoned are hooked on drugs, but only a quarter get help in overcoming their addiction.[6]

At the same time, government spending on corrections has skyrocketed, climbing sixfold in twenty years.[7] In some states, imprisonment is so costly that taxpayers could have, for the same price, put each inmate through an Ivy League college![8]

Yet harsher treatment is not proving more effective, either in making us feel safer or in changing criminal behavior. Most released prisoners go on to offend again, and states with high rates of prison growth have not experienced correspondingly large drops in crime. As crime declined nationally during the 1990s, West Virginia, for example, had one of the highest prison growth rates even as its violent crime rate went up.[9]

So what is effective?

Across the political spectrum, a multilayered movement is taking shape—from California's Republican governor to Ohio's chief of prisons to citizen innovators in communities nationwide—that builds on the key insights of Living Democracy. Security grows from a culture of connection based on mutual respect and accountability, including the engagement of those most affected. As Sachi's redemption came through her relationship with the one person who did not reject her, solutions for our society are emerging as citizens are fostering a culture of inclusion.

What works are efforts addressing the two emotions at the root of our growing pain: fear and shame.

Let me begin with fear, for I believe that fear can give rise to the very threats it most wants to dispel.

Two taxi drivers—one Russian, one Greek—on opposite sides of the country recently responded with virtually the same words when I asked (as I typically do when I encounter a newcomer to our nation), "What do you think of America?"

"You're all afraid," they said, and they were not referring to the impact of 9/11. They each added, "You're all afraid of each other."

Taken aback to hear the same observation from people from very different parts of the world, I've gradually come to understand what they were telling me. Even as violent crime has dropped dramatically since the early 1990s and property crime has fallen for over twenty-five years—today more than half of us believe that crime is on the rise.[10]

Even as crime decreases, a culture of fear deepens. One reason is that our media of communication, as we've seen in Chapter Nine, has become primarily a medium for selling, and crime sells. According to Barry Glassner's book *The Culture of Fear*, network news homicide coverage from 1990 to 1998 leapt almost sixfold—not even counting the O. J. Simpson trial.[11] Yet the actual murder rate over this time fell by a third.[12]

I believe, however, that something even more insidious is at work: what I think of as the "ambient fear" in our culture flows directly from the antidemocratic premise of the Far Right I outlined in Chapter Two: that ours is a dog-eat-dog world in which we are each fundamentally competitors we cannot trust, not neighbors with common needs whom we can trust.

Americans live with the prospect that any day we might lose out in the ceaseless race for good jobs, schools, homes, mates, parking spots—all presumed to be scarce. This premise creates a milieu of fear (the words *scarce* and *scare* seem oddly similar). In this high-stakes game of musical chairs, some of us end up not just without a seat but out on the street.

We fear the shame of being cast out.

This fear is fed by an underlying uneasiness and disorientation as the dominant market-can-do-no-wrong dogma tramples familiar values that sustain communities. What sells seems to trump everything. Little wonder so many Americans sense they're "being robbed" of "the country they had known growing up," as *Atlanta Journal-Constitution* editor Jay Bookman puts it.

"That fear—that sense of being under assault in your own country—is a powerful thing," he continues. We feel the assault in everything from the barrage of sexually explicit ads on family-time TV to the relentless announcements of "mass layoffs and a tax-subsidized move overseas. However, the root cause of those changes," Bookman concludes, is "just business, chasing a dollar with little or no attention to what its impact will be."[13]

Unable to name the fear flowing from this primal sense of loss of home, we pin it on sources presented—crime we see on the evening news, terrorists that could strike at any second. We seek protection by violent means if necessary and by banishing offenders. We buy more guns (now one in every four of us has one) and security systems.[14] We build more prisons. With one in six prisons now privately run, we've created a booming new industry whose profits per bed are 80 percent greater than the Marriott Hotels enjoy.[15] Like the gun lobby, the new prison lobby's vested interest lies in fanning our fear.

WHERE THE JUST-GET-TOUGH APPROACH HAS TAKEN US . . .

- *Incarceration*. Though a mere 5 percent of the world's people live in the United States, we lock up nearly a quarter of all those imprisoned worldwide.[16] This nation's incarceration rate is five to eight times greater than that of the industrialized countries most similar to us, including Canada, England, and France.[17] During the 1980s and 1990s, mandatory sentencing sent ever more nonviolent perpetrators to jail—in 2000, fully 81 percent of those sentenced to state prisons.[18]

- *Costs of imprisonment*. In 2001, U.S. states spent as much as $38,000 per inmate, making it cheaper to have sent each prisoner to Harvard.[19] Government spending on corrections (not including police or courts) has jumped sixfold in the past twenty years, to nearly $60 billion—42 percent more than we spend on education.[20]
- *Executions*. The United States is one of only a handful of nations that executes offenders. Others include Iran, Vietnam, and China. Together, these four countries were responsible for 84 percent of all recorded executions in 2003.[21] Yet U.S. states with the death penalty have higher murder rates than those without it.[22]

. . . AND THE CYCLE OF CRIME IT CREATES

- *Crime rates*. Although rates here have declined, the murder rate in the United States is still four times higher than in Western Europe, Canada, Australia, and Japan. The United States has the sixth worst reported crime rate in the world, at 8,517 crimes per 100,000 inhabitants. Even Mexico and Colombia have lower crime rates than we do.[23]
- *Recidivism*. Within three years of release, 68 percent of ex-convicts are rearrested for a felony or serious misdemeanor.[24]
- *Toll on families*. More than half of all prisoners had to leave behind a child under the age of eighteen.[25] Over two million American children currently have a parent in prison.[26] Boys without a father at home are twice as likely to one day end up in jail as boys with both parents at home.[27]

Our culture of fear, and the banishment approach to crime it inspires, ends up generating the very crime that so frightens us.

a culture of shame

Striking cross-culture contrasts in the incidence of crime tell us there is nothing inevitable about the high rates we suffer.[28] If crime isn't caused simply by miscreants plaguing all societies more or less equally, what is the cause?

For understanding, I turned to psychiatrist James Gilligan, who headed the study of violence at Harvard Medical School and has devoted more than thirty years to working closely with violent criminals. His groundbreaking books *Violence* and *Preventing Violence* address the root of the failures captured in the previous box.[29]

Our problem is that we've been asking the wrong questions about crime, Gilligan tells us. Typically we ask only, How evil is the action, and how much punishment does it deserve?

Gilligan thinks we should be asking a different question: What's at the root of the violence? And his answer: shame.

"I have yet to see a serious act of violence," Gilligan reports "that was not provoked by the experience of feeling shamed and humiliated, disrespected and ridiculed."[30] He recounts horrifying stories of vicious murders triggered by a single slur. I say "triggered" because Gilligan's deeper point is that such triggers spark violence because ours is a shaming culture.

Accepting the four "givens" capsulated in Chapter Four, our society increasingly traps those at the bottom on a treadmill of deadening schools, poverty-wage jobs, and hardscrabble neighborhoods. All are insults to self-regard. Adding to the humiliations of poverty itself is America's persistent Horatio Alger myth, the bootstrap notion that anyone with spunk can lift oneself out of the hole. In reality, social mobility—lower-income people climbing to society's higher rungs—is *less* real here than in European societies that Americans assume to be more rigid than ours.[31]

It is through work that most of us come to feel valued as members of a community. Without a job or with pay so meager that it tells us we're devalued, we feel humiliated.

If you deprive "a man of a job or an income," said Martin Luther King Jr., "you are in substance saying to that man that he has no right to exist. . . . It is murder, psychologically."[32]

Almost two-thirds of U.S. prisoners are poor—earning less than $1,000 a month before their arrest.[33]

Thus feelings of shame predate any trigger, and frequently all it takes is even a mild put-down to release rage. "The word 'disrespect' is so central in the vocabulary" of chronically violent men, says Gilligan, "that they have abbreviated it into the slang term, 'he dissed me.'" Violence is the only avenue to respect these men see, he says, quoting a violent inmate in a running battle with correction officers: "I've got to have my self-respect, and I've declared war on the whole world till I get it!"[34]

Economists recently confirmed the link between poverty and crime, finding in a detailed analysis of recent decades that wages of non-college-educated men are "almost a mirror image of crime patterns." So strong is the link that the researchers concluded that "a sustained long-term decrease in crime rates will depend on . . . the wages of less skilled men."[35]

Seeing low wages, joblessness, and homelessness as potent stimuli of shame and therefore key to the politics of violence helps us understand why the United States, with a much larger share of people living in poverty compared to other wealthy countries, also suffers the highest rates of violent crime.[36] Moreover, given that it is one's sense of inferior status relative to others that engenders shame, Gilligan isn't surprised that the "most powerful predictor" of a society's murder rate is "the size of the disparities in income and wealth" and that among advanced industrial nations, the United States suffers the most unequal income spread.[37] Earlier I noted that the ratio of top CEO salary to average worker pay here is thirty to fifty times greater than in Europe and Japan.

To this shaming culture in the outside world, U.S. prisons add shaming treatment on the inside.

Even though an official study reports that fewer than one in ten inmates is raped in U.S. prisons, Gilligan's insider experience tells him that rape in prison is nearly universal.[38] U.S. prison conditions, he writes, "force prisoners to engage in acts of serious violence in order to avoid being mutilated, raped, or murdered themselves."[39]

"We profess to rely on the prison for our safety; yet it is directly responsible for much of the damage that society suffers at the hands of offenders," Ralph Banay, head of Sing Sing Prison's psychiatric clinic, said half a century ago.[40]

In sum, the fear-driven premise of our competitive economic life, combined with a willingness to tolerate extreme inequities of opportunity—all the while clinging to the myth that we all have an equal chance—leads to widespread feelings of shame. Our approach to punishment compounds that shame, inciting more violence. The media blast us with high-ratings violent "news," frightening us further and confirming for us that crime is the cause of the unease we feel. We get still "tougher" on crime, and the cycle of needless misery is perpetuated.

emerging solutions: what real security feels like

Emerging answers—creatively dissolving each link of this deadly cycle—are taking shape across our country. Prior chapters have pointed to movements that address demeaning wages and degrading housing, as well as predatory lending facing poor people; we learned of a political party representing the interests of working families. All these efforts help break the cycle of fear, shame, and violence.

Following are glimpses of people with the courage to admit that our current path to security is failing.[41] They are remaking prisons, showing that we can hold transgressors accountable for the harm they've done and require restitution where possible without severing their community ties and further shaming them.

Just as many of us are coming to realize that in relation to our ecological home there is no "away" to which we can throw our trash, so too there is no "away" to which we can banish offenders. We can resist the temptation to expel and instead engage.

To stoke our confidence that change is possible, it's worth noting that the get-tough frame with its horrendous human and dollar costs took hold in the mid-1970s partly as a result of a *single* survey for the New York legislature claiming that rehabilitating criminals doesn't work. It got big media attention at the time, including by CBS's *60 Minutes*. Panned by scholars, the survey was nonetheless promoted by those who wanted to cut rehab programs. It fit their frame, and they used it to convince the public that the get-tough strategy was the only realistic approach.[42]

My point is that frames are made, sometimes quickly, and they can be remade. Here are five ways.

SEEING THROUGH THE EXCLUSION ILLUSION: FIVE WAYS AMERICANS ARE CREATING SECURITY

- Enabling prisoners to rebuild self-respect and to find a contributing place for themselves in communities
- Reknitting communities as citizens take on responsibility for safety and become partners with police
- Enabling nonviolent offenders to avoid prison and make amends to their victims and the community
- Spreading practices that resolve minor breaches and disputes *before* they escalate into crime
- Strengthening community connections—including economic exchanges—that enhance mutual respect, trust, and support and therefore our feelings of safety.

Several of the following glimpses draw on stories written for the American News Service.

when inmates get help, we all become safer

"I often ask the question, 'Who would you rather sit next to on a bus? A person who is very, very angry about their prison experience and untrained and uneducated? Or a person who obtained a GED and vocational training in prison and is on his or her way to work?"

So says Reginald Wilkinson, chief of Ohio's prison system since 1991. In his state, prisoners are required to use their time to develop job skills and receive drug treatment.[43]

The new (old) wisdom that rehabilitation should take center stage is even taking off in California—a notorious example of the failure of the lock-'em-up strategy. California has seriously overcrowded prisons compounded by the country's worst rate of reincarceration. Six out of ten prisoners return.[44]

This failure and skyrocketing prison costs have not been lost on Governor Arnold Schwarzenegger. In 2004, he asked the legislature to approve a complete reorganization that elevates rehabilitation to equal standing with overall prison operations.[45] And he took other "radical" steps, adding the word *rehabilitation* to the department's title and appointing Jeanne Woodward, fifty, to head the Department of Corrections.

Woodward began as a San Quentin Prison guard twenty-five years ago and rose through the ranks to become its first female warden. Under her direction, with the help of some three thousand volunteer teachers and counselors, San Quentin came to run more self-improvement programs than any other state prison—at practically no extra cost.[46]

One program, the "Success Dorm," houses two hundred inmates who agree to follow the dorm's rules. They hold jobs in the prison during the day, and they must take at least three classes at night. In classes, inmates learn about the "fatal peril," the moment just before anger can lead to violence. Using Dr. Seuss stories, they learn how to read to their children when they go home.

"True public protection is making sure we send inmates out of our prisons in better shape than when they come in," says Woodward.[47]

No doubt some of the lessons the new corrections chief will be applying come from the San Francisco County Jail's highly effective Resolve to Stop the Violence Project (RSVP).

In 1997, RSVP selected several dozen men convicted of violent offenses to spend twelve hours a day, six days a week, in such programs as victim-offender mediation, mentoring, community theater, gardening, poetry writing, acupuncture, yoga, and guided meditation.[48] The men are offered substance abuse treatment, education, and job training. Group counseling calls the men to vigorous self-examination about the role of violence in their lives. Unfortunately, only 62 beds, out of 2,085 total, are designated for the program.[49]

After release, the men help restore the community they've hurt through work that includes violence prevention education. Some involve theater productions in schools and community centers.[50] RSVP also offers newly released prisoners six months of antiaddiction support and education.[51]

After only four months of this intense immersion, graduates are 83 percent less likely to be rearrested for a violent crime one year after release.[52] On the outside, inmates who were most responsive in prison get more training to become RSVP mediators and facilitators themselves.

RSVP focuses at least as much on restoring the victim as on reclaiming the perpetrator. It helps victims understand the impact of the crime on their lives and restore their losses. RSVP's goal is for victims to come through not only as survivors but also as advocates for safer communities.

The program is strikingly cost-effective. It adds 15 percent to per-inmate costs, but it is so successful in reducing rearrests that taxpayers save $4 for every $1 spent.[53]

Despite proof that inmate rehabilitation classes are cost-effective, California spends less than 3 percent of its corrections budget on them, and less than a third of inmates have access.[54] This is what Schwarzenegger says he wants to change.

RSVP-type evidence seems to be cracking the grip of get-tough dogma.

Ohio has taken the lead in the search for effective rehabilitation. Corrections Chief Wilkinson says that in Ohio reentry "begins the day the offender arrives." Officials there help convicts maintain family ties while in prison and when they leave prison provide halfway houses and organized community help—called "citizen circles"—to find housing and jobs.[55]

WHAT WORKS: MORE SNAPSHOTS[56]

- *Read novels, cut crime*. Taking part in Changing Lives Through Literature—in its fifteenth year—thirty-five hundred convicts in Massachusetts have now done at least part of their prison time around seminar tables on college campuses. In small groups, sitting with probation officers and often a judge, participants share thoughts about a book they've all read. One Esteban Velez reflected on characters such as Wolf Larsen, the brutal ship captain in Jack London's *Sea Wolf*. "I started to see myself in him, and I didn't like what I saw," Velez told the American News Service. He'd been arrested for drug possession and breaking and entering.[57] The program costs $500 per convict; and by cutting recidivism in half, it is saving Massachusetts an estimated $3 million each year.[58]
- *Missouri offers unprisonment*. While most of the country still confines youth offenders in large correctional insti-

tutions with as many as two thousand youths, in 1983 Missouri decided to give it up. Now three-quarters of its youth offenders participate in nonresidential rehab programs or live in groups of ten to twelve young people—in dorms, not cells.

In this smaller-scale, personalized around-the-clock approach, youth are treated as part of communities and families. At least two highly trained professionals oversee the young people at all times and everyone participates in academic classes and group therapy. Many tend their own pets—dogs, turtles, rabbits. Colorful bulletin boards designed by the residents cover most walls.

This shift in approach, say the experts, helps explain why Missouri's average recidivism rate of 11 percent is dramatically lower than elsewhere. Despite the intensive attention the young people receive, it costs Missouri one-third *less* per youth than the average of eight surrounding states still locked into the prison paradigm.[59]

- *Prisoners learn to mediate, not to fight*. At the Washington State Reformatory in Monroe, prisoners wanting to become peacemakers attend a forty-hour course that features lectures, demonstrations, and role-playing. The program teams volunteer community peacemakers with inmate negotiators when problems arise between prisoners. In the vast majority of the cases, everyone has left the room satisfied, said Jim Newman, on the staff there. "They shake hands rather than taking it out in the big yard where there might be a fight or a stabbing."[60]
- *Ex-prisoners grow food and selves*.[61] In San Francisco, ex-convicts work as "garden apprentices" and "tree

> corps apprentices" while also attending computer and literacy classes and counseling.[62] They earn $11 per hour and get medical and dental benefits. Since 1992, tree corps apprentices have planted more than ten thousand street trees in the San Francisco Bay Area. In 2002, the garden apprentices grew and distributed sixty thousand pounds of organic vegetables, mostly for poor families and seniors. Whereas statewide, two-thirds of released offenders eventually return to jail, of those who've worked in the Garden Project, only about one-quarter do.[63]

citizens and police partnering

Outside of prison, a movement began in the early 1990s to re-embed law enforcement within community relationships. Called community policing, it's cited as one of the reasons for the marked decline in violent crime since then.

Before volunteering as a neighborhood crime fighter in Spokane, Washington, Cheryl Steele never thought she would be instrumental in catching the Bad Tooth Bandit. The armed robber, known for his visibly poor dental work, had been on a one-man crime spree for over a year, holding up a score of stores and frustrating the police.[64]

His mistake was holding up a store in the west-central Spokane neighborhood where Steele helped organize an active community policing program. That night, now over a decade ago, the neighborhood network buzzed with reports to the local substation, giving the police the information needed to apprehend the Bad Tooth Bandit only nine blocks from the crime scene.

Community policing—police and citizens partnering to reduce crime—was introduced in the 1980s but really took off in 1994 when the Clinton administration created an arm of the Justice Department to provide grants to cities for neighborhood policing.

In Steele's case, it was a personal tragedy that had ignited her. "When a friend of my daughter's was abducted and murdered, I realized that it was time to get involved," Steele told the American News Service. She's now the community mobilization manager for Oregon's department of corrections and on the board of a regional community policing effort.

In Spokane, volunteers photograph gang-related graffiti and report its location. After a rash of bicycle thefts, citizen volunteers began a bicycle registration drive. They are even trained to take latent fingerprints from cars that have been broken into or vandalized.

From one volunteer center in the early 1990s, there are now eleven community-oriented policing centers—called "COPS shops"—including the only one in the country housed within a high school and staffed by volunteer high school students. Overall, about five hundred citizens volunteer.[65]

Community policing is as much about keeping problems from entering the criminal justice doorway as it is about nabbing criminals. It is also about addressing underlying triggers to crime, Lieutenant Larry Powell, fifty-four, a thirty-one-year veteran of the Cincinnati police force, explained to me. He spoke with pride of his city's Citizens on Patrol, which started in four neighborhoods in 1997 and has spread to more than twenty-five.

"Here, over eight hundred citizens are being trained twenty hours in observation skills, how to use radios," he explained. "We give them special shirts, caps, and jackets. They are the eyes and ears—but not the hands. We don't want them confronting anyone. They report quality-of-life things like litter as well as crime and abandoned cars." Currently, almost three thousand volunteers patrol 120 sections of the city.[66]

Patrols of at least three people typically walk for two to four hours through their neighborhoods a couple of times a week.

"Besides reporting," Lieutenant Powell said, "Citizens on Patrol sends a message: These people care enough to get out and walk. People think, 'Hey, if they can get out and walk, maybe I should get involved, too.'"

Then Lieutenant Powell told me a story.

In 2001, a young African American was killed by the police, and Cincinnati was torn apart by civil unrest, he said. "And in the same neighborhood, Over-the-Rhine, where the riots occurred, a problem came up recently at a service station.

"Kids would come up and beg patrons. They'd pump gas, wash windows, and ask for money. The patrons would complain, and the kids would run. Then they'd take the station's squeegees and throw them on top of the building. The manager got really upset."

The citizens involved in community policing "sat down with the service station manager and came up with something," Powell told me. "There was a car wash attached to the station, so on Fridays the kids were invited to wipe the cars, and patrons put tips in a bucket. At the end of the day, the kids divided up the tips.

"The solution also connected youngsters with agencies that gave them some experiences they'd never had—like visiting Kings Island amusement park a few miles from here. They even got to go to the zoo for the first time.

"The police could have come in and called it trespassing, and these kids would be in the justice system."

But, Lieutenant Powell stressed, "solutions are not always police intervention." The goal is not making arrests but avoiding them.

"I used to be a recruiting supervisor," he added, "and I'd ask, 'Why do you want this job?' And 99 percent of new recruits would say, 'Because I want to help people.' So here, I would tell them, is another vehicle for that—community policing."

Sadly, in his first term, President Bush cut community policing funds, and his 2006 budget would virtually wipe out federal support, leaving less than 5 percent of the current level.[67] But in cities like

Spokane, support for community policing is so high that they've found alternate sources of funds to keep the program thriving.

"community parenting"

Beyond community policing and outside the official realm of law enforcement is a movement that so grabbed me, I chose it as the subject of the first story I wrote for the American News Service in 1995.

Recently, I caught up with Eddie Staton, now fifty-seven, who was the centerpiece of that story. A dad in Omaha, Nebraska, in 1989, Eddie saw his close friend lose a son—beaten up on the street by a gang when he'd come home from college. Grief and shock propelled Staton to launch MAD DADS—Men Against Destruction-Defending Against Drugs and Social Disorder.[68]

In their signature green polo shirts and black baseball caps, its volunteers walk the city streets as late as 1:00 A.M. and approach people loitering, possibly selling drugs. "We talk to them right on the street, counsel them, cry with them, ask questions, pray with them," said Frank May, a program development coordinator in the Omaha office in the 1990s. "We are a presence. We're not trying to intimidate. We're trying to help."

MAD DADS has grown to sixty chapters in sixteen states. It involves more than sixty-five thousand parents who work to address the underlying problems that lead to drug use and crime. "In a sense," May said, "we're street parents, not street police. Drug problems can come from the parenting these kids have had or not had."

In Los Angeles, a MAD DADS bicycle patrol pedals up and down streets, helping young people avoid gang harassment and make it to school. Other chapters of MAD DADS operate gun buy-back programs and chaperone teen dances.

Eddie stresses that MAD DADS is much more than late-night street patrols. The members counsel incarcerated men, mentor, and lead after-school activities. In Jacksonville, Florida, now the national headquarters, MAD DADS is part of alternative sentencing that offers juvenile offenders the chance to work in community gardens to grow produce for seniors.

The tack is not punitive. We approach "with a smile and a kind word," said Eddie. Volunteers commonly tell young people they run into, "I love you, I care about you, I don't want you to get hurt," he said. Just being out at night is a statement, he noted, that says to the kids that these volunteers think the kids are important.

The members even apologize to the youth they meet, he told us, saying, "I'm sorry that your daddy wasn't there for you, but I love you enough to help you." They connect by sharing their own lives: "A lot of us have come up through tough situations, but someone has given us a spark to get us to do the right thing, and that's all we're trying to pass on to them."

MAD DADS also talks to single moms who may be benefiting from their teenager's drug-dealing income. Volunteers take the mothers to penitentiaries to see for themselves what will happen to their kids if they continue. MAD DADS also visits prisons to counsel, encourage, and prepare inmates. They tell them that their old neighborhood has changed and that it won't accept crime anymore. They offer to help them but also warn, if you do commit crime, "you not only got to worry about police, you got to worry about us."

MAD DADS chapters offer grief counseling as well. "Kids see people killed right in front of them—then we expect them to go to school and do a good job," said Eddie. When someone is shot, "both families, the shooter and the shot, are getting in touch with us and want us to help. . . . Two lives are lost here. You don't need a Ph.D. to do this—what you need is a lot of sensitivity, a lot of love, to put yours arms around someone and let them cry."

You could have two kids from the same family, he stressed, and one will go to college and the other to jail. The difference is that one "ran into somebody who cared," whereas the other "lived their life based on what they saw on TV." Eddie tells youth who imagine themselves as "gangbangers on TV" that if they continue on the streets, "You're not going to wake up tomorrow and make it to the next episode!"

For Eddie, it is "surrogate parenting from the streets."

restoring justice

Another approach taking off here at home and abroad allows nonviolent offenders to make amends and correct their course before they are forced to "do time," avoiding the harm that could occur if they were severed from their community and exposed to hardening forces.

When James Talbot got into trouble some years ago, the Vermont teenager might have come up against the impersonal face of traditional American justice: a black-robed judge sternly pronouncing a sentence from a courtroom bench.[69]

But instead of facing a judge, James found himself sitting across a conference room table from Don Pfister, an unemployed therapist with a ponytail and a sympathetic attitude. "I want to compliment you on what you've done so far," Pfister said, as his fellow Community Reparative Board members—an engineer, a state employee, a restaurant manager—nodded in agreement.

James, eighteen, had met most requirements of the agreement with the board that he had signed ninety days earlier in Barre, Vermont, in an approach in which local citizens volunteer to help sentence and supervise nonviolent offenders.

At the time, the mid-1990s, this approach, called community justice, was in its infancy in the United States, and Vermont was in the lead. Today it has spread nationwide.

"People are better in touch with the problems in their local communities," Michael Dooley, formerly with the Vermont Department of Corrections, told the American News Service in 1995. "When we asked the community to volunteer for these boards, the response was beautiful."

Vermont judges can transfer to these boards nonviolent offenders who would otherwise get probation and a fine but not much supervision from overworked probation officers.

"They wouldn't be jumping through all the hoops" that community boards put them through, Pfister told the ANS. Among those hoops are restitution to their victims, completing community service, meeting the victim in face-to-face mediation, and taking a driver improvement course.

Offenders can also be required to meet with victim empathy panels, where, for example, an alcohol-related offender would hear directly from people victimized by drunk drivers.

"I think victims are finding more satisfaction with this system," said Catherine Waltz, a victims' rights advocate at the Franklin County District Attorney's Office in Saint Albans, Vermont.

For James Talbot, charged with underage drinking while on probation for an unlawful-mischief conviction, the community itself was considered the victim. He performed twenty hours of community service and wrote a report on what a drunk driving charge could do to his car insurance rates.

He failed, however, to spend a patrol shift riding along with officers of a local police department, as required by the board. They gave him another month to get it done.

"They're trying to help and not screw you over. They have you think about what you did. I've learned a lot from it," James said. "They seem to care more because they're volunteering. The judge, it's just his job."

"We're moving from an adversarial, win-lose approach to a problem-solving resolution process. We're learning as we go," said Dooley.

In one Vermont case, the restitution required of a young man for snatching a woman's purse was to help out in her garden. The two became friends. Repairing the harm one has caused can help save perpetrators from a downward spiral of humiliation, self-loathing, and more harm.

In New Zealand, all but the most serious youth offenses are handled in this way.[70] Here in the United States, over seven hundred restorative justice programs for youth dot the map.[71]

holding kids accountable without losing them

Teen courts are a related approach to restorative rather than punitive justice. Here young people face a true jury of their peers.

Imagine this: a thirteen-year-old boy stands before a jury to hear his sentence for stealing two packs of cigarettes from the local Wal-Mart. In another court, the judgment might have been less severe. But here the boy sits before a jury of other teenagers.[72]

The six jurors—all between the ages of ten and seventeen—in a community north of Tampa called Brooksville, sentence him to twenty-eight hours of community service, plus an apology to the Wal-Mart store. They also require a two-page report on the health hazards of smoking and the effect of stealing on the economy.

Such is a day at Hernando County Teen Court—an alternative now offered in roughly a thousand communities in almost every state from Florida to Alaska.[73] If the boy had turned down the teen court option for the traditional court system and charges had been pressed, he might have ended up with a record that could have hurt his chances of getting a job or being accepted to college.

"It's a second chance," the boy said just before he heard his sentence.

His peers also decided that he should serve eight jury duties with the teen court, pulling him in to help the system that helped him.

In most teen courts, first used in the early 1980s, youngsters serve not only as jurors but also as defense attorneys and prosecutors. In some places such as Anchorage, Alaska, they even act as judges. In each case, parents must consent to the option and show up for the court date, usually in the evening.

"Peer pressure seems to be the most important factor in whether a kid commits a crime," David Silverstein, the presiding judge in the Florida case, told the American News Service. "Here you have a whole room of peer pressure, trying to turn you around."

"So many of the students have no idea, except for what they see on TV, about what is really truly involved" when a crime is committed, said Sharon Leon, executive director of the Anchorage Youth Court. The teens learn, for instance, that stores pass along the cost of shoplifting to consumers.

Texas and New York lead in the teen and youth courts movement.

Rehabilitating and reintegrating convicts and working with nonviolent offenders to keep them out of jail and free of a criminal record—all this cuts through our culture's cycle of fear and violence. Another approach is enabling people to resolve conflict before it escalates. In a fast-growing mediation movement, any citizen who gets the training can help out, just as they can by volunteering for a community board in the restorative justice movement.

acting before all trust is lost

It was a humid evening in Brevard, North Carolina, but the atmosphere between the two neighbors was still frosty. Their last discussion had turned into an argument over the property line and ended in a fistfight.[74]

The district court judge in this community of seven thousand had hesitated to hear their case. Yes, he could have found one of them guilty, but they would still be angry and still be next-door neighbors. So the judge instead referred them to the Dispute Settlement Center in first-floor offices donated by the local Methodist church.

In two hours, the neighbors had solved the conflict themselves. All it had taken was a little help from two trained volunteers, who in Brevard could range from a retired IBM executive to a worker at the local paper mill, to get them talking and listening.

"We find that if we can get people to sit down and talk, we typically get an 85 to 90 percent success rate," said John Fenner, the center's director.

The process is community mediation, around only since the 1970s, addressing everything from disputes over barking dogs to child custody battles. By the mid-1980s, there were around 100 centers. Now 550 centers across the country handle almost one hundred thousand disputes every year.

Their track record? Eighty-five percent of mediations result in agreements, and disputants uphold them nine out of ten times.[75] Not bad for our litigious-happy culture. The relief this approach offers to overburdened courts has not gone unnoticed: New York State now funds centers serving all sixty-two of its counties, which receive more than forty-four thousand referrals a year, and Michigan uses $3 civil court filing fees to help fund its twenty-four centers.[76]

giving and getting

To feel a sense of belonging that dissolves fear, most of us need to know that we have something to contribute that's valued. That feeling can be elusive for many in our increasingly money-dominated culture. A movement is under way that enables exchanges of assistance, not money.

Twenty-five years ago, law school professor Edgar Cahn found himself in an intensive care unit recovering from a major heart attack, suddenly reliant on others. He felt useless and started to wonder about other so-called throwaway people—the elderly, the young, the sick, the poor. He imagined that many felt like he did. They didn't want to be treated like helpless victims, and they hungered to contribute.

Edgar began looking for ways that all people, regardless of their station in life, could give of themselves. He questioned the market economy's narrow presumption that some people's time is worth more than that of others and sought an exchange system that would encourage cooperation.

A lean and serious man, Edgar, now seventy, invented an elegantly simple tool, a tax-exempt "currency" not for buying more stuff but one that anyone "could earn by helping others and spend by getting help."

He called it "time dollars," whereby one hour of service provided to another earns oneself one hour of service in return. What is offered and received can be very different—a lift to the doctor's, help at tax time, a leaky pipe fixed, a hot meal prepared. The key for Edgar is that all services are afforded equal value.

Recognizing everyone as having something to offer, Edgar's approach eases the humiliation and shame that plague our culture. It creates a zone where every person feels valued. And the resulting relationships ease fear as people know others to whom they can turn if the need arises.

"The first need and opportunity appeared with the elderly," Edgar explained in a phone hookup in 2004 with dozens of people around the country eager to learn about time dollars. "How to keep them out of nursing homes and in their own homes in the community where they often do better." They feel more connected and safer in familiar settings.

With this tool, suddenly people realized that many who in a market economy are seen as dependents—teenagers, the elderly, recent immigrants—can participate on an equal footing, beyond volunteering.[77]

His idea, as they say, had legs. It has taken hold, for example, in the Washington, D.C., teen court, where by serving on a jury, offenders earn time dollars that they can then use to buy a recycled computer. The University of the District of Columbia is arranging for applicants to put time dollars earned on the court toward gaining entry and financial aid in its criminal justice program.[78]

In Washington, each year about a quarter of the one thousand first-offense juveniles are referred to the youth court.[79] In 2004, what is now called the Time Dollar Youth Court handled four hundred cases, and only 11 percent of those offenders got into trouble again.[80] Imagine the revolutionary potential of the youth court in this city where more than *half* of all young black men aged eighteen to twenty-four are under court jurisdiction—in prison, on parole, or on probation.[81]

Edgar Cahn's approach is alive in schools, too, where it addresses the humiliation youngsters experience when they feel "labeled" and useless.

Believing that the need to give is as deep for kids as for adults, he told Chicago school authorities, "Find us any fifth- and sixth-graders willing to put in about a hundred hours tutoring younger kids and win a recycled computer. The schools sent us the special education kids and those with attention deficit problems," Edgar said.[82]

"But these kids respond to higher expectations. Attendance went up on tutoring days. And as a result of becoming tutors, they were no longer categorized as special education students. Fighting after school stopped—tutors didn't let anyone beat up their tutees," Edgar noted.[83]

Students went from being underachievers to becoming mentors. All it took was acknowledgment that they had something to give. Time dollars provided that reinforcement in a tangible way.

In other ways, too, neighbors are reconnecting and creating a new economy based on people-to-people swaps. They are reducing the fear some people have of teenagers or immigrants by welcoming and involving them in exchange networks.

They have names like "time credit," "care shares," or "neighbor-to-neighbor programs,"[84] all rewarding simple roles: raising a family, being a good citizen, caring—"the tasks we need the most," as Edgar characterizes them.

Consider Louis Peretz. He may have extended his own life by driving around his Brooklyn neighborhood for most of a decade. Louis took part in a voluntary member-to-member time-dollars-type plan. As his neighbors' chauffeur, he earned credits so that when his own health started to fail, he could use them to get the supplemental at-home care he needed without depleting his own savings.[85]

"If I didn't have all those credits for driving people here and there, I'd probably be on welfare right now—or worse," said Louis in an interview with the American News Service in the mid-1990s. At the time, he was in his eighties and one of the tens of thousands of people across the country who then—and even more now—trade shopping, gardening, plumbing, and other everyday services.

Many service exchanges are coordinated by a hospital, church, or community organization that acts as a central bank.

Earning credits can spur other possibilities. People who exchange services begin to hold potluck lunches and organize neighborhood crime watch systems, Edgar pointed out. They begin looking after each other and checking in, building alliances.

Since its birth in 1985, Edgar Cahn's time dollar system has taken hold in about a hundred sites in thirty states, from small-town Ohio to New York City.[86]

For Louis Peretz, it was the simple pleasure of friendship with the woman he took shopping or the man he drove to the welfare office. "I'm a friendly person, but I'm not looking for any heroics. I'm just doing everything that would make me feel OK," said Louis.

"Market prices," Edgar told us, are based on scarcity. "The more scarce, the more valuable. What is abundant becomes dirt cheap. So everything that's allowed humans to thrive—hugging our kids, taking care of the frail, grieving, these basic human capacities—are devalued, yet they are what have enabled the species to survive. No wonder we're in trouble.

"The real wealth of society is not money. Money is a substitute for trust. We can work for the real thing," he declared.

We think our security lies in more prisons, but for Louis Peretz it came in the form of knowing he had others to whom he could turn because he'd been able to offer help to them. And for young tutors, security is gaining skills and respect, helping them become effective adults.

americans create feelings of safety in community

Opening this chapter, I reflected on what I feel is our culture of fear—widespread feelings of isolation and vulnerability that we respond to by punishing and banishing. These reactions themselves contribute to violence that then engenders more fear.

The antidote is trust, a common thread throughout the diverse stories in this book. Trust dissolves fear, and it begins with the most common of human experiences—talk.

When I was growing up in the 1950s in Texas, "visiting" didn't mean going somewhere; it meant conversation. With the coffee percolating on the stove, my parents and their friends spent endless hours visiting in our kitchen around the yellow Formica table, as I related at the start of this book. Down a short hallway, I'd lie awake for hours listening to the hum from the kitchen as the grown-ups talked about the "big important things"—what I hoped I could do someday.

Ambient fear in our culture, I believe, flows in part from our lack of opportunity to take part in the kind of grown-up talk that wrapped me in feelings of security as a child. The proportion of one-person households jumped from 17 percent in 1970 to more than a quarter in 2003.[87] We spend more than a third less time visiting with friends than we did thirty years ago.[88]

Warning our children not to talk to strangers, perhaps we begin to think that aversion is normal for grown-ups too. And today's long commutes, home entertainment centers, Internet, gated communities, TV-ad-driven politics, hate-talk radio, and suburban sprawl with no gathering places all conspire to make conversation with people we don't know less likely.

Suspicion fills the vacuum.

Ironically, our fear of each other lifted briefly in 2001 after the terrorist attacks of September 11.[89] Americans experienced an all-time low in concern about crime as fear was replaced fleetingly with a uniting sense of "us."

Now many Americans are determined to stimulate the talk that nurtures that sense of strong community.

"Tired of small talk? Try some *big* talk!" So goes the snappy slogan of Seattle-launched Conversation Cafés, now a national movement of small-group hosted topical conversations in coffee shops. The idea had been brewing in founder Vicki Robin for some time, but after 9/11, Vicki told me, "within a week, I was grabbed with the passion. When you put strangers, caffeine, and ideas in the same room, brilliant things can happen."[90]

The idea is to make conversation "fun, simple, clear, and inviting," Vicki added. "Talking to strangers is certainly risky—they might hurt you, reject you, ridicule you, or follow you home. At Conversation Cafés, you are safe because there's a host who will be friendly, manage the weirdos, and keep things going."

Conversation Cafés clearly feed a hunger, spreading in three years to twenty-five cities in fourteen states and five other countries.

Conversation Café mottos communicate that the experience is both serious and fun: "We are the talk show!" "Mama was wrong—talk to strangers!" "Conversation—soul food for hungry minds!" "Think globally, talk locally!"

"A Conversation Café is like a dinner party," Vicki explained, "where the host just wants the guests to all enjoy themselves." Some coffee shop owners also see the advantage for them and publicize their establishment as a Conversation Café site.

Hosts are trained and in Seattle join in a "host learning circle" to celebrate successes and track conversational themes. They find that posing three questions works well—one for the head, one for the heart, and one for the need to act. At the Cafés, "people of diverse views reflect philosophically, politically, and personally. . . . They are places to make meaning with other thoughtful citizens," Vicki said. For her, the "conversation is an antidote to loneliness and social isolation; it's democracy in action."

Conversation Cafés are only one of many related connections efforts you can learn about at the National Coalition for Dialogue and Deliberation Web site.[91]

The meteoric takeoff of one, Meetup.com, surprised even its founders. It's so simple—an Internet site that makes it easy for people with common interests to find each other and schedule gatherings in public places, such as Chihuahua owners in New York City, human rights activists in Fort Worth, Texas, or knitting enthusiasts in Milwaukee. In less than three years, it's hooked up a million and a half members worldwide in nearly two hundred thousand Meetup groups on over five thousand topics.

Howard Dean's presidential primary campaign's much-touted use of the Internet in 2004 would not have had nearly its impact without Meetup, enabling supporters to gather face to face in sometimes hundreds of sites across the country on any given night.

Another reflection of the hunger for conversation is the September Project commemorating 9/11. In 2004, almost five hundred libraries in fifty states and in eight countries created opportunities for strangers to converse and undertake an array of actions from voter registration to study groups on foreign policy.[92]

In these simple gatherings, Americans are re-creating the "belonging" so central to our real security, as Jeremy Rifkin reminds us in his observation that opens this chapter.

connection and shame

Psychologists might well diagnose our culture as one "in denial," stubbornly blind to the ways in which we needlessly provoke the violence we fear. Framing violence only as a moral deficiency to be corrected by punishment, we intensify the shame that incubates violence.

Perhaps stories such as those in this chapter can shake us awake—can help us see that the security so essential to our freedom and happiness is possible only if we build inclusive communities and get serious about uprooting the sources of shaming, from racism to poverty to abusive prisons.

Blocking our path to security is a rigid economic determinism I describe in Chapter Two, so pervasive it is now like an ether we breathe. Sadly, it leads inexorably to a society divided between a minority of wealthy families and majority of ever more insecure families who feel excluded and devalued.

There is no safety for any of us. We have only to look at Latin America, to the fortress walls, literally, that surround the homes of the wealthy. They struggle to separate themselves from the poor, yet they still live in fear.

It's easy to despair even as in these pages we see the tracks made by tens of thousands of citizens who are obviously neither hopeless nor helpless. They're acting from the insight in Martin Luther King Jr.'s famous letter written in his jail cell in Birmingham, Alabama: "We are caught in an inescapable network of mutuality, tied in a single garment of destiny. Whatever affects one directly affects all indirectly."[93]

Seeing life as this single garment makes possible the ultimate empowerment: knowing that our every act to erase the causes of violence helps generate safety for all.

On this note, let me end the chapter by sharing a simple story of my friend Susan Baird.

Susan was on a cross-country flight and trying to read, but she couldn't help but overhear a few aisles away a father's harsh words to his middle-school-aged son. The tone of his voice was biting; his criticism, unrelenting. Susan began to feel uncomfortable, as she imagined the child's embarrassment.

Then, suddenly, the boy rushed past her, with his father in pursuit. Without thinking, Susan simply flung an arm across the aisle in front of the father. Shocked, the man turned to my friend and scolded her for involving herself in what was none of her business.

"When you speak so loudly that we can all hear, you've made it our business," Susan said quietly. She then told him firmly that humiliating a child backfires; it won't produce a caring, confident adult—what we all need. After a bit, another passenger chimed in to support Susan, and the man returned to his seat. He quieted down.

Much later at Dulles airport in the bus delivering passengers to the terminal, the man made a point of seeking Susan out. He initiated a handshake and made small talk, speaking to her respectfully. His very act of approaching Susan told me that he also wanted her respect.

Susan will never know whether her action changed this man and thus altered his child's future. But it may well have. She may have cut, or at least weakened, a chain of humiliation and anger leading to violence. Her act was observed by fellow passengers; how might it affect them as well?

I only know that I still feel awe at what Susan did so automatically and still wonder whether in such a moment I would have her courage. I am not sure. But I do know that her action makes it more likely that I could act. Knowing what Susan did makes me, and perhaps others who watched her on the plane that day, more able to believe that we might find the courage to do the right thing, too.

Such is the nature of our personal destiny once we see ourselves, as King does, woven in a "single garment."

12

THE INVITATION

finding ourselves in democracy's walk

The most serious threat to democracy is the notion that it has already been achieved.

ANONYMOUS

In these pages, I've shared a causal pattern that I see drawing us right to democracy's edge, a pattern that's taken me decades to wrestle into focus. It starts with our culture's messages about our very nature.

Encouraged to see ourselves as isolated, materialistic, and competitive, *of course* we want to believe in a market that works automatically, one requiring nothing from us but working and shopping! Caught in this caricature of our nature, we assume we'd only muck up any attempt to create a fairer, more democratic economy. And we come to accept an equally false idea about political democracy: that it can meet today's challenges while understood as simply a particular structure of government, working on its own, without us.

The result is what I call "thin democracy," incapable of stirring our positive passions because it disrespects and excludes so many of us. Thin democracy makes America frighteningly vulnerable to extremists of all stripes, including those willing to sacrifice their own and others' lives for their causes. Thin democracy cannot compete with visions of glorious states of moral certainty here and in the afterlife, promised to those who accept the extremists' dogmas.

The solutions that fill this book flow from very different assumptions. They offer a vision more powerful and compelling than either our thin democracy or the dogmas promoted by extremists here in America and around the world.

They have to do with belief in ourselves.

The promise of Living Democracy arises from a more complex view of our nature. Human beings are social creatures who crave connection; we thrive best in trusting communities. We are not encapsulated egos, detached and numb to the suffering of others.

Neither are we couch potatoes, thrilled to turn over our fate to politicians and CEOs. Our species would never have made it this far if we weren't by nature problem solvers, creatures with a deep need for effectiveness in the wider world. We are most energized when our lives have purpose and meaning.

We humans yearn for transcendent meaning within community, and Living Democracy is rich enough to satisfy a big part of that yearning: for it is a vision of connectedness to each other and of work larger than ourselves—a secular calling that is at the same time deeply rooted in virtually all religious traditions. It stirs our highest passions.

The fulfillment of these richer aspects of our humanity is the greatest adventure of our time.

I hope that throughout this book, you've registered the joy in the voices of Americans who are cutting through the false messages to claim their fuller selves. They're discarding the outdated, disproved notion that engagement is only for officials and experts. They are insisting that without us, there are no solutions.

Only we citizens, for example, can put "values boundaries" around the market to protect that which has inherent value, not just market value: our health and the health of our communities. Monopoly is no game. It is what markets do without citizens who are awake and engaged. So even when it comes to distributing commodities, a competitive, freedom-serving marketplace depends on us to keep wealth widely dispersed so all citizens can participate.

reframing fear

Many of today's calls for change, I fear, point fingers of blame: We should just work harder on ourselves to become less darn selfish. That's not my frame, nor, I would guess, is it the frame of most of the people in this book.

Pushing forward democracy's edge doesn't require that we change our nature, becoming "better" people. It does require that we become more fully ourselves.

Yes, ourselves—but with one new twist.

In his 2005 book *Collapse*, Jared Diamond reminds us that great civilizations have fallen not from inexorable forces of nature but from specific human choices, choices to persist in a pattern that's clearly failing.[1]

Our simple and false ideas about capitalism and democracy are not working. Can we choose Living Democracy? Can we choose to eliminate money's corrupting grip on our electoral process? Can citizens infuse their voices, and with them principles of mutual accountability, in all dimensions of public life, from our schools and workplaces to the media and the marketplace?

Choosing new ideas, new pathways, is frightening. Yet we know today that not changing is what we should most fear.

It takes effort and careful attention to change—to be true to democracy. Let me share with you a personal moment in which the challenge hit home.

It is the final week before the 2004 election, and I'm seated in the social hall of a synagogue in suburban Philadelphia. A debate between Lois Murphy, the candidate I've traveled here to support in her race for Congress, and the Republican incumbent, Jim Gerlach, is about to begin.

The large room is overflowing, and I am eager to get my first glimpse of Gerlach, the man who had just released a message going to thousands of area telephones linking my candidate, an upstanding community member and strong advocate for women, to the Taliban!

I know his ad has had an impact. The day before, as I approached one house to leave campaign literature, an agitated man at the door asked, "Are you with the Taliban, lady?" When I tried to explain, he threatened to unleash his angry dog.

Murphy opens by asking Gerlach to disown his dishonest ad. He refuses, no one objects, and the debate proceeds. The audience has been told to submit questions in advance but not to speak.

Only later do I realize what democracy demanded of me that morning.

Instead of going up to Gerlach afterward and telling him his ad was an assault on democracy—something I prided myself for doing at the time—I could have simply stood up when he refused to disown his ad. I could have announced that I would remain standing until Mr. Gerlach acknowledged his mistake. My voice would have quivered as my heart pounded. But my example might have enabled others to stand. And even if not one person had joined me, at least there would have been an inescapable message in the room about the preciousness of democratic principle. Beyond focusing on policy differences, everyone there would have been called to reflect on the need to defend democracy itself.

I didn't even think of doing this at the time. And if I had, my fear of embarrassment might well have stopped me.

In the 1950s, psychologist Solomon Asch presented subjects with a set of lines and simply asked them to say which lines were the same length. Seems easy, but there were six other people in the room—all deliberately giving the wrong answer. In that situation, Asch found that a third of the subjects went along with those giving the wrong answer. Being accepted was so important that it overrode what their own eyes told them.[2]

Note, however, that if even *one* of the others agreed with the subject, the person was much more likely to give the answer he or she knew to be correct. This simple experiment confirms what we already know about ourselves. It is much easier to tell the truth if we see others doing it. Even one other person!

Thus every time we tell the difficult truth in what George Orwell would call this time of "universal lies," it becomes easier for someone else to be a truth teller. Courage is contagious.

To move an unjust, life-denying order, history has shown that sometimes we have to break the law and suffer the consequences. It's called civil disobedience, and we can thank, among others, the Society of Friends (Quakers) for showing us over centuries the power of its nonviolent practice—helping, for example, end the scourge of slavery.

Civil disobedience also has a violent form, as when high-order German clergy plotted to assassinate Adolf Hitler. They were discovered and executed.

But what I could have done at the debate in the synagogue that late October morning is different. It breaks no law. I think of it as the practice of "civic obedience"—obeying what democracy asks of us even if it means risking embarrassment and creating distance between ourselves and others.

Civic obedience is available to each of us, and I doubt whether we can pull our society back from the precipice without embracing its practice.

To cultivate such courage, on which Living Democracy depends, requires a new understanding of the role of fear in our lives. Here's the "twist" on our nature to which I hinted earlier.

Humans are hardwired through eons of evolutionary experience to sense that our survival depends on staying on the "inside"—with the tribe. We thrive on the approval of others; we dread humiliation above all else. So it's hard for human beings to say, "No, the whole pack is heading toward catastrophe!" We fear being cast out. So we hold back.

Yet our dominant tribe *is* about to paddle over Victoria Falls—as we melt ice caps, obliterate species, pollute the air, speed wealth's concentration, and build ever more weapons of mass destruction. Thus it could well be that unless humans are able to work creatively with fear, we *are* doomed.

In our 2004 book *You Have the Power,* coauthor Jeffrey Perkins and I argue—based on our experience and on hard science—that despite our biological heritage, we can *choose* how we respond to fear.[3] In fact, this may be the most important choice of our lives.

We can learn to experience fear not as a verdict but as a signal. Whereas eons ago, breaking with the pack meant death, perhaps in today's circumstances, it means just the opposite—it may be the only path to life. With this insight, we can come to interpret fear sensations as telling us not that we're off track but that we are precisely where we should be. We can see fear as pure energy, a tool we can work with. We can expect our voices to quiver, our hearts to pound, as mine did when I approached Jim Gerlach after the debate that disturbing morning.

Pounding hearts are OK. It is in those moments that we can even celebrate that we are at our own and democracy's growing edge.

paying attention

I am learning that it's so much easier to live at this edge, to feel exhilaration, not panic, the more I know I'm surrounded—surrounded by millions braver than me who are breaking the ground. Therefore, what this era requires of me is commitment to attention. It takes focused attention to perceive the new worlds emerging.

I was struck by former Czech Republic president Vaclav Havel's frustration with those who fail to attend to the real lessons of history—what citizens are creating worldwide.

"Some politicians and pundits maintain that communism merely collapsed under its own weight—again, owing to 'objective laws' of history," Havel lamented in 2004. "Again individual responsibility and individual actions are belittled. Communism, we are told, was only one of the dead ends of Western rationalism; therefore, it was sufficient to wait passively for it to fail."[4]

No, says Havel, as one who did *not* wait passively.

It takes work to even see, much less to absorb, the real lessons of what regular citizens are accomplishing right here, right now.

It requires putting ourselves in the company of those who are already in motion, maybe a bit ahead of us. We can do this literally or by turning to independent news sources such as those described in Chapter Nine, to find their stories. In the Entry Points for Living Democracy section I include my own magazine suggestions.

By paying attention I also mean watching our words.

"How forcible are right words," says Job 6:25. Yet while we have a language of capitalism, a language of Marxism, and most recently a language of the Far Right (from "death tax" to "ownership society"), we have no language of Living Democracy. We cannot create what we cannot imagine, and to imagine, we humans need stories and we need words to tell them.

We need words projecting the new perspective that Living Democracy suggests. Linguists call this "framing."

The current language of those seeking democratic reform is locked in an old, too often weak or negative frame. And it sometimes backfires: To criticize corporate interests, for example, for championing "free markets" sounds bizarre: Why would anyone oppose what's "free"? Even attacking the free market adds weight to the notion that such a thing exists when it doesn't. Our choice is between and a fair or unfair market. The term *globalization*, as I mentioned earlier, focuses us on the scale and scope of activity rather than on who's in control, the heart of the matter. Even the word *democracy* can be a barrier to communication.

To create the world we want, we need to be consciously creating a new, powerful frame—democracy as a living practice—and choosing words that evoke it. Because I believe this work to be so critical, I offer alternative words and phrases (see "Toward a Language of Democracy"). Read, react, reject, invent. Invite others to debate and to devote disciplined attention to framing our vision with language that will be heard.

And our reward for paying attention?

Hope—with all its generative power. As we pay attention, we discover the emergent world this book chronicles. We gain effectiveness as we absorb the lessons. We also learn that hope is not an individual talent—you have it or you don't—or something one just happens to bump into. Hope is what grows as we pay attention to the causes behind the symptoms so that we find satisfying entry points into the patterns that create needless suffering—and then engage with others as savvy problem solvers. Hope is a project, a community project.

walking with bold humility

Finally, a lesson of this book is humility.

We think we know, but we don't. We think we can assess probabilities, but we can't. We humans have never been here before: we've never been so able to look over the edge, to see the possibility of our fall, or collapse, to use Diamond's term, or the possibility of reframing this edge as a new beginning.

We can't predict outcomes. One thing I love most about making it to my sixties is that I can look back at all the things emerging that I would have given almost zero probability of success when I was my children's age.

Each of the initiatives you've encountered in this book began with one person or a small handful of people—whether it was Wade Rathke with the pit in his stomach "the size of a grapefruit" knocking on doors in Little Rock, never imagining three decades later that 175,000 low-income people across the country would be bettering corporate practice through ACORN; or Dan Cantor and friends in New York just seven years ago asking themselves, "Wouldn't it be nice if workers had a party of their own?" and already the Working Families Party has brought big returns to the lowest-paid; or Deborah Meier, the teacher in East Harlem who trusted her gut to create one school that's since ignited a democratic school reform movement nationwide; or George Siemon and buddies in 1988 in tiny Viroqua, Wisconsin, dreaming up a democratic dairy co-op that has become a multimillion-dollar, organic trendsetter. Or think of the four thirty-somethings three decades ago on the South Side of Chicago sharing a few beers as they cooked up the country's first community development bank, now influencing even corporate banking practices.

Virtually every breakthrough in this book marks its birth little more than thirty years ago. And many are more recent. This in historical time is no time at all. The rapidity of their growth, the parallels in the lessons they are learning, suggests that we would be naïve—just plain silly—to underestimate their potential.

It is not possible to know what's possible. *That's* what I mean by humility. And because this is true, we are free. We are free to act assuming that our action—no matter how "small" it appears to us—could be the tipping point setting off tectonic shifts of consciousness and creativity.

In this spirit of bold humility, this book asks us to pay attention. To consciously let go of defeating and false messages telling us that it's all over or that there's no place for us in this great human drama. It asks us to admit that we can't judge our chances of success, but we can learn to see the richness that's been made invisible to us and then to make it visible . . . so that its ripples radiate.

Most of all, this book proves that not one of us is alone as we set out on the exhilarating *experience of democracy*—this satisfying and very human walk in which we go on risking belief in ourselves.

TWO FRAMES FOR DEMOCRACY

Thin Democracy: A Structure of Government	*Living Democracy: A Way of Life*
What is it?	
Democracy is a form of government. It's something we "have." It's a structure—multiple parties, three branches of government—that we were lucky enough to have inherited. Ours is complete, its structure unchanging.	Democracy is more than a particular form of government. It is a way of living, an evolving culture of trust grounded in the values of inclusivity and mutuality. We shape its norms and expectations as workers, students, employers, parents, community members, clients, and citizens. Living Democracy is something we *do*. It is never finished.
How does it work?	
Ordinary citizens had best let the free market and better-qualified officials and experts make the decisions. Citizens' role is to elect others to solve our problems and to protest if we have to.	The market and government can only function to create strong, healthy communities if guided by the insights and engagement of citizens closest to the problems. Citizens share responsibility for public problem solving.
Who gets involved?	
Public life is nasty and alienating. It's for those with thick skins and big egos. Only officials and celebrities have public lives.	We each play public roles and can experience the rewards of engagement as we practice the "arts of democracy"—active listening, creatively using conflict, negotiation, mediation, mentoring, and so on.
What's the motivation?	
Public involvement is a necessary evil to protect our private lives. Getting involved in public affairs is simply a means to an end. It's a way for someone to get what he or she wants.	Public engagement can enrich our private lives. Indeed, it is the only way to fulfill certain deep needs and to develop uniquely human capacities: to connect with others in common purpose, to make a difference in the wider community, to express our values, and to fully respect ourselves.

TOWARD A LANGUAGE OF DEMOCRACY

How forcible are right words.

JOB 16:25

Living Democracy is a new way of seeing ourselves and our world—a new frame, as linguists would say. Knowing that words shape perceptions and expectations, we can consciously generate language that communicates what is emerging and what we want to bring into being. It takes work!

In this spirit, here are my initial suggestions:

Currently Used Terms	*(Problematic Connotations)*	*More Accurate Alternatives*
Activist	(Rabble-rouser, extremist with own agenda)	Engaged citizen, active citizen, empowered citizen
Antiglobalization	(Backward, selfish, isolationist)	Prodemocracy, pro-strong communities, anti-corporate control, anti-economic concentration
Citizenship	(Burden, duty, boring)	Public engagement, community engagement
Conventional farming	(Sounds benign and time-tested when it is neither)	Chemically dependent farming, industrial agriculture, factory farming
Conservatives (applied to those in power today)	(Incorrectly implies a devotion to the preservation of the environment and communities)	Far Right, antidemocratic Right
Democracy	(Limited to voting and government)	Living Democracy—a way of life that includes economic democracy and assumes citizen participation
Environmental movement	(Focuses on nature, not people)	Healthy communities movement

Currently Used Terms	*(Problematic Connotations)*	*More Accurate Alternatives*
Free trade	(Implies absence of government control, automatic regulatory mechanism; doesn't exist)	Corporation-favoring trade, corporate trade, unfair trade
Globalization	(Implies interdependence, more connection, free trade, cheaper goods)	Global corporatization, global corporatism, economic centralization, economic feudalism, downward pressure on global wages
Justice, social justice	(Radical, Left, forced equality)	Democracy, fair opportunity, freedom
Liberal	(Favoring big government)	Progressive, democratic
Low-wage workers	(Lacks insight)	Underpaid workers
Minimum wage	(Sounds technical, ignores the human aspect)	Poverty wage versus living wage
National debt per person	(Lacks meaning to most people)	"Birth tax"—share of nation's debt each newborn faces, $150,000 in 2005
Nonprofit organization	(Says what it is not but not what it is)	Social-benefit organization, citizens' organization
Organic farming	(Focuses on the absence of pesticides, going backward)	Ecological farming—using the science of ecology to increase quality and productivity while enhancing the environment; progress
Pro-choice movement	(Selfish women only thinking of themselves)	Pro-child movement including the right of every child to be wanted with opportunities for a full life; focus on universal access to birth control and prenatal care, child nutrition, and child care

Currently Used Terms	*(Problematic Connotations)*	*More Accurate Alternatives*
Protest, demonstration	(Negative)	Civic disobedience (positive act to defend democratic values)
Public life	(Restricted to officials and celebrities)	Roles we each play (as a consumer, investor, worker, employer, parent, voter, and more that shape our world)
Regulation	(Big Brother, top-down intrusive government, inefficiency)	Standards protecting ownership diversity, competition, health, and the environment; public protections; "values boundaries" around the market
Right to same-sex marriage	(Focuses on sexuality)	Freedom to marry, equal marriage
Social safety net	(Sounds like welfare)	Opportunity protection, family protection
Taxes	(Burden, rip-off of "our" money)	Membership dues for a strong, healthy society
Unions	(Self-interest, big bosses, special interests)	Workers' organizations, workers' rights organizations
Welfare	(Paternalistic, takes care of lazy people)	Fair opportunities for the able and care for the ill and disabled
Welfare state	(Coddling people, big bureaucracy)	Fair-opportunity society

NOTES

The Path

1. Elsie R. Pamuk and others, *Health, United States, 1998: Socioeconomic Status and Health Chartbook* (Hyattsville, Md.: National Center for Health Statistics, 1998), pp. 5–7 [http://www.cdc.gov/nchs/data/hus/hus98cht.pdf], accessed on March 21, 2005. Among low-income men, an additional $15,000 of income ends up adding six or seven years of life.
2. Jeff Harrison, "Study: Nation Wastes Nearly Half Its Food," University of Arizona, Tucson, November 18, 2004 [http://uanews.org/cgi-bin/WebObjects/UANews.woa/wa/MainStoryDetails?ArticleID=10144], accessed on February 22, 2005.
3. "Solutions News Stories: American News Service Now Searchable Online," Small Planet Institute [http://www.smallplanetinstitute.org/ans.php], accessed on March 3, 2005.

Chapter One: The Frame

1. Dee Hock, *Birth of the Chaordic Age* (San Francisco: Berrett-Koehler, 1999), p. 3.
2. "Government Documents on Torture/Freedom of Information Act," American Civil Liberties Union, January 21, 2005 [http://www.aclu.org/International/International.cfm?ID=13962&c=36], accessed on March 3, 2005; Susan Milligan, "Back-Room Dealing a Capitol

Trend," *Boston Globe*, October 3, 2004; "Shattering the Myth: An Initial Snapshot of Voter Disenfranchisement in the 2004 Elections," People for the American Way Foundation, National Association for the Advancement of Colored People, and Lawyers' Committee for Civil Rights Under Law, December 2004 [http://www.pfaw.org/pfaw/dfiles/file_477.pdf], accessed on March 23, 2005; "George W. Bush's War on Women: A Chronology," Planned Parenthood Federation of America, March 27, 2003 [http://www.ppslr.org/Public_affairs/WaronWomenChronology.pdf], accessed on April 6, 2005; David Barstow and Robin Stein, "Under Bush, a New Age of Prepackaged TV News," *New York Times*, March 13, 2005; Jim VandeHei and Peter Baker, "Social Security: On with the Show," *Washington Post*, March 12, 2005.

3. William H. Hastie, quoted in *The Great Quotations*, ed. George Seldes (New York: Pocket Books, 1967).
4. Pippa Norris, *Democratic Phoenix: Reinventing Political Activism* (New York: Cambridge University Press, 2002), fig. 3.2.
5. "Voter Turnout from 1945 to Date: A Global Report on Political Participation," International Institute for Democracy and Electoral Assistance, Stockholm, Sweden: "Regional Differences" [http://www.idea.int/vt/survey/voter_turnout_pop2–2.cfm] and "Turnout in the World—Country by Country Performance (1945–98)" [http://www.idea.int/vt/survey/voter_turnout2.cfm], accessed on February 8, 2005.
6. "NES Guide to Public Opinion and Electoral Behavior," National Election Studies, Center for Political Studies, University of Michigan: "Care Who Wins Congressional Election 1970–2002" [http://www.umich.edu/~nes/nesguide/toptable/tab6d_8.htm], accessed on February 4, 2005.
7. Ibid., "Worked for a Party or Candidate 1952–2002" [http://www.umich.edu/~nes/nesguide/toptable/tab6b_3.htm], accessed on February 7, 2005.
8. Jimmy Carter, "Still Seeking a Fair Florida Vote," *Washington Post*, September 27, 2004. See also "Existing Commitments for Democratic Elections in OSCE Participating States," Organization for Security and Cooperation in Europe, Office for Democratic Institutions and Human Rights October 2003 [http://www.osce.org/documents/odihr/2003/10/772_en.pdf], accessed June 24, 2005.

9. Robert D. Putnam, *Bowling Alone* (New York: Simon & Schuster, 2000), p. 45.
10. Gary Orren, "Fall from Grace: The Public's Loss of Faith in Government," in *Why People Don't Trust Government,* ed. Joseph S. Nye Jr., Philip D. Zelikow, and David C. King (Cambridge, Mass.: Harvard University Press, 1997), pp. 80–81.
11. United States Senate, Office of the Secretary, Office of Public Records, "Secretary of the Senate Compiled Statistics," faxed February 25, 2005.
12. Edward N. Wolff, "Changes in Household Wealth in the 1980s and 1990s in the U.S.," Working Paper No. 47, Levy Economics Institute of Bard College, May 2004 [http://www.levy.org/modules/pubslib/files/wp407.pdf], p. 31, accessed on February 2, 2005.
13. Tom Waldron and others, *Working Hard, Falling Short: America's Working Families and the Pursuit of Economic Security* (Chevy Chase, Md.: Brandon Roberts + Associates, for the Working Poor Families Project, Annie E. Casey Foundation, October 2004) [http://www.aecf.org/publications/data/working_hard_new.pdf], accessed on April 21, 2005; Jeff Chapman, "States Move on Minimum Wage," Issue Brief No. 195, Economic Policy Institute, Washington, D.C., June 11, 2003 [http://www.epinet.org/content.cfm/issuebriefs_ib195], accessed on February 8, 2005.
14. "U.S. Bankruptcy Filings 1980–2003," American Bankruptcy Institute [http://www.abiworld.org/ContentManagement/ContentDisplay.cfm?ContentID=13743], accessed on March 26, 2005; David U. Himmelstein and others, "Illness and Injury as Contributors to Bankruptcy," *Health Affairs*, February 2, 2005 [http://content.healthaffairs.org/cgi/content/abstract/hlthaff.w5.63v1], accessed on April 6, 2005.
15. Institute of Medicine of the National Academies, *Insuring America's Health: Principles and Recommendations* (Washington, D.C.: National Academies Press, 2004), p. 8 [http://www.nap.edu/books/0309091055/html/], accessed on March 24, 2005; Peter Franks, Carolyn M. Clancy, and Marthe R. Gold, "Health Insurance and Mortality: Evidence from a National Cohort," *Journal of the American Medical Association*, 1993, *270*, 737–741; Paul D. Sorlie, Norman J. Johnson, Eric Backlund, and Douglas D. Bradham, "Mortality in the Uninsured Compared with That in Persons with Public and Private Health Insurance," *Archives of Internal Medicine*, 1994, *154*, 2409–2416.

16. Nicholas D. Kristof, "Health Care? Ask Cuba," *New York Times*, January 12, 2005; "Rank Order—Infant Mortality Rate," *World Factbook 2004* (Washington, D.C.: Central Intelligence Agency, February 10, 2005) [http://www.cia.gov/cia/publications/factbook/rankorder/2091rank.html], accessed on March 23, 2005.
17. Mark Nord, Margaret Andrews, and Steven Carlson, *Household Food Security in the United States, 2003*, Food Assistance and Nutrition Research Report Number 42 (Washington, D.C.: Economic Research Service, U.S. Department of Agriculture, October 2004), sec. 1, tab. 1 [http://www.ers.usda.gov/publications/fanrr42/fanrr42.pdf], accessed on January 26, 2005.
18. Cynthia Bergman, "EPA Issues Designations on Ozone Health Standards," U.S. Environmental Protection Agency, April 15, 2004 [http://yosemite.epa.gov/opa/admpress.nsf/0/f2673d2323be58b385256e77005aa9af?OpenDocument], accessed on March 7, 2005.

Chapter Two: The Long Arc

1. Martin Luther King Jr., "Letter from Birmingham Jail," April 16, 1963 [http://www.thekingcenter.org/prog/non/Letter.pdf], accessed on February 15, 2005.
2. "Visitation Statistics, 2005, Liberty Bell," Independence National Historical Park, National Park Service [http://www.nps.gov/inde/stats/stats02.html], accessed on February 16, 2005.
3. William H. Hastie, quoted in *The Great Quotations*.
4. Ann Burkhart, "The Constitutional Underpinnings of Homelessness," *Houston Law Review*, 1997, *34*, 213 [http://www.houstonlawreview.org/archive/downloads/40-2%20pdf%20files/(1)Burkhartg3.pdf], accessed on March 3, 2005.
5. Alexander Hamilton, speech to the Constitutional Convention concerning the United States Senate, June 19, 1787, quoted in Robert Yates, "Notes of the Secret Debates of the Federal Convention of 1787," May 30, 1787–July 5, 1787.
6. Adam Smith, *Theory of Moral Sentiments*, ed. D. D. Raphael and A. L. Macfie (Indianapolis, Ind.: Liberty Classics, 1982), pt. 2, sec. 2, 1:80.
7. "Government Documents on Torture," accessed on March 3, 2005.
8. Brian Baird, "We Need to Read the Bills," *Washington Post*, November 27, 2004, p. A31.

9. Milligan, "Back-Room Dealing."
10. "Teachers' T-Shirts Bring Bush Speech Ouster," Bend.com [http://www.bend.com/news/ar_view.php?ar_id=18712], accessed on March 30, 2005.
11. VandeHei and Baker, "Social Security," p. A3.
12. Seth Borenstein, "EPA to Cut Protection of Seasonal Waterways," *Pittsburgh Post-Gazette*, January 7, 2003, p. A6; "EPA Chief Leavitt Should Act to Guard Clean-Water Measure," *Tampa Tribune*, November 1, 2003, p. 14; "2006 Budget Proposal: Agency Breakdown," *Washingon Post*, February 7, 2005; Sharon Parrott and others, "Where Would the Cuts Be Made Under the President's Budget? An Analysis of Reductions in Education, Human Services, Environment, and Community Development Programs," Center on Budget and Policy Priorities, February 28, 2005 [http://www.cbpp.org/2-22-05bud.pdf], accessed on March 9, 2005.
13. Ray McGovern, "It Sounds Crazy, but . . . ," *Asia Times*, March 3, 2005 [http://atimes.com/atimes/Middle_East/GC03Ak03.html], accessed on April 6, 2005.
14. Paul Krugman, *The Great Unraveling: Losing Our Way in the New Century* (New York: Norton, 2003), p. 6.
15. Sheldon Rampton and John Stauber, *Banana Republicans: How the Right Wing Is Turning America into a One-Party State* (New York: Tarcher/Penguin, 2004), p. 3.
16. David Brock, *The Republican Noise Machine: Right Wing Media and How It Corrupts Democracy* (New York: Crown/Random House, 2004); Amy Goodman and David Goodman, *The Exception to the Rulers* (New York: Hyperion, 2004); Krugman, *The Great Unraveling*; Greg Palast, *The Best Democracy Money Can Buy: The Truth About Corporate Cons, Globalization, and High-Finance Fraudsters* (New York: Plume/Penguin, 2003); Rampton and Stauber, *Banana Republicans*.
17. David Brock, *The Real Anita Hill* (New York: Free Press, 1993); David Brock, *Blinded by the Right: The Conscience of an Ex-Conservative* (New York: Random House, 2002), pp. 110, 124, 126.
18. Brock, *The Republican Noise Machine*.
19. "Top Corporate PACs Favored GOP," CBS News, November 26, 2004 [http://cbsnews.cbs.com/stories/2004/11/26/politics/main657844.shtml], accessed on February 17, 2005.

20. Jim VandeHei, "Business Sees Gain in GOP Takeover," *Washington Post*, March 27, 2005.
21. Interview of Grover Norquist, *The 700 Club*, Christian Broadcast Network, May 2, 2001.
22. "The Budget and Economic Outlook: Fiscal Years 2006 to 2015," Congressional Budget Office, January 25, 2005), tab.7 [http://www.cbo.gov/showdoc.cfm?index=1821&sequence=0#table7], accessed on February 20, 2005; Halliburton Co., "Form 10-K," filed with the U.S. Securities and Exchange Commission on March 1, 2005, p. 33 [http://phx.corporate-ir.net/phoenix.zhtml?c=67605&p=irol-SECText&TEXT=aHR0cDovL2NjYm4uMTBrd2l6YXJkLmN-vbS94bWwvZmlsaW5nLnhtbD9yZXBvPXRlbmsmaXBhZ2U9MzMwMzE5NyZkb2M9MCZhdHRhY2g9b24=], accessed on March 14, 2005; "Map and Graph: Military: Expenditures—Dollar Figure," NationMaster.com [http://www.nationmaster.com/graph-T/mil_exp_dol_fig&int=-1], accessed on June 20, 2005; Sheryl Gay Stolberg, "The Revolution That Wasn't," *New York Times*, February 13, 2005.
23. Stolberg, "The Revolution That Wasn't."
24. Marc A. Miles, Edwin J. Feulner Jr., and Mary Anastasia O'Grady, "2005 Index of Economic Freedom: The Link Between Economic Opportunity and Prosperity," Heritage Foundation, 2005; "United States" [http://www.heritage.org/research/features/index/country.cfm?id=Unitedstates], accessed on March 24, 2005.
25. Jay Stanley and Barry Steinhardt, "Bigger Monster, Weaker Chains: The Growth of an American Surveillance Society," American Civil Liberties Union, January 2003 [http://www.aclu.org/Files/OpenFile.cfm?id=11572], p. 9, accessed on March 23, 2005; Neil Lewis, "Court Overturns Limits on Wiretaps to Combat Terror," *New York Times*, November 19, 2002, p. A1.
26. Isaac Shapiro and Joel Friedman, "Tax Returns: A Comprehensive Assessment of the Bush Administration's Record on Cutting Taxes," Center on Budget and Policy Priorities, April 23, 2004 [http://www.cbpp.org/4–23–04tax.pdf], p. iv, accessed on March 12, 2005; "Final Tax Plan Tilts Even More Toward Richest," Citizens for Tax Justice, May 22, 2003, revised June 5, 2003 [http://www.ctj.org/pdf/sen0522.pdf], accessed on March 5, 2005.

27. "Budget of the United States Government, Fiscal Year 2006," Office of Management and Budget, 2005: "Analytical Perspectives" [http://www.whitehouse.gov/omb/budget/fy2006/pdf/spec.pdf], p. 245, accessed on February 19, 2005; "Budget of the United States Government, Fiscal Year 2006": "Summary Tables" [http://www.whitehouse.gov/omb/budget/fy2006/tables.html], tab. S-1, accessed on March 7, 2005; *The Budget for Fiscal Year 2006*, "Historical Tables" (Washington, D.C.: Office of Management and Budget, 2005), p. 76 [http://www.whitehouse.gov/omb/budget/fy2006/pdf/hist.pdf], accessed on June 20, 2005; Nicholas Kristof, "A Glide Path to Ruin," *New York Times*, June 26, 2005.
28. Parrott and others, "Where Would the Cuts Be Made?"
29. Franklin Delano Roosevelt, speech to the Democratic National Convention, June 27, 1936. He was quoting Lord Chancellor Northington, who in the 1762 case of *Vernon* v. *Bethell*, wrote, "Necessitous men are not, truly speaking, free men."
30. "Merging with Gulf," Chevron Corporation [http://www.chevron.com/learning_center/history/time/1980-now/pg2.asp], accessed on February 19, 2005.
31. Tony Karon, "Welcome! Why You've Now Got AOL Time Warner," CNN, January 20, 2000 [http://archives.cnn.com/2000/US/01/20/aol.warner.time.merger/], accessed on March 27, 2005.
32. See Chapter Five for statistics on corporate concentration in a range of sectors. See Chapter Eight for concentration in food and agriculture. See Chapter Nine for concentration in the media.
33. Chuck Collins, Chris Hartman, and Holly Sklar, "Divided Decade: Economic Disparity at the Century's Turn," United for a Fair Economy, December 15, 1999 [http://www.faireconomy.org/press/archive/1999/Divided_Decade/DivDec.pdf], accessed on July 1, 2004; Mark Nord, Margaret Andrews, and Steven Carlson, *Household Food Security in the United States, 2003* (Washington, D.C.: Economic Research Service, October 2004), sec. 1, tab. 1 [http://www.ers.usda.gov/publications/fanrr42/fanrr42.pdf], accessed on January 26, 2005.
34. Robert F. Kennedy Jr., *Crimes Against Nature: How George W. Bush and His Corporate Pals Are Plundering the Country and Hijacking Our Democracy* (New York: HarperCollins, 2004), p. 191.

35. Thomas Jefferson, letter to George Logan, in *The Works of Thomas Jefferson*, fed. ed., vol. 12, ed. Paul Leicester Ford (New York: Putnam, 1905), p. 44.
36. Dwight D. Eisenhower, "Farewell Address," January 17, 1961 [http://www.ourdocuments.gov/doc.php?doc=90&page=transcript], accessed on March 24, 2005.
37. Eric Eckholm, "The Conflict in Iraq: The Contractors: Excess Fuel Billing by Halliburton in Iraq Is Put at $108 Million in Audit," *New York Times*, March 15, 2005, p. A12.
38. Waldron and others, *Working Hard, Falling Short*.
39. George W. Bush, "Remarks by the President on Iraq," Cincinnati Museum Center, Cincinnati Union Terminal, Cincinnati, Ohio, October 7, 2002 [http://www.whitehouse.gov/news/releases/2002/10/20021007-8.html], accessed on March 18, 2005; Warren P. Strobel, Jonathan S. Landay, and John Walcott, "Doubts Cast on Efforts to Link Saddam, al-Qaida," Knight-Ridder/Tribune News Service, March 3, 2004; Thom Shanker, "Rumsfeld Sees Lack of Proof for Qaeda-Hussein Link," *New York Times*, October 5, 2004, p. A10; Walter Pincus and Peter Baker, "Data on Iraqi Arms Flawed, Panel Says," *Washington Post*, April 1, 2005, p. 1.
40. Anthony Lappé and Stephen Marshall, *True Lies* (New York: Penguin/Plume, 2004), ch. 6; James Glanz, "The Reach of War: Missing Explosives," *New York Times*, October 31, 2004.
41. "Estimates show that up to 70 percent of the 2 million nongovernmental organizations in the United States have been created in the last three decades. The number of nongovernmental organizations operating internationally—those with a significant presence in three or more countries—has quadrupled to 20,000 in that same period." Curtis Runyan, "Action on the Front Lines," *WorldWatch*, November-December 1999 [http://www.worldwatch.org].
42. Between 1989 and 1998, the number went from 464,002 to 734,000. "Number of Tax-Exempt Organizations Registered with the IRS, 1989–1998," National Center for Charitable Statistics, Urban Institute [http://nccs2.urban.org/n_taxexempt.pdf], accessed on March 7, 2005.

43. Rachel Carson, *Silent Spring* (Boston: Houghton Mifflin, 1962).
44. See Fritjof Capra, *Web of Life* (New York: Anchor/Random House, 1996).
45. James V. Grimaldi and R. Jeffrey Smith, "Gambling Interests Funded DeLay Trip," *Washington Post,* March 12, 2005, p. A1.
46. "How Are the Toxics Release Inventory Data Used?" Toxics Release Inventory Program Division, U.S. Environmental Protection Agency, May 2003 [http://www.epa.gov/tri/guide_docs/2003_datausepaper.pdf], accessed on February 8, 2005. TRI data are available to the public through Web sites like TRI Explorer [http://www.epa.gov/triexplorer], Envirofacts [http://www.epa.gov/enviro], and Environmental Defense's Scorecard [http://www.scorecard.org].
47. "The Bump-Up Suit," Louisiana Environmental Action Network, August 29, 2001 [http://www.leanweb.org/airproj.html#auditpet], accessed on March 7, 2005.
48. Archon Fung and Dara O'Rourke, "Reinventing Environmental Regulation from the Grassroots Up: Explaining and Expanding the Success of the Toxics Release Inventory," *Environmental Management,* 2000, *25,* 115 [http://www.archonfung.net/papers/FungORourke TRI00.pdf], accessed on February 8, 2005.
49. "American Voters Say Urgent Moral Issues Are Peace, Poverty and Greed," Zogby International, Center for American Progress, Res Publica, and Pax Christie USA, November 12, 2004 [http://www.zogby.com/soundbites/ReadClips.dbm?ID=10389], accessed on February 24, 2005.
50. Morris P. Fiorina, with Samuel J. Abrams and Jeremy C. Pope, *Culture War? The Myth of a Polarized America* (New York: Longman, 2005), p. 20, citing "Issues and Continuity Now Working for Gore," Pew Research Center for the People and the Press, September 14, 2000 [http://www.people-press.org/reports/display.php3?ReportID=33], accessed on December 13, 2004.
51. Laurie Goodstein, "Evangelical Leaders Swing Influence Behind Effort to Combat Global Warming," *New York Times,* March 10, 2005.
52. "Americans Favor Malpractice Reform and Drug Importation but Rank Them Low on Health Priority List for the Congress and

President," Henry J. Kaiser Family Foundation and Harvard School of Public Health, January 11, 2005 [http://www.kff.org/kaiserpolls/pomr011105nr.cfm], accessed on March 30, 2005; "Religion and Politics: Contention and Consensus," Pew Research Center for the People and the Press and Pew Forum on Religion and Public Life, July 24, 2003, p. 20 [http://pewforum.org/publications/surveys/religion-politics.pdf], accessed on June 17, 2005.

53. Fiorina, *Culture War?* pp. 18–19, citing "Issues and Continuity Now Working for Gore."
54. "Large Majorities Believe Big Companies, PACs, Media and Lobbyists Have Too Much Power and Influence in Washington," Harris Interactive, April 10, 2002 [http://www.harrisinteractive.com/news/allnewsbydate.asp?NewsID=447], accessed on June 23, 2004.
55. Harry C. Boyte, *Everyday Politics: Reconnecting Citizens and Public Life* (Philadelphia: University of Pennsylvania Press, 2004), p. 190.

Chapter Three: Power Is Not a Four-Letter Word

1. Alexis de Tocqueville, *Democracy in America,* ed. Richard D. Heffner (New York: Signet Classics, 2001), p. 109. Originally published in 1835.
2. Michael D. Yapko, "The Art of Avoiding Depression," *Psychology Today*, May-June 1997 [http://cms.psychologytoday.com/articles/pto-19970501–000029.html], accessed on February 5, 2005; G. L. Klerman and M. M. Weissman, "Increasing Rates of Depression," *Journal of the American Medical Association,* 1989, *261,* 2229–2235.
3. Richard Layard, *Happiness: Lessons from a New Science* (New York: Penguin, 2005); Claudia Wallis, "The New Science of Happiness," *Time,* January 17, 2005.
4. Erich Fromm, *The Anatomy of Human Destructiveness* (New York: Henry Holt, 1992), p. 264. Originally published in 1973.
5. Abraham Maslow, *The Farther Reaches of Human Nature* (New York: Penguin, 1993), p. 262. Originally published in 1971.
6. Natalie Angier, "Why We're So Nice: We're Wired to Cooperate," *New York Times,* July 23, 2002, p. F1.
7. Quoted in Marilyn Berlin Snell, "The Power of Protest," *Sierra Magazine,* May-June 2003 [http://www.sierraclub.org/sierra/200305/lol1.asp], accessed on March 6, 2005.

8. See Edward T. Chambers, *Roots for Radicals: Organizing for Power, Action, and Justice* (New York: Continuum, 2003); Michael Gecan, *Going Public* (Boston: Beacon Press, 2002); and Mark Warren, *Dry Bones Rattling: Community Building to Revitalize American Democracy* (Princeton, N.J.: Princeton University Press, 2001).
9. Neal St. Anthony, "Advocates for Lower-Income People Analyze New Mortgage Data from Fed," *Minneapolis Star Tribune*, October 23, 1991, p. 1D.
10. "Banks' Minority Loans Up," *New York Times*, August 13, 1993, p. D12.
11. Dorothy Stoneman, *Leadership Development: A Handbook from the Youth Action Program of the East Harlem Block Schools* (New York: Youth Action Program), pp. 161–162.
12. "History and Facts," YouthBuild USA [http://www.youthbuild.org/about_history.html], accessed on February 26, 2005. For more information, contact YouthBuild USA, 58 Day Street, P.O. Box 440322, Somerville, MA 02144, tel. (617) 623-9900, ybinfo@youthbuild.org, http://www.youthbuild.org.
13. Allan Luks with Peggy Payne, "Helper's High: The First Phase," in *The Healing Power of Doing Good* (New York: Ballantine Books, 1992).
14. Bernard Crick, *In Defense of Politics* (Chicago: University of Chicago Press, 1993), p. 25. Originally published in 1962.
15. "The Arts of Democracy," Small Planet Institute [http://www.smallplanetinstitute.org/arts.php].

Part Two: Democracy Growing Up

1. Vaclav Havel, president of the Czech Republic, in an address to the U.S. Congress, February 1990.

Chapter Four: Our Coat

1. Thomas Jefferson, letter to Samuel Kercheval, June 12, 1816, *Writings*, ed. Merrill D. Peterson (New York: Library of America, 1984), p. 1401.
2. "Voter Turnout May Slip Again," Pew Research Center for the People and the Press, July 13, 2000 [http://people-press.org/reports/print.php3?PageID=201], accessed on March 6, 2005.

3. Fiorina, *Culture War?* p. 18, citing "Issues and Continuity Now Working for Gore."
4. "Fusion Beyond New York," Working Families Party [http://www.workingfamiliesparty.org/elections/elsewhere.html], accessed on February 26, 2005.
5. "Election Returns, 2003: Results and Highlights," Working Families Party, 2003 [http://www.workingfamiliesparty.org/elections/compendium.pdf], pp. 3–5, accessed on March 6, 2005.
6. John B. Anderson, "Former 'Spoiler' Touts Merits of Instant Runoff Balloting," *Milwaukee Journal Sentinel,* February 29, 2004, p. J4.
7. "Large Majorities Believe Big Companies, PACs, Media and Lobbyists Have Too Much Power and Influence in Washington," Harris Interactive, April 10, 2002 [http://www.harrisinteractive.com/news/allnewsbydate.asp?NewsID=447], accessed on June 23, 2004.
8. "FEC Reports on Congressional Activity for 2000," Federal Election Commission, May 15, 2001 [http://www.fec.gov/press/press2001/051501congfinact/051501congfinact.html], accessed on February 25, 2005.
9. "2004 Presidential Campaign Financial Activity Summarized," Federal Election Commission, February 3, 2005 [http://www.fec.gov/press/press2005/20050203pressum/20050203pressum.html], accessed on February 25, 2005.
10. Micah L. Sifry and Nancy Watzman, *Is That a Politician in Your Pocket? Washington on $2 Million a Day* (Hoboken, N.J.: Wiley, 2004), p. 13.
11. "2004 Election Outcome: Money Wins," Center for Responsive Politics, November 3, 2004 [http://www.opensecrets.org/pressreleases/2004/04results.asp], accessed on February 3, 2005.
12. "Chemical Plant Insecurity," *60 Minutes*, CBS, originally aired November 16, 2003, recap rebroadcast June 13, 2004; "U.S. Plants: Open to Terrorists," *60 Minutes*, CBS, June 13, 2004 [http://www.cbsnews.com/stories/2003/11/13/60minutes/main583528.shtml], accessed on March 6, 2005.
13. Sifry and Watzman, *Is That a Politician in Your Pocket?* p. 25.
14. Ibid., p. 70. Sifry and Watzman, of Public Campaign, used FDA data to estimate that five major drugs rushed to market in the 1990s and later banned are suspected in over one thousand deaths.

15. Ibid., p. 19.
16. Greg Palast, *The Best Democracy Money Can Buy: The Truth About Corporate Cons, Globalization, and High-Finance Fraudsters* (New York: Plume/Penguin, 2003).
17. *Buckley* v. *Valeo*, 424 U.S. 1 (1976); Louise D. Wides, Gregory J. Scott, Robert W. Biersack, and R. Blake Lange, *Twenty Year Report* (Washington, D.C.: Federal Elections Commission, April 1995), pp. 8–9 [http://www.fec.gov/pdf/20year.pdf], accessed on March 25, 2005.
18. "Clean Elections Update," Public Campaign, October 28, 2004 [http://www.publicampaign.org/pressroom/pressreleases/release2004/edmemo_10_28_04.htm], accessed on November 22, 2004.
19. "Clean Elections Works!" Clean Elections Institute, August 9, 2004 [http://azclean.org/documents/8–9–042002SuccessStats.doc], accessed on February 17, 2005.
20. "Record Number of 'Clean' Candidates Elected in Maine and Arizona, System Also Takes Hold in North Carolina," Public Campaign, November 5, 2004 [http://www.publicampaign.org/pressroom/press releases/release2004/release_11_05_04.htm], accessed on November 22, 2004.
21. Micah Sifry, "Clean Elections," *Yes! Magazine*, Winter 2003 [http://www.yesmagazine.com/article.asp?ID=571], accessed on March 25, 2005.
22. Robbie Sherwood, "Arizona: Clean Elections Challenge Is Off Ballot for Nov. 2," *Arizona Republic*, August 13, 2004 [http://www.fair elections.us/article.php?id=240], accessed on March 25, 2005.
23. Personal communication from Nancy Watzman, Public Campaign, Washington, D.C., March 1, 2005.
24. Chuck Collins, Chris Hartman, and Holly Sklar, "Divided Decade: Economic Disparity at the Century's Turn," United for a Fair Economy, December 15, 1999 [http://www.faireconomy.org/press/archive/1999/Divided_Decade/DivDec.pdf], accessed on July 1, 2004.
25. "The Wal-Mart Story," Wal-Mart USA [http://www.walmart.com/cservice/aw_story.gsp?NavMode=9], accessed on March 6, 2005; Luisa Kroll and Lea Goldman, "Special Report: The World's Richest People," *Forbes*, February 26, 2004 [http://www.forbes.com/billionaires], accessed on February 20, 2005. The five Waltons have an estimated $20 billion each in assets; Sakiko Fukuda-Parr and others, *Human*

Development Report 2004: Cultural Liberty in Today's Diverse World (New York: United Nations Development Programme, 2004), p. 30 [http://hdr.undp.org/reports/global/2004/pdf/hdr04_complete.pdf], accessed on March 5, 2005. It's estimated that 1.2 billion of the world's people make less than $1 a day.

26. Thomas Jefferson, letter to James Madison, October 28, 1785, in *The Founders' Constitution*, ed. Philip B. Kurland and Ralph Lerner (Chicago: University of Chicago Press, 2000), vol. 1, ch. 15, doc. 32 [http://press-pubs.uchicago.edu/founders/documents/v1ch15s32.html], accessed on March 7, 2005.
27. Franklin Delano Roosevelt, "Rendezvous with Destiny," Democratic National Convention, Philadelphia, June 27, 1936.
28. Cass Sunstein, "Evident Truths," *Harper's*, July 2004, p. 19.
29. Lewis F. Powell Jr., "Confidential Memorandum: Attack of American Free Enterprise System," August 23, 1971, reproduced as "The Powell Memo," ReclaimDemocracy, April 3, 2004 [http://reclaimdemocracy.org/corporate_accountability/powell_memo_lewis.html], accessed on March 25, 2005.
30. Ralph Nader, *Unsafe at Any Speed: The Designed-In Dangers of the American Automobile* (New York: Grossman, 1965).
31. David Callahan, *$1 Billion for Ideas: Conservative Think Tanks in the 1990s* (Washington, D.C.: National Committee for Responsive Philanthropy, 1999).
32. "About Campus Progress," Center for American Progress [http://www.campusprogress.org/about], accessed on March 8, 2005; personal communication from Ben Hubbard, campus programs director, Center for American Progress, March 7, 2005. Estimate of $35 million is based on the 2003 IRS Form 990s of the top twelve conservative youth development organizations, such as Young America's Foundation, the Leadership Institute, and the Intercollegiate Studies Institute. The additional tens of millions of dollars go toward endowing professorships, chairs, academic centers and programs, and scholarships for graduate study.
33. Waldron and others, *Working Hard, Falling Short*.
34. "Minimum Wage: Frequently Asked Questions," Economic Policy Institute July 2004 [http://www.epinet.org/content.cfm/issueguides_minwage_minwagefaq], accessed on February 6, 2005.

35. Nicholas Riccardi, "'Living Wage' Law OK'd by County Supervisors," *Los Angeles Times*, June 16, 1999.
36. "Living Wage Impact Research Summaries and Citations," Living Wage Resource Center, January 2001 [http://www.livingwagecampaign.org/index.php?id=1953], accessed on March 25, 2005, citing Robert Pollin and Stephanie Luce, *The Living Wage: Building a Fair Economy* (New York: New Press, 1998).
37. Dana L. Jackson and Laura L. Jackson, eds., *The Farm as Natural Habitat* (Washington, D.C.: Island Press, 2002), pp. 28–29.
38. For more information, contact the Land Stewardship Project, 2200 Fourth Street, White Bear Lake, MN 55110, tel. (651) 653-0618, cathye@landstewardshipproject.org, http://www.landstewardshipproject.org.
39. Nebraska constitution, art. 12, sec. 8, (adopted 1982); proclamation by the governor occurred on November 29, 1982 [http://statutes.unicam.state.ne.us/Corpus/chapC/CXII-8.html], accessed on February 28, 2005.
40. Rick Welsh and Thomas A. Lyson, "Anti-Corporate Farming Laws, the 'Goldschmidt Hypothesis' and Rural Community Welfare," revised version of paper presented at the Rural Sociological Society in Albuquerque, N.M., August 2001 [http://wwwi300.org/I-300%20report.pdf], accessed on June 30, 2004.
41. Circuit Judge Bowman, "Appeals from the United States District Court for the District of South Dakota," *South Dakota Farm Bureau et al.* v. *Joyce Hazeltine et al.*, No. 02-2366 (8th Cir. Ct. App., 2003) [http://www.ca8.uscourts.gov/opndir/03/08/022366P.pdf], accessed on March 15, 2005.
42. "Executive Briefing," Millennium Poll on Corporate Social Responsibility, Environics International, September 1999, p. 2 [http://www.pwcglobal.com/extweb/ncpressrelease.nsf/84f5f51d361fe04e8525665f00506220/07eab72b718ee1ee852567fc005ee5df/$FILE/Millennium_Exec.A4.pdf], accessed on March 25, 2005.
43. "*Business Week*/Harris Poll: How Business Rates: By the Numbers," *Business Week*, September 11, 2000 [http://www.businessweek.com/2000/00_37/b3698004.htm], accessed on March 17, 2005.
44. "Don't Buy Old Growth," Rainforest Action Network [http://www.ran.org/ran_campaigns/old_growth/], accessed on June 30, 2005.

45. Rebecca Gardyn, "Eco Friend or Foe?" *American Demographics*, 2003, *25*(8), 12.
46. Ed Ring, "A Man for All Forests," *EcoWorld*, October 30, 2000 [http://www.ecoworld.com/Home/Articles2.cfm?TID=328], accessed on July 1, 2004.
47. "Wake Up Weyerhaeuser: Protect Forests Now!" Rainforest Action Network, February 19, 2004 [http://www.ran.org/news/newsitem.php?id=920&area=oldgrowth], accessed on March 6, 2005.

Chapter Five: The Elephant

1. Edward S. Mason, "Corporation," in *International Encyclopedia of Social Sciences*, ed. David L. Sills (New York: Macmillan, 1968), p. 397.
2. Sarah Anderson and John Cavanagh, *Top 200: The Rise of Corporate Global Power* (Washington, D.C.: Institute for Policy Studies, 2000), pp. 6, 13–16 [http://www.ips-dc.org/downloads/Top_200.pdf], accessed on March 1, 2005. Based on 1999 data; "United States," *The World Factbook 2000* (Washington, D.C.: Central Intelligence Agency, 2000) [http://www.umsl.edu/services/govdocs/wofact2000/geos/us.html], accessed on March 10, 2005; *The World Factbook 2005* (Washington, D.C.: Central Intelligence Agency, 2005) [http://www.cia.gov/cia/publications/factbook/], accessed on July 1, 2005; *General Motors Corporation 2004 Annual Report* (Detroit: General Motors Corp., 2005) [http://www.gm.com/company/investor_information/docs/fin_data/gm04ar/index.html], accessed on July 1, 2005.
3. Stacy Mitchell, "Independent Businesses Unite!" *In Business*, July-August 2003, pp. 16–18 [http://amiba.net/pdf/inbusiness_9.03.pdf], accessed on March 25, 2005; Stacy Mitchell, *The Hometown Advantage: How to Defend Your Main Street Against Chain Stores . . . and Why It Matters* (Minneapolis, Minn.: Institute for Local Self-Reliance, 2000).
4. Benjamin Franklin, "Queries and Remarks Respecting Alterations in the Constitution of Pennsylvania," in *Democracy, Liberty, and Property*, ed. Francis W. Coker (Old Tappan, N.J.: Macmillan, 1949), p. 90.
5. Thomas Jefferson, letter to James Madison.
6. Charles Lindblom, *Politics and Markets* (New York: Basic Books, 1977), p. 356.

7. "Minute Maid Park," Houston Astros [http://houston.astros.mlb.com/NASApp/mlb/hou/ballpark/hou_ballpark_history.jsp#name], accessed on February 26, 2005; Chris Isidore, "Astros Strike Out Enron," *CNN Money*, February 27, 2002 [http://money.cnn.com/2002/02/27/companies/enron_astros/], accessed on February 26, 2005.
8. Thomas Jefferson, letter to George Logan, p. 44.
9. Thom Hartmann, *Unequal Protection* (New York: Rodale Press, 2002), pp. 70–73.
10. Christopher Schwarzen, "Enron Cost Utilities $1.8 Billion, Feds Say," *Seattle Times*, February 1, 2005, p. B1; Jef Feeley, "Enron Workers Win $86 Million Settlement in Pension Suits," *Seattle Times*, May 13, 2004, p. E2; William Greider, *The Soul of Capitalism* (New York: Simon & Schuster, 2003), p. 112.
11. "Toxic Ignorance: The Continuing Absence of Basic Health Testing for Top-Selling Chemicals in the United States," Environmental Defense Fund, 1997 [http://www.environmentaldefense.org/documents/243_toxicignorance.pdf], pp. 14, 16, accessed on March 16, 2005.
12. The portion of the U.S. population suffering from asthma has increased from 2.9 percent in 1980 (6.7 million Americans) to 7.1 percent in 2001 (20.3 million Americans). David M. Mannino and others, "Surveillance for Asthma—United States, 1960–1995," *Morbidity and Mortality Weekly Report,* April 24, 1998 [http://www.cdc.gov/mmwr/preview/mmwrhtml/00052262.htm#00003083.htm], accessed on March 12, 2005; "Asthma," Centers for Disease Control and Prevention, November 11, 2003 [http://www.cdc.gov/communication/tips/asthma_gnrl.htm], accessed on March 12, 2005; "Section 1: Population," *Statistical Abstract of the United States, 2001* (Washington, D.C.: U.S. Census Bureau, 2002) [http://www.census.gov/prod/2002pubs/01statab/pop.pdf], accessed on March 12, 2005; "Table US-2001EST-01: Time Series of National Population Estimates, April 1, 2000 to July 1, 2001," U.S. Census Bureau, December 27, 2001 [http://www.census.gov/popest/archives/2000s/vintage_2001/US-2001EST-01.html], accessed on March 12, 2005.
13. David Bollier, *Silent Theft: The Private Plunder of our Common Wealth* (New York: Routledge, 2003), p. 87, citing Mineral Policy Center, "The Last American Dinosaur: The 1872 Mining Law," undated fact sheet.

14. Ibid., citing USPIRG, *Green Scissors '98: Cutting Wasteful and Environmentally Harmful Spending* (Washington, D.C.: USPIRG, 1998), p. 24.
15. Nanette Byrnes and Louis Lavelle, "The Corporate Tax Game," *Business Week*, March 31, 2003 [http://www.businessweek.com/magazine/content/03_13/b3826058.htm], accessed on March 26, 2005.
16. "Corporate Welfare," Public Citizen [http://www.citizen.org/congress/welfare/index.cfm], accessed on March 6, 2005.
17. "Inventory of U.S. Greenhouse Gas Emissions and Sinks, 1990–2002," U.S. Environmental Protection Agency, April 15, 2004 [http://yosemite.epa.gov/OAR/globalwarming.nsf/UniqueKeyLookup/RAMR5WNMGY/$File/04_complete_report.pdf], pp. ES-5, ES-7, ES-9, accessed on March 13, 2005.
18. "Impact of Climate Change to Cost the World $US 300 Billion a Year," United Nations Environmental Programme, February 3, 2001 [http://www.unep.org/Documents/Default.asp?DocumentID=192&ArticleID=2758], accessed on March 3, 2005.
19. "Safe Drinking Water Act 30th Anniversary: U.S. EPA's Program to Regulate the Placement of Waste Water and other Fluids Underground," Environmental Protection Agency, June 2004 [http://www.epa.gov/safewater/sdwa/30th/factsheets/uic.html], accessed on March 12, 2005.
20. Isaac Shapiro and David Kamin, "Share of Economy Going to Wages and Salaries Drops for Unprecedented 14th Straight Quarter," Center on Budget and Policy Priorities, October 29, 2004 [http://www.cbpp.org/10-29-04pov.pdf], accessed on March 30, 2005.
21. Juliet S. Schor, *The Overworked American* (New York: Basic Books, 1992); "The State of Working America, 2004–2005: Work Hours," Economic Policy Institute, September 5, 2004 [http://www.epinet.org/books/swa2004/news/swafacts_workhours.pdf], p. 2, accessed on March 26, 2005; "The Parenting Deficit: Council of Economic Advisers Analyze the 'Time Crunch,'" Council of Economic Advisers, May 1999 [http://www.newecon.org/ParentingDeficitCEA-May99.html], accessed on February 23, 2005.
22. Gardiner Harris, "Drug Firms' 'Bad' Year Wasn't So Bad," *Wall Street Journal*, February 21, 2003; Neal Pattison and Luke Warren, "2002

Drug Industry Profits," Public Citizen, June 2003 [http://www.citizen.org/documents/Pharma_Report.pdf], p. 2, accessed on March 8, 2005; Peter Rost, "Bush Report on Drug Imports: Good Data, Bad Conclusions," *CounterPunch*, January 20, 2005 [http://www.counterpunch.org/rost01202005.html], accessed on June 24, 2005. Rost is vice-president of marketing at Pfizer.

23. Democratic Staff of the Committee on Education and the Workforce, for Rep. George Miller (D-Calif.), Senior Democrat, "Everyday Low Wages: The Hidden Price We All Pay for Wal-Mart," U.S. House of Representatives, February 16, 2004 [http://edworkforce.house.gov/democrats/WALMARTREPORT.pdf], accessed on February 21, 2005.
24. Ibid, p. 4.
25. Jeffrey McCracken and Jamie Butters, "Election-Year Issue: Democratic Candidates Back Pro-Union Proposal," *Detroit Free Press*, February 7, 2004 [http://www.freep.com/news/politics/union7_20040207.htm], accessed on February 22, 2005; "Union Members Summary," Bureau of Labor Statistics, January 27, 2005 [http://stats.bls.gov/news.release/union2.nr0.htm], accessed on February 22, 2005.
26. "Traditional Growth Moves: The Old Approaches Are Losing Steam," Mercer Management Consulting, 2002 [http://www.mercermc.com/Books/HowToGrow/pdfs/Traditionalgrowthmoves.pdf], accessed on February 19, 2005.
27. "Antitrust Fares Relatively Well in President's FY 2003 Budget, but Slowing Merger Pace Can Spell a Problem," American Antitrust Institute, February 13, 2002 [http://www.antitrustinstitute.org/recent2/168.cfm], accessed on March 8, 2005; Kevin J. Clancy and Peter C. Krieg, "Surviving Innovation: Common Testing Mistakes Can Derail a Promising New Product Launch," *Marketing Management*, March-April 2003 [http://www.copernicusmarketing.com/about/docs/surviving_innovation.htm], accessed on March 9, 2005.
28. Personal communication from Alexandra Lejoux, National Association of Corporate Directors, Washington, D.C.
29. Pennsylvania Consolidated Statutes, 15 Pa.C.S. 1715 (2004).
30. Arnie Cooper, "Twenty-Eight Words That Could Change the World," *Sun*, September 2004, pp. 4–7.

31. Robert Hinkley, "28 Words to Redefine Corporate Duties: The Proposal for a Code for Corporate Citizenship," *Multinational Monitor,* July-August 2002 [http://multinationalmonitor.org/mm2002/02julyaug/july-aug02corp4.html], accessed on March 10, 2005.
32. MATP, "Law Change to Force Hardie to Pay Up," *Sydney Daily Telegraph*, October 29, 2004; Chris Merritt, "Options Canvassed for Hardie Law Changes," *Australian Financial Review*, November 12, 2004, p. 59.
33. Patrick McGeehan, "No Democracy on These Ballots," *New York Times*, February 13, 2005, sec. 3, p. 4.
34. Marjorie Kelly, *The Divine Right of Capital* (San Francisco: Berrett-Koehler, 2003), p. 33.
35. Eric Wahlgren, "Spreading the Yankee Way of Pay," *Business Week Online*, April 18, 2001 [http://www.businessweek.com/careers/content/apr2001/ca20010419_812.htm], accessed June 26, 2005.
36. *Dartmouth College* v. *Woodward*, 17 U.S. 518 at 636 (1819).
37. Ibid.
38. For an overview of the history of corporate personhood and concerns about it, see Dean Ritz, ed., *Defying Corporations, Defining Democracy* (New York: Apex Press, 2001).
39. Charles Wallace Collins, *The 14th Amendment and the States* (Boston: Little, Brown, 1912), pp. 137–138.
40. *Marshall* v. *Barlow's*, 436 U.S. 307 (1978).
41. *International Dairy Foods Association* v. *Amestoy*, 92 F.3d 67 (2d Cir. 1996).
42. *First National Bank* v. *Bellotti*, 435 U.S. 765 (1978).
43. Jeffrey Kaplan and Jeff Milchen, "Ballot Initiatives Hijacked by Corporations," ReclaimDemocracy, March 7, 2004 [http://reclaimdemocracy.org/corporate_speech/overturn_bellotti_initiatives.html], accessed April 6, 2005.
44. Thomas A. Lindzey and Richard L. Grossman, "Edited Selections from FROST Briefs Submitted to the U.S. District Court for the Middle District of Pennsylvania, Honorable Yvette Kane, Presiding," *By What Authority*, Fall 2004 [http://www.poclad.org/bwa/Fall04.htm], accessed on April, 5, 2005.

45. Ellen Z. Harrison and Summer Rayne Oakes, "Investigation of Alleged Health Incidents Associated with Land Application of Sewage Sludges," *New Solutions*, 2002, *12*, pp. 390, 403–404 [http://cwmi.css.cornell.edu/Sludge/Newsolutions.pdf], accessed on March 1, 2005.
46. Community Environmental Legal Defense Fund, "In U.S. First, Local Government Refuses to Recognize Corporate Claims to Civil Rights," ReclaimDemocracy, December 13, 2002 [http://reclaimdemocracy.org/corporate_accountability/porter_township_ordinance.html], accessed on February 23, 2005; "Berkeley Becomes Latest U.S. Municipality to Oppose Corporate Constitutional 'Rights,'" ReclaimDemocracy, June 16, 2004 [http://reclaimdemocracy.org/personhood/berkeley_resolution.html], accessed on February 23, 2005; Community Environmental Legal Defense Fund, "Confronting Corporations: Two Townships Adopt Ordinances Limiting Corporate Rights," *Community Solicitor*, July 2003 [http://www.celdf.org/caucus/csolicitor_0707.asp], accessed on March 18, 2005.
47. Alan B. Krueger, "A Study Looks at What the Public Knows, or Doesn't Know, About Economics and Why," *New York Times*, April 1, 2004, p. C2, citing Alan S. Blinder and Alan B. Krueger, "What Does the Public Know About Economic Policy, and How Does It Know It?" working paper, May 2004 [http://www.irs.princeton.edu/pubs/pdfs/496.pdf], accessed on March 26, 2005.
48. "Global Tobacco Treaty," Corporate Accountability International [http://www.stopcorporateabuse.org/cms/page1143.cfm], accessed on June 30, 2005.
49. Robert F. Kennedy Jr., "Better Gas Mileage, Greater Security," *New York Times*, November 24, 2001, p. A27.
50. "Store Size Caps," Institute for Local Self-Reliance [http://www.newrules.org/retail/size.html], accessed April 5, 2005. See also Mitchell, *Hometown Advantage*.
51. "Formula Restaurant Ban: Arcata, California," Institute for Local Self-Reliance [http://www.newrules.org/retail/arcata.html], accessed on March 26, 2005; Daniel Mintz, "City Council Introduces Chain Restaurant Cap, 4–1," *Arcata Eye*, May 21, 2002 [http://www.arcata-eye.com/top/020521top02.shtml], accessed on February 2, 2005.

52. Paul Hawken, Amory Lovins, and L. Hunter Lovins, *Natural Capitalism: Creating the Next Industrial Revolution* (New York: Little, Brown, 1999), pp. 14–15, citing R. U. Ayres, *Technology and Environment* (Washington, D.C.: National Academy of Sciences, 1989), and *Efficient Use of Energy: American Physical Society Studies on the Technical Aspects of the More Efficient Use of Energy*, Conference Proceedings No. 25 (New York: American Institute of Physics, 1975).
53. "What's Happening with Businesses Around the World?" *Eco-Cycle Times*, Spring-Summer 2004, p. 5 [http://www.ecocycle.org/newsletters/pdfs/2004spring_summer.pdf], accessed on February 18, 2005.
54. Christopher Flavin and Gary Gardner, "Good News: Look What Political Will Can Do," *International Herald Tribune*, January 9, 2003.
55. "Waste Electrical and Electronic Equipment," European Union, May 28, 2004 [http://europa.eu.int/scadplus/leg/en/lvb/l21210.htm], accessed on August 24, 2004; "European Union (EU) Electrical and Electronic Products Directives," INFORM, Inc., June 2003 [http://www.informinc.org/fact_WEEEoverview.pdf], accessed on August 19, 2004.
56. Der Grüne Punkt [http://www.green-dot.org], accessed on July 11, 2005.
57. "Recycling Rates Remain at a High Level," *Green Dot*, May 2004 [http://www.gruener-punkt.de/Recycling_rates_remain_at_a_high_level.1061+B6Jkw9MSZub0ZsYXNoPQ_.0.html], accessed on February 18, 2005.
58. Jeffrey Hollender and Stephen Fenichell, *What Matters Most* (New York: Basic Books, 2004), pp. 136–137.
59. Sam Cole and Eric Vozick, "Zero Waste Around the World," *Eco-Cycle Times*, Fall-Winter 2002 [www.ecocycle.org/TimesFall2002/ZeroWasteAroundWorld.cfm], accessed on November 29, 2004.
60. "Maine Auto Manufacturer Takes Back Law," Institute for Local Self-Reliance [http://www.newrules.org/environment/mercuryme.html], accessed on March 26, 2005.
61. *Alliance of Automobile Manufacturers* v. *Martha Kirkpatrick*, 2004 U.S. Dist. LEXIS 2225 (D.Me. Feb. 17, 2004).
62. E. F. Schumacher, *Small Is Beautiful* (New York: HarperCollins, 1973).
63. Hawken, Lovins, and Lovins, *Natural Capitalism;* Günter Pauli, *Upsizing: The Road to Zero Emissions, More Jobs, More Income and No Pollution* (Sheffield, England: Greenleaf, 2000); Herman Daly,

Toward a Steady State Economy (New York: Freeman, 1973); William McDonough and Michael Braungart, *Cradle to Cradle: Remaking the Way We Make Things* (New York: North Point Press, 2002).

64. Navin Nayak, *Redirecting America's Energy: The Economic and Consumer Benefits of Clean Energy Policies* (Washington, D.C.: USPIRG Education Fund, 2005), p. 16 [http://www.apolloalliance.org/doc Uploads/redirectingamericasenergy%2Epdf], accessed on March 17, 2005.
65. Miguel Bustillo, "A Shift to Green," *Los Angeles Times*, June 12, 2005, p. C1.
66. William Greider, *The Soul of Capitalism: Opening Paths to a Moral Economy* (New York: Simon & Schuster, 2003), pp. 105, 107. Public employee pension funds held $2.6 trillion in 2003, and twelve hundred pension funds were union-managed.
67. "The Center," AFL-CIO Center for Working Capital [http://www.centerforworkingcapital.org/who/index.html], accessed on March 12, 2005.
68. Greider, *The Soul of Capitalism*, p. 106.
69. Ibid, p. 107.
70. Personal communication from Tim Smith, senior vice president, Walden Asset Management, Boston, March 21, 2005.
71. "Impact of Climate Change."
72. "Direct and Indirect Costs of Diabetes in the United States," American Diabetes Association [http://www.diabetes.org/diabetes-statistics/cost-of-diabetes-in-us.jsp], accessed on February 1, 2005; American Diabetes Association, "Economic Costs of Diabetes in the U.S. in 2002," *Diabetes Care*, 2003, 26, 917–932 [http://care.diabetesjournals.org/cgi/content/full/26/3/917], accessed on February 1, 2005.
73. Corine P. Bucker and others, "Proxy Voting Decisions," CalPERS, August 21, 2000 [http://www.calpers-governance.org/alert/proxy/Item10i.asp], accessed on February 15, 2005; "CalPERS Issues Statement on Tyco Reincorporation to America," *Corporate Governance News*, March 6, 2003 [http://www.calpers-governance.org/news/2003/tyco030603.asp], accessed on February 15, 2005.
74. Mary Williams Walsh, "CalPERS Ouster Puts Focus on How Funds Wield Power," *New York Times*, December 2, 2004, p. C1.

75. Joe Keefe and Steven D. Lydenberg, *Corporate Governance, Social Responsibility, and Obligations of Ownership: Background Paper for State Treasurers and Legislators* (Providence, R.I.: Domini Social Investments, 2003), p. 10 [http://www.socialinvest.org/areas/research/other/012004_treasurers.pdf], accessed on March 12, 2005. "Up to 80% of the market value of companies in today's marketplace can be accounted for by these intangibles, up from only 20% two decades ago": Robert G. Eccles and Samuel A. Di Piazza, *Building Public Trust: The Future of Corporate Reporting* (New York: Wiley, 2002), p. 36. "Measures That Matter," Ernst & Young Center for Business Innovation, 1998: This study found that nonfinancial performance criteria account for as much as 35 percent of investors' buy-side decisions, confirming that share price is affected by—and shareowners place a value on—such nonfinancial criteria.
76. "McDonald's Corporation Case Summary," Natural Step, 2003 [http://www.naturalstep.org/learn/docs/cs/mcdonalds_case.pdf], accessed on November 29, 2004; Jill Rosenblum, "McDonald's Sweden: A Case Study," Natural Step, 1999 [http://www.naturalstep.org/learn/docs/articles/mcdsweden_story.pdf], accessed on November 29, 2004.
77. "McDonald's Corporation Case Summary."
78. The Natural Step, founded in 1989 in Sweden, works with seventy municipalities and sixty companies worldwide, including Home Depot, Starbucks, and Bank of America. For more information, see "History," Natural Step [http://www.naturalstep.org/about/history.php], accessed on February 18, 2005; Karl-Henrik Robèrt, *The Natural Step Story: Seeding a Quiet Revolution* (Gabriola Island, Canada: New Society, 2002); Brian Nattrass and Mary Altomare, *Dancing with the Tiger: Learning Sustainability Step by Natural Step* (Gabriola Island, Canada: New Society, 2002); "McDonald's Corporation Case Summary."
79. "McDonald's Serves Organic Milk Drinks," *Eurofood*, August 29, 2002.
80. "Menu Choice Around the World: It's What I Eat," McDonald's Corporation [http://www.mcdonalds.com/corp/values/balance/menu_choices.html], accessed on March 26, 2005.
81. "About Us: History," Coalition for Environmentally Responsible Economies [http://www.ceres.org/about/history.htm], accessed on

March 26, 2005; "About Us: Endorsing Companies," Coalition for Environmentally Responsible Economies [http://www.ceres.org/about/endorsing_companies.htm], accessed on March 12, 2005; "Our Work: The CERES Principles," Coalition for Environmentally Responsible Economies [http://www.ceres.org/our_work/principles.htm], accessed on March 12, 2005.

82. For more information, contact Verité, 44 Belchertown Road, Amherst, MA 01002, tel. (413) 253-9227, verite@verite.org, http://www.verite.org.
83. "About Social Accountability International," Social Accountability International [http://www.sa-intl.org/AboutSAI/AboutSAI.htm], accessed on March 26, 2005; "Corporate Involvement Program (CIP)," Social Accountability International [http://www.sa-intl.org/SA8000/CIP.htm], accessed on March 20, 2005; "SA8000 Certified Facilities," Social Accountability International, December 31, 2004 [http://www.sa-intl.org/Accreditation/CertifiedFacilities.xls], accessed on February 2, 2005. Social Accountability International accredits certifying bodies to audit factories regularly to make sure they are SA8000 compliant.
84. Steven Greenhouse, "Groups Reach Agreement for Curtailing Sweatshops," *New York Times*, November 5, 1998, p. A20; "Participating Colleges and Universities," Fair Labor Association [http://www.fairlabor.org/all/colleges/list.html], accessed on March 16, 2005.
85. "Participating Companies and Licensees," Fair Labor Association [http://www.fairlabor.org/all/companies/index.html], accessed on March 26, 2005; "Charter Document, Fair Labor Association," Fair Labor Association, July 27, 2004, pp. 4, 19, 27–29 [http://www.fairlabor.org/all/about/FLAcharter.pdf], accessed on March 13, 2005.
86. "History," United Students Against Sweatshops [http://www.studentsagainstsweatshops.org/about/history.php], accessed on March 10, 2005; Nattrass and Altomare, *Dancing with the Tiger*.
87. Ibid.; "Affiliates," United Students Against Sweatshops [http://www.studentsagainstsweatshops.org/about/chapters.php], accessed on February 23, 2005.
88. "Codes, Monitoring, and Verification: Why the CCC Is Involved," Clean Clothes Campaign [http://www.cleanclothes.org/codes.htm], accessed on June 30, 2005.

89. "Dow Jones Sustainability World Index (DJSI World) Fact Sheet," Dow Jones Sustainability Indexes, December 31, 2004 [http://www.sustainability-index.com/djsi_pdf/publications/Factsheets/DJSI World_20041231.pdf], accessed on March 26, 2005.
90. Alexander Gourevitch, "No Justice, No Contract: The Worker Rights Consortium Leads the Fight Against Sweatshops," *American Prospect*, June 29, 2001, p. 3 [http://www.workersrights.org/Amer_Pros_6–29–01.pdf], accessed on March 10, 2005; "WRC-Affiliated Colleges and Universities," Worker Rights Consortium March 9, 2005 [http://www.workersrights.org/as.asp], accessed on March 26, 2005.
91. "GRI at a Glance," Global Reporting Initiative [http://www.globalreporting.org/about/brief.asp], accessed on March 26, 2005.
92. "Power Hungry: Six Reasons to Regulate Global Food Corporations," ActionAid International, 2005 [http://www.actionaid.org.uk/wps/content/documents/power_hungry.pdf], p. 5, accessed on March 26, 2005.
93. "About Us," Fair Labor Association [http://www.fairlabor.org/all/about], accessed on March 12, 2005.
94. Harold Meyerson, "Wal-Mart Loves Unions (in China)," *Washington Post*, December 1, 2004, p. A25.
95. Democratic Staff, "Everyday Low Wages."
96. James Goldsborough, "Yet Another Challenge to Wal-Mart," *San Diego Union-Tribune*, April 12, 2004; Jim Hightower, "Giving the Gipper His Due," *Texas Observer*, July 16, 2004; Jonathan Tasini, "The Wal-Mart Myth," TomPaine.com, April 12, 2004 [http://www.tompaine.com/feature2.cfm/ID/10226], accessed on March 13, 2005; James Flanigan, "Costco Sees Value in Higher Pay," *Los Angeles Times*, February 15, 2004.
97. "About FSC," Forest Stewardship Council [http://www.fsc.org/en/about/what_is], accessed on February 2, 2005.
98. Nigel Cope, "Thailand Accuses Tesco of Ripping Off Local Suppliers," *London Independent*, September 24, 2002.
99. "The 2003 Sustainability Report," Carrefour, 2004: "Key Performance Indicators" [http://www.carrefour.com/english/nosengagements/rdd2003_7.jsp] and "Message from the Chairman and CEO"

[http://www.carrefour.com/english/nosengagements/rdd2003_2.jsp], accessed on March 26, 2005.

100. "Changes at the Top of Carrefour: Daniel Bernard Leaves, Luc Vandevelde Takes Over," Union Network International, February 4, 2005 [http://www.union-network.org/UNIsite/Sectors/Commerce/Multinationals/Carrefour_Bernard_leaves.htm], accessed on March 26, 2005; "Socially Responsible Manufacturing," Carrefour [http://www.carrefour.com//english/nosengagements/rdd2_1_4.jsp], accessed on March 26, 2005.
101. "Key-Figures," Carrefour, December 31, 2004 [http://www.carrefour.com/english/infosfinancieres/chiffresCles.jsp#], accessed on March 26, 2005; "Annual Report 2003: Financial Report," Carrefour [http://www.carrefour.com/docs/ra2003_interconsolides_en.pdf], p. 69, accessed on March 26, 2005.

Chapter Six: Attention

1. Judy Wicks's restaurant is the White Dog Café, 3420 Sansom Street, Philadelphia, PA 19104, tel. (215) 386-9224, http://www.whitedog.com. Her forthcoming book is tentatively titled *Table for Six Billion, Please*.
2. "Philadelphia Café Serves Up Wind Power," Renewable Energy Access, March 26, 2002 [http://www.renewableenergyaccess.com/rea/news/story?id=6246], accessed on March 6, 2005.
3. "Local Business Networks," Business Alliance for Local Living Economies, [http://www.livingeconomies.org/BALLE/viewPage.cfm?pageId=1051], accessed on February 1, 2005. All types of businesses are members of BALLE networks, including retailers, financial services companies, realtors, and therapists. See a sample chapter's member companies at "Our Members," Salt Lake Vest Pocket Business Coalition, [http://www.vestpocket.org/members1c.html], accessed on March 26, 2005.
4. Tim Kasser, *The High Price of Materialism* (Cambridge, Mass.: MIT Press, 2002), p. 11.
5. Christopher D. Cook, *Diet for a Dead Planet: How the Food Industry Is Killing Us* (New York: New Press, 2004), p. 7, citing Mary Hendrickson and others, "Consolidation in Food Retailing and Dairy:

Implications for Farmers and Consumers in a Global Food System," report to the National Farmers Union, University of Missouri, 2001.

6. Chuck Collins, Chris Hartman, and Holly Sklar, "Divided Decade: Economic Disparity at the Century's Turn," United for a Fair Economy, December 15, 1999 [http://www.faireconomy.org/press/archive/1999/Divided_Decade/DivDec.pdf], p. 2, accessed on April 6, 2005.
7. Joseph Stiglitz, *Globalization and Its Discontents* (New York: Norton, 2003), p. 9.
8. Thomas L. Friedman, "Small and Smaller," *New York Times*, March 4, 2004, p. A29.
9. John Cavanagh and Jerry Mander, eds., *Alternatives to Economic Globalization: A Better World Is Possible*, 2nd ed. (San Francisco: Berrett-Koehler, 2004); Robin Broad, "The Washington Consensus Meets the Global Backlash: Shifting Debates and Policies," *Globalizations*, December 2004, pp. 129–154.
10. Saritha Rai, "Protests in India Deplore Soda Maker's Water Use," *New York Times*, May 21, 2003; Paul Vallely, Jon Clarke, and Liz Stuart, "Coke Adds Life? In India, Impoverished Farmers Are Fighting to Stop Drinks Giant Destroying Livelihoods," *London Independent*, July 25, 2003.
11. "Dumping Without Borders: How U.S. Agricultural Policies Are Destroying the Livelihoods of Mexican Corn Farmers," Oxfam International, August 2003 [http://www.oxfaminternational.org/eng/pdfs/pp030827_corn_dumping.pdf], p. 2, accessed on March 8, 2005; Sophia Murphy, "Managing the Invisible Hand: Markets, Farmers, and International Trade," Institute for Agriculture and Trade Policy, April 2002) [http://www.tradeobservatory.org/library/uploadedfiles/Managing_the_Invisible_Hand_2.pdf], p. 14, accessed on March 9, 2005; "The Ten-Year Track Record of the North American Free Trade Agreement: U.S., Mexican, and Canadian Farmers and Agriculture," Public Citizen, December 16, 2003 [http://www.citizen.org/documents/NAFTA_10_ag.pdf], p. 2, accessed on March 8, 2005.
12. "Foreign Service," *Now*, PBS, August 29, 2003 [http://www.pbs.org/now/politics/jobflight.html], accessed on March 21, 2005, citing Forrester Research, November 2002.
13. Lorenzo Becawtini, businessman from Florence, Italy, quoted in Terry Tempest Williams, "Engagement," *Orion*, July-August 2004 [http://

www.oriononline.org/pages/om/04–2om/TempestWilliams.html], accessed on February 22, 2005.

14. Wendy Priesnitz, "The Market for Healthy, Sustainable Living," *Natural Life*, November-December 2003 [http://www.life.ca/nl/94/LOHAS.html], accessed on February 16, 2005.
15. "Backgrounder: Fair Trade Certified Coffee," TransFair USA [http://www.transfairusa.org/pdfs/backgrounder_coffee.pdf], accessed on August 2, 2004.
16. Ros Davidson, "Organic Regs Shaking Up Coffee Industry, Growth Seen," Reuters, October 11, 2002; Kim Mitchell and Phil Wells, "Spilling the Beans on the Coffee Trade," Fairtrade Foundation, March 2002) [http://www.fairtrade.org.uk/downloads/pdf/spilling_the_beans.pdf], p. 9, accessed on February 1, 2005.
17. Charis Gresser and Sophia Tickell, "Mugged: Poverty in Your Coffee Cup," Oxfam America, 2002 [http://www.oxfamamerica.org/newsandpublications/publications/research_reports/mugged], p. 20, accessed on March 17, 2005.
18. "Fair Trade Market Achieves Record Growth in 2003," TransFair USA, March 29, 2004 [http://www.transfairusa.org/content/about/pr_040329.php], accessed on February 1, 2005.
19. "2003 Report on Fair Trade Trends in U.S., Canada, and the Pacific Rim," Fair Trade Federation, International Federation for Alternative Trade, and Co-Op America, 2004 [http://www.fairtradefederation.org/2003_trends_report.pdf], p. 2, accessed on February 10, 2005.
20. "Supermarket Report Card," Oxfam America, October 2004 [http://www.oxfamamerica.org/newsandpublications/publications/campaign_materials/ftc_reportcard], accessed on February 15, 2005.
21. "Fair Trade Farmers Worldwide," TransFair USA [http://www.transfairusa.org/content/about/global_reach.php], accessed on March 17, 2005. For more information, contact TransFair USA, 1611 Telegraph Avenue, Suite 900, Oakland, CA 94612, tel. (510) 663-5260, info@transfairusa.org, http://www.transfairusa.org.
22. Personal communication from Lina Musayev, United Students for Fair Trade, February 23, 2005.
23. Check out the following Web sites for more information: Fair Labor Association [http://www.fairlabor.org], Worker Rights Consortium [http://www.workersrights.org], Clean Clothes Campaign [http://

www.cleanclothes.org], Social Accountability International [http://www.cepaa.org], Rainforest Alliance [http://www.rainforest-alliance.org], Global Reporting Initiative [http://www.globalreporting.org].

24. Bella English, "No Sweat Leader Is Passionate About Newton Company's Union-Only Apparel," *Boston Globe*, May 1, 2004.
25. Linda Baker, "The Goal: 'Sweatshop Free.' The Problem: Defining It," *New York Times*, December 14, 2003.
26. Jenny Strasburg, "Politically Correct Upstart Challenges Nike," *San Francisco Chronicle*, May 7, 2004.
27. Marshall Glickman and Marjorie Kelly, "Working Capital," *E Magazine*, March-April 2004 [http://www.emagazine.com/view/?1398], accessed on January 15, 2005. Three useful Web sites on social investing are http://www.socialinvest.org, http://www.socialfunds.com, and http://www.responsibleinvesting.org.
28. Ibid.
29. For more information, contact Advocacy and Public Policy Program, 1612 K Street NW, Suite 650, Washington DC, 20006, tel. (202) 872-5313, traceyrembert@socialinvest.org, http://www.shareholder action.org.
30. Marjorie Kelly, "Holy Grail Found: Absolute, Definitive Proof That Responsible Companies Perform Better Financially," *Business Ethics*, Winter 2004 [http://www.business-ethics.com/current_issue/winter_2005_holy_grail_article.html], accessed on March 26, 2005.
31. Marc Orlitzky, Frank L. Schmidt, and Sara L. Rynes, "Corporate Social and Financial Performance: A Meta-Analysis," *Organization Studies*, 2003, *24*, 403–411 [http://business.auckland.ac.nz/newstaffnet/profile/publications_upload/000000556_orlitzkyschmidtrynes2003os.pdf], accessed on March 1, 2005; Andrew White and Matthew Kiernan, "Corporate Environmental Governance," U.K. Environment Agency, September 2004 [http://www.innovestgroup.com/pdfs/2004-11-09-Environmental_Governance.pdf], accessed on March 1, 2005.
32. Glickman and Kelly, "Working Capital."
33. "Benchmarks: The Domini 400 Social Index," KLD Research & Analytics [http://www.kld.com/benchmarks/dsi.html], accessed on March 2, 2005.
34. "12,000 Students Pledge to Boycott Citigroup Credit Cards," Rainforest Action Network, October 22, 2001 [http://www.ran.org/news/

newsitem.php?id=437&area=finance], accessed on March 2, 2005; "RAN: Rainforest Action Network and Citigroup Announce Enhanced Citigroup Environmental Policy," Rainforest Action Network, January 22, 2004 [http://www.ran.org/news/newsitem.php?id=886&area=finance], accessed on March 2, 2005; "World's Largest Bank Makes Huge Step Toward Sustainability," Rainforest Action Network, [http://www.ran.org/ran_campaigns/global_finance/citi_victory.html], accessed on March 2, 2005.

35. Glickman and Kelly, "Working Capital."
36. Ibid., quoting Siew Hong Teoh, Ivo Welch, and C. Paul Wazzan, "The Effect of Socially Activist Investment Policies on the Financial Markets: Evidence from the South African Boycott," *Journal of Business*, 1999, *72*(1).
37. Glickman and Kelly, "Working Capital."
38. "An Interview with Founder Robert Rubinstein," *GreenMoney Journal*, Fall 2004 [http://www.greenmoneyjournal.com/article.mpl?newsletterid=30&articleid=322], accessed on March 19, 2005.
39. Glickman and Kelly, "Working Capital."
40. "Hawken Critique of Socially Responsible Investing Misses Key Trends and Impacts," Social Investment Forum, October 5, 2004 [http://www.socialinvest.org/Areas/News/041005.html], accessed on February 23, 2005.
41. "New York City Pension Fund Victorious in Urging Four More Companies to Bar Discrimination Based on Sexual Orientation," Human Rights Campaign, February 5, 2004 [http://www.hrc.org/ExxonMobilTemplate.cfm?Section=News_Releases1&CONTENTID=16141&TEMPLATE=/ContentManagement/ContentDisplay.cfm], accessed on March 26, 2005. Ninety-six of the Fortune 100 companies now have nondiscrimination policies.
42. "Private Pensions and Their Importance," Women's Institute for a Secure Retirement [http://www.wiser.heinz.org/private_pensions.html], accessed on March 6, 2005.
43. "The Center," AFL-CIO Center for Working Capital [http://www.centerforworkingcapital.org/who/index.html], accessed on March 12, 2005.
44. "Look for the Union Label—in Finance," *Business Week*, March 28, 2005 [http://www.businessweek.com/magazine/content/05_13/b3926111.htm], accessed on May 27, 2005.

45. "Industry Financial, Employment Statistics," Securities Industry Association [http://www.sia.com/research/pdf/keystats.pdf], accessed on March 8, 2005.
46. For more information, contact AFL-CIO Center for Working Capital, 888 16th Street NW, Washington, DC 20006, tel. (202) 974-8020, fax: (202) 974-8029, CWC@centerforworkingcapital.org, http://www.centerforworkingcapital.org.
47. "McDonald's USA Nutrition Facts for Popular Menu Items," McDonald's USA [http://www.mcdonalds.com/app_controller.nutrition.index1.html], accessed on February 1, 2005; U.S. Department of Health and Human Services and U.S. Department of Agriculture, *Dietary Guidelines for Americans, 2005*, 6th ed. (Washington, D.C.: U.S. Government Printing Office, January 2005), p. 11 [http://www.health.gov/dietaryguidelines/dga2005/document/pdf/DGA2005.pdf], accessed on March 19, 2005.
48. Thomas L. Friedman, *The Lexus and the Olive Tree* (New York: First Anchor Books, 2000), p. 104.
49. World Trade Organization, *Annual Report, 1998* (Geneva: World Trade Organization, 1998), p. 33 [http://www.wto.org/english/res_e/booksp_e/anrep_e/anre98_e.pdf], accessed on February 23, 2005.
50. Energy Information Administration, *International Energy Outlook, 2004* (Washington, D.C.: Energy Information Administration, April 2004), pp. 7, 30 [http://www.eia.doe.gov/oiaf/ieo/pdf/0484(2004).pdf], accessed on March 27, 2005; Energy Information Administration, *International Energy Outlook, 2000* (Washington, D.C.: Energy Information Administration, March 2000), p. 135 [http://tonto.eia.doe.gov/FTPROOT/forecasting/04842000.pdf], accessed on March 27, 2005.
51. Energy Information Administration, *International Energy Outlook, 2004*, pp. 163, 177.
52. Energy Information Administration, *Annual Energy Review, 2003* (Washington, D.C.: Energy Information Administration, September 2004), p. 5 [http://www.eia.doe.gov/emeu/aer/pdf/aer.pdf], accessed on March 27, 2005.
53. Ibid. pp. 5, 9.
54. Joel Schwartz, "Harvesting and Long-Term Exposure Effects in the Relation Between Air Pollution and Mortality," *American Journal of*

Epidemiology, 2000, *151*, 440–448. "Air pollution kills about 70,000 Americans each year."

55. Aaron Naparstek, "The Coming Energy Crunch," *New York Press*, June 2, 2004 [http://www.nypress.com/17/22/news&columns/AaronNaparstek.cfm], accessed on March 14, 2005.
56. Ibid., quoting James Howard Kunstler; see also Kunstler, *The Long Emergency: Surviving the End of the Oil Age, Climate Change, and Other Converging Catastrophes of the Twenty-First Century* (New York: Atlantic Monthly Press, 2005).
57. Personal communication from Michael Shuman; see also Shuman, *Going Local: Creating Self-Reliant Communities in a Global Age* (New York: Free Press, 1998).
58. "2003 Report on Socially Responsible Investing Trends in the United States," Social Investment Forum, December 2003, p. ii [http://www.socialinvest.org/areas/research/trends/sri_trends_report_2003.pdf], accessed on March 14, 2005.
59. Personal communication from Justin Conway, coordinator of the Community Investment Program, Co-Op America and Social Investment Forum, March 15, 2005.
60. "CDFIs: Bridges Between Capital and Communities: 2001 Member Statistics and Information, National Community Capital Association, 2002 [http://www.communitycapital.org/National_Community_Capital_Association_statistics_brochure.pdf], accessed on February 24, 2005.
61. Christine Canabou, "Center for Community Self-Help," *Fast Company*, January 2004, p. 56 [http://www.fastcompany.com/magazine/78/social_cfcsh.html], accessed on February 2, 2005.
62. Lynn Adler and Jim Mayer, "Martin Eakes, Self-Help, Durham, North Carolina" (interview), *Faith, Hope and Capital*, PBS, originally broadcast on March 31, 2000 [http://www.pbs.org/capital/stories/martin-eakes-print.html], accessed on March 27, 2005.
63. Canabou, "Center for Community Self-Help"; "Summary of NC Predatory Lending Law," Coalition for Responsible Lending, February 2002 [http://www.responsiblelending.org/pdfs/shortsumm.pdf], accessed on February 8, 2005; "N.C. Predatory Mortgage Lending Law: FAQs," Center for Responsible Lending [http://www.responsiblelending.org/predlend_nc/faqs.cfm#two], accessed on March 3, 2005.

64. Canabou, "Center for Community Self-Help."
65. Ibid., p. 56.
66. "Conservation," 2003 Annual Report, ShoreBank Corp. [http://www.shorebankcorp.com/bins/site/templates/child.asp?area_4=pages/nav/about/right_side.dat&area_2=pages/about/annual_reports.dat&area_7=pages/titles/about_title.dat], accessed on February 2, 2005.
67. "Buy Local Campaign Launched in Northwest Washington," New Rules Project, Institute for Local Self-Reliance, February 1, 2004 [http://www.newrules.org/retail/news_archive.php?browseby=slug&slugid=213], accessed on March 4, 2005.
68. "Unchaining for One Day Means Millions for Communities," American Independent Business Alliance, November 10, 2004 [http://amiba.net/Unchained_national_release.html], accessed on February 25, 2005, citing "The Economic Impact of Locally Owned Businesses vs. Chains: A Case Study in Midcoast Maine," Institute for Local Self-Reliance, September 2003 [http://www.newrules.org/retail/midcoaststudy.pdf], accessed on March 20, 2005; "Executive Summary, Economic Impact Analysis: A Case Study: Local Merchants vs. Chain Retailers," Civic Economics, prepared for LiveableCity Austin, December 2002 [http://amiba.net/pdf/Economic_Impact_study_tx.pdf], accessed on March 20, 2005.
69. "Unchaining," American Independent Business Alliance.
70. Personal communication from Susan Witt, executive director, E. F. Schumacher Society, February 21, 2005.
71. Ibid. For more information on local currencies, see "Local Currencies," E. F. Schumacher Society [http://www.schumachersociety.org/frameset_local_currencies.html], accessed on March 5, 2005.
72. Michelle Nijhuis, "For Sale by Owners," *Smithsonian*, October 2004 [http://www.smithsonianmag.si.edu/smithsonian/issues04/oct04/poi.html], accessed on February 5, 2005. The Mercantile consists of a 7,500-square-foot retail store with a 2,500-square-foot annex.
73. Allison Batdorff, "Powell Mercantile Serves as Model for Others," *Caspar* (Wyo.) *Star Tribune*, November 16, 2004 [http://www.casperstartribune.net/articles/2004/11/16/news/wyoming/c1d16119668eeda987256f4e0011b15a.txt], accessed on February 23, 2005.
74. Nijhuis, "For Sale by Owners."

75. Ibid.
76. Batdorff, "Powell Mercantile."
77. Marjorie Kelly, *The Divine Right of Capital: Dethroning the Corporate Aristocracy* (San Francisco: Berrett-Koehler, 2003), p. 43.
78. "What Your Disaffected Workers Cost," *Gallup Management Journal*, March 15, 2001 [http://gmj.gallup.com/content/default.asp?ci=439], accessed on March 30, 2005.
79. Christopher Mackin, "Wealth at Work: Employee Ownership and Responsible Accumulation," June 22, 2004, paper presented at the Real Utopias Conference, University of Wisconsin, June 25–27, 2004 [http://www.havenscenter.org/real_utopias/2004documents/Mackin%20paper.pdf], p. 2, accessed on February 16, 2005.
80. "Table 1: Participation in Shared Capitalism Programs, from Survey of Individuals," National Center for Employee Ownership [http://www.nceo.org/library/widespread_tables.html], accessed on March 27, 2005.
81. Jeff Gates, *Democracy at Risk: Rescuing Main Street from Wall Street* (Cambridge, Mass.: Perseus, 2000); Jeff Gates, *The Ownership Solution: Toward a Shared Capitalism for the Twenty-First Century* (New York: Perseus, 1998).
82. "ESOP Facts and Figures," ESOP Association [http://www.esopassociation.org/pubs/stats.html], accessed on February 13, 2005.
83. "The Employee Ownership 100," National Center for Employee Ownership [http://www.nceo.org/library/eo100.html], accessed on March 1, 2005; "Corporate Culture," UPS [http://sustainability.ups.com/social/culture.html], accessed on March 27, 2005.
84. Robert Barker, "The Key Word in Google's IPO: Risky," *Business Week*, August 9, 2004 [http://www.businessweek.com/magazine/content/04_32/b3895134_mz026.htm], accessed on March 27, 2005.
85. Mackin, "Wealth at Work," p. 5, citing Peter A. Kardas, Adria L. Scharf, and Jim Keogh, "Wealth and Income Consequences of Employee Ownership: A Comparative Study from Washington State," *Journal of Employee Ownership Law and Finance*, 1998, *10*(4), 3–52.
86. Corey Rosen, "Employee Ownership Update for February 19, 2004," National Center for Employee Ownership [http://www.nceo.org/columns/cr155.html], accessed on March 7, 2005.

87. "Wal-Mart Fact Sheets," Wal-Mart Corp. [http://www.walmart facts.com/doyouknow/default.aspx], accessed on February 1, 2005; "Wal-Mart: An Example of Why Workers Remain Uninsured and Underinsured," AFL-CIO, October 2003 [http://www.aflcio.org/issues politics/healthpolicy/upload/Wal-Mart_final.pdf], accessed on February 1, 2005.
88. Personal communication from Don Leber, director of advertising, Bi-Mart, Eugene, Oregon.
89. McKay Nursery Company, P.O. Box 185, 750 South Monroe Street, Waterloo, WI 53594, tel. (920) 478-2121 or (800) 236-4242, fax: (920) 478-3615, info@mckaynursery.com, http://www.mckaynursery.com.
90. Darren Waggoner, "Migrant Laborers Seize the American Dream," American News Service, 1996. To search the complete archive of ANS stories, see http://www.smallplanetinstitute.org/ans.php.
91. "About Cooperatives," National Cooperative Business Association [http://www.ncba.coop/abcoop_work.cfm], accessed on March 7, 2005; personal communication from Peggy Powell, director of workforce strategies, Paraprofessional Healthcare Institute, March 10, 2005.
92. Steven Greenhouse, "Health Aides Who Get Sick Days? Ownership Is Good for Co-Op Workers, but Union Complicates Mix," *New York Times*, February 14, 2004; Linda R. Prout, "In Burgeoning Home Health Care Industry, Small Worker-Owned Firms Shows the Way," American News Service, 1996.
93. "Programs: Cooperative Restaurants Project," Restaurant Opportunities of New York [http://www.rocny.org/programs-cooperative restaurantsproject.htm], accessed on March 1, 2005.
94. "Surviving WTC Restaurant Staff Starting New Eatery," CNN, January 19, 2005 [http://www.cnn.com/2005/US/01/19/wtc.restaurant.ap/], accessed on March 7, 2005. For more information on worker ownership, contact U.S. Federation of Worker Cooperatives, 2129 Franklin Avenue East, Minneapolis, MN 55404, tel. (415) 379-9201, http://www.usworkercoop.org.
95. Carmen Sirianni and Lewis Friedland, *Civic Innovation in America: Community Empowerment, Public Policy, and the Movement for Civic Renewal* (Berkeley: University of California Press, 2001), p. 59.

96. "Digital Press Kit," New Community Corporation [http://www.newcommunity.org/pressKitFrame.htm], accessed on February 22, 2005; Darvin Ayre, Gruffie Clough, and Tyler Norris, with Dixie Griffin Good, *Trendbenders: Building Healthy and Vital Communities* (Chicago: Health Research & Educational Trust, 2002), pp. 21–23.
97. Luther K. Snow, *Community Transformation: Turning Threats into Opportunities* (Evanston, Ill.: Asset-Based Community Development Institute, Institute for Policy Research, Northwestern University, 2001), pp. 21–27.
98. Ibid., pp. 15–20.
99. Jeffrey McCracken and Jamie Butters, "Election-Year Issue: Democratic Candidates Back Pro-Union Proposal," *Detroit Free Press*, February 7, 2004 [http://www.freep.com/news/politics/union7_20040207.htm], accessed on February 22, 2005; Lance Compa, "Unfair Advantage: Workers' Freedom of Association in the United States Under International Human Rights Standards," Human Rights Watch, August 2000 [http://hrw.org/reports/pdfs/u/us/uslbr008.pdf], accessed on February 26, 2005; "Union Members Summary," Bureau of Labor Statistics, January 27, 2005 [http://stats.bls.gov/news.release/union2.nr0.htm], accessed on February 22, 2005.
100. Jennifer Gordon, *Suburban Sweatshops: The Fight for Immigrant Rights* (Cambridge, Mass.: Harvard University Press, 2005).
101. "Slavery in the 21st Century," *New Internationalist*, August 2001 [http://www.newint.org/issue337/facts.htm], accessed on February 1, 2005; Mike Kaye, *Forced Labour in the 21st Century* (West Sussex, England: Anti-Slavery International and the International Confederation of Free Trade Unions, 2001), p. 8 [http://www.antislavery.org/homepage/resources/forcedlabour.pdf], accessed on February 1, 2005; "Contemporary Forms of Slavery," Fact Sheet No.14, Office of the United Nations High Commissioner for Human Rights [http://www.ohchr.org/english/about/publications/docs/fs14.htm], accessed on February 8, 2005.
102. "World Employment Report, 2004–05: Employment, Productivity and Poverty Reduction," International Labor Organization, 2005 [http://www.ilo.org/public/english/employment/strat/download/wr04c1en.pdf],, ch. 1, p. 23, accessed on February 7, 2005.

103. Karen Mazurkewich, "A Wealth of Happiness: Tashi Wangyal," *Wall Street Journal*, October 8, 2004, p. A14.
104. "Calvert-Henderson Quality of Life Indicators," Calvert Group [http://www.calvert-henderson.com], accessed on March 16, 2005; Jason Venetoulis and Cliff Cobb, *The Genuine Progress Indicator, 1950–2002*, 2004 update (Oakland, Calif.: Redefining Progress, March 2004) [http://www.rprogress.org/newpubs/2004/gpi_march 2004update.pdf], accessed on March 16, 2005.
105. Redefining Progress, 1731 Connecticut Ave. NW, Suite 500, Washington, DC [http://www.redefiningprogress.org/projects/gpi], accessed on August 3, 2005.

Chapter Seven: Action

1. Gail Sheehy, "Personal Action is Political: Introduction," in MoveOn.org, *MoveOn's 50 Ways to Love Your Country* (Makawao, Hawaii: Inner Ocean, 2004), p. 104.
2. Ibid.
3. Paul Goldberger, "The Case for Architecture," keynote address, Fourteenth Annual Accent on Architecture Gala, American Architectural Foundation, March 8, 2003 [http://www.archfoundation.org/about/news.article.1.htm], accessed on February 24, 2005. See also "Listening to the City," AmericaSpeaks [http://www.americaspeaks.org/projects/cases/ltc/index.htm], accessed on February 24, 2005.
4. Carolyn Lukensmeyer, *AmericaSpeaks Network News*, July 20, 2004 [http://www.thataway.org/news/archives/000244.html], accessed on March 6, 2004.
5. "American Democracy in an Age of Rising Inequality," Task Force on Inequality and American Democracy, American Political Science Association, 2004 [http://www.apsanet.org/imgtest/taskforcereport.pdf], accessed on June 19, 2005.
6. Robert D. Putnam, "The Strange Disappearance of Civic America," *American Prospect*, December 1, 1996 [http://www.prospect.org/print/V7/24/putnam-r.html], accessed on March 13, 2005; Robert D. Putnam, *Bowling Alone: The Collapse and Revival of American Community* (New York: Simon & Schuster, 2000); Robert D. Putnam, *Democracies in Flux: The Evolution of Social Capital in Contemporary*

Society (Oxford: Oxford University Press, 2002); Robert D. Putnam, *Better Together: Restoring the American Community* (New York: Simon & Schuster, 2003).

7. Personal communication from Martha McCoy, April 2004.
8. *Meet the Press with Tim Russert*, NBC, November 28, 2004 [http://www.msnbc.msn.com/id/6601018/], accessed on February 24, 2005. See also Jim Wallis, *God's Politics: Why the Right Gets It Wrong and the Left Doesn't Get It* (San Francisco: HarperSanFrancisco, 2005).
9. Mark R. Warren and Richard L. Wood, *Faith-Based Community Organizing: The State of the Field* (Jericho, N.Y.: Interfaith Funders, 2001) [http://comm-org.utoledo.edu/papers.htm], accessed on February 11, 2005. Most of the 133 local networks are themselves members of one of four national networks: the Industrial Areas Foundation (IAF), the Pacific Institute for Community Organization (PICO), the Gamaliel Foundation, and the Direct Action Research and Training Center (DART).
10. Mark R. Warren, "Building Democracy: Faith-Based Community Organizing Today," Shelterforce Online, National Housing Institute, January-February 2001 [http://www.nhi.org/online/issues/115/Warren.html], accessed on February 16, 2005.
11. Quoted in Cheryl Dahle, "Social Justice: Ernesto Cortes Jr.," *Fast Company*, December 1999, p. 294 [http://www.fastcompany.com/magazine/30/cortes.html], accessed on March 9, 2005.
12. Ernesto Cortes Jr., "The Politics of Philio: Political Friendship" (unpublished paper), October 7, 2002.
13. Theda Skocpol, *Diminished Democracy: From Membership to Management in American Civic Life* (Norman: University of Oklahoma Press, 2004), p. 176.
14. Josh Barbanel, "Steady Focus, Evolving Vision," *New York Times*, May 16, 2004; "Nehemiah Homeownership Program," New York City Department of Housing Preservation and Development, November 4, 2004 [http://www.nyc.gov/html/hpd/html/for-homebuyers/nehemiah.html], accessed on February 10, 2005.
15. "Minimum Wage: Frequently Asked Questions," Economic Policy Institute, July 2004 [http://www.epinet.org/content.cfm/issueguides_minwage_minwagefaq], accessed on February 6, 2005.

16. "Wage Commission," City of Baltimore [http://www.ci.baltimore.md.us/government/wage/], accessed on February 10, 2005.
17. William Bole, "Citizens Define Their Own 'Living Wage,'" American News Service, 1995.
18. Personal communication from Carrie Laughlin, Southwest Industrial Areas Foundation, Austin, March 24, 2005.
19. Personal communication from Regina Botterill, cofounder of NICWJ, Chicago, February 14, 2005.
20. Ibid.
21. John Laidler, "Breakthrough in Job Training Defies Spotty Record," American News Service, 1995.
22. Ibid.
23. Personal communication from Carrie Laughlin, March 15, 2005. For more information, contact Project QUEST, Inc., 301 South Frio, Suite 400, San Antonio, TX 78207, tel. (210) 270-4690, fax (210) 270-4691, http://www.questsa.com.
24. Mark R. Warren, "Building Democracy."
25. Patrice Pascual, "Organizing for Education: The Alliance Schools in Texas," *AdvoCasey: Documenting Programs that Work for Kids and Families*, Spring 1999 [http://www.aecf.org/publications/advocasey/organizing], accessed on February 25, 2005.
26. "Leadership Training for Public Life," Metropolitan Alliance for Common Good [http://www.macg.org/takeaction/ltpl], accessed on February 25, 2005.
27. The Oakland-based Pacific Institute for Community Organization (PICO) ranks second in scope behind the Industrial Areas Foundation, with more than a thousand affiliated religious congregations, schools, and neighborhood institutions engaging a million families in 150 cities and towns. PICO California, for example, developed enough clout to succeed in 2000 in getting the state to increase funds for primary care health clinics by $50 million. Another member of the PICO network, Baton Rouge Working Interfaith Network, has a membership of thirty-four congregations representing forty-one thousand families. For more information, contact Pacific Institute for Community Organizing (PICO) National Network, 171 Santa Rosa Avenue, Oakland, CA 94610, tel. (510) 655-2801, fax (510) 655-

4816, sreedsd@earthlink.net, http://www.piconetwork.org. A similar effort, the Chicago-based Gamaliel Foundation, boasts over forty affiliates in seventeen states, including four affiliates in South Africa. For more information, contact Gamaliel Foundation, 203 North Wabash Avenue, Suite 808, Chicago, IL 60601, tel. (312) 357-2639, fax (312) 357-6735, shazel@gamaliel.org, http://www.gamaliel.org. The Direct Action and Research Training (DART) Network is made up of twenty-one metropolitan organizations spread throughout Indiana, Michigan, Ohio, Florida, Virginia, and Kentucky representing over 450 local member institutions, 95 percent of which are religious congregations (including Muslim, Christian, and Jewish faiths). For more information, contact DART Network, 314 N.E. 26th Terrace, Miami, FL 33137, tel. (305) 576-8020, fax (305) 576-0789, dartcenter@aol.com, http://www.thedartcenter.org.

28. "Gale Cincotta, 'Mother of Community Reinvestment Act,' Passes Away," Shelterforce Online, National Housing Institute, September-October 2001 [http://www.nhi.org/online/issues/119/industrynews.html], accessed on March 6, 2005.
29. Steven Erlanger, "New York Turns Squatters into Homeowners," *New York Times*, October 12, 1987, p. A1.
30. "History of CRA," National Training and Information Center, April 22, 2003 [http://www.ntic-us.org/issues/cra/cra-history.htm], accessed on February 25, 2005.
31. David W. Chen, "U.S. Set to Alter Rules for Banks Lending to Poor," *New York Times*, October 20, 2004.
32. "New York Reaches Unprecedented $484 Million Agreement with Predatory Lender; Household to Refund Consumers Nationwide and Reform Its Business Practices," press release, Office of New York State Attorney General Eliot Spitzer, October 11, 2002 [http://www.oag.state.ny.us/press/2002/oct/oct11a_02.html], accessed on February 28, 2005.
33. "What Is Predatory Mortgage Lending?" Community Action Project [http://www.captc.org/pubpol/predlending/Pred.Lend.pdf], accessed on April 5, 2005.
34. "ACORN Launches National Campaign Against Tax Refund Loan Rip-Offs and Their Largest Promoter, H&R Block," Association of

Community Organizations for Reform Now, January 14, 2004 [http://www.acorn.org/index.php?id=8539&tx_ttnews[pointer]=1&tx_ttnews[tt_news]=13270&tx_ttnews[backPid]=8538&cHash=2647ded7a9], accessed on February 27, 2005.

35. "H&R Block and ACORN Partner to Help Working Families Claim and Keep More of What They've Earned This Tax Season," Association of Communities Organizations for Reform Now, January 14, 2005 [http://acorn.org/index.php?id=1196&tx_ttnews[tt_news]=13207&tx_ttnews[backPid]=1096&cHash=93e94a48bf], accessed on February 25, 2005.
36. *Statistical Abstract of the United States, 2001* (Washington, D.C.: U.S. Census Bureau, 2002), p. 734 [http://www.census.gov/prod/2002pubs/01statab/banking.pdf], accessed on April 5, 2005; *Statistical Abstract of the United States, 2004–2005* (Washington, D.C.: U.S. Census Bureau, 2004), p. 745 [http://www.census.gov/prod/2004pubs/04statab/banking.pdf], accessed on April 5, 2005; Elizabeth Warren and Amelia Warren Tyagi, *The Two-Income Trap: Why Middle-Class Mothers and Fathers Are Going Broke* (New York: Basic Books, 2003) pp. 6, 194.
37. "ACORN Celebrates Signing of Massachusetts Predatory Lending Law," Association of Community Organization for Reform Now, August 10, 2004 [http://acorn.org/index.php?id=1200&tx_ttnews[tt_news]=3735&tx_ttnews[backPid]=1181&cHash=70812a708e], accessed on February 27, 2005. The enacted law will protect borrowers by ensuring that they talk with a certified housing counselor prior to taking out a loan over the high-cost threshold, prohibiting prepayment penalties on high-cost loans, and limiting the amount of fees financed into the loan to 5 percent of the loan amount.
38. Sheila Muto, "Residents Have Their Say on LAX Expansion Plans," *Wall Street Journal*, December 15, 2004.
39. Dushaw Hockett and others, "The Crisis in America's Housing: Confronting Myths and Promoting a Balanced Housing Policy," Center for Community Change, Center for Economic and Policy Research, Children's Defense Fund, Community Learning Project, and National Low Income Housing Coalition, January 2005 [http://www.nlihc.org/research/housingmyths.pdf], p. 11, accessed on February 28, 2005.

40. "Housing Trust Fund Project," Center for Community Change, [http://www.communitychange.org/issues/housing/trustfundproject/downloads/htfbrochure.pdf], accessed on February 28, 2005; personal communication from Mary E. Brooks, director of the Housing Trust Fund Project, Center for Community Change, Frazier Park, Calif., March 5, 2005.
41. Carmen Sirianni and Lewis Friedland, *Civic Innovation in America* (Berkeley: University of California Press, 2001), p. 76.
42. Rebecca S. Krantz, "Cycles of Reform in Porto Alegre and Madison," in *Deepening Democracy*, ed. Archon Fung and Erik Olin Wright (New York: Verso, 2003), p. 227.
43. For more information, see "2005 Adopted Capital Improvement Budget (CIB)," Office of Financial Services, City of Saint Paul, Minn. [http://www.stpaul.gov/depts/ofs/cib/2005budget], accessed on February 28, 2005.
44. For more information, see "About the Neighborhood Matching Fund," Seattle Department of Neighborhoods [http://www.seattle.gov/neighborhoods/nmf/about.htm], accessed on February 28, 2005.
45. "All 2004 Awarded Projects," Neighborhood Matching Fund, Department of Neighborhoods, City of Seattle [http://www.seattle.gov/neighborhoods/nmf/2004%20awards.pdf], accessed on March 16, 2005. For an overview of Seattle's experience with citizen participation and more, see Jim Diers, *Neighborhood Power* (Seattle: University of Washington Press, 2004).
46. For more information, see Leonard P. Oliver, *Study Circles: Coming Together for Personal Growth and Social Change* (Washington, D.C.: Seven Locks Press, 1987).
47. "Our History," Days of Dialogue, Santa Monica, Calif. [http://home.earthlink.net/~daysofdialogue/d8573oh.html], accessed on February 28, 2005; Jack Crowl, "Some Try a Deceptively Simple Strategy to Defuse Racial Tension: Talking," American News Service, 1995.
48. Bella English, "Study Circles: Tool for Democracy: Getting New People Involved in Civic Issues," *UUWorld Magazine*, November-December 2000 [http://www.uua.org/world/1100feat2.html], accessed on February 20, 2005.
49. Julie Fanselow, *What Democracy Looks Like: Kuna, Idaho* (Pomfret, Conn.: Study Circles Resource Center, 2004), pp. 4–5 [http://www.

studycircles.org/pdf/SCRC_Kuna%20Story.pdf], accessed on February 20, 2005. See also Gloria Mengual, "What Works: Study Circles in the Real World," Topsfield Foundation, 2003, adapted from Rona Roberts, "Toward Competent Communities: Best Practices for Producing Community-Wide Study Circles," Roberts & Kay, 2000 [http://www.studycircles.org/pdf/best_practices.pdf], accessed on March 19, 2005.

50. James Surowiecki, *The Wisdom of Crowds* (New York: Doubleday, 2004), p. 30.
51. "The Tennessee Aquarium: Inspiring Wonder and Appreciation for the Natural World," Tennessee Aquarium and Imax 3D Theater, Chattanooga, 2004 [http://www.tnaqua.org/Newsroom/faqsripple.asp], accessed on February 21, 2005; Katharine Whittemore, "Can a Thousand 'Chattanoogas' Bloom?" American News Service, 1995.
52. Personal communication from Tyler Norris, former director of the U.S. Coalition for Healthier Cities and Communities, November 14, 2004.
53. Gianpaolo Baiocchi, "Participation, Activism, and Politics: The Porto Alegre Experiment," in *Deepening Democracy*, ed. Archon Fung and Erik Olin Wright (New York: Verso, 2003), pp. 47–50.
54. Gianpaolo Baiocchi, *Militants and Citizens: The Politics of Participation in Porto Alegre* (Stanford, Calif.: Stanford University Press, 2005).
55. "Party Identification 7-Point Scale, 1952–2002," *NES Guide to Public Opinion and Electoral Behavior* (Ann Arbor: National Election Studies, Center for Political Studies, University of Michigan, 1995–2000) [http://www.umich.edu/~nes/nesguide/toptable/tab2a_1.htm], accessed on February 1, 2005.
56. Micah L. Sifry, "The Rise of Open-Source Politics," *Nation*, November 4, 2004 [http://www.thenation.com/doc.mhtml?i=20041122&s=sifry], accessed on November 13, 2004.
57. Brian Faler, "Election Turnout in 2004 Was Highest Since 1968," *Washington Post*, January 15, 2005.
58. Personal communication from Naina Khanna, field director, League of Independent Voters, New York, March 7, 2005.
59. Jim Hightower and Phillip Frazer, eds., "Reasons to Celebrate and Be Hopeful!" *Hightower Lowdown*, November 2004.

60. William Upski Wimsatt with Gary Dauphin, "The Alisha Thomas Story How a 24-Year-Old Got Elected to the Georgia State House," Brooklyn Rail, February 2004 [http://www.thebrooklynrail.org/express/feb04/alishathomas.html], accessed on March 1, 2005, excerpted from Adrienne Brown and William Upski Wimsatt, eds., *How to Get Stupid White Men out of Office: The Anti-Politics, Unboring Guide to Power* (New York: Soft Skull Press, 2004).
61. Ibid.
62. "The Dean Dozen 2004 Election Results," Democracy for America, 2005 [http://democracyforamerica.com/dd_returns.php], accessed on June 11, 2005.
63. Wimsatt with Dauphin, "Alisha Thomas Story."
64. Keith Kelleher and Madeline Talbott, "The People Shall Rule, Holding Public Officials Accountable in Chicago," Shelterforce Online, National Housing Institute, November-December 2000 [http://www.nhi.org/online/issues/114/kelleher.html], accessed on February 28, 2005.
65. Ibid.
66. Sharon Parrott and others, "Where Would the Cuts Be Made Under the President's Budget? An Analysis of Reductions in Education, Human Services, Environment, and Community Development Programs," Center on Budget and Policy Priorities, February 28, 2005 [http://www.cbpp.org/2-22-05bud.pdf], accessed on March 9, 2005.
67. Mike Wallace, "A New New Deal," address at New York 2050, Gotham Center, New York [http://www.ny2050.org/documents/newdeal], accessed on June 23, 2005.
68. Gecan, *Going Public*, p. 7.

Chapter Eight: Choice

1. Alexander Hamilton, *Federalist Papers*, no. 79 (1787).
2. Etienne G. Krug and others, eds., "World Report on Violence and Health," World Health Organization, 2002 [http://www.who.int/violence_injury_prevention/violence/world_report/en/full_en.pdf], p. 10, accessed on February 23, 2005.
3. Mark Nord, Margaret Andrews, and Steven Carlson, "Household Food Security in the United States, 2003," Food Assistance and

Nutrition Research Report No. 42, Economic Research Service, U.S. Department of Agriculture, October 2004 [http://www.ers.usda.gov/publications/fanrr42/fanrr42.pdf], p. 6, accessed on April 4, 2005.

4. Katherine M. Flegal, Barry I. Graubard, David F. Williamson, and Mitchell H. Gail, "Excess Deaths Associated with Underweight, Overweight, and Obesity," *Journal of American Medical Association*, 2005, *293*, 1861–1867; Kenneth E. Thorpe and others, "The Rising Prevalence of Treated Disease: Effects on Private Health Insurance Spending," *Health Affairs—Web Exclusive*, June 27, 2005, p. W5-322 [http://content.healthaffairs.org/cgi/reprint/hlthaff.w5.317v1], accessed on June 27, 2005; Eric A. Finkelstein, Ian C. Fiebelkorn, and Guijing Wang, "National Medical Spending Attributable to Overweight and Obesity: How Much, and Who's Paying?" *Health Affairs*, May 13, 2003. Dr. Walter Willett at the Harvard School of Public Health argues that studies suggest a much higher toll.
5. Thomas A. Lyson and Annalisa Lewis Raymer, "Stalking the Wily Multinational: Power and Control in the U.S. Food System," *Agriculture and Human Values*, 2000, *17*, 199–208.
6. Greg Toppo, "Obesity Weighs Down Progress in Index of Youth Well-Being," *USA Today*, March 29, 2005 [http://www.usatoday.com/news/health/2005-03-29-youth-well-being_x.htm], accessed on March 29, 2005.
7. Calculations based on the current market price of corn at $2.20 per bushel (56 pounds) and the current supermarket price of Kellogg's Original Corn Flakes at $3.33 per pound, based on a store visit to Shaw's Supermarket, Belmont, Mass., March 6, 2005.
8. "*Fortune* 500 Largest U.S. Corporations," *Fortune*, April 16, 2001.
9. Sharon S. Elliott and others, "Fructose, Weight Gain, and the Insulin Resistance Syndrome," *American Journal of Clinical Nutrition*, 2002, *76*, 911–922 [http://www.ajcn.org/cgi/content/full/76/5/911], accessed on March 5, 2005.
10. John P. Bantle, Susan K. Raatz, William Thomas, and Angeliki Georgopoulos, "Effects of Dietary Fructose on Plasma Lipids in Healthy Subjects," *American Journal of Clinical Nutrition*, 2000, *72*, 1128–1134 [http://www.ajcn.org/cgi/content/full/72/5/1128], accessed on March 5, 2005.

11. Kim Severson and Melanie Warner, "Fat Substitute, Once Praised, Is Pushed Out of the Kitchen," *New York Times*, February 13, 2005.
12. "Wholly Good for You," *UC Berkeley Wellness Letter*, March 2005, p. 3, citing a new Harvard University study; "The Whole Grain Story," *Tufts University Health and Nutrition Letter*, July 2005, pp. 4–5.
13. "Coca-Cola," Coca-Cola Company [http://www2.coca-cola.com/brands/brands_coca-cola.html], accessed on March 1, 2005.
14. Mary Hendrickson and William Heffernan, "Concentration of Agricultural Markets," University of Missouri, Department of Rural Sociology, February 2005 [http://www.agribusinessaccountability.org/pdfs/311_Concentration-Tables-2004.pdf], accessed on July 20, 2005.
15. "Wal-Mart Food: Big and Getting Bigger," *Retail Forward*, September 2003 [http://www.retailforward.com/freecontent/Walmart_food.asp], accessed on April 5, 2005.
16. Federal Trade Commission, *Slotting Allowances in the Retail Grocery Industry: Selected Case Studies in Five Product Categories* (Washington, D.C.: Federal Trade Commission, 2003) [http://www.ftc.gov/os/2003/11/slottingallowancerpt031114.pdf], accessed on April 5, 2005.
17. Hendrickson and Heffernan, "Concentration of Agricultural Markets," February 2005; "The B.L.T. and the C.P.I.," *New York Times*, July 6, 2004, p. C1.
18. Kimberly Morland and others, "Neighborhood Characteristics Associated with the Location of Food Stores and Food Service Places," *American Journal of Preventive Medicine*, 2002, *22*, 23–29.
19. Marion Nestle, *Food Politics* (Berkeley: University of California Press, 2002), p. 25.
20. Stuart Elliott, "Upbeat Forecast in Advertising," *New York Times*, June 23, 2004, quoting Robert J. Coen, "Insider's Report: Robert Coen Presentation on Advertising Expenditures," Universal McCann, December 2004, p. 8 [http://www.universalmccann.com/Insiders1204.pdf], accessed on January 26, 2005.
21. International Labor Organization, *World Employment Report 2004–05: Employment, Productivity and Poverty Reduction* (Geneva: International Labor Organization, 2005), ch. 1 [http://www.ilo.org/public/english/employment/strat/wer2004.htm], accessed on February 7, 2005.

22. Elliott, "Upbeat Forecast in Advertising"; Anthony E. Gallo, "Food Advertising in the United States," in *America's Eating Habits: Changes and Consequences*, ed. Elizabeth Frazao (Washington, D.C.: Economic Research Service, U.S. Department of Agriculture, 1999), pp. 173–180 [http://www.ers.usda.gov/publications/aib750/aib750i.pdf], accessed on March 1, 2005.
23. Jim Kirk, "New Campaign at McDonald's Has Lovin' Feeling," *Chicago Tribune*, June 12, 2003.
24. Kelly D. Brownell and David S. Ludwig,"Fighting Obesity and the Food Lobby," *Washington Post,* June 9, 2002, p. B7.
25. Clive Thompson, "There's a Sucker Born in Every Medial Prefrontal Cortex," *New York Times*, October 26, 2003.
26. "Dietary Guidelines Committee Criticized," Center for Science in the Public Interest, August 19, 2003 [http://cspinet.org/new/200308191.html], accessed on March 14, 2005; Kristine Kieswer, "PCRM Wins USDA Lawsuit," *Physicians Committee for Responsible Medicine Magazine*, 2001, *10*(1) [http://www.pcrm.org/magazine/GM01Winter/GM01Win4.html], accessed on April 2, 2005.
27. Marion Nestle, *Safe Food: Bacteria, Biotechnology, and Bioterrorism* (Berkeley: University of California Press, 2003), pp. 76–77.
28. "Power Hungry: Six Reasons to Regulate Global Food Corporations," ActionAid International, 2005, [http://www.actionaid.org.uk/wps/content/documents/power_hungry.pdf], p. 13, accessed on February 23, 2005.
29. Jeffrey Smith, *Seeds of Deception: Exposing Industry and Government Lies About the Safety of Genetically Engineered Foods* (Fairfield, Iowa: Yes! Books, 2003).
30. "Are You Eating Genetically Modified Foods?" *CNN Health,* March 24, 2005 [http://www.cnn.com/2005/HEALTH/diet.fitness/03/24/genetic.foods.ap/], accessed on April 1, 2005; William K. Hallman and others, "Americans and GM Food: Knowledge, Opinion, and Interest in 2004," Food Policy Institute, Cook College, Rutgers University, 2004 [http://www.foodpolicyinstitute.org/docs/reports/NationalStudy2004.pdf], p. 3, accessed on February 24, 2005.
31. Gary Langer, "Behind the Label: Many Skeptical of Bioengineered Food," *ABC News*, June 19, 2001 [http://abcnews.go.com/sections/scitech/DailyNews/poll010619.html], accessed on March 20, 2005.

32. Based on figures from the official 2002 contribution and expenditure reports for ballot measures in Oregon. According to Pat McCormick, from the communications firm Conkling Fiskum & McCormick, who worked on the campaign against the labeling, "The report shows that committees supporting Measure 27, which would have required the labeling of genetically engineered foods in Oregon, spent a total of about $163,000 advocating for the measure after it was certified to the ballot. The Coalition Against the Costly Labeling Law raised and spent just about $5.4 million opposing the measure, which voters rejected overwhelmingly (71 percent voted against it)."
33. Geoffrey Lean, "Revealed: Health Fears over Secret Study into GM Food," *Independent on Sunday*, May 22, 2005.
34. Dennis T. Avery, *The Hidden Dangers in Organic Food* (Washington, D.C.: American Outlook, Hudson Institute, 1998); Mitchell Cohen, statement, Centers for Disease Control and Prevention, January 14, 1999; "CDC Has Never Compared *E. coli* Risks of Organic, Traditional Food," *Alternative Agriculture News*, February 1999; "*E. coli* and the Safety of Organic Food," Soil Association, October 10, 2001 [http://www.soilassociation.org/web/sa/saweb.nsf/0/80256ad800554549802567fc00389c5f?OpenDocument], accessed on March 21, 2005; "FAIR's Correspondence with ABC re John Stossel's February 4 Report on Organic Food," Fairness and Accuracy in Reporting, February 22, 2000 [http://www.fair.org/activism/stossel-organics.html], accessed on March 21, 2005.
35. "2002 Hudson Institute Annual Report," Hudson Institute, February 5, 2004 [http://www.hudson.org/files/publications/Hudson2002AnnualReportFinal.pdf], pp. 23–24, accessed on March 20, 2005.
36. "Food-Disparagement Laws: State Civil and Criminal Statutes," FoodSpeak Coalition for Free Speech, Center for Science in the Public Interest [http://www.cspinet.org/foodspeak/laws/existlaw.htm], accessed on March 12, 2005.
37. "Judge Chucks Suit Maligning Beef Industry," Reporters Committee for Freedom of the Press, September 20, 2002 [http://www.rcfp.org/news/2002/0920cactus.html], accessed on March 1, 2005.
38. For more information about this case, go to http://www.foxbghsuit.com.
39. Campbell R. McConnell and Stanley L. Brue, *Economics*, 16th ed. (New York: McGraw-Hill/Irwin, 2005), p. 468.

40. Hendrickson and Heffernan, "Concentration of Agricultural Markets," February 2005; figures in the chapter referring to concentration among corn exporters and soybean processors are from the 2002 report by the same authors.
41. Quoted in Dan Carney, "Dwayne's World," *Mother Jones*, July-August 1995 [http://www.motherjones.com/news/special_reports/1995/07/carney.html], accessed on April 5, 2005.
42. "Power Hungry," p. 4.
43. Ibid., p. 13.
44. Personal communication from Matthew Shane, Economic Research Service, U.S. Department of Agriculture, December 2004. Using 1975 as the base, current (2002) agricultural export prices are only 42 percent of what they were in 1975.
45. Howard Elitzak, "Indicators," *Amber Waves*, February 2004, p. 43 [http://www.ers.usda.gov/amberwaves/february04/pdf/indicators.pdf], accessed on February 24, 2005.
46. Between 1999 and 2003, the United States lost on average fifteen thousand farms per year. "Number of Farms, Average Size of Farm, and Land in Farms, United States, 1974–2003," National Agricultural Statistics Service [http://www.nass.usda.gov/ky/B2004/p010.pdf], accessed on June 29, 2005.
47. U.S. Department of Agriculture, *Food and Agricultural Policy: Taking Stock for the New Century* (Washington, D.C.: U.S. Department of Agriculture, 2001), p. 23 [http://www.usda.gov/news/pubs/farmpolicy01/fullreport.pdf], accessed on April 5, 2005.
48. Zili Sloboda, "Drug Abuse in Rural America: A Growing Problem," *Counselor,* December 2002, pp. 16–20; Michael R. Rosmann, "Agriculture Mental Health," National Agricultural Safety Database, Southern Coastal Agromedicine Center, National Institute for Occupational Safety and Health, October 2004 [http://www.cdc.gov/nasd/docs/d001701-d001800/d001769/d001769.html], accessed on April 6, 2005.
49. Personal communication, C. Robert Taylor, Auburn University.
50. "Tyson Foods Fails to Honor the Term of the Contract for Certain Growers," E-Bulletin #20, Rural Advancement Foundation International-USA (RAFI-USA), February 2004 [http://www.rafiusa.org/pubs/pubebulletins/e-Bulletin20.html], accessed on March 2, 2005.

51. "USDA Subsidies for farms in the United States totaled $131,313,000,000 from 1995 through 2002." "EWG Farms Subsidy Database," Environmental Working Group [http://www.ewg.org/farm/regionsummary.php?fips=00000], accessed on April 5, 2005.
52. "What's the Plan? U.S. Farm Subsidies, 1995 through 2003," Environmental Working Group [http://www.ewg.org/farm/findings.php], accessed on February 28, 2005.
53. "Foodborne Illness: Frequently Asked Questions," Centers for Disease Control and Prevention, January 10, 2005 [http://www.cdc.gov/ncidod/dbmd/diseaseinfo/files/foodborne_illness_FAQ.pdf], p. 5, accessed on February 28, 2005.
54. "Preventing Diabetes and Its Complications," Centers for Disease Control and Prevention, August 2003 [http://www.cdc.gov/nccdphp/pe_factsheets/pe_ddt.htm], accessed on March 7, 2005.
55. Eric A. Finkelstein, Ian C. Fiebelkorn, and Guijing Wang, "National Medical Spending Attributable to Overweight and Obesity: How Much, and Who's Paying?" *Health Affairs*, May 14, 2003 [http://www.healthaffairs.org].
56. "Pesticide Injury and Illness Surveillance," National Institute for Occupational Safety and Health [http://www.cdc.gov/niosh/topics/pesticides/], accessed on February 28, 2005.
57. Kristin S. Schafer and others, "Chemical Trespass Pesticides in Our Bodies and Corporate Accountability" [http://panna.org/campaigns/docsTrespass/chemicalTrespass2004.dv.html], executive summary, pp. 4–5, accessed June 24, 2005. The report is an analysis of Centers for Disease Control data.
58. B. Eskanazi and others, "Exposure of Children to Organophosphate Pesticides and Their Potential Adverse Health Effects," June 1999, cited in ibid.
59. Frances Moore Lappé, *Diet for a Small Planet*, 20th anniv. ed. (New York: Ballantine Books, 1991), p. 69; Peter H. Gleick, "Making Every Drop Count," *Scientific American*, February 2001; David Pimentel, Laura Westra, and Reed Noss, eds., *Ecological Integrity: Integrating Environment, Conservation and Health* (Washington, D.C.: Island Press, 2001).
60. Pimentel, Westra, and Noss, *Ecological Integrity*.
61. Calculations based on "Summary Report, 1992 National Resources Inventor," Soil Conservation Service, U.S. Department of Agriculture,

1994 [http://www.nrcs.usda.gov], accessed March 30, 2005; Andy Jerardo, "Import Share of U.S. Food Consumption Stable at 11 Percent," Economic Research Service, U.S. Department of Agriculture, July 2003 [http://www.ers.usda.gov/publications/fau/july03/fau7901/fau7901.pdf], accessed on April 4, 2005.

62. "Animal Waste Report: Entire United States," Scorecard [http://www.scorecard.org/env-releases/aw/us.tcl], accessed on March 19, 2005, based on 1997 agricultural census data.
63. Jonathan Patz and Marjorie L. Share, "Livestock: Old MacDonald Doesn't Live Here Anymore," EcoHealth, Johns Hopkins Bloomberg School of Public Health [http://www.ecohealth101.org/whats_left/eat3.html], accessed on March 21, 2005.
64. Dan Ferber, "Hypoxia in the Gulf of Mexico: Progress Toward the Completion of an Integrated Assessment," National Centers for Coastal Ocean Science, National Ocean Service, National Oceanic and Atmospheric Administration, November 1, 2000 [http://oceanservice.noaa.gov/products/pubs_hypox.html], accessed on February 25, 2005.
65. "Organic Foods Offer a Better Way to Farm and a Better Way to Eat—So Why Are They Under Siege?" *Food Safety Review,* Spring 2005, p. 4.
66. David Pimentel and Marcia Pimentel, "Sustainability of Meat-Based and Plant-Based Diets and the Environment," *American Journal of Clinical Nutrition,* 2003, *78,* 660S–663S [http://www.ajcn.org/cgi/reprint/78/3/660S], accessed on February 3, 2005; Elysa Hammond, "Fight Global Warming with Your Knife and Fork," *Moving Toward Sustainability* (newsletter), Summer 2004, citing "Inventory of U.S. Greenhouse Gas Emissions and Sinks, 1990–2001," U.S. Environmental Protection Agency, April 15, 2003 [http://yosemite.epa.gov/oar/globalwarming.nsf/content/ResourceCenterPublicationsGHGEmissionsUSEmissionsInventory2003.html], accessed on February 3, 2005. EPA reports on annual emissions by sector show agricultural industries emitting 7 to 8 percent of all industrial emissions. Hammond rounded up to 10 percent because these data do not include energy expended to manufacture chemical fertilizers.
67. Erin M. Tegtmeier and Michael D. Duffy, "External Costs of Agricultural Production in the United States," *International Journal of*

Agricultural Sustainability, 2004, *2*, 1–20 [http://www.leopold.iastate.edu/pubs/staff/files/externalcosts_IJAS2004.pdf.], accessed on March 16, 2005.

68. Ibid.
69. "Prices Received by Farmers, All Milk," Daily Yearbook, Economic Research Service, U.S. Department of Agriculture [http://usda.mannlib.cornell.edu/data-sets/livestock/89032/mlkallvf.xls], accessed on April 5, 2005.
70. Phil Howard, "Organic Industry Structure," Center for Agroecology and Sustainable Food Systems, University of California, Santa Cruz, November 2003 [http://www.agribusinessaccountability.org/pdfs//253_Organic%20Industry%20Structure.pdf], accessed on April 5, 2005.
71. Personal communication from Phil Howard, Center for Agroecology and Sustainable Food Systems, University of California, Santa Cruz, April 20, 2005.
72. See also Lee Egerstrom, "Obstacles to Cooperation," in *Cooperatives and Local Development: Theory and Applications for the 21st Century*, ed. Christopher Merrett and Norman Walzer (New York: Sharpe, 2003).
73. Damien Cave, "Now, She's 'Organic' (That's a Plus)," *New York Times*, August, 1, 2004.
74. Hammond, "Fight Global Warming."
75. Ibid.
76. Laurie E. Drinkwater, "Legume-Based Cropping Systems Have Reduced Carbon and Nitrogen Losses," *Nature*, November 18, 1998, pp. 262–265; Cass Petersen, Laurie E. Drinkwater, and Peggy Wagoner, *The Rodale Institute Farming Systems Trial: The First 15 Years* (Kutztown, Pa.: Rodale Institute, 1999).
77. Ibid.
78. Virginia Worthington, "Nutritional Quality of Organic Versus Conventional Fruits, Vegetables, and Grains," *Journal of Alternative and Complementary Medicine*, 2001, *7*, 151–193. The article reviews findings of forty-one published articles showing higher levels of key nutrients in organic food; Bill Liebhardt, "Get the Facts Straight: Organic Yields Are Good," Organic Farming Research Foundation, *Information Bulletin*, Summer 2001, p. 1.

79. Daniel Lass, G. W. Stevenson, John Hendrickson, and Kathy Ruhf, *CSA Across the Nation: Findings from the 1999 CSA Survey* (Madison: Center for Integrated Agricultural Systems, College of Agricultural and Life Sciences, University of Wisconsin-Madison, 2003) [http://www.cias.wisc.edu/pdf/csaacross.pdf], p. i, accessed on March 24, 2005; personal communication from Laura Brown, Madison Area CSA Coalition.
80. "About Cooperatives," National Cooperative Business Association [http://www.ncba.coop/abcoop_food.cfm], accessed on February 23, 2005.
81. Economic Research Service, *Macroeconomics and Agriculture: The Importance of Income Growth for U.S. Agriculture* (Washington, D.C.: U.S. Department of Agriculture, 2002); Judith Jones Putnam and Jane E. Allshouse, *Food Consumption, Prices, and Expenditures, 1970–97* (Washington, D.C.: Economic Research Service, 1999).
82. Kim T. B. Knoops and others, "The Mediterranean Diet, Lifestyle Factors, and 10-Year Mortality in Elderly European Men and Women," *Journal of the American Medical Association*, 2004, *292*, 1433 ff.
83. Jane Reed, Elizabeth Frazão, and Rachel Itskowitz, *How Much Do Americans Pay for Fruits and Vegetables?* Agriculture Information Bulletin No. 790 (Washington, D.C.: Economic Research Service, 2004) [http:/ers.usda.gov/publications/aib790/aib790.pdf], accessed on March 19, 2005.
84. Calculations based on prices and servings as listed on Stop & Shop's Peapod Web site, http://www.peapod.com, and based on a phone call to Whole Foods in Brighton, Massachusetts, on July 1, 2005, and the assumption that a serving size of organic uncooked oatmeal is one-third of a cup.
85. Michael Penn, "Will Power," *Wisconsin Academy Review*, Winter 2003 [http://wisconsinacademy.org/review/vol49_1/willpower.html], accessed on March 20, 2005; Will Allen, "Food Power: Central City Program Teaches Food Growing and Life Skills," *Wisconsin Foodshed*, July 1998 [http://www.cias.wisc.edu/pdf/foodshed/foodshed4.pdf], accessed on March 20, 2005.
86. Wayne Roberts, "Ex-Basketball Star's Urban Agro-Project a New Kind of Entrepreurialism with Kind Profits," *Now Magazine*, October 28,

2004 [http://www.nowtoronto.com/issues/2004-10-28/news_story3.php], accessed on March 20, 2005. For more information, contact Growing Power, 5500 West Silver Spring Road, Milwaukee, WI 53218, tel. (414) 527-1546, fax (414) 527-1908, staff@growingpower.org, http://www.growingpower.org.

87. "1st Quarter 2003 Department of Housing Report," Chicago Rehab Network, July 16, 2003 [http://www.chicagorehab.org/policy/pdf/1stquarter2003report.pdf], p. 4, accessed on April 5, 2005.
88. Katherine H. Brown and Anne Carter, "Urban Agriculture and Community Food Security in the United States: Farming from the City Center to the Urban Fringe," Community Food Security Coalition, North American Urban Agriculture Committee, October 2003 [http://www.foodsecurity.org/primercfscuac.pdf], p. 10, accessed on April 5, 2005.
89. "School Vending Machines 'Dispensing Junk,'" Center for Science in the Public Interest, May 11, 2004 [http://www.cspinet.org/new/200405111.html], accessed on April 5, 2005.
90. Stuart Reeves, "Study Links Vending Machines, Obesity," *Austin Daily Texan*, August 28, 2003 [http://www.dailytexanonline.com/news/2003/08/28/WorldNation/Study.Links.Vending.Machines.Obesity-454067.shtml], accessed on March 12, 2005.
91. Personal communication from Kristin Barnhart, who handles public relations for McDonald's western division.
92. Meredith May, "Teachers Sizzle over Fast-Food Fundraiser; Some Say It Promotes Unhealthy Choices," *San Francisco Chronicle*, October 15, 2002, A1.
93. California Senate Bill 677, introduced by Sen. Deborah V. Ortiz (D-Sacramento) on February 21, 2003 [http://www.asu.edu/educ/epsl/CERU/Legislation/CERU-0305-65-RL.pdf], accessed on March 14, 2005. For more information, see http://www.nojunkfood.org.
94. Cathy Shufro, "Green Menus College Campuses Opt for Sustainable Dining," *E Magazine*, July-August 2004 [http://www.emagazine.com/view/?1853&src=], accessed on March 1, 2005.
95. "World Agriculture: Trends and Indicators," Economic Research Service, U.S. Department of Agriculture, 1995 [http://www.ers.usda.gov/data/sdp/view.asp?f=international/89024/], accessed on April 5, 2005.

96. Pimentel and Pimentel, "Sustainability."
97. Richard Manning, "The Oil We Eat," *Harper's*, February 2004 [http://www.harpers.org/TheOilWeEat.html], accessed on February 25, 2005.
98. Janet L. Sawin, *Mainstreaming Renewable Energy in the 21st Century*, Worldwatch Paper No.169 (Washington, D.C.: WorldWatch Institute, 2004); Paul Roberts, *The End of Oil: On the Edge of a Perilous New World* (Boston: Houghton Mifflin, 2004); David Goodstein, *Out of Gas: The End of the Age of Oil* (New York: Norton, 2004); David Francis, "Has Global Oil Production Peaked?" *Christian Science Monitor*, January 29, 2004 [http://www.csmonitor.com/2004/0129/p14s01-wogi.html], accessed on February 25, 2005.
99. "Bacteria Fears Prompt Largest Ever U.S. Meat Recall," *New York Times*, October 14, 2002.
100. Doug Grow, "Puny Township 1, Big Ag 0," *Minneapolis Star Tribune*, June 11, 2005.
101. Personal communication from Betsy Johnson, interim director, American Community Gardening Association, New York.
102. "Table 8. Farms, Land in Farms, Value of Land and Buildings, and Land Use, 2002 and 1997," *2002 Census of Agriculture* (Washington, D.C.: U.S. Department of Agriculture, 2003), vol. 1, ch. 2 [http://www.nass.usda.gov/census/census02/volume1/us/st99_2_008_008.pdf], accessed on March 28, 2005.

Chapter Nine: Voice

1. Alexis de Tocqueville, *Democracy in America*, p. 309.
2. Thomas Jefferson, letter to Colonel Edward Carrington, January 16, 1787, in *The Life and Selected Writings of Thomas Jefferson*, ed. Adrienne Koch and William Peden (New York: Modern Library/Random House, 1998), p. 381.
3. "Future of the First Amendment: What America's High School Students Think About Their Freedoms: Results," John S. and James L. Knight Foundation, January 31, 2005 [http://firstamendment.jideas.org/results/students/studentsurvey4.php], accessed on February 19, 2005.
4. "Table of Global Press Freedom Rankings," Freedom House [http://www.freedomhouse.org/research/pressurvey/allscore2005.pdf], accessed June 24, 2005.

5. "Azerbaijan: Editor of Opposition Weekly Gunned Down," Committee to Protect Journalists, March 2, 2005 [http://www.cpj.org/news/2005/Azer02mar05na.html], accessed on March 9, 2005.
6. Christine Y. Chen, "Clear Channel: Not the Bad Boys of Radio," *Fortune*, February 18, 2003 [http://www.fortune.com/fortune/ceo/articles/0,15114,423802,00.html], accessed on March 4, 2005.
7. "Reason Interview: Mark S. Fowler," *Reason*, November 1981.
8. Tony Karon, "Welcome! Why You've Now Got AOL Time Warner," CNN, January 20, 2000 [http://archives.cnn.com/2000/US/01/20/aol.warner.time.merger/], accessed on March 27, 2005.
9. Matthew T. Felling, "The Incredible Shrinking Sound Bite," Center for Media and Public Affairs, September 28, 2000 [http://oregonstate.edu/Dept/pol_sci/fac/sahr/ps415/cmpa2000.pdf], accessed on February, 23, 2005.
10. *Statistical Abstract of the United States, 2004–2005* [http://www.census.gov/prod/2004pubs/04statab/infocomm.pdf], p. 717, accessed on March 4, 2005.
11. Grace Kim, "Three out of Four Americans Have Access to the Internet, According to Nielsen/NetRatings," Nielsen//NetRatings, March 18, 2004 [http://www.nielsennetratings.com/pr/pr_040318.pdf], accessed on March 2, 2005.
12. "50th Anniversary of 'Wonderful World of Color' TV," U.S. Census Bureau, March 11, 2004 [http://www.census.gov/Press-Release/www/releases/archives/facts_for_features/001702.html], accessed on February 23, 2005; *Radio Today: How America Listens to Radio*, 2004 ed. (New York: Arbitron, 2004), p. 3 [http://www.arbitron.com/downloads/radiotoday04.pdf], accessed on March 29, 2005; "Research Nation Fact Sheet," Onfolio [http://www.onfolio.com/press/ResearchNation.doc], accessed on February 23, 2005.
13. Mark Crispin Miller, "What's Wrong with This Picture," *Nation*, December 20, 2001 [http://www.thenation.com/doc.mhtml?i=20020107&s=miller], accessed on March 12, 2005. For more information on media concentration, go to http://www.mediachannel.org/ownership.
14. Robert McChesney, *The Problem of the Media* (New York: Monthly Review Press, 2004), p. 178, citing Tim Burt and Peter Thal Larsen,

"Sony and BMG Sign Music Merger Deal," *Financial Times*, December 12, 2003.

15. "How the Studios Stack Up in '97," *Variety*, January 5, 1998, p. 96.
16. Robert McChesney, *Rich Media, Poor Democracy: Communication Politics in Dubious Times* (New York: New Press, 1999), p. 166, citing "Ma Bell Convenience Store," *Economist*, June 27, 1998, pp. 61–62.
17. Joel S. Yudken and Christine Owens, "Reply Comments of the American Federation of Labor and Congress of Industrial Organizations," in "In the Matter of Cross-Ownership of Broadcast Stations and Newspaper/Radio Cross-Ownership Waiver Policy," Federal Communications Commission, February 19, 2002 [http://www.cwa-union.org/issues/telecom/aflcio_reply.pdf], p. 6, accessed on March 12, 2005, citing Ben Bagdikian, *The Media Monopoly*, 6th ed. (Boston: Beacon Press, 2000), p. xxxii; Thomas Kunkel and Gene Roberts, "Leaving Readers Behind: The Age of Corporate Newspapering," *American Journalism Review*, 2001, *23*(4).
18. Kunkel and Roberts, "Leaving Readers Behind."
19. "Clear Channel Radio Fact Sheet," Clear Channel Communications [http://www.clearchannel.com/fact_sheets/radio_factsheet.pdf], accessed on March 12, 2005.
20. "Television: Stations," Clear Channel Communications [http://www.clearchannel.com/Television/Stations.aspx], accessed on March 12, 2005; "Clear Channel Outdoor Awarded Franchise to Provide Advertising on NCTD Buses Operating Within North San Diego County," Clear Channel Outdoor, July 1, 2004 [http://www.clearchanneloutdoor.com/corp/prDetail.asp?id=37], accessed on March 12, 2005; "International Radio," Clear Channel Communications [http://www.clearchannel.com/InternationalRadio/home.aspx], accessed on March 12, 2005; "Entertainment: Venue List," Clear Channel Communications [http://www.clearchannel.com/Entertainment/ent_venue_list.aspx], accessed on March 12, 2005.
21. "Clear Channel Entertainment Fact Sheet," Clear Channel Entertainment, February 2, 2005 [http://www.clearchannel.com/fact_sheets/entertainment_factsheet.pdf], accessed on March 12, 2005.
22. Charles Lewis, "Profiteering from Democracy," *Public I*, October 2000 [http://www.publicintegrity.org/docs/publici/pi_2000_10.pdf], accessed on March 15, 2005.

23. Matthew T. Felling, "The Incredible Shrinking Sound Bite," Center for Media and Public Affairs, September 28, 2000 [http://oregon state.edu/Dept/pol_sci/fac/sahr/ps415/cmpa2000.pdf], accessed on February, 23, 2005.
24. "Changing Definitions of News: What Was Studied," Project for Excellence in Journalism, March 6, 1998 [http://www.journalism.org/resources/research/reports/definitions/studied.asp], accessed on March 15, 2005.
25. Ibid.
26. Beth Gillin, "Product Placement Turns TV Programs into Commercials," Knight-Ridder, January 24, 2005.
27. David Barstow and Robin Stein, "Under Bush, a New Age of Prepackaged TV News," *New York Times*, March 13, 2005.
28. John Stauber and Sheldon Rampton, *Toxic Sludge is Good for You!: Lies, Damn Lies, and the Public Relations Industry* (Monroe, Maine: Common Courage Press, 1995).
29. "Political Ad Spending on Television Sets New Record: $1.6 Billion," Alliance for Better Campaigns, November 24, 2004 [http://www.bettercampaigns.org/press/release.php?ReleaseID=65], accessed on March 21, 2005.
30. Find media political ad purchases in your community through the Alliance for Better Campaigns at http://www.bettercampaigns.org.
31. Steven Manning, "Channel One Enters the Media Literacy Movement," *Rethinking Schools*, Winter 1999 [http://www.rethinking schools.org/archive/14_02/chan142.shtml], accessed on March 16, 2005.
32. Roy F. Fox, *Harvesting Minds: How TV Commercials Control Kids* (Westport, Conn.: Praeger, 1996). For more details of the sort presented in the box, see Robert McChesney's *Rich Media, Poor Democracy*.
33. Sheldon Rampton and John Stauber, *Weapons of Mass Deception: The Uses of Propaganda in Bush's War on Iraq* (New York: Tarcher/Penguin, 2003), p. 66.
34. Steven Kull, "Americans Continue to Believe Iraq Supported al-Qaeda, Had WMD," April 22, 2004 [http://www.pipa.org/Online Reports/Iraq/IraqPressRelease4_22_04.pdf], accessed on June 23, 2005.
35. Lawrence Soley, "The Power of the Press Has a Price," *Extra!* July-August 1997 [http://www.fair.org/index.php?page=1387], accessed on

May 12, 2005. See also Bill Kovach, Tom Rosenstiel, and Amy Mitchell, "Commentary: A Crisis of Confidence," in *How Journalists See Journalists in 2004: Views on Profits, Performance and Politics* (Washington, D.C.: Pew Research Center for the People and the Press and Project for Excellence in Journalism, 2004), p. 28 [http://people-press.org/reports/pdf/214.pdf], accessed on May 2, 2005; and Bob Papper, *2003 Local Television News Study of News Directors and the American Public* (Washington, D.C.: Radio and Television News Directors Foundation, 2003), p. 88 [http://www.rtndf.org/ethics/2003survey.pdf], accessed on May 12, 2005.

36. "Public Confidence in War Effort Falters but Support for War Holds Steady," Pew Research Center for the People and the Press, March 25, 2003 [http://people-press.org/reports/display.php3?ReportID=177], accessed on February 21, 2005; Amy Goodman, "An Hour with CNN's Aaron Brown on the Network's Coverage of the Antiwar Movement, the Sanitization of the War in Iraq, and Why He Feels This Is an Inappropriate Time for Reporters to Ask Questions About War," *Democracy Now!* April 4, 2003 [http://www.democracynow.org/article.pl?sid=03/04/16/2156256&mode=thread&tid=11], accessed on February 19, 2005.
37. Tom Valtin, "Zuni Salt Lake Saved," *Planet Newsletter*, October-November 2003 [http://www.sierraclub.org/planet/200307/zuni.asp], accessed on March 9, 2005.
38. Anne Robertson, "Clear Channel and Viacom Refuse Sierra Club Ads," *Phoenix Business Journal*, February 7, 2003 [http://www.bizjournals.com/phoenix/stories/2003/02/10/newscolumn4.html], accessed on March 9, 2005.
39. U.S. Congress, 73rd Congress, "Communications Act of 1934," passed June 19, 1934 [http://www.fcc.gov/Bureaus/OSEC/library/legislative_histories/47.pdf], accessed on February 24, 2005.
40. "Cable Communications Act of 1984," Public Law 98-549, October 30, 1984, 98 Stat. 2780, Amendment of Communications Act of 1934.
41. "The Fairness Doctrine: In the Matter of Editorializing by Broadcast Licensees," in *Documents of American Broadcasting*, 3rd ed., ed. Frank J. Khan (Upper Saddle River, N.J.: Prentice Hall, 1978), pp. 217–

231; Ford Rowan, *Broadcast Fairness: Doctrine, Practice, Prospects* (New York: Longman, 1984); William B. Ray, *FCC: The Ups and Downs of Radio-TV Regulation* (Ames: Iowa State University Press, 1990), ch. 4; Philip Abrams and Jeffrey Cunard, "The Media: Liberty and Licence—the FCC Controversy," *Guardian*, January 18, 1988.

42. McChesney, *Rich Media, Poor Democracy*, p. 276, citing Kahn, *Documents*, ch. 39.
43. Kennedy, *Crimes Against Nature*, p. 176, citing *Friends of the Earth* v. *FCC*, 449 F.2d 1164 (D.C. Cir. 1971).
44. Ibid., p. 177.
45. McChesney, *Problem of the Media*, p. 213.
46. Transcript of proceedings before the Federal Communications Commission, December 12, 1995 [http://64.233.161.104/search?q=cache:mPC7QiXXQjEJ:www.fcc.gov/Bureaus/Mass_Media/Informal/ilmm6001.txt+beachfront+property+on+the+cybersea&hl=en], accessed April 1, 2005.
47. "Statement of Media Access Project Executive Director Gigi B. Sohn," Media Access Project, April 2, 1997 [http://www.mediaaccess.org/programs/digitaltv/releases/4297rel.htm], accessed on March 23, 2005.
48. Yochi J. Dreazen, "FCC's Powell Quickly Marks Agency as His Own," *Wall Street Journal*, May 1, 2001.
49. Michael K. Powell, "The Public Interest Standard: A New Regulator's Search for Enlightenment," presentation at the American Bar Association's Seventeenth Annual Legal Forum on Communications Law, Las Vegas, Nevada, April 5, 1998 [http://www.fcc.gov/Speeches/Powell/spmkp806.html], accessed on March 28, 2005.
50. "American Public Opinion on Media Violence," Mediascope, March 15, 2000 [http://www.mediascope.org/pubs/ibriefs/apomv.htm], accessed on March 14, 2005; F. Lunz, "Press to Press: Cool It," *Brill's Content*, March 2000; Robert W. Welkos, "The Times Poll: Public Echoes Dole View on Sex, Violence;" *Los Angeles Times*, June 14, 1995.
51. "News Media," Polling Report, 2005 [http://www.pollingreport.com/media.htm], accessed on February 26, 2005, referring to a poll for the Pew Research Center for the People and the Press conducted by Princeton Survey Research Associates, July 8–16, 2002.

52. "State of the News Media, 2005—Overview: Economics," Project for Excellence in Journalism, 2005 [http://www.stateofthenewsmedia.org/2005/narrative_overview_economics.asp?cat=4&media=1], accessed on March 16, 2005.
53. *Standard & Poor's 2004 Review: Global Indices* (New York: McGraw-Hill, 2004) [http://www2.standardandpoors.com/spf/pdf/index/GIR_Global2004.pdf], accessed on March 23, 2005.
54. "Political Ad Spending on Television Sets New Record: $1.6 Billion," Alliance for Better Campaigns, November 24, 2004 [http://www.bettercampaigns.org/press/release.php?ReleaseID=65], accessed on March 21, 2005.
55. Barstow and Stein, "Under Bush."
56. Ibid.
57. Sheldon Rampton, "Fake News: We Told You So," Center for Media and Democracy [http://www.prwatch.org/node/3518], accessed April 1, 2005.
58. Joseph Carroll, "Local TV and Newspapers Remain Most Popular News Sources," Gallup Organization, December 20, 2004 [http://www.gallup.com/poll/content/default.aspx?ci=14389&pg=3], accessed on February 26, 2005.
59. Ina Howard, "Power Sources: On Party, Gender, Race and Class, TV News Looks to the Most Powerful Groups," *Extra!* May-June 2002 [http://www.fair.org/index.php?page=1109], accessed on March 20, 2005.
60. Ibid.
61. Anthony Lappé and Stephen Marshall, *True Lies* (New York: Penguin/Plume, 2004).
62. Norman Solomon, "The P.U.-litzer Prizes for 2004," AlterNet, December 10, 2004 [http://www.alternet.org/mediaculture/20714/], accessed on March 22, 2005.
63. Anne E. Kornblut, "Doubts on White House Reporter Are Recalled," *New York Times*, February 17, 2005, p. A22; Andrew Buncombe, "White House's Loyal Reporter Once Worked as Gay Hooker," *London Independent*, February 20, 2005, p. 22.
64. Erik Galatas, "Free Speech Television," Media Alliance [http://www.media-alliance.org/article.php?story=20031109003248161], accessed

on March 9, 2005; for more information on Free Speech Television, go to http://www.freespeech.org. "Company Profile," DISH Network [http://www.dishnetwork.com/content/aboutus/company_profile/index.shtml], accessed on March 16, 2005; for more information on DISH Network, go to http://http://www.dishnetwork.com.

65. "How the Studios Stack Up," p. 96.
66. Jeremiah Bauman, "Protecting Our Future: Policy Directions and Strategies to Protect Children's Development Against Toxic Chemicals," American Association on Mental Retardation, 2003 [http://www.aamr.org/ToxinsandMentalRetardation/pdf/Web_Paper_9_Baumann.pdf], accessed on March 16, 2005; "Get Your Hands on Plastic!" American Plastics Council [http://www.teachingplastics.org], accessed on March 16, 2005.
67. Personal communication from Diane Hatz, director of marketing and special projects, Global Resource Action Center for the Environment, New York, March 8, 2005. View *The Meatrix* at http://www.themeatrix.com.
68. Tim Connor, "From Bad to Worse," *Camas Magazine*, September 4, 2003; Ron C. Judd, "Newspaper Part of the Story in Spokane Fight," *Seattle Times*, October 20, 2003.
69. Judd, "Newspaper Part of the Story."
70. "Our Story," Thin Air Radio [http://www.thinairradio.org/history1.htm], accessed on February 18, 2005.
71. "All Politics Is Local, But You Wouldn't Know It by Watching Local TV," Alliance for Better Campaigns, October 2003 [http://bettercampaigns.org/reports/display.php?ReportID=12], accessed on March 23, 2005; Jennifer Harper, "Study Finds 'Near Blackout' of Local Public Issues on TV," *Washington Times*, October 28, 2003.
72. "Statement of FCC Chairman William Kennard on District Court Upholding Radio Licensing Requirements in Dunifer Pirate Radio Case," Federal Communications Commission, June 17, 1998 [http://ftp.fcc.gov/Speeches/Kennard/Statements/stwek847.html], accessed on February 23, 2005.
73. "Radio," *Chronicle of Philanthropy*, January 6, 2005.
74. Hannah Sassaman, "Presente! A Radio Station Barn Raising," *YES!* Spring 2005, p. 32.

75. William Baue, "Taco Bell Agrees to Pay Florida Tomato Pickers a Penny More per Pound to End Boycott," Socialfunds.com [http://www.socialfunds.com/news/article.cgi/article1581.html], accessed on April 2, 2005.
76. "A Nation Online: Entering the Broadband Age," National Telecommunications and Information Administration, U.S. Department of Commerce, September 2004 [http://www.ntia.doc.gov/reports/anol/NationOnlineBroadband04.htm], accessed on March 9, 2005. In 2003, 65 percent of white Americans had access to the Internet, compared to only 45 percent of black Americans. Among those making over $75,000 a year, 80 percent had Internet access, while only 25 percent of those making less than $15,000 a year could say the same.
77. "Community Wireless Networks: Building Tomorrow's Public Service Communications Infrastructure," Free Press, [http://www.freepress.net/wifi/guideintro.php], accessed on February 25, 2005.
78. Marc Levy, "Telecom Companies Fighting Competition," *San Francisco Chronicle*, February 27, 2005.
79. Jonathan Krim, "Fast Internet Service for the People," *Washington Post*, December 2, 2004.
80. Ibid.
81. Josh McHugh, "The Firefox Explosion," *Wired*, February 2005 [http://wired.com/wired/archive/13.02/firefox.html?pg=1&topic=firefox&topic_set], accessed on March 9, 2005.
82. "About Community Media," Alliance for Community Media [http://www.alliancecm.org/index.php?page_id=2], accessed on March 15, 2005. For more information, contact Alliance for Community Media, 666 Eleventh Street N.W., Suite 740, Washington, DC 20001, tel. (202) 393-2650, fax (202) 393-2653, acm@alliancecm.org, http://www.alliancecm.org.
83. For more information, contact Media Access Project, 1625 K Street N.W., Suite 1000, Washington, DC 20006, tel. (202) 232-4300, info@mediaaccess.org, http://www.mediaaccess.org; Center for Digital Democracy, 1718 Connecticut Avenue N.W., Suite 200, Washington, DC 20009, tel. (202) 986-2220, jeff@democraticmedia.org, http://democraticmedia.org.

84. For more information, contact Allied Media Projects, P.O. Box 20128, Toledo, OH 43610, info@alliedmediaprojects.org, http://www.alliedmediaprojects.org; Free Press, 100 Main Street, P.O. Box 28, Northampton, MA 01061, tel. (866) 666-1533, fax (413) 585-8904, info@freepress.net, http://www.freepress.net. See also Center for International Media Action, 1276 Bergen Street, Suite 4, Brooklyn, NY 11213, tel. (646) 249-3027, fax (815) 642-0801, cima@mediaactioncenter.org, http://www.mediaactioncenter.org.
85. For more information, contact MediaRights, 104 West Fourteenth Street, 4th Floor, New York, NY 10011, tel. (646) 230-6288, fax (646) 230-6328, http://www.mediarights.org; Working Films, 602 South Fifth Avenue, Wilmington, NC 28401, tel. (910) 342-9000, fax (910) 342-9003, mramey@workingfilms.org, http://www.workingfilms.org.
86. For more information, contact In the Mix, 114 East Thirty-Second Street, Suite 903, New York, NY 10016, tel. (212) 288-2150, (800) 597-9448, IntheMix@pbs.org, http://www.pbs.org/inthemix.
87. Jeff Perlstein, "The Independent Media Center Movement," *Media-File*, January-February 2001 [http://www.media-alliance.org/mediafile/20-1/perlstein.html], accessed on March 28, 2005.
88. McChesney, *Problem of the Media*, p. 213.
89. "Radio Deregulation: Has It Served Citizens and Musicians?" Future of Music Coalition, November 18, 2002 [http://www.futureofmusic.org/research/radiostudyexecsum.cfm], accessed on March 14, 2005.

Part Four: Democracy in Our Bones

1. Benjamin Barber, "America Skips School," *Harper's*, November 1993.
2. Rene A. Spitz, "Hospitalism," in *The Psychoanalytic Study of the Child*, vol. 1., ed. R. S. Eissler (New York: International Universities Press, 1945); Rene A. Spitz, "Hospitalism: A follow-up report," in *The Psychoanalytic Study of the Child*, vol. 2, ed. R. S. Eissler (New York: International Universities Press, 1946). Psychologist Rene Spitz observed that orphaned babies in a foundling home, who had only limited interaction with nurses, had lowered resistance rates to sickness, and 37 percent died within two years, despite otherwise impeccable

hygiene, shelter, warmth, and food. A host of other studies have confirmed these findings.

3. Giacomo Rizzolatti and Michael A. Arbib, "Language Within Our Grasp," *Trends in Neurosciences*, 1998, *21*, 188–194.
4. "The Arts of Democracy," Small Planet Institute [http://www.smallplanetinstitute.org/arts.php].

Chapter Ten: Learning

1. Horace Mann, *The Republic and the School: The Education of Free Men* (New York: Teachers College Press, 1957), p. 58. Originally published in 1845. Horace Mann (1796–1859) became the first secretary of the Massachusetts Board of Education in 1837 and spearheaded the common school movement, which ensured that every child could receive a basic education funded by local taxes.
2. "Table 2: Trends in New York State High School Graduates Entering Institutions of Higher Education Within and Outside New York State, 1990 to 2004," State Education Department, University of the State of New York, 2004 [http://www.emsc.nysed.gov/irts/educationstats/hsgrads/table2-hsgrads.html#public], accessed on June 14, 2005.
3. "A League Table of Educational Disadvantage in Rich Nations," *Innocenti Report Card*, November 2002 [http://www.unicef-icdc.org/publications/pdf/repcard4e.pdf], p. 4, accessed on March 29, 2005.
4. Andrew Sum, Irwin Kirsch, and Robert Taggart, "The Twin Challenges of Mediocrity and Inequality: Literacy in the U.S. from an International Perspective," Policy Information Center, Educational Testing Service, February 2002 [http://www.ets.org/research/pic/twinchall.pdf], p. 10, accessed on January 3, 2005.
5. "Dropouts Concentrated in 35 Cities While Federal Data on Dropouts Underestimate Problem," Harvard Graduate School of Education, January 13, 2001 [http://www.gse.harvard.edu/news/features/conf01132001.html], accessed on January 4, 2005.
6. "U.S. Lags in Graduation Rates," *CBS News*, September 16, 2004 [http://www.cbsnews.com/stories/2004/09/16/world/main643934.shtml], accessed on January 4, 2005.

7. Sum, Kirsch, and Taggart, "Twin Challenges," p. 30; Herbert J. Walberg, *Spending More While Learning Less* (Washington, D.C.: Thomas B. Fordham Foundation, 1998).
8. Deborah Meier and George Wood, *Many Children Left Behind* (Boston: Beacon Press, 2004), p. 6.
9. Mark Stricherz, "Many Teachers Ignore Cheating, Survey Finds," *Education Week*, May 9, 2001 [http://www.edweek.org/ew/articles/2001/05/09/34cheat.h20.html], accessed on December 29, 2004.
10. Jill F. DeVoe and others, "Indicators of School Crime and Safety, 2004," U.S. Departments of Education and Justice, November 2004 [http://nces.ed.gov/pubs2005/crime_safe04/indicator_07.asp], p. 24, accessed on December 22, 2004.
11. "School Facilities: Condition of America's Schools," Government Accountability Office, February 1, 1995 [http://www.gao.gov/archive/1995/he95061.pdf], p. 2, accessed on February 17, 2005.
12. For more information, contact Coalition of Essential Schools, 1814 Franklin Street, Suite 700, Oakland, CA 94612, tel. (510) 433-1251, http://www.essentialschools.org; Center for Collaborative Education, 1 Renaissance Park, 1135 Tremont Street, Suite 490, Boston, MA 02120, tel. (617) 421-0134, http://www.ccebos.org; New England Small Schools Network, 1 Renaissance Park, 1135 Tremont Street, Suite 490, Boston, MA 02120, tel. (617) 421-0134; http://www.nessn.org; Big Picture Schools, 17 Gordon Avenue, Suite 104, Providence, RI 02905, tel. (401) 781-1873, http://www.bigpicture.org; Institute for Student Achievement, 1 Hollow Lane, Suite 100, Lake Success, NY 11042, tel. (516) 812-6700, http://www.studentachieve ment.org/home.htm; School Redesign Network, Stanford University, School of Education, 520 Galvez Mall, Stanford, CA 94305, tel. (650) 725-0703, mrgurney@stanford.edu, http://www.schoolredesign.net; Forum for Education and Democracy, P.O. Box 216, Amesville, OH 45711, tel. (740) 448-3402, info@forumforeducation.org, http://www.forumforeducation.org.
13. "Coalition of Essential Schools Receives $18.7M from Bill and Melinda Gates Foundation," Coalition of Essential Schools, September 2003 [http://www.essentialschools.org/pub/ces_docs/about/org/

pr_sept03.html], accessed on February 15, 2005. For more information, contact Bill and Melinda Gates Foundation, P.O. Box 23350, Seattle, WA 98102, tel. (206) 709-3100, info@gatesfoundation.org, http://www.gatesfoundation.org.

14. "No Child Left Behind Act of 2001," U.S. Department of Education, January 7, 2002 [http://www.ed.gov/nclb/overview/intro/execsumm.pdf], accessed on January 14, 2005; "Fact Sheet: NCLB and Adequate Yearly Progress," Florida Department of Education [http://www.fldoe.org/NCLB/FactSheet-AYP.pdf], accessed on January 14, 2005; "Consequences for Schools and Systems Not Making Adequate Yearly Progress (AYP)," Georgia Department of Education [http://www.doe.k12.ga.us/support/plan/nclb/ayp_consequences.asp], accessed on January 14, 2005.
15. Dennis Littky with Samantha Grabelle, *The Big Picture: Education Is Everyone's Business* (Alexandria, Va.: Association for Supervision and Curriculum Development, 2004), p. 26.
16. Deborah Meier, *In Schools We Trust: Creating Communities of Learning in an Era of Testing and Standardization* (Boston: Beacon Press, 2002), p. 28.
17. Robert Gladden, "The Small School Movement: A Review of the Literature," in *Small Schools, Big Imaginations: A Creative Look at Urban Public Schools*, ed. Michelle Fine and Janis I. Somerville (Chicago: Cross City Campaign for Urban School Reform, 1998), pp. 113–137; Kathleen Cotton, "School Size, School Climate, and Student Performance," Northwest Regional Educational Laboratory, May 1996 [http://www.nwrel.org/scpd/sirs/10/c020.html], accessed on March 20, 2005; Patricia A. Wasley and others, *Small Schools, Great Strides* (Chicago: Bank Street College of Education, 2000) [http://www.bankstreet.edu/gems/publications/SmallSchoolsStudy.pdf], accessed on February 17, 2005; Craig Howley and Robert Bickel, "Results of Four-State Study: Smaller Schools Reduce Harmful Impact of Poverty on Student Achievement," Rural School and Community Trust, February 2000 [http://www.ruraledu.org/docs/sapss/sapss.html], accessed on February 22, 2005.
18. Robert Bickel and Craig Howley, "The Influence of Scale on Student Performance: A Multilevel Extension of the Matthew Principle," in

Education Policy Analysis Archives, 2000, 8(22) [http://olam.ed.asu.edu/epaa/v8n22/], accessed on February 24, 2005; Howley and Bickel, "Results of Four-State Study."

19. "Lehman Alternative Community School: What Makes Us Alternative?" [http://www.icsd.k12.ny.us/acs/info.html#Family%20Groups], accessed on June 15, 2005. For further information, contact Lehman Alternative Community School, 111 Chestnut Street, Ithaca, NY 14850, tel. (607) 274-2183, http://www.icsd.k12.ny.us/acs.
20. "How We Work with Schools," Institute for Student Achievement [http://www.studentachievement.org/how_we_work.htm], accessed on February 2, 2005.
21. Interview with Anthony Rhodes, student support coordinator, Fenway High School, Roxbury, Mass., January 2005.
22. "Fenway High School," National Association of Secondary School Principals [http://www.principals.org/s_nassp/sec.asp?CID=66&DID=47034], accessed on March 29, 2005.
23. "Breakthrough High Schools," National Association of Secondary School Principals [http://www.principals.org/breakthrough/], accessed on January 14, 2005.
24. "Power Readers," Boston Arts Academy/Fenway High School Library [http://fenway.boston.k12.ma.us/library/for_students/power_readers.htm], accessed on February 2, 2005.
25. Meier, *In Schools We Trust*.
26. Littky and Grabelle, *The Big Picture*, p. 20.
27. Richard Cohen is the founder and director of School Mediation Associates, 134 Standish Road, Watertown, MA 02472, tel. (617) 926-0994, sma@schoolmediation.com, http://www.schoolmediation.com.
28. Estimated by Richard Cohen, January 11, 2005.
29. Nancy A. Burrell, Cindy S. Zirbel, and Mike Allen, "Evaluating Peer Mediation Outcomes in Educational Settings: A Meta-Analytic Review," *Conflict Resolution Quarterly*, 2003, *21*, 7–26.
30. John Dewey, "My Pedagogic Creed," *School Journal*, January 1897.
31. Rebecca Skinner and Chris Chapman, "Service-Learning and Community Service in K–12 Public Schools," National Center for Educational Statistics, September 1999 [http://nces.ed.gov/pubs99/1999043.pdf], p. 4, accessed on March 29, 2005.

32. Katy Anthes, "Institutionalized Service Learning in the 50 States," Education Commission of the States, March 2001 [http://www.ecs.org/clearinghouse/23/77/2377.htm], accessed on January 3, 2005; Martha Naomi Alt and Katharin Peter, "Private Schools: A Brief Portrait," National Center for Education Statistics, August 2002 [http://nces.ed.gov/pubs2002/2002013.pdf], p. 22, tab. 12, accessed on April 4, 2005.
33. Mark Hugo Lopez, "Youth Attitudes Toward Civic Education and Community Service Requirements," Center for Information and Research on Civic Learning and Engagement, University of Maryland School of Public Affairs, October 2002 [http://www.civicyouth.org/PopUps/FactSheets/FS_Youth_Attitudes_Civic_Education.pdf], p. 2, accessed on March 7, 2005.
34. Diane Loupe, "The Legal Authority Behind Service," *School Administrator,* August 2000 [http://www.aasa.org/publications/sa/2000_08/loupe_side_litigation.htm], accessed on January 12, 2005.
35. Skinner and Chapman, "Service-Learning and Community Service," p. 1.
36. For exemplary programs enabling students to experience real-life problem solving and learn the arts of democratic dialogue, goal setting, reflection, and negotiation, see "Entry Points for Living Democracy" at the back of this book.
37. Alison Gopnik, "How We Learn," *New York Times Book Review,* January 16, 2005, p. 26.
38. "Service to Civics," Grantmaker Forum on Community and National Service, October 2003 [http://www.pacefunders.org/publications/pubs/Service%20to%20Civics%202003.pdf], p. 20, accessed on February 15, 2005.
39. Shay Bilchik, "Violence After School," Office of Juvenile Justice and Delinquency Prevention, November 1999 [http://www.ncjrs.org/pdffiles1/ojjdp/178992.pdf], accessed on January 18, 2005.
40. "CIS/MCYC," GEAR UP Waco [http://www.gearupwaco.org/cis-mcyc.htm], accessed on January 18, 2005.
41. "Lighted Schools Program Is So Popular Parents Come, Too," American News Service, 1997.

42. Personal communication from Martin Blank, staff director of the Coalition for Community Schools, Washington, D.C., January 2005. For more information on his organization, go to http://www.communityschools.org. The estimate of the number of Lighted Schools was confirmed by other leaders in the field.
43. "Principles at Work," Coalition of Essential Schools, 2001 [http://www.essentialschools.org/pdfs/PAW3.pdf], accessed on February 2, 2005.
44. Leanna Stiefel, Patrice Iatarola, Norm Fruchter, and Robert Berne, "The Effects of Size of Student Body on School Costs and Performance in New York City High Schools," Robert F. Wagner Graduate School of Public Service, Institute for Education and Social Policy, New York University, April 1998 [http://www.nyu.edu/iesp/publications/effects/effects.pdf], p. 11, accessed on February 2, 2005.
45. Michael Dobbs, "Critics Are Saying Education Dept. Favors Right Wing: School Privatization Pushed, Report Finds," *San Francisco Chronicle*, January 3, 2004; Stan Karp, "Let Them Eat Tests," Rethinking Schools Online, Summer 2002 [http://www.rethinkingschools.org/special_reports/bushplan/Eat164.shtml], accessed on March 9, 2005; Sally West Johnson, "Mathis Rips Feds over School Act," *Rutland* (Vt.) *Herald*, February 5, 2003; Jim Hightower, "The Hidden Push to Privatize Public Schools," Common Dreams, September 23, 2004 [http://www.commondreams.org/views04/0923-13.htm], accessed on March 9, 2005.
46. Greg Toppo, "Education Dept. Paid Commentator to Promote Law," *USA Today*, January 7, 2005.
47. Hastie, quoted in *The Great Quotations*, ed. Seldes.
48. Deborah Meier, "On Unions and Education," *Dissent Magazine*, Winter 2004 [http://www.dissentmagazine.org/menutest/articles/wi04/meier.htm], accessed on December 21, 2004.
49. Marina A. Piscolish, "Reflecting on Conflict and Its Resolution in Our School Community: Recommended Content of the Three-Hour Introductory Session for Staff," Ohio Commission on Dispute Resolution and Conflict Management, Columbus [http://

disputeresolution.ohio.gov/schools/piscolishinservice.htm], accessed on February 2, 2005.

50. Meier, *In Schools We Trust*, p. 5.

Chapter Eleven: Security

1. Jeremy Rifkin, "The European Dream: The New Europe Has Its Own Cultural Vision—and It May Be Better Than Ours," *Utne*, September-October 2004 [http://www.utne.com/pub/2004_125/promo/11349-1.html], accessed on February 19, 2005.
2. Gail Tsukiyama, *The Samurai's Garden: A Novel* (New York: St. Martin's Press, 1995).
3. *Sourcebook of Criminal Justice Statistics Online*, 30th ed. (Washington, D.C.: Bureau of Justice Statistics, 2002) [http://www.albany.edu/sourcebook/pdf/t622.pdf], sec. 6, tab. 6.22, accessed on March 29, 2005.
4. "Number of Persons Under Correctional Supervision," Bureau of Justice Statistics, November 7, 2004 [http://www.ojp.usdoj.gov/bjs/glance/tables/corr2tab.htm], accessed on January 20, 2005; "Table 1: Annual Estimates of the Population by Sex and Five-Year Age Groups for the United States, April 1, 2000 to July 1, 2004," U.S. Census Bureau, June 9, 2005 [http://www.census.gov/popest/national/asrh/NC-EST2004/NC-EST2004-01.xls], accessed on June 21, 2005.
5. Milton S. Eisenhower Foundation, *To Establish Justice, to Insure Domestic Tranquility* (Washington, D.C.: Milton S. Eisenhower Foundation, 1999) [http://www.eisenhowerfoundation.org/aboutus/publications/justice.html], accessed on March 31, 2005.
6. "Correctional Populations in the United States, 1997," Bureau of Justice Statistics, November 2000 [http://www.ojp.usdoj.gov/bjs/pub/pdf/cpus97.pdf], p. vi, accessed on April 6, 2005.
7. "Direct Expenditures by Criminal Justice Function, 1982–2001," Bureau of Justice Statistics, February 6, 2004 [http://www.ojp.usdoj.gov/bjs/glance/tables/exptyptab.htm], accessed on April 5, 2005.
8. James J. Stephan, "State Prison Expenditures, 2001," Bureau of Justice Statistics, June 2004 [http://www.ojp.usdoj.gov/bjs/pub/pdf/spe01.pdf], p. 3, accessed on April 5, 2005; "Tuition and Fees, 2001–2002," *Handbook for Students, Faculty of Arts and Sciences*

(Cambridge, Mass.: Harvard University, 2001) [http://www.registrar.fas.harvard.edu/handbooks/student.2001-2002/chapter6/tuition.html], accessed on April 5, 2005.

9. Jason Ziedenberg, "Deep Impact: Quantifying the Effect of Prison Expansion in the South," Justice Policy Institute, April 4, 2003 [http://www.justicepolicy.org/article.php?id=124], accessed on March 31, 2005.
10. "National Crime Victimization Survey Property Crime Trends, 1973–2003," Bureau of Justice Statistics [http://www.ojp.usdoj.gov/bjs/glance/tables/proptrdtab.htm], accessed on March 26, 2005. The rate of property crimes has declined from 519.9 per thousand population in 1973 to 163.2 crimes per thousand population in 2003; "National Crime Victimization Survey Violent Crime Trends, 1973–2003," Bureau of Justice Statistics [http://www.ojp.usdoj.gov/bjs/glance/tables/viortrdtab.htm], accessed on March 26, 2005. The rate of violent crimes has fallen from 47.7 per thousand population in 1973 to 22.3 crimes per thousand population in 2003; Lydia Saad, "U.S. Crime Problem Less Troubling to Americans," Gallup News Service, November 9, 2004 [http://www.gallup.com/poll/content/default.aspx?ci=13987&pg=1], accessed on January 21, 2005.
11. Barry Glassner, *The Culture of Fear: Why Americans Are Afraid of the Wrong Things* (New York: Basic Books, 2000), especially "Introduction: Why Americans Fear the Wrong Things."
12. "Homicide Rates from the Vital Statistics," Bureau of Justice Statistics, January 30, 2004 [http://www.ojp.usdoj.gov/bjs/glance/tables/hmrttab.htm], accessed on April 5, 2005.
13. Jay Bookman, "Greatest Fear Isn't Terrorists, It's Change," *Atlanta Journal-Constitution*, November 15, 2004, p. A11.
14. "Police Foundation Releases Most Comprehensive Information to Date on America's Private Stock of Firearms," Police Foundation, May 5, 1997 [http://www.policefoundation.org], accessed on January 20, 2005, citing Philip J. Cook and Jens Ludwig, *Guns in America: Results of a Comprehensive National Survey on Firearms Ownership and Use* (Washington, D.C.: Police Foundation, 1996).
15. James J. Stephan and Jennifer C. Karberg, "Census of State and Federal Correctional Facilities, 2000," Bureau of Justice Statistics,

August 2003, rev. October 15, 2003 [http://www.ojp.usdoj.gov/bjs/pub/pdf/csfcf00.pdf], accessed on February 7, 2005; *2003 Annual Report* (Washington, D.C.: Marriott International, 2004) [http://ir.shareholder.com/mar/downloads/2003annualreport.pdf], accessed on February 7, 2005; *2003 Annual Report* (Nashville, Tenn.: Corrections Corporation of America, 2004) [http://www.shareholder.com/cxw/downloads/cca2003ar_final.pdf]. Marriott Hotels' 490,600 rooms brought in operating income of $702 million in 2003, while the Corrections Corporation's 65,000 beds produced an operating income of $168 million.

16. Home page, U.S. Census Bureau [http://www.census.gov/], accessed on January 19, 2005; Roy Walmsley, *Findings: World Prison Population List,* 5th ed. (London: Home Office, 2003) [http://www.nicic.org/Library/019412], accessed on January 19, 2005.
17. "Entire World: Prison Population Rates per 100,000 of the National Population," International Centre for Prison Studies, King's College, London, updated January 11, 2004 [http://www.prisonstudies.org/], accessed on March 18, 2005.
18. "Facts About Prisons and Prisoners," Sentencing Project, November 2004 [http://www.sentencingproject.org/pdfs/1035.pdf], accessed on January 21, 2005.
19. James J. Stephan, "State Prison Expenditures, 2001," p. 3; "Tuition and Fees, 2001–2002," Harvard University.
20. "Direct Expenditures by Criminal Justice Function"; "Department of Education," Budget of the United States Government, Fiscal Year 2003 [http://www.gpoaccess.gov/usbudget/fy03/pdf/bud13.pdf], p. 116, accessed on March 30, 2005.
21. "Death Penalty," Amnesty International USA [http://www.amnestyusa.org/abolish/document.do?id=3E4211D4A5E4D9A080256E67005A4CAE], accessed on January 20, 2005.
22. Raymond Bonner and Ford Fessenden, "States with No Death Penalty Share Lower Homicide Rates," *New York Times*, September 22, 2000, p. A1. See also "Facts About Deterrence and the Death Penalty," Death Penalty Information Center [http://www.deathpenaltyinfo.org/article.php?scid=12&did=167], accessed on January 20, 2005.

23. "Seventh United Nations Survey of Crime Trends and Operations of Criminal Justice Systems, Covering the Period 1998–2000," United Nations, April 2001 [http://www.unodc.org/unodc/crime_cicp_survey_seventh.html], accessed on April 5, 2005.
24. Patrick A. Langan and David J. Levin, "Recidivism of Prisoners Released in 1994," Bureau of Justice Statistics, June 2002 [http://www.ojp.usdoj.gov/bjs/abstract/rpr94.htm], accessed on April 5, 2005.
25. Christopher J. Mumola, "Incarcerated Parents and Their Children," Bureau of Justice Statistics, August 2000 [http://www.ojp.usdoj.gov/bjs/pub/pdf/iptc.pdf], accessed on January 27, 2005.
26. "Federal Resource Center for Children of Prisoners," Child Welfare League of America, [http://www.cwla.org/programs/incarcerated/], accessed on January 27, 2005.
27. "Fatherless Youth at Higher Risk for Jail—Study," Reuters, August 20, 1998 [http://www.prisonactivist.org/pipermail/prisonact-list/1998-August/002185.html], accessed on June 15, 2005.
28. Seventh United Nations Survey of Crime Trends and Operations of Criminal Justice Systems, covering the period 1998–2000 (New York, NY: United Nations, April 2001) [http://www.unodc.org/unodc/crime_cicp_survey_seventh.html], accessed on April 5, 2005.
29. James Gilligan, *Violence: Reflections on a National Epidemic* (New York: Vintage Books/Random House, 1997). See also note 33.
30. Ibid., p. 110.
31. Lawrence Mishel, Jared Bernstein, and John Schmitt, *The State of Working America, 2000–2001* (Ithaca, N.Y.: Economic Policy Institute, 2001), executive summary; Samuel Bowles, Herbert Gintis, and Melissa Osborne Groves, eds., *Unequal Chances: Family Background and Economic Success* (Princeton, N.J.: Princeton University Press, 2005).
32. Martin Luther King Jr., *The Trumpet of Conscience* (New York: HarperCollins, 1968), p. 55.
33. "Facts About Prisons and Prisoners."
34. Gilligan, *Violence*, pp. 105–107.
35. Eric D. Gould, Bruce A. Weinberg, and David B. Mustard, "Crime Rates and Local Labor Market Opportunities in the United States, 1979–1997," *Review of Economics and Statistics*, 2002, 84, 48, 58

[http://www.terry.uga.edu/~dmustard/labor.pdf], accessed on March 26, 2005.

36. James Gilligan, *Preventing Violence* (New York: Thames & Hudson, 2001), p. 45, citing Mishel, Bernstein and Schmitt, *State of Working America, 2000–2001*.
37. Ibid., pp. 39, 45.
38. Cindy Struckman-Johnson and David Struckman-Johnson, "Sexual Coercion Rates in Seven Midwestern Prison Facilities for Men," *Prison Journal*, 2000, *80*, 379–390 [http://www.spr.org/pdf/struckman.pdf], accessed on October 11, 2004; Gilligan, *Violence*, p. 165.
39. Gilligan, *Violence*, p. 163.
40. Ralph Banay, "Should Prisons Be Abolished?" *New York Times Magazine*, January 30, 1955.
41. Several of the glimpses draw on stories written for the American News Service (1995–2000), founded by Frances Moore Lappé and Paul Martin Du Bois. To search the complete archive, go to http://www.smallplanetinstitute.org/ans.php.
42. Jenifer Warren, "State Is Joining Shift on Prisons," *Los Angeles Times*, March 27, 2005.
43. Ibid.
44. Marcus Nieto, "Adult Parole and Probation in California," California Research Bureau, September 2003 [http://www.library.ca.gov/crb/03/09/03-009.pdf], p. 1, accessed on February, 15, 2005.
45. "Reforming Corrections: Report of the Corrections Independent Review Panel," June 2004 [http://cpr.ca.gov/report/indrpt/corr/index.htm], accessed on March 14, 2005.
46. Dana King, "San Quentin Inmates Serving Time on a Yoga Mat?" CBS 5, March 10, 2005 [http://www2.cbs5.com/30minutesbayarea/local_story_069163552.html], accessed March 31, 2005.
47. Quoted in Mark Martin, "New Director of State Prisons Believes in Rehabilitating, Not Recycling, Inmates," *San Francisco Chronicle*, June 21, 2004, p. A1.
48. "Resolve to Stop the Violence Project," Reentry National Media Outreach Program, [http://www.reentrymediaoutreach.org/sp_public_rsvp.htm], accessed on February 10, 2005; personal communication from

Jerry Scoggins, RSVP, San Francisco, February 8, 2005. RSVP participants are required to participate in the program as part of their sentence or condition of probation, are recruited from a county jail, or can request to participate in the program. All participants must have been charged with a violent offense.

49. Personal communication from Jerry Scoggins, February 3, 2005.
50. "RSVP: Resolve to Stop the Violence Project," San Francisco Sheriff's Department [http://www.sfgov.org/site/sheriff_index.asp?id=25413], accessed on February 10, 2005.
51. "Resolve to Stop the Violence Project."
52. James Gilligan and Bandy Lee, "The Resolve to Stop the Violence Project: Reducing Violence Through a Jail-Based Initiative," unpublished article received from Jerry Scoggins, February 3, 2005.
53. Ibid.
54. Martin, "New Director of State Prisons."
55. Warren, "State Is Joining Shift."
56. Many of these innovations are promoted by National Crime Prevention Council [http://www.ncpc.org].
57. William Bole, "Novel Approach to Sentencing Has Criminals Hitting the Books, Going Straight," American News Service, 1996.
58. "Alternative Sentencing Program Honored with New England Board of Higher Education Excellence Award," Supreme Judicial Court, February 27, 2004 [http://cltl.umassd.edu/pdf/outreachpress3c.pdf], accessed on February 24, 2005.
59. "Reforming the Juvenile Justice System," Center on Juvenile and Criminal Justice, [http://www.cjcj.org/jjic/reforming.php], accessed on February 25, 2005.
60. Mieke H. Bomann, "Prison Tensions Cool When Inmates Seek Training as Mediators," American News Service, 1998.
61. The Garden Project's motto is "We don't just grow plants; we grow people too!"
62. "Programs," Garden Project [http://www.gardenproject.org/grow people/programs/programs.htm], accessed on February 26, 2005.
63. Nieto, "Adult Parole and Probation," p. 1; "Sowing the Seeds: Community Rehabilitation Through Gardening," forum moderated by Rev. Alan Jones, Grace Cathedral, San Francisco, October 26, 2003

[http://www.gracecathedral.org/forum/for_20031026.shtml], accessed on February 15, 2005.

64. Story adapted from James V. O'Connor, "Citizens Put the Community in Community Policing," American News Service, 1996.
65. Personal correspondence from Mike Erp, executive director, Washington State Institute for Community Oriented Policing, Spokane, Wash., March 30, 2005.
66. Interview with Lieutenant Larry Powell, January 14, 2005.
67. "2006 Budget Proposal: Agency Breakdown," *Washingon Post*, February 7, 2005.
68. "MAD DADS to Move Headquarters from Omaha," *Grand Island* (Nebr.) *Independent*, March 29, 2001 [http://www.theindependent.com/stories/032901/new_maddadmove29.html], accessed on March 7, 2005. For more information, contact: MAD DADS, 555 Stockton Street, Jacksonville, FL 32204, tel. (904) 388-8171, http://www.maddads.com.
69. Mark Lewis, "A New Approach to Nonviolent Crime," American News Service, 1995. Name of offender has been changed.
70. "About Youth Justice: Overview of Principles and Process," Youth Court of New Zealand [http://www.justice.govt.nz/youth/aboutyj.html], accessed on February 28, 2005.
71. Gordon Bazemore and Mara Schiff, *Juvenile Justice Reform and Restorative Justice* (Devon, England: Willan, 2005), p. 101.
72. Story adapted from Nancy Weil, "In Teen Courts, Young People Set Their Peers Straight," American News Service, 1996.
73. "Youth Court List by State," National Youth Court Center, American Probation and Parole Association [http://www.youthcourt.net/national_listing/overview.htm], accessed on January 26, 2005.
74. Story adapted from Paul Bush, "Forgoing the Courtroom, More Americans Try Do-It-Yourself Approach to Justice," American News Service, 1996.
75. "Overview of Community Mediation," National Association for Community Mediation [http://www.nafcm.org/pg5.cfm], accessed on September 15, 2004.
76. Ibid.; "Community Dispute Resolution Program Annual Report, 2003" Office of Dispute Resolution, Michigan State Court Admin-

istrative Office, 2003 [http://www.courts.michigan.gov/scao/resources/publications/reports/CDRPAnnualReport2003V2.pdf], accessed on January 24, 2005.

77. Edgar S. Cahn, *No More Throw-Away People: The Co-Production Imperative* (Washington, D.C.: Essential Books, 2000), p. 7. For more information, contact Time Dollar USA, 5500 Thirty-Ninth Street N.W., Washington, DC 20015, tel. (202) 686-5200, contact@timedollar.org, http://www.timedollar.org.
78. Edgar S. Cahn, "The Time Dollar Youth Court: Salvaging Throw-Away Juveniles," *Criminal Justice Magazine*, 2000, *15*(1) [http://www.abanet.org/crimjust/cjmag/15-1/cahn.html], accessed on July 9, 2004.
79. Courtland Milloy, "Reprimands That Resonate," *Washington Post*, March 17, 1999, p. B1.
80. Personal communication from Carolyn Dallas, executive director, Time Dollar Youth Court, Washington, D.C., January 18, 2005.
81. Cahn, "Time Dollar Youth Court."
82. Personal communication from Edgar S. Cahn, June 8, 2004.
83. Ibid. See also Edgar S. Cahn, "Time Dollars: A New Currency in Community Building" [http://www.islandcounty.net/health/time_dollars.htm], accessed on July 7, 2004.
84. Jane Braxton Little, "New System of Swapping Services Brings Neighbors and Needs Together," American News Service, 1996.
85. Ibid.
86. For more information on time-dollar-type services, contact Time Dollar Youth Court, 409 East Street N.W., Building B, Washington, DC 20001, tel. (202) 508-1612, zfowlk@cs.com, http://www.timedollar.org; Ethan Allen Institute, 4836 Kirby Mountain Road, Concord, VT 05824, tel. (802) 695-1448, http://www.ethanallen.org; Member-to-Member, Elderplan, Inc., 745 Sixty-Fourth Street, Brooklyn, NY 11220, tel. (718) 921-7909, customerservice@elderplan.org, http://www.elderplan.org/programs/member_to_member.shtml.
87. Jason Fields, "America's Families and Living Arrangements, 2003," U.S. Census Bureau, November 2004 [http://www.census.gov/prod/2004pubs/p20-553.pdf], accessed on January 21, 2005.
88. Putnam, *Bowling Alone*.
89. Saad, "U.S. Crime Problem Less Troubling."

90. For more information, contact Conversation Cafés, New Road Map Foundation, P.O. Box 15320, Seattle, WA 98115, tel. (206) 527-0437, info@conversationcafe.org, http://www.conversationcafe.org.
91. Contact National Coalition for Dialogue and Deliberation, P.O. Box 402, Brattleboro, VT 05302, tel. (802) 254-7341, ncdd@thataway.org, http://www.thataway.org.
92. "Event Ideas," September Project, Seattle [http://www.theseptember project.org/events.htm], accessed on February 13, 2005.
93. Martin Luther King Jr., "Letter from Birmingham Jail," April 16, 1963 [http://www.thekingcenter.org/prog/non/Letter.pdf], accessed on February 15, 2005.

Chapter Twelve: The Invitation

1. Jared Diamond, *Collapse: How Societies Choose to Fail or Succeed* (New York: Viking, 2005).
2. Solomon E. Asch, "Opinions and Social Pressure," *Scientific American*, November 1955, pp. 31–35.
3. Frances Moore Lappé and Jeffrey Perkins, *You Have the Power: Choosing Courage in a Culture of Fear* (New York: Tarcher/Penguin, 2004).
4. Vaclav Havel, "The European Experiment," TomPaine.com, November 15, 2004 [http://www.tompaine.com/articles/the_european_exper iment.php], accessed on March 23, 2005.

ENTRY POINTS FOR LIVING DEMOCRACY

Thousands of citizen organizations nationwide are making our democracy come alive to solve real problems. Space allows us to list only organizations and resources highlighted in the book, with a few exceptions. Please visit our Web site for additional suggestions. Many have newsletters and other publications. Some have training programs. Get in touch!

Also, search the American News Service online archive for stories of citizens solving some of the country's biggest problems—from health care to reforming prisons—at http://www.smallplanetinstitute.org/ans.php.

National Multi-Issue

Association of Community Organizations for Reform Now (ACORN)
(Local chapters all over the United States)
739 Eighth Street, S.E.
Washington, DC 20003
Tel.: (877) 55ACORN
E-mail: natacorndc@acorn.org
Web site: http://www.acorn.org

Bioneers
6 Cerro Circle
Lamy, NM 87540
Tel.: (877) BIONEER
E-mail: info@bioneers.org
Web site: http://www.bioneers.org

The Gamaliel Foundation
203 North Wabash Avenue, Suite 808
Chicago, IL 60601
Tel.: (312) 357–2639
E-mail: gamalielus@sbcglobal.net
Web site: http://www.gamaliel.org

Industrial Areas Foundation (IAF)
220 West Kinzie Street, 5th Floor
Chicago, IL 60610
Tel.: (312) 245–9211
E-mail: iaf@industrialareasfoundation.org
Web site: http://www.industrialareasfoundation.org

National People's Action (NPA)
810 Milwaukee Avenue
Chicago, IL 60622
Tel.: (312) 243–3038
E-mail: npa@npa-us.org
Web site: http://www.npa-us.org

National Training and Information Center (NTIC)
810 North Milwaukee Avenue
Chicago, IL 60622
Tel.: (312) 243–3035
E-mail: NTIC@NTIC-US.ORG
Web site: http://www.ntic-us.org

Pacific Institute for Community Organization (PICO)
171 Santa Rosa Avenue
Oakland, CA 94610
Tel.: (510) 655–2801
Web site: http://www.piconetwork.org

Affiliated with the Industrial Areas Foundation

Allied Communities of Tarrant (ACT)
P.O. Box 3565
Fort Worth, TX 76113
Tel.: (817) 332–1830
E-mail: actpower@swbell.net

Baltimoreans United in Leadership Development (BUILD)
2114 North Charles Street
Baltimore, MD 21218
Tel.: (410) 528–0305
E-mail: buildiaf@erols.com
Web site: http://www.buildiaf.org

Communities Organized for Public Service (COPS)
925 San Pedro Avenue
San Antonio, TX 78212
Tel.: (210) 222–2367
E-mail: copsmetro@sbcglobal.net
Web site: http://www.industrialareasfoundation.org/iafaffiliates/iafaffiliatessw.htm

East Brooklyn Congregations (EBC)
440 Watkins Street
Brooklyn, NY 11212
Tel.: (718) 498–4099
E-mail: ebcteam@aol.com
Web site: http://www.industrialareasfoundation.org/iafaffiliates/iafaffiliatesne.htm

Greater Boston Interfaith Organization
307 Bowdoin Street
Dorchester, MA 02122
Tel.: (617) 825–5600
E-mail: office@gbio.org
Web site: http://www.gbio.org

Metro Alliance
925 San Pedro Avenue
San Antonio, TX 78212
Tel.: (210) 222–8562

Shelby County Interfaith
1300 Monroe Avenue
Memphis, TN 38104
Tel.: (901) 278–6800

Regional and Citywide Multi-Issue

Hartford Areas Rally Together (HART)
423 Washington Street
Hartford, CT 06106
Tel.: (860) 525–3449
Web site: http://www.hartnet.org/hart

InterValley Project
95 Fair Oaks Avenue
Newton, MA 02460
Tel.: (617) 796–8836
E-mail: intervalleyp@aol.com
Web site: http://www.intervalleyproject.org

Kentuckians for the Commonwealth (KFTC)
P.O. Box 1450
London, KY 40743
Tel.: (606) 878–2161
E-mail: kftc@adelphia.net
Web site: http://www.kftc.org

Pennsylvania Environmental Network (PEN)
P.O. Box 92
Fombell, PA 16123
Tel.: (724) 910–0660
E-mail: pen@penweb.org
Web site: http://www.penweb.org

Working for a More Democratic Political System (Chapter Four)

National

The Alliance for Democracy
P.O. Box 540115
760 Main Street
Waltham, MA 02454
Tel.: (781) 894–1179
E-mail: afd@theallianceforddemocracy.org
Web site: http://www.theallianceforddemocracy.org

Center for Responsive Politics
1101 Fourteenth Street, N.W., Suite 1030
Washington, DC 20005
Tel.: (202) 857–0044
E-mail: info@crp.org
Web site: http://www.opensecrets.org

Center for Voting and Democracy
6930 Carroll Avenue, Suite 610
Takoma Park, MD 20912
Tel.: (301) 270–4616
E-mail: irv@fairvote.org
Web site: http://www.fairvote.org/irv

Clean Elections Institute, Inc.
2702 North Third Street, Suite 4010
Phoenix, AZ 85004
Tel.: (602) 840–6633
Web site: http://www.azclean.org

Common Cause
1250 Connecticut Avenue, N.W., Suite 600
Washington, DC 20036
Tel.: (202) 833–1200
Web site: http://www.commoncause.org

InstantRunoff.com
Midwest Democracy Center
325 West Huron Avenue, Suite 304
Chicago, IL 60610
Tel.: (312) 587–7060
Web site: http://www.instantrunoff.com

League of Independent Voters/League of Pissed-Off Voters
226 West 135th Street, 4th Floor
New York, NY 10030
Tel.: (212) 283–8879
E-mail: Contactus@indyvoter.org
Web site: http://www.indyvoter.org

League of Women Voters
1730 M Street, N.W., Suite 1000
Washington, DC 20036
Tel.: (202) 429–1965
Web site: http://www.lwv.org

Public Campaign
1320 Nineteenth Street, N.W., Suite M1
Washington, DC 20036
Tel.: (202) 293–0222
E-mail: info@publicampaign.org
Web site: http://www.publicampaign.org

Public Citizen
1600 Twentieth Street, N.W.
Washington, DC 20009
Tel.: (202) 588–1000
Web site: http://www.citizen.org

Working Families Party
88 Third Avenue
Brooklyn, NY 11217
Tel.: (718) 222–3796
E-mail: wfp@workingfamiliesparty.org
Web site: http://www.workingfamiliesparty.org

Midwest

Dakota Rural Action
P.O. Box 549
Brookings, SD 57006
Tel.: (605) 697–5204
E-mail: action@dakotarural.org
Web site: http://www.dakotarural.org

Northeast

Maine Citizens for Clean Elections
1 Pleasant Street
Portland, ME 04101
Tel.: (207) 780–8657
E-mail: info@mainecleanelections.org
Web site: http://www.mainecleanelections.org

Working for a More Democratic Economy (Chapter Six)

National

American Independent Business Alliance (AMIBA)
222 South Black Avenue
Bozeman, MT 59715
Tel.: (406) 582–1255
E-mail: info@AMIBA.net
Web site: http://www.amiba.net

As You Sow Foundation
311 California Street, Suite 510
San Francisco, CA 94104
Tel.: (415) 391–3212
E-mail: asyousow@asyousow.org
Web site: http://www.asyousow.org

Business Alliance for Local Living Economies (BALLE)
275 Fifth Street
San Francisco, CA 94103
Tel.: (415) 348–6284
E-mail: sean@livingeconomies.org
Web site: http://www.livingeconomies.org

Center for Working Capital
888 Sixteenth Street, N.W.
Washington, DC 20006
Tel.: (202) 974–8020
E-mail: CWC@centerforworkingcapital.org
Web site: http://www.centerforworkingcapital.org

Citizens Trade Campaign
P.O. Box 77077
Washington, DC 20013
Tel.: (202) 778–3320
E-mail: info@citizenstrade.org
Web site: http://www.citizenstrade.org

Clean Clothes Connection
Peace Through Interamerican Community Action
170 Park Street
Bangor, ME 04401
Tel.: (207) 947–4203
E-mail: info@pica.ws
Web site: http://www.cleanclothesconnection.org/search.asp

Coalition for Environmentally Responsible Economies (CERES)
99 Chauncy Street, 6th Floor
Boston, MA 02111
Tel.: (617) 247–0700
Web site: http://www.ceres.org

Co-op America
1612 K Street NW, Suite 600
Washington, DC 20006
Tel: (800) 584–7336
Web site: http://www.coopamerica.org

Corporate Accountability International
46 Plympton Street
Boston, MA 02118
Tel.: (617) 695–2525
Web site: http://www.stopcorporateabuse.org

The Corporation
Web site: http://www.thecorporation.com/

Domini Social Investments
P.O. Box 9785
Providence, RI 02940
Tel.: (800) 762–6814
Web site: http://www.domini.com

Dow Jones Sustainability World Index (DJSI World)
SAM Indexes GmbH
Seefeldstrasse 215
8008 Zurich, Switzerland
Tel.: (+41–1) 395–2828
E-mail: info@sustainability-indexes.com
Web site: http://www.sustainability-index.com

Ecological Footprint Quiz
Web site: http://www.myfootprint.org

E. F. Schumacher Society
140 Jug End Road
Great Barrington, MA 01230
Tel.: (413) 528–1737
E-mail: efssociety@smallisbeautiful.org
Web site: http://www.schumachersociety.org

Fair Labor Association (FLA)
1505 Twenty-Second Street, N.W.
Washington, DC 20037
Tel.: (202) 898–1000
Web site: http://www.fairlabor.org

Fair Trade Resource Network
P.O. Box 33772
Washington, DC 20033
Tel.: (202) 234–6797
Web site: http://www.fairtraderesource.org

GreenMoney Journal
P.O. Box 469078
Escondido, CA 92046
Tel.: (800) 849–8751
E-mail: greenmoney@pcspublink.com
Web site: http://www.greenmoney.com

Greenpeace, Inc.
United States Office
702 H Street, N.W., Suite 300
Washington, DC 20001
Tel.: (800) 326–0959
E-mail: info@wdc.greenpeace.org
Web site: http://www.greenpeaceusa.org

IdealsWork.com
Web site: http://www.idealswork.com

Institute for Local Self-Reliance
1313 Fifth Street S.E.
Minneapolis, MN 55414
Tel.: (612) 379–3815
Web site: http://www.ilsr.org; http://www.newrules.org

International Labor Organization
United States Office
1828 L Street, N.W., Suite 600
Washington, DC 20036
Tel.: (202) 653–7652
E-mail: washilo@ilowbo.org
Web site: http://www.us.ilo.org

National Center for Employee Ownership (NCEO)
1736 Franklin Street, 8th Floor
Oakland, CA 94612
Tel.: (510) 208–1300
E-mail: nceo@nceo.org
Web site: http://www.nceo.org

National Cooperative Business Association
1401 New York Avenue, N.W., Suite 1100
Washington, DC 20005
Tel.: (202) 638–6222
E-mail: ncba@ncba.coop
Web site: http://www.ncba.coop

National Interfaith Coalition for Worker Justice (NICWJ)
1020 West Bryn Mawr Avenue, 4th Floor
Chicago, IL 60660
Tel.: (773) 728–8400
E-mail: bridget@nicwj.org
Web site: http://www.nicwj.org

Natural Step
50 Osgood Place, Penthouse
San Francisco, CA 94105
Tel.: (415) 318–8170
E-mail: services@naturalstep.org
Web site: http://www.naturalstep.org

Program on Corporations, Law and Democracy (POCLAD)
P.O. Box 246
South Yarmouth, MA 02664
Tel.: (508) 398–1145
E-mail: people@poclad.org
Web site: http://www.poclad.org

Rainforest Action Network (RAN)
221 Pine Street, Suite 500
San Francisco, CA 94104
Tel.: (415) 398–4404
E-mail: rainforest@ran.org
Web site: http://www.ran.org

ReclaimDemocracy.org
222 South Black Avenue
Bozeman, MT 59715
Tel.: (406) 582–1224
Web site: http://reclaimdemocracy.org

Redefining Progress
1904 Franklin Street, 6th Floor
Oakland, CA 94612
Tel.: (510) 444–3041
E-mail: info@rprogress.org
Web site: http://www.rprogress.org

Social Accountability International (SAI)
220 East Twenty-Third Street, Suite 605
New York, NY 10010
Tel.: (212) 684–1414
E-mail: info@sa-intl.org
Web site: http://www.cepaa.org

Social Investment Forum
1612 K Street, N.W., Suite 650
Washington, DC 20006
Tel.: (202) 872–5319
Web site: http://www.socialinvest.org; http://www.communityinvest.org; http://www.shareholderaction.org

Sustainable Connections
Bellingham Towers
119 North Commercial Street, Suite 350
Bellingham, WA 98225
Tel.: (360) 647–7093
Web site: http://www.sconnect.org

TransFair USA
1611 Telegraph Avenue, Suite 900
Oakland, CA 94612
Tel.: (510) 663–5260
E-mail: info@transfairusa.org
Web site: http://www.transfairusa.org

Trillium Asset Management
711 Atlantic Avenue
Boston, MA 02111
Tel.: (800) 548–5684
Web site: http://www.trilliuminvest.com

Unionwear
E-mail: resource@unionwear.com
Web site: http://www.unionwear.com

United Nations Global Reporting Initiative (GRI)
Keizersgracht 209
Postbus 10039
N-1001 EA Amsterdam, Netherlands
Tel.: (+31–0–20) 531 00 00
Fax: (+31–0–20) 531 00 31
E-mail: info@globalreporting.org
Web site: http://www.globalreporting.org

United Students Against Sweatshops (USAS)
1150 Seventeenth Street, N.W., Suite 300
Washington, DC 20036
Tel.: (202) 667–9328
E-mail: organize@usasnet.org
Web site: http://www.studentsagainstsweatshops.org

United Students for Fair Trade
E-mail: linam@gwu.edu
Web site: http://www.usft.org

Verité
44 Belchertown Road
Amherst, MA 01002
Tel.: (413) 253–9227
E-mail: verite@verite.org
Web site: http://www.verite.org

Workers Rights Consortium (WRC)
5 Thomas Circle, N.W., 5th Floor
Washington, DC 20005
Tel.: (202) 387–4884
E-mail: wrc@workersrights.org
Web site: http://www.workersrights.org

Midwest

Bethel New Life, Inc.
4950 West Thomas Street
Chicago, IL 60651
Tel.: (773) 473–7870
Fax: (773) 473–7871
Web site: http://www.bethelnewlife.org

Land Stewardship Project
2200 Fourth Street
White Bear Lake, MN 55110
Tel.: (651) 653–0618
Web site: http://www.landstewardshipproject.org

McKay Nursery
P.O. Box 185
Waterloo, WI 53594
Tel.: (800) 236–4242
E-mail: info@mckaynursery.com
Web site: http://www.mckaynursery.com

Powell Mercantile
227 North Bent Street
Powell, WY 82435
Tel.: (307) 754–5888

ShoreBank Corporation
7054 South Jeffery Boulevard
Chicago, IL 60649
Tel.: (800) 669–7725
E-mail: Information@shorebankcorp.com
Web site: http://www.shorebankcorp.com

Northeast

Coastal Enterprises, Inc.
36 Water Street
P.O. Box 268
Wiscasset, ME 04578
Tel.: (207) 882–7552
E-mail: cei@ceimaine.org
Web site: http://www.ceimaine.org

Community Environmental Legal Defense Fund
675 Mower Road
Chambersburg, PA 17201
Tel.: (717) 709–0457
E-mail: info@celdf.org
Web site: http://www.celdf.org

Cooperative Home Care Associates
349 East 149th Street
Bronx, NY 10451
Tel.: (718) 993–7104
Web site: http://www.chcany.org

Friends and Residents of Saint Thomas (FROST)
P.O. Box 457
Saint Thomas, PA 17252
Web site: http://www.friendsandresidents.com

Ithaca Hours
Web site: http://www.ithacahours.com

Justice Clothing
48 Main Street
Bangor, ME 04401
Tel.: (207) 941–9912
E-mail: info@justiceclothing.com
Web site: http://www.justiceclothing.com

Member-to-Member
Elderplan
745 Sixty-Fourth Street
Brooklyn, NY 11220
Tel.: (718) 921–7909
E-mail: info@elderplan.org
Web site: http://www.elderplan.org

New Community Corporation
233 Market Street
Newark, NJ 07103
Tel.: (973) 623–2800
E-mail: info@newcommunity.org
Web site: http://www.newcommunity.org

No Sweat Apparel
14B Felton Street
Waltham, MA 02453
Tel.: (877) 992–7827
E-mail: info@nosweatapparel.com
Web site: http://www.nosweatapparel.com

Restaurant Opportunities Center of New York (ROC-NY)
99 Hudson Street, 3rd Floor
New York, NY 10013
Tel.: (212) 343–1771
E-mail: siby@rocny.org
Web site: http://www.rocny.org

Walden Asset Management
40 Court Street
Boston, MA 02108
Tel.: (617) 726–7250
Web site: http://www.waldenassetmgmt.com

White Dog Café
3420 Sansom Street
Philadelphia, PA 19104
Tel.: (215) 386–9224
E-mail: info@whitedog.com
Web site: http://www.whitedog.com

South

Center for Community Self-Help/Self-Help Credit Union
P.O. Box 3619
Durham, NC 27702
Tel.: (919) 956–4400
Web site: http://www.self-help.org

Quality Employment Through Skills Training
(Project QUEST, Inc.)
301 South Frio Street, Suite 400
San Antonio, TX 78207
Tel.: (210) 270–4690
Web site: http://www.questsa.com

West

Bi-Mart
220 South Seneca Road
Eugene, OR 97402
Tel.: (800) 456–0681
E-mail: comments@bimart.com
Web site: http://www.bimart.com

California Public Employees' Retirement System (CalPERS)
Lincoln Plaza
400 P Street
Sacramento, CA 95814
Tel.: (888) 225–7377
Web site: http://www.calpers.ca.gov

Democracy Unlimited of Humboldt County
P.O. Box 610
Eureka, CA 95502
E-mail: info@DUHC.org
Web site: http://www.duhc.org

Los Angeles Alliance for a New Economy (LAANE)
215 West Sixth Street, Suite 1204
Los Angeles, CA 90014
Tel.: (213) 486–9880
E-mail: info@laane.org
Web site: http://www.laane.org

Salt Lake Vest Pocket Business Coalition
P.O. Box 521357
Salt Lake City, UT 84152
Tel.: (801) 596–8977
E-mail: info@vestpocket.org
Web site: http://www.vestpocket.org

Working for a More Democratic, Sustainable Approach to Food (Chapter Eight)

National

American Community Garden Association
Council on the Environment of New York City
51 Chambers Street, Suite 228
New York, NY 10007
Tel.: (877) 275–2242
Web site: http://www.communitygarden.org

American Corn Growers Association
P.O. Box 18157
Washington, DC 20036
Tel.: (202) 835–0330
E-mail: ACGA@ACGA.org
Web site: http://www.acga.org

Community Food Security Coalition
P.O. Box 209
Venice, CA 90294
Tel.: (310) 822–5410
Web site: http://www.foodsecurity.org

EarthSave International
P.O. Box 96
New York, NY 10108
Tel.: (800) 362–3648
E-mail: information@earthsave.org
Web site: http://www.earthsave.org

Food First/Institute for Food and Development Policy
398 Sixtieth Street
Oakland, CA 94618
Tel.: (510) 654–4400
E-mail: foodfirst@foodfirst.org
Web site: http://www.foodfirst.org

Global Resource Action Center for the Environment (GRACE)
215 Lexington Avenue, Suite 1001
New York, NY 10016
Tel.: (212) 726–9161
E-mail: info@gracelinks.org
Web site: http://www.gracelinks.org

Heifer International
P.O. Box 8058
Little Rock, AR 72203
Tel.: (800) 422–0474
Web site: http://www.heifer.org

Institute for Agriculture and Trade Policy
2105 First Avenue South
Minneapolis, MN 55404
Tel.: (612) 870–0453
E-mail: iatp@iatp.org
Web site: http://www.iatp.org

Local Harvest
220 Twenty-First Avenue
Santa Cruz, CA 95062
Tel.: (831) 475–8150
E-mail: gpayet@localharvest.org
Web site: http://www.localharvest.org

National Campaign for Sustainable Agriculture
P.O. Box 396
Pine Bush, NY 12566
Tel.: (845) 361–5201
E-mail: campaign@sustainableagriculture.net
Web site: http://www.sustainableagriculture.net

National Cooperative Grocers Association
1 Timber Way, Suite 101
Daphne, AL 36526
Tel.: (251) 621–7675
Web site: http://www.ncga.coop

National Farm to School Program
Center for Food and Justice
Urban and Environmental Policy Institute
Occidental College
1600 Campus Road
Mail Stop M1
Los Angeles, CA 90041
Tel.: (323) 341–5095
Web site: http://www.farmtoschool.org

National Gardening Association
1100 Dorset Street
South Burlington, VT 05403
Tel.: (800) 538–7476
Web site: http://www.kidsgardening.com

Organic Consumers Association
6101 Cliff Estate Road
Little Marais, MN 55614
Tel.: (218) 226–4164
Web site: http://www.organicconsumers.org

Midwest

George Jones Farm
Ecological Design Innovation Center
Lewis Center for Environmental Studies
Oberlin College
122 Elm Street
Oberlin, OH 44074
Tel.: (440) 775–8409
Web site: http://www.neofoodshed.org/jonesfarm

Growing Power
5500 West Silver Spring Road
Milwaukee, WI 53218
Tel.: (414) 527–1546
Web site: http://www.growingpower.org

Land Stewardship Project
2200 Fourth Street
White Bear Lake, MN 55110
Tel.: (651) 653–0618
E-mail: cathye@landstewardshipproject.org
Web site: http://www.landstewardshipproject.org

Organic Valley
1 Organic Way
La Farge, WI 54639
Tel.: (888) 444–6455
E-mail: organic@organicvalley.com
Web site: http://www.organicvalley.com

Vermont Valley Community Farm
4628 City Highway FF
Blue Mounds, WI 53517
Tel.: (608) 767–3860
E-mail: farm@vermontvalley.com
Web site: http://www.vermontvalley.com

Northeast

Food Project
P.O. Box 256141
Dorchester, MA 02125
Tel.: (617) 442–1322
E-mail: info@thefoodproject.org
Web site: http://www.thefoodproject.org

Just Food
P.O. Box 20444
Greeley Square Street
New York, NY 10001
Tel.: (212) 645–9880
E-mail: info@justfood.org
Web site: http://www.justfood.org

Northeast Organic Farming Association (NOFA)
P.O. Box 135
Stevenson, CT 06491
Tel.: (203) 888–5146
E-mail: bduesing@cs.com
Web site: http://www.nofa.org

Yale Sustainable Food Project
246 Church Street
P.O. Box 208261
New Haven, CT 06511
Tel.: (203) 432–2084
E-mail: sustainablefoodproject@yale.edu
Web site: http://www.yale.edu/sustainablefood

South

Howard Lyman
Voice for a Viable Future
P.O. Box 22903
Alexandria, VA 22304
Tel.: (703) 461–3393
E-mail: hlyman@aol.com
Web site: http://www.madcowboy.com

Jane Akre and Steve Wilson
The Jane and Steve Fund
P.O. Box 3553
Ponte Vedra Beach, FL 32004
Tel.: (904) 273–0345; (727) 943–8970
E-mail: akre@foxBGHsuit.com; wilson@foxBGHsuit.com
Web site: http://www.foxbghsuit.com

West

The Edible Schoolyard
Martin Luther King Jr. Middle School
1781 Rose Street
Berkeley, CA 94703
Tel.: (510) 558–1335
E-mail: info@edibleschoolyard.org
Web site: http://www.edibleschoolyard.org

Niman Ranch
1025 East Twelfth Street
Oakland, CA 94606
Tel.: (866) 808–0340
E-mail: info@nimanranch.com
Web site: http://www.nimanranch.com

Reclaiming the Media (Chapter Nine)

Alliance for Community Media
666 Eleventh Street, N.W., Suite 740
Washington, DC 20001
Tel.: (202) 393–2650
E-mail: acm@alliancecm.org
Web site: http://www.alliancecm.org

Allied Media Projects
P.O. Box 20128
Toledo, OH 43610
E-mail: info@alliedmediaprojects.org
Web site: http://www.clamormagazine.org/allied/about.html

Center for Digital Democracy
1718 Connecticut Avenue, N.W., Suite 200
Washington, DC 20009
Tel.: (202) 986–2220
Web site: http://www.democraticmedia.org

Center for International Media Action
1276 Bergen Street, Suite 4
Brooklyn, NY 11213
Tel.: (646) 249–3027
E-mail: cima@mediaactioncenter.org
Web site: http://www.mediaactioncenter.org

Center for Media & Democracy (publisher of PR Watch)
520 University Avenue, Suite 227
Madison, WI 53703
Tel.: (608) 260-9713
E-mail: editor@prwatch.org
Web site: http://www.prwatch.org

Fairness and Accuracy in Reporting (FAIR)
112 West Twenty-Seventh Street
New York, NY 10001
Tel.: (212) 633–6700
E-mail: fair@fair.org
Web site: http://www.fair.org

Future of Music Coalition
1615 L Street, N.W., Suite 520
Washington, DC 20036
Tel.: (202) 429–8855
Web site: http://www.futureofmusic.org

Low Power Radio Association
Excelsiorlaan 91
B-1930 Zaventem, Belgium
Tel.: (+32–2) 714 54 90
E-mail: info@lpra.org
Web site: http://www.lpra.org

Media Access Project
1625 K Street, N.W., Suite 1000
Washington, DC 20006
Tel.: (202) 232–4300
E-mail: info@mediaaccess.org
Web site: http://www.mediaaccess.org

MediaRights
104 West Fourteenth Street, 4th Floor
New York, NY 10011
Tel.: (646) 230–6288
Web site: http://www.mediarights.org

Media Tenor
15 West Twenty-Sixth Street, 5th Floor, R
New York, NY 10010
Tel.: (212) 448–0793
E-mail: r.jekielek@mediatenor.com
Web site: http://www.mediatenor.com

Microcinema International
1706 Church Street, Suite 1222
San Francisco, CA 94131
Tel.: (415) 864–0660
E-mail: info@microcinema.com
Web site: http://www.microcinema.com

MoveOn.org
Web site: http://www.moveon.org

Openflows Networks, Ltd.
40 Follis Avenue
Toronto, ON M6G 1S3, Canada
Tel.: (416) 531–5944
E-mail: info@openflows.org
Web site: http://openflows.org

PR Watch
Center for Media & Democracy
520 University Avenue, Suite 227
Madison, WI 53703
Tel.: (608) 260–9713
E-mail: editor@prwatch.org
Web site: http://www.prwatch.org

Prometheus Radio Project
P.O. Box 42158
Philadelphia, PA 19101
Tel.: (215) 727–9620
E-mail: info@prometheusradio.org
Web site: http://www.prometheusradio.org

Reclaim the Media
927 Twenty-Second Avenue
Seattle, WA 98122
E-mail: universaldeclaration@reclaimthemedia.org
Web site: http://www.reclaimthemedia.org

Third World Majority
369 Fifteenth Street
Oakland, CA 94612
Tel.: (510) 682–6624
E-mail: info@cultureisaweapon.org
Web site: http://www.cultureisaweapon.org

Media Practicing Living Democracy (Chapter Nine)

AlterNet
Web site: http://www.alternet.org

Coalition of Immokalee Workers/Radio Conciencia
P.O. Box 603
Immokalee, FL 34143
Tel.: (239) 657–8311
E-mail: workers@ciw-online.org
Web site: http://www.ciw-online.org

Common Dreams News Center
Web site: http://www.commondreams.org

Democracy Now!
P.O. Box 693
New York, NY 10013
Tel.: (212) 431–9090
E-mail: mail@democracynow.org
Web site: http://www.democracynow.org

Free Press
100 Main Street
P.O. Box 28
Northampton, MA 01061
Tel.: (866) 666–1533
Web site: http://www.freepress.net

Free Speech TV
P.O. Box 6060
Boulder, CO 80306
Tel.: (303) 442–8445
Web site: http://www.freespeech.org

Guerrilla News Network/GNN.tv
Web site: http://www.guerrillanews.com

Hometown Utilicom (public Internet utility)
45 Railroad Street
Kutztown, PA 19530
Tel.: (610) 683–6131
E-mail: services@kutztownboro.org
Web site: http://www.hometownutilicom.org

Independent Media Center
Web site: http://www.indymedia.org/en/index.shtml

In the Mix
114 East Thirty-Second Street, Suite 903
New York, NY 10016
Tel.: (800) 597–9448
E-mail: inthemix@pbs.org
Web site: http://www.pbs.org/inthemix

KRBS-lp 107.1 FM
P.O. Box 9
Oroville, CA 95965
Tel.: (530) 534–1200
E-mail: krbs@cncnet.com
Web site: http://www.radiobirdstreet.org

The Meatrix
Web site: http://www.themeatrix.com

Pacifica Radio
1925 Martin Luther King Jr. Way
Berkeley, CA 94704
Tel.: (510) 849–2590
E-mail: contact@pacifica.org
Web site: http://www.pacifica.org

Rooftop Films
232 Third Street, Studio E103
Brooklyn, NY 11215
Tel.: (877) 786–1912
E-mail: info@rooftopfilms.com
Web site: http://www.rooftopfilms.com

Simple Machines Records
3819 Beecher Street, N.W.
Washington, DC 20007
Tel.: (703) 351–7507
E-mail: info@simplemachines.net
Web site: http://www.simplemachines.net

Thin Air Radio
35 West Main Street, Suite 340E
Spokane, WA 99201
Tel.: (509) 747–3807
Web site: h8ttp://www.thinairradio.org

Tompaine.com
Web site: http://www.tompaine.com

TruthOut
Web site: http://truthout.org

Working Films
602 South Fifth Avenue
Wilmington, NC 28401
Tel.: (910) 342–9000
E-mail: mramey@workingfilms.org
Web site: http://www.workingfilms.org

Facilitating Collaborative Problem Solving (Chapter Seven)

National

Coalition for Healthier Cities and Communities
1 North Franklin
Chicago, IL 60606
Tel.: (312) 422–2618
E-mail: info@healthycommunities.org
Web site: http://www.healthycommunities.org

Community Initiatives
2119 Mapleton Avenue
Boulder, CO 80304
Tel.: (303) 444–3366
E-mail: info@communityinitiatives.com
Web site: http://www.communityinitiatives.com

National Civic League
1445 Market Street, Suite 300
Denver, CO 80202
Tel.: (303) 571–4343
E-mail: ncl@ncl.org
Web site: http://www.ncl.org

National League of Cities
1301 Pennsylvania Avenue, N.W., Suite 550
Washington, DC 20004
Tel.: (202) 626–3000
E-mail: info@nlc.org
Web site: http://www.nlc.org

City Offices Promoting Citizen Participation

Portland Office of Neighborhood Involvement
1221 S.W. Fourth Avenue, Room 110
Portland, OR 97204
Tel.: (503) 823–4519
E-mail: oni@ci.portland.or.us
Web site: http://www.portlandonline.com/oni

Saint Paul Department of Planning and Economic Development
1400 City Hall Annex
25 West Fourth Street
Saint Paul, MN 55102
Tel.: (651) 266–6700
Web site: http://www.stpaul.gov/depts/ped

Seattle's Department of Neighborhoods
700 Third Avenue, Suite 400
Seattle, WA 98104
Tel.: (206) 684–0464
Web site: http://www.ci.seattle.wa.us/neighborhoods

Furthering Education for Living Democracy (Chapter Ten)

Big Picture Schools
17 Gordon Avenue, Suite 104
Providence, RI 02905
Tel.: (401) 781–1873
Web site: http://bigpicture.org

Center for Collaborative Education
1 Renaissance Park
1135 Tremont Street, Suite 490
Boston, MA 02120
Tel.: (617) 421–0134
E-mail: info@ccebos.org
Web site: http://www.ccebos.org

Coalition of Essential Schools
1814 Franklin Street, Suite 700
Oakland, CA 94612
Tel.: (510) 433–1451
Web site: http://www.essentialschools.org

Educators for Social Responsibility
23 Garden Street
Cambridge, MA 02138
Tel.: (617) 492–1764
E-mail: educators@esrnational.org
Web site: http://www.esrnational.org

Forum for Education and Democracy
P.O. Box 216
Amesville, OH 45711
Tel.: (740) 448–3402
E-mail: info@forumforeducation.org
Web site: http://www.forumforeducation.org

Institute for Student Achievement
1 Hollow Lane, Suite 100
Lake Success, NY 11042
Tel.: (516) 812–6700
Web site: http://www.studentachievement.org

KIDS Consortium
215 Lisbon Street, Suite 12
Lewiston, ME 04240
Tel.: (207) 784–0956
E-mail: kap@kidsconsortium.org
Web site: http://www.kidsconsortium.org

Lighted Schools
Communities in Schools/McLennan County Youth Collaboration, Inc. (CIS-MCYC, Inc.)
425 Austin Avenue, 5th Floor
Waco, TX 76701
Tel.: (254) 753–6002
Web site: http://www.mcycwaco.org/Lighted%20Schools.htm

Public Achievement
Center for Democracy and Citizenship
Humphrey Institute of Public Affairs
301 Nineteenth Avenue South
Minneapolis, MN 55455
Tel.: (612) 625–0142
E-mail: eeschenbacher@hhh.umn.edu
Web site: http://www.publicachievement.org

School Mediation Associates
134 Standish Road
Watertown, MA 02472
Tel.: (617) 926–0994
E-mail: sma@schoolmediation.com
Web site: http://www.schoolmediation.com

School Redesign Network
Stanford University School of Education
520 Galvez Mall
Stanford, CA 94305
Tel.: (650) 725–0703
E-mail: mrgurney@stanford.edu
Web site: http://www.schoolredesign.net

Texas Interfaith Education Fund (IEF)
1106 Clayton Lane, Suite 120W
Austin, TX 78723
Tel.: (512) 459–6551
Web site: http://www.industrialareasfoundation.org/iafaffiliates/iafaffiliatessw.htm

Schools Highlighted in This Book

Central Park East Secondary School
1573 Madison Avenue
New York, NY 10029
Tel.: (212) 860–8935

Federal Hocking Local Schools
8461 State Route 144
Stewart, OH 45778
Tel.: (740) 662–6691
Web site: http://www.federalhocking.k12.oh.us

Fenway High School
174 Ipswich Street
Boston, MA 02215
Tel.: (617) 635–9911
E-mail: fenway@boston.k12.ma.us
Web site: http://fenway.boston.k12.ma.us

Holbrook School
570 Main Road
Holden, ME 04429
Tel.: (207) 843–7769
Web site: http://www.sad63.k12.me.us/hbk.html

Hudson High School
155 Apsley Street
Hudson, MA 01749
Tel.: (978) 567–6100
Web site: http://www.hudson.k12.ma.us

Lehman Alternative Community School
111 Chestnut Street
Ithaca, NY 14850
Tel.: (607) 274–2183
Web site: http://www.icsd.k12.ny.us/acs

Morningside Middle School
2751 Mississippi Street
Fort Worth, TX 76104
Tel.: (817) 922–6680
E-mail: btrimble@fortworthisd.org
Web site: http://www.fortworthisd.org/profile/054mp.html

Involving Youth in Democratic Living and Learning (Chapters Seven and Ten)

Youth Action Program and Homes, Inc.
1325 Fifth Avenue
New York, NY 10029
Tel.: (212) 860–8170

YouthBuild USA
58 Day Street
P.O. Box 440322
Somerville, MA 02144
Tel.: (617) 623–9900
E-mail: ybinfo@youthbuild.org
Web site: http://www.youthbuild.org

Promoting Public Dialogue (Chapters Seven and Eleven)

Conversation Cafés
New Road Map Foundation
P.O. Box 15320
Seattle, WA 98115
Tel.: (206) 527–0437
E-mail: info@conversationcafe.org
Web site: http://www.conversationcafe.org

Meetup, Inc.
632 Broadway, 10th Floor
New York, NY 10012
Tel.: (212) 255–7327
Web site: http://www.meetup.com

National Coalition for Dialogue and Deliberation
P.O. Box 402
Brattleboro, VT 05302
Tel.: (802) 254–7341
E-mail: ncdd@thataway.org
Web site: http://www.thataway.org

September Project
E-mail: info@theseptemberproject.org
Web site: http://www.theseptemberproject.org

Study Circles Resource Center
697 Pomfret Street
P.O. Box 203
Pomfret, CT 06258
Tel.: (860) 928–2616
E-mail: scrc@studycircles.org
Web site: http://www.studycircles.org

Promoting Security Through Connection

National

Justice Policy Institute
4455 Connecticut Avenue, N.W., Suite B500
Washington, DC 20008
Tel.: (202) 363–7847
E-mail: info@justicepolicy.org
Web site: http://www.justicepolicy.org

Men Against Destruction-Defending Against Drugs and Social Disorder (MAD DADS)
555 Stockton Street
Jacksonville, FL 32204
Tel.: (904) 388–8171
E-mail: national@maddads.com
Web site: http://maddads.com

National Association for Community Mediation
1527 New Hampshire Avenue, N.W.
Washington, DC 20036
Tel.: (202) 667–9700
E-mail: nafcm@nafcm.org
Web site: http://www.nafcm.org

National Youth Court Center
American Probation and Parole Association
P.O. Box 11910
Lexington, KY 40578
Tel.: (859) 244–8193
E-mail: nycc@csg.org
Web site: http://www.youthcourt.net

Sentencing Project
514 Tenth Street, N.W., Suite 1000
Washington, DC 20004
Tel.: (202) 628–0871
Web site: http://www.sentencingproject.org

Time Dollar USA
5500 Thirty-Ninth Street, N.W.
Washington, DC 20015
Tel.: (202) 686–5200
E-mail: contact@timedollar.org
Web site: http://www.timedollar.org

Midwest

Citizens on Patrol Project (COPP)
City of Cincinnati Police Department
310 Ezzard Charles Drive
Cincinnati, OH 45214
Tel.: (513) 352–2972
Web site: http://www.cincinnati-oh.gov/police/pages/-9496-

Northeast

Changing Lives Through Literature
Department of English
University of Massachusetts
285 Westport Road
North Dartmouth, MA 02747
Tel.: (508) 999–8752
E-mail: cltl@umassd.edu
Web site: http://cltl.umassd.edu

Community Justice Exchange
520 Eighth Avenue
New York, NY 10018
Tel.: (212) 373–1690
E-mail: info@communityjustice.org
Web site: http://www.communityjustice.org

Time Dollar Youth Court
409 E Street, N.W., Building B
Washington, DC 20001
Tel.: (202) 508–1612
E-mail: zfowlk@cs.com
Web site: http://www.timedollar.org

Vermont Community and Restorative Justice System
Vermont Agency of Human Services, Department of Corrections
103 South Main Street
Waterbury, VT 05671
Tel.: (802) 241–2261
Web site: http://www.doc.state.vt.us/community_and_restorative_justice

South

Dispute Settlement Center
302 Weaver Street
Carrboro, NC 27510
Tel.: (919) 929–8800
E-mail: ocdsc@disputesettlement.org
Web site: http://www.disputesettlement.org

West

Garden Project
P.O. Box 24292
San Francisco, CA 94124
Tel.: (650) 266–9513
E-mail: cathrinesneed@yahoo.com
Web site: http://www.gardenproject.org

Insight Prison Project
P.O. Box 888
Woodacre, CA 94973
Tel.: (415) 488–1348
E-mail: Jverduin@comcast.net
Web site: http://www.insightprisonproject.org

Resolve to Stop the Violence Project (RSVP)
425 Seventh Street
San Francisco, CA 94103
Tel.: (650) 266–9337
Web site: http://www.sfgov.org/site/sheriff_index.asp?id=25413

Washington State Institute for Community Oriented Policing
Washington State University at Spokane
P.O. Box 1495
Spokane, WA 99210
Tel.: (509) 358–7500
E-mail: WSICOP@wsu.edu
Web site: http://www.spokane.wsu.edu/research&service/WSICOP/wsicop.asp

Selected Magazines for Living Democracy

Adbusters magazine
1243 West 7th Avenue
Vancouver, BC
V6H 1B7
Canada
Tel: (800) 663–1243
E-mail: info@adbusters.org
Web site: http://www.adbusters.org

Ode magazine
98 Main Street, Suite 220
Tiburon, CA 94920
Tel: (888) 633–6242
E-mail: ode@odemagazine.com
Web site: http://www.odemagazine.com

Orion Magazine
The Orion Society
187 Main Street
Great Barrington, MA 01230
Tel: (888) 909–6568
E-mail: editor@orionsociety.org
Web site: http://www.oriononline.org/

Resurgence magazine
Rocksea Farmhouse
St. Mabyn, Bodmin
Cornwall PL30 3BR
United Kingdom
Tel: (+44) 0–1208–841824
Web site: http://www.resurgence.org

The Sun magazine
P.O. Box 469061
Escondido, CA 92046–9061
Tel.: (888) 732–6736
E-mail: TheSunMagazine@pcspublink.com
Web site: http://www.thesunmagazine.org

Utne magazine
Box 7460
Red Oak, IA 51591–0460
Tel: (800) 736–8863
Web site: http://www.utne.com

WorldWatch magazine
World Watch Institute
P.O. Box 188
Williamsport, PA 17703–9913
Tel: (888) 544–2303
E-mail: wwpub@worldwatch.org
Web site: http://www.worldwatch.org/pubs/mag/

Yes! magazine
Positive Futures Network
P.O. Box 10818
Bainbridge Island, WA 98110–0818
Tel: (800) 937–4451
E-mail: subs@yesmagazine.org
Web site: http://www.yesmagazine.org/

Some Favorite Newsletters

Food Safety Now!
Web site: http://www.centerforfoodsafety.org

Lowdown
Web site: http://www.hightowerlowdown.org

Nutrition Action Health Letter
Web site: http://www.cspinet.org/nah

THE AUTHOR

FRANCES MOORE LAPPÉ is the author or coauthor of fifteen books. Her 1971 three-million-copy best-seller, *Diet for a Small Planet*, continues to awaken readers to the human-made causes of hunger and the power of our everyday choices to create the world we want.

Democracy's Edge is the completion of a trilogy that began in 2002 with *Hope's Edge*, written with her daughter Anna Lappé. It is the thirtieth-anniversary sequel to Lappé's first book. Jane Goodall said of *Hope's Edge*, "Absolutely one of the most important books as we enter the twenty-first century." Second in the trilogy is *You Have the Power: Choosing Courage in a Culture of Fear*, written with Jeffrey Perkins.

Frances and Anna Lappé lead the Cambridge-based Small Planet Institute (http://www.smallplanetinstitute.org), a collaborative network for research and popular education to bring democracy to life. Together they founded the Small Planet Fund (http://www.smallplanetfund.org), which solicits and channels resources to democratic social movements, especially those featured in *Hope's Edge*.

In 1975, with Joseph Collins, Lappé launched the California-based Institute for Food and Development Policy (Food First). Its publications continue to shape the international debate on the root causes of hunger and poverty. The institute was described by the *New York Times* as one of the nation's "most respected food think tanks."

In 1990, Lappé co-founded the Center for Living Democracy, a ten-year initiative to help accelerate the spread of democratic innovations. She served as founding editor of the center's American News Service, which placed solutions-oriented news stories in almost three hundred newspapers nationwide.

Lappé's books have been used in a broad array of courses in hundreds of colleges and universities and in more than fifty countries. Her articles and opinion pieces have appeared in publications as diverse as the *New York Times*, *O, The Oprah Magazine*, and *Christian Century*. Her television and radio appearances have included PBS with Bill Moyers, the *Today* show, CBS Radio, and National Public Radio.

Lappé is a sought-after public speaker and has received seventeen honorary doctorates from distinguished institutions. In 1987 in Sweden, Lappé became the fourth American to receive the Right Livelihood Award, sometimes called the "Alternative Nobel," for her "vision and work healing our planet and uplifting humanity."

She welcomes readers to contact her at fmlappe@smallplanetinstitute.org.

INDEX

A

ActionAid, 105
Activists, 6; reframing terminology for, 321; socially responsible shareholder, 126
Adbusters magazine, 447
Adelphia, 88
Advertisers, media content influenced by, 221–222, 225
Advertising: for food products, 189–190; media as medium for, 220–221; political, 223–224, 229, 383n30
Against the Grain (M. Lappé), 193
Agribusiness corporations: efforts to fight, 67–69, 95; farm subsidies to, 198; farmers' disadvantageous position with, 186, 194–197, 374nn44, 46; intimidation of truth tellers by, 193–194. *See also* Farming; Food industry
Agriculture. *See* Farming
Aicher, Paul, 171–172
Air quality, 8, 80
Akre, Jane, 194, 429
Alinsky, Saul, 39, 156
Allen, Erika, 207–209, 216
Allen, Will, 207–209, 216
Alliance for Community Media, 430
Alliance for Democracy, 409
Allied Communities of Tarrant (ACT), 35, 36–37, 407
Allied Media Projects, 244, 430
AlterNet, 433
Altria, 118, 188
America Online–Time-Warner, 21, 221, 222
American Community Garden Association, 424
American Corn Growers Association (ACGA), 424
American Independent Business Alliance (AMIBA), 412
American Meat Institute, 191
American News Service (ANS): history of, xv, 230; interviewee's statements to, 201, 286, 288, 291, 295, 298, 302; stories published by, 157, 293, 400n41, 405
Anderson, John, 58
Arcata, California, chain restaurants in, 95
Archer Daniels Midland, 193, 195
Arizona, campaign spending reform in, 60–63
The Art of Political War (DeLay), 17
As You Sow Foundation, 412
Asch, Solomon, 312
Association of Community Organizations for Reform Now (ACORN),

316; contact information, 405; electoral political involvement of, 179–180; history of, 164–167, 366n37; power of banking knowledge of, 38–39; Working Families Party and, 55
Asthma rates, 80, 341n12
AT&T, 222
Attention. *See* Paying attention
Australia, Corporations Act of, 87
Automobiles, recycling of, 96, 97
Avery, Dennis, 192–193
Avon, 103

B

Bachar, Joel, 235
Baird, Susan, 306–307
Ballinger, Jeff, 122
Baltimoreans United in Leadership Development (BUILD), 157–158, 407
Banay, Ralph, 284
Bank of America, 103, 348n78
Banking: ACORN's efforts for fair practices in, 38–39, 165–166, 366n37; community, 127, 131–135
Bankruptcies, personal, 8, 18
Banks, Kim, 275
Barber, Benjamin, 249
Barclays, 125
Barnes & Noble, 78
Baton Rouge Working Interfaith Network, 364n27
Becawtini, Lorenzo, 117
Beef industry, 193, 199
Ben Asher, Moshe, 42
Benoit, Elder, 41–42, 155
Berger, David, 173
Berman, Shelley, 275
Bertelsmann, 222
The Best Democracy Money Can Buy (Palast), 176
Betancourt, Nicole, 236
Bethel New Life, Inc., 145, 420
Big Picture Schools, 438
Bill and Melinda Gates Foundation, 254
Billenness, Simon, 125
Billionaires for Bush, 40
Bi-Mart, 141, 423
Bioneers, 406
Blaming: accompanying calls for change, 311; ending, with participation in power, 35
Blank, Arthur, 73
Blinded by the Right (Brock), 18
Blockbuster, 78
Bloggers, 233
Blue states, red states vs., 26–27
Blue Vinyl, 236
Boggs, Terry, 36–37
Boise Cascade, 73, 74, 75
Bolin, Keith, 195, 196, 197
Bookman, Jay, 280
Borders, 78
Botterill, Regina, 159
Bottle recycling, 96–97
Bowling Alone (Putnam), 153
Boyte, Harry, 27
Brancaccio, David, 91
Breitbart, Joshua, 234, 235
Brock, David, 18
Brooks, Garth, 69
Brune, Michael, 71–75
Buckley v. Valeo, 60
Building in Good Faith, 236
Burton, Betsy, 135–137
Bush, George W., 6, 17, 40, 292–293
Bush administration: assault on democratic values by, 15–18; federal budget under, 19–20; news segments produced by, 229; No Child Left Behind Act of, 255, 273–274
Business Alliance for Local Living Economies (BALLE), 112, 351n3, 412
Buycotts, 105. *See also* Power shopping

C

Cahn, Edgar, 299–302
California, criminal rehabilitation efforts in, 286–288, 289–290, 401n48

California for the Industrial Areas Foundation, 39
California Public Employees' Retirement System (CalPERS), 100, 423
Campaign spending: corporate influence in current system of, 58–59; First Amendment and, 60; state reforms of, 60–63
Campbell, Colin, 129
Cantor, Dan, 55, 57, 316
Capital punishment, 281
Capitalism: democracy and, 145–147. *See also* Market
Capra, Fritjof, 25
Cargill, 195, 197
Carrefour, 107
Carson, Rachel, 24
Caruso, Frank, 242–243
Cascadian Farm, 201
Center for Collaborative Education, 438
Center for Community Self-Help, 132–133, 423
Center for Digital Democracy, 244, 430
Center for International Media Action, 430
Center for Living Democracy, xiv, 109
Center for Media & Democracy, 431
Center for Responsive Politics, 409
Center for Voting and Democracy, 410
Center for Working Capital, 127, 413
Central Park East Secondary School (Harlem), 251–253, 259–262, 274, 440
CEOs, compensation of, 88, 283
Change: conflict accompanying, 266, 275–276; potential for, 316–317; reframing fear accompanying, 311–314
Changing Lives Through Literature, 288, 445
Channel One, 224
Chattanooga, Tennessee, community visioning in, 174–175
Chemical industry, security in, 59
Cheney, Dick, 25
Children: diabetes rate in, 211; food advertising aimed at, 190; hungry, 23; obese, 187; with parents in prisons, 278, 281; pesticides in food of, 198. *See also* Schools
Chiquita, 103
Choices: food, 185–199, 216–217; personal, public impact of, 32; spending, environmental impact of, 117
Cincotta, Gale, 163, 165
Citibank credit cards, 125
Citigroup, 132
Citizen organizations: faith-in-action, 154–159, 163, 363n9, 364n27; increasing number of, 24, 332nn41–42; job training by, 159–161
Citizens: increasing participatory role of, 180–182; in neighborhood councils of city governments, 169–171; noninvolvement vs. participation of, 152–154; power of organized, 39, 151–152
Citizens' movement: community benefits initiatives of, 167–168; community visioning initiatives of, 174–176; housing trust funds advocated by, 168–169; study circle initiatives of, 171–174
Citizens on Patrol Project (COPP), 291–292, 444
Citizens Trade Campaign, 413
Civic obedience, 313
Civil disobedience, 313
Clean Clothes Campaign, 104
Clean Clothes Connection, 413
Clean Election Act (Arizona), 62–63
Clean Elections Institute, Inc., 410
Clean elections movement, 60–63
Clean Water Act, 16
Clear Channel, 222–223, 225, 239, 245–246
Clothes, fair labor production of, 104, 105, 121–123
Coalition for Environmentally Responsible Economies (CERES), 103, 413

Coalition for Healthier Cities and Communities, 436
Coalition of Essential Schools, 254, 272, 438
Coastal Enterprises, Inc. (ME), 145, 421
Coca-Cola, 96, 104, 116, 188, 190, 201
Coffee, Fair Trade, 118–121
Cohen, Richard, 266–267
Collapse (Diamond), 311
Colleges and universities: antisweatshop advocacy at, 104, 105, 121–122; Fair Trade coffee at, 119–121; Far Right funding programs at, 66, 338n32; locally produced food served by, 212–213. *See also* Schools
Collins, Joseph, xiv
Colors restaurant (NY), 143–144
Comcast, 242
Common Cause, 59, 410
Common Dreams News Center, 433
Communities: encouraging conversation in, 303–305; human need to function in, 30; school programs involving students in, 267–271
Communities Organized for Public Service (COPS), 156–157, 160–161, 407
Community banking, 127, 131–135
Community benefits initiatives, 167–169
Community development corporations, 144–145
Community Environmental Legal Defense Fund, 421
Community Food Security Coalition, 214, 425
Community Initiatives, 176, 437
Community investing, 131–132. *See also* Community banking
Community Justice Exchange, 445
Community media centers, 243–244
Community mediation, 298–299, 443
Community organizations: engaging low-income people outside institutions, 163–167; faith-based, 154–159, 163, 363n9, 364n27; job training efforts of, 159–161; study circles as, 171–174
"Community parenting," 293–295
Community policing, 290–293
Community Reinvestment Act, 163, 165
Community service programs, in schools, 268
Community supported agriculture, 203–205, 209. *See also* CSAs
Community visioning initiatives, 174–176
Compassion, power from arousing, 41–42
Conflict: accompanying change, 266, 275–276; creative, as skill for democracy, 265–266; mediation for resolving, 266–267, 276, 298–299
Connection: as antidote to culture of fear, 305–307; culture of, in schools, 256–265, 273; human need for, 31, 154, 310; security as based on, 278, 285. *See also* Relationships
Consumer food cooperatives, 205
Conversation Cafés, 304–305, 442
Co-op America, 123, 413
Cooperation: exchange system encouraging, 300–302; human brain structured for, 30, 249
Cooperative Home Care Associates, 142–143, 421
Cooperatives: consumer food, 205; farmer, 200–202; worker ownership in, 139–144
Corporate Accountability International, 414
Corporate disclosure, 105
Corporate globalization, 115–117, 128–129
The Corporation, 414
Corporations, 77–108; aligned with Far Right, 18; community development, 144–145; concern about power of, 27, 52, 301; controlling

food industry, 187–189; court decisions on rights of, 88–94; cultural norms and expectations shaping, 101–105, 106–107; myths about, 87–88; political campaign contributions of, 18, 58–59; property rights championed by, 15; public consequences of concentration of, 80–81; reforming values of, 70–75; rules governing, 78–79, 85–87; setting "values boundaries" on, 67, 94–98, 158, 310; size and influence of, 77–78, 82–83; socially responsible investment's impact on, 125; workers as owners of, 139–145. *See also* Agribusiness corporations; Shareholders
Corrections: get-tough approach in, 278, 280–281, 285; government spending on, 278, 281; industry devoted to, 280, 398n15; rehabilitation efforts in, 285, 286–290, 401n48. *See also* Prisons
Cortes, Ernie, 155–156, 160
Costco, 107, 118
Crick, Bernard, 44
Crime: get-tough approach to, 278, 280–281, 285; innovative approaches to, 284–285; rates of, 279, 281, 397n10; relationship between poverty and, 282–284; shame as root of, 282–284
CSAs, 203–205, 209. See also Community supported agriculture
Culture: of connection, in schools, 256–265, 273; corporate behavior shaped by norms of, 101–105, 106–107; of fear, 279–280, 303; of shame, 282–284
The Culture of Fear (Glassner), 279
Cynicism, communicating to overcome, 42

D

Dakota Rural Action, 68–69, 411
Daly, Herman, 97, 214
Davis, Milton, 133
Dean, Howard, 177, 178, 305
DeAngelis, Larry, 56–57
Death penalty, 281
Debus, Robert, 87
Defense spending, 20, 27
DeLay, Tom, 17, 25
DeLeon, Florinda, 143
Democracy: believers vs. nonbelievers in, 3–4, 16–17; capitalism and, 145–147; common perception of, 5–6; continual development of, 13–14; fragility of, 4; learning, 249, 251; mistrust of, 14–18; as powerful tool, 5, 9; reframing vocabulary for, 322; scarcity of, xiii; two frames for, 319–320. *See also* Living Democracy; Thin democracy
Democracy Now!, 234, 434
Democracy Unlimited of Humboldt County (CA), 424
Dependence, with globalization, 116–117
Depression, rates of, 29, 112
Dewey, John, 267
Diamond, Jared, 311
Diener, Ed, 148
Diers, Jim, 170, 171
Diet for a Small Planet (F. Lappé), xiii, 187, 206
Direction Action Research and Training (DART) Network, 363n9, 365n27
Discipline, power in, 40–41
Disney, 222
Dispute Settlement Center (Carrboro, North Carolina), 298–299, 446
Diversity: of food products, 188; of media ownership, 222, 226, 227, 231, 246–247; relationships of, 38; schools and, 256
Documentaries, cutting-edge, 235–237
Dole, 103
Domini 400 Social Index (DSI 400), 124

Domini Social Investments, 414
Dooley, Michael, 295, 296
Dow Chemical, 193, 198
Dow Jones Sustainability World Index (DJSI World), 105, 414
Drugs: cost of, 81; unsafe, rushed to market, 59, 336n14
Drury, John, 30
DuBois, Paul Martin, xiv

E

E. F. Schumacher Society, 138, 414
Eakes, Martin, 132–133
Earhart, Sharon, 139
EarthSave International, 425
East Brooklyn Congregations (EBC), 157, 407
Ecological footprint, 117, 414
Ecology, 24–25
Economics: as relationships, 112–117. *See also* Local economies
Edible Schoolyard, 212, 429
Edmonds, Beth, 61
Educators for Social Responsibility, 438
Egerstrom, Lee, 201, 202, 217
Eileen Fisher, 103
Eisenhower, Dwight, 22
Elderplan, 422
Elections: Americans working for, of political parties, 7; campaign spending in, 58–63; congressional, lack of voter interest in, 7; presidential, voter turnout in, 7, 178–180; U.S., fairness standards unmet in, 7
Emigh, Pam, 1, 34
Employee stock ownership plans (ESOPs), 140, 142
Energy consumption: with corporate globalization, 128–129; with globalized food system, 214–215
Engagement: de Tocqueville on need for, 29; false cultural ideas about, 31; as key to Living Democracy, 9–11; lack of, with thin democracy, 7–8
Enron, 80, 88, 99
Environment: bank concerned about, 134; concern about protection of, 26; corporate accountability for, 103; impact of spending choices on, 117, 414
Environmental Protection Agency (EPA): standards of, 94–95; Toxics Release Inventory, 25–26
European Union (EU), recycling required by, 96
Expectations: shaping corporate behavior, 101–105, 106–108; of Wall Street, 83
Externalities, 82–83
ExxonMobil, 87

F

Fahrenheit 9/11, 236
Fair Labor Association (FLA), 103–104, 106, 415
Fair Trade movement, 118–121
Fair Trade Resource Network, 415
Fairness and Accuracy in Reporting (FAIR), 225, 431
Fairness Doctrine, 226, 227, 231
Faith-based community organizations, 154–159, 163, 363n9, 364n27
Far Right: academic program funding by, 66, 338n32; antigovernment myth of, 19–21; assault on democratic values by, 15–18; boundary setting on corporations rejected by, 98; federal housing initiatives targeted by, 134; government reduction as goal of, 19; government vs. market myth of, 21–23; unions labeled as special interests by, 158
Farmer cooperatives, 200–202
Farmers' markets, 205
Farming: community supported agriculture model of, 203–205, 209; contract, 196–197; factory, sustainability of, 215–216; federal subsidies for, 198; financial statistics on, 195–196, 374nn44, 46; fish, 207–208; negative impacts of current system

of, 198–199, 376n70; organic, 202–203, 377n82; reframing terminology for, 321, 323; in urban communities, 207–210. *See also* Agribusiness corporations
Fats, in American diet, 188, 189
Fayetteville, North Carolina, study circles in, 174
Fear: culture of, 279–280, 303; reframing, accompanying change, 311–314
Federal Communications Commission (FCC): low-power radio stations and, 239, 242; media ownership rules of, 226, 246–247; public interest protected by, 225–227
Federal Hocking High School (Stewart, Ohio): conflict at, 276; contact information, 440; culture of connection at, 256–257, 258, 259–260, 263–265; internship program at, 267–268; as participant in Coalition of Essential Schools, 272; testing and assessment at, 262–263, 274
Fenner, John, 299
Fenway High School (Boston), 259, 263, 441
Films, cutting-edge, 235–237
Firefox, 243
First Amendment, 60
Fish farming, 207–208
Fishing, sustainable, 145
Fletcher, James, 133
Food, 183–217; advertising for, 189–190; changing current system of producing and distributing, 184–185; choice of, 185–199, 216–217; Fair Trade movement and, 118–121; globalization and, 214–215; illnesses related to, 198, 215; importance of power over, 183–184; junk, and schools, 210–212; pesticides used in production of, 198. *See also* Farming
Food and Drug Administration (FDA), 59, 336n14
Food First, xiv, 425
Food industry: effect of corporate control in, 187–189; global warming increased by, 199, 376n70; influence of, on government policies, 190–193. *See also* Agribusiness corporations
Food Project (Boston), 209–210, 428
Food Safety Now!, 449
Ford, 128
Ford, Henry, 65
Forum for Education and Democracy, 439
Fourteenth Amendment, 89, 97
Fourth Amendment, 89
Fowler, Mark, 221
Frank, Barb, 201–202
Frank, Becky, 202
Franklin, Benjamin, 78
Free market, 15, 63–64. *See also* Market
Free Press, 244, 245, 434
Free Speech TV, 434
Friedman, Milton, 22
Friedman, Thomas, 115, 128
Friends and Residents of Saint Thomas (FROST), 90–91, 421
Fromm, Erich, 30
Fusion voting, 54, 57
Future of Music Coalition, 245, 246, 247, 431

G

Galdston, Ken, 10, 37–38, 174
Gamaliel Foundation, 363n9, 365n27, 406
Gannon, Jeff, 233
Garden Project (San Francisco), 289–290, 446
Garner, James, 180
Garza, Bernardo, 142
Gates, Chris, 181
Gates, Jeff, 140
Gecan, Michael, 181
General Electric, 222
General Mills, 116, 192, 201
General Motors, 77, 103

Genetically modified organisms (GMOs), 191–192, 193, 195, 372n32
Genuine Progress Indicator, 148
The Geography of Nowhere (Kunstler), 129
George Jones Farm, 213, 427
Gerlach, Jim, 311–312, 314
Germany, "Green Dot" trademark in, 96
Giadone, Dulcie, 35–36
Gilligan, James, 282, 283, 284
Glassner, Barry, 279
Glazier, Andrew, 211
Gleason, Susan, 246–247
Global Reporting Initiative (GRI), 105, 419
Global Resource Action Center for the Environment (GRACE), 237, 425
Global Tobacco Treaty, 94
Global warming: Christian groups concerned about, 26; costs of, 80–81, 100; increased by U.S. farming practices, 199, 376n70; Kyoto Protocol limiting, 94, 98
Globalization: corporate., 115–117, 128–129; of food system, 214–215; reframing terminology for, 322
Globalization and Its Discontents (Stiglitz), 115
Going Local (Shuman), 131
Goldberger, Paul, 152
Goodman, Amy, 234
Google, 140
Gorelick, Jamie, 151
Government: Americans' belief in big interests running, 7; citizen participation in, 152–154; community policing funding by, 292–293; corporate concentration and, 80–81; corrections spending by, 278, 281; Far Right's goal of reducing, 19; federal, budget of, 19–20; food corporations' influence on policies of, 190–193; food recall power of, 215; labor standards ignored by, 106; market vs., 18–19, 21–23, 64; neighborhood councils advising, 169–171; news stories approved and produced by, 220, 229; nutrition education budget of, 190
Graduation rates, high school, 253
Grains, processed vs. whole, 188, 206
The Great Unraveling (Krugman), 17
Greater Boston Interfaith Organization, 41, 408
Greed, 18, 26
Green, Katie, 275
"Green Dot" trademark, 96
GreenMoney Journal, 415
Greenpeace, Inc., 415
Greider, William, 99
Gross, Matthew, 177
Growing Power, 207–208, 427
Growth hormone, in milk, 89, 193–194
Grzywinski, Ronald, 133, 134
Guckert, James, 233
Guerrilla News Network (GNN), 232–233, 234

H

H&R Block, 166
H. J. Heinz, 192
Halliburton, 19, 22–23
Hamilton, Alexander, 14, 183
Hanggi, Elena, 38
Happiness, factors contributing to, 29–30
Harrigan, Sean, 100
Hartford Areas Rally Together (HART), 35–36, 408
Hastie, William, 4, 13, 275
Hatz, Diane, 237
Havel, Vaclav, 49, 314
Health care, cost of, 8, 27
Health Care Without Harm, 236
Health insurance, 8
Heifer International, 425
Helfand, Judith, 236
Helping, emotional gain from, 44
High-fructose corn syrup, 187–188

Hill, Anita, 18
Hinkley, Robert, 64, 82, 86–87
Hock, Dee, 3
Holbrook School (Holden, Maine), 269–271, 441
Holm, Glen, 139
Home Depot, 78; Natural Step and, 348n78; Rainforest Action campaign targeting, 71, 72–73, 74, 75, 102, 126
The Hometown Advantage (Mitchell), 77–78
Hometown Utilicom, 434
Horizon, 201
Horowitz, David, 17, 225
Hostile takeovers, 82, 85
Houghton, Mary, 133, 134
Household Finance, 165–166
Housing trust funds, 168–169
Howard, Ina, 231
Hudson High School (Massachusetts), 274–275, 441
Hudson Institute, 193
Human nature: false beliefs about, 29–31; view of, underlying by Living Democracy, 310
Humility, 316–317
Humor, power in, 39–40
Hundt, Karen, 175
Hundt, Reed, 226
Hunger: in America, xiv, 8, 185; caused by scarcity of democracy, xiii

I

IdealsWork.com, 123, 415
Illnesses: food-related, 198, 215; obesity-related, 185, 198; personal bankruptcy as result of, 8
Immokalee, Florida, low-power radio station in, 240–241, 433
In the Mix, 435
Inaba, Ian, 232
Incarceration. *See* Corrections; Prisons
Income, life expectancy and, 325n
Independent Media Center, 244–245, 434
Independents, Americans identifying themselves as, 176
Industrial Areas Foundation (IAF), 363n9; affiliates of, 156–158, 407–408; contact information, 406; founding of, 156; philosophy of, 44, 161–163; as "power organization," 181
Infants: mortality rates for, 8; nurturance needed by, 249, 389n2
Insight Prison Project, 446
Instant run-off voting, 58
InstantRunoff.com, 410
Institute for Agriculture and Trade Policy, 426
Institute for Food and Development Policy, xiv, 425
Institute for Local Self-Reliance, 415
Institute for Student Achievement, 258, 439
Institutional investors, 98–101, 347n66
Intangibles, shareholders' concern with, 101, 348n75
Interdependence, with globalization, 116–117
International Labor Organization (ILO), 147; contact information, 416; humane labor conventions of, 103, 106, 107, 146
Internet: average daily use of, 221; corporate control of Web sites on, 222; Firefox browser for searching, 243; news services via, 232–233; politics affected by, 177; publicly provided access to, 242–243; statistics on access to, 242, 388n76
InterValley Project, 37–38, 408
Iraq war: democratic values overlooked in, 15, 23–24; media reporting about, 224, 225, 229, 233
Ithaca (New York) Hours, 138, 421

J

Janis-Aparicio, Madeline, 167–168
Japan, recycling laws in, 96

Jefferson, Thomas, 22, 51, 65, 78, 79–80, 219
Jenkins, Jerry, 171
Job training, 40–41, 159–161
Johnson, Charlie, 68–69, 238
Judge, Tom, 269–270
Junk food, schools and, 210–212
Just Food (New York), 428
Just Food Northfield Community Co-Op (Minnesota), 205
Justice Clothing, 122, 421
Justice Policy Institute, 443

K

Kellogg's, 187, 370n7
Kelly, Marjorie, 124, 125, 139
Kennedy, Robert Jr., 22
Kentuckians for the Commonwealth (KFTC), 34, 36, 39–40, 409
Kern, Jen, 164, 165–166, 179, 180
KIDS Consortium (Lewiston, Maine), 268–271, 439
King, Martin Luther Jr., 13, 27, 283, 306
Kleinberg, Mindy, 152
Knight, Phil, 104
Knobloch, Kyle, 275
Knorzer, Erv, 241
Knorzer, Marianne, 241
Knowledge, as power, 38–39
Kraft, 188
Kristof, Nicholas, 20
Kroger, 118
Krugman, Paul, 17
Kuna, Idaho, study circles in, 173
Kunstler, James Howard, 129
Kutztown, Pennsylvania, wireless Internet access in, 242–243
Kyoto Protocol, 94, 98

L

Labor standards, 106. *See also* Fair Labor Association (FLA); International Labor Organization (ILO)
Labor unions. *See* Unions
Lajoux, Alexandra, 98–99, 100–101
Land Stewardship Project, 67, 420, 427
Language, for Living Democracy, 315, 321–324
Lappé, Anna, 55
Lappé, Anthony, 232
Lappé, Marc, 193
League of Independent Voters/League of Pissed-Off Voters, 179, 410
League of Women Voters, 61–62, 411
Learning: to become powerful, 46–47; democracy, 249, 251; to handle conflict in schools, 266–267. *See also* Colleges and universities; Schools
Leber, Don, 141
Lehman Alternative Community School (Ithaca, New York), 258, 265, 441
Leon, Sharon, 298
Letters to Congress, 7
The Lexus and the Olive Tree (Friedman), 128
Liberty Media, 222
Licensed to Kill, Inc., 86
Life expectancy, poverty and, xi, xiii, 325n
Lifestyles of health and sustainability (LOHAS), 117
Lighted School (Waco, Texas), 271, 439
Lima, Ohio, study circles in, 173
Lindblom, Charles, 79
Linzey, Tom, 90, 92, 93
Living Democracy: economic relationships in, 113–115; engagement as key to, 9–11; factors driving emergence of, 23–26; food choices with, 216–217; foundation of security in, 278; origin of concept of, xiv–xv; paying attention as element of, 47, 128, 314–316; reframing fear for, 311–314; thin democracy contrasted to, 7; view of human nature underlying, 310; vocabulary for, 315, 321–324

Living wages, 66–67, 157–158, 164, 167. *See also* Wages
Lobbyists, 7, 223
Local currencies, 137–138. *See also* Time dollars programs
Local economies: as alternative to corporate globalization, 129–131; benefits of, 130–131; community banking for, 127, 131–135; local currency supporting, 137–138; local organizations promoting shopping at, 135–137; organization encouraging, 112, 351n3; restaurant dedicated to, 111–112, 351n1
Local Harvest (Santa Cruz, California), 426
Locke, John, 15
Lohan, Gabriella, 160
Long, Michelle, 135
Long, Russell, 140
Los Angeles: community benefits agreement in, 167–169; living wage campaign in, 67, 167; MAD DADs in, 293; school district certification of food products, 211–212; study circles in, 172
Los Angeles Alliance for a New Economy (LAANE), 424
Lovins, Amory, 97
Lovins, Hunter, 97
Low Power Radio Association, 431
Lowdown, 499
Lowe's, 78
Low-power radio, 239–243
Lula da Silva, Luis Inacio, 153
Lumber companies, reforming values of, 71–75
Lyman, Howard, 193, 429

M

Maine: campaign spending reform in, 61; KIDS Consortium in (Lewiston), 268–271, 439; recycling laws in, 97; sustainable fishing in, 145
Maine Citizens for Clean Elections, 412
Mann, Horace, 251, 390n1
Manning, Richard, 214
Market: "free," 15, 63–64; government vs., 18–19, 21–23, 64; movements to limit negative impact of, 66–69; Reagan's championing of, 19, 64; wealth concentration and, 64–66
Marshall, John, 88
Marshall, Stephen, 232
Martin, Kevin, 227
Masi, Brad, 213
Maslow, Abraham, 30
Mason, Edward S., 77
Mason, Griff, 147
Materialism, 26, 29, 112
May, Frank, 293
Mays, Lowry, 220–221
MBNA Corporation, 18
McCoy, Martha, 151, 154, 172–173, 174, 181–182
McDonald's, 102, 128, 190, 210, 237
McDonough, William, 97
McGovern, Ray, 17
McKay Nursery, 141–142, 420
Mead, Marge, 61–63
The Meatrix, 237, 435
Media, 219–248; advertising's influence on, 190, 220–222, 225; agribusiness corporations' intimidation of truth tellers in, 193–194; average American daily "consumption" of, 221; Bush administration payments to commentators in, 18; citizen pressure to change rules governing, 245–248; concentration of, 222–224, 226; democratic alternative forms of, 237–245; influences on content of, 225, 227–228, 229–230; Iraq war reports in, 224, 225, 229, 233; market vs. government message in, 18–19; as news source, 231, 232–234; ownership of, 222, 226, 227, 231, 246–247; press freedom and, 219–220, 230; profitability of, 228–229. *See also* Federal Communications Commission (FCC)

Media Access Project, 226, 244, 247, 431
Media Tenor, 231, 432
MediaRights, 244, 432
Mediation: community, 298–299, 443; training for, in schools, 266–267, 276
Meetup.com, 305, 442
Meier, Deborah, 253–254, 257, 259, 262, 276, 316
Member-to-Member Elderplan, 422
Men Against Destruction-Defending Against Drugs and Social Disorder (MAD DADs), 293–295, 443
Mendocino County, California, anti-GMO initiative in, 192
Mergers and acquisitions, 82
Merrett, Sam, 213
Merrick, Scott, 178
Metro Alliance (San Antonio, Texas), 160, 408
Microcinema International, 432
Microcinemas, 235
Miles, Doug, 157, 158
Milk, growth hormone in, 89, 193–194
Mineral rights, government sale of, 80
Minimum wage: decreased enforcement of, 146; decreasing buying power of, 8, 66; increased in New York, 54–55; reframing terminology for, 322. *See also* Wages
Minot, North Dakota, lack of radio personnel in, 238–239
Missouri, youth offender rehabilitation efforts in, 288–289
Mitchell, Stacy, 77–78
Money: local currencies as variation of, 138–139; as substitute for trust, 302; time dollars as alternative to, 299–302, 444, 445
Monford, Lamont, 173
Monsanto: GMO technology of, 191, 192, 195; growth hormone of, 89, 193–194
Montague, Read, 190
Moore, Margaret, 35
Morgan, Daymon, 39–40
Morningside Middle School (Fort Worth, Texas), 441
MoveOn.org, 432
Mozilla Firefox, 243
Murphy, Lois, 311–312
Musayev, Lina, 119–121
Myths: about blue vs. red states, 26–27; about corporations, 87–88; about cost of organic foods, 206, 378n88; about government vs. market, 21–23, 64; of Far Right as antigovernment, 19–21

N

Nader, Ralph, 53, 65–66
National Association for Community Mediation, 443
National Association of Broadcasters, 242
National Campaign for Sustainable Agriculture, 426
National Cattlemen's Beef Association, 193
National Center for Employee Ownership (NCEO), 416
National Civic League, 437
National Coalition for Dialogue and Deliberation, 304, 442
National Cooperative Business Association, 416
National Cooperative Grocers Association, 426
National Farm to School Program, 426
National Gardening Association, 427
National Interfaith Coalition for Worker Justice (NICWJ), 158–159, 416
National League of Cities, 437
National People's Action, 163, 165, 406
National Training and Information Center (NTIC), 406
National Youth Court Center, 444
Natural Step, 102, 104, 348n78, 416
Nebraska: farmland purchasing restricted in, 68, 95; MAD DADS in, 293–295
Needs, human, 29–30

Neighborhood councils, 169–171, 437
Neiman, Adam, 122–123
Neoconservatives, 17
Nestle, Marion, 191
New Community Corporation (Newark, New Jersey), 144–145, 422
New Jersey, junk food banned in schools in, 212
New Party, 55
Newman, Jim, 289
News: alternatives to corporate sources of, 232–234; corporate media as source of, 231; government production of segments billed as, 229
News Corporation, 222
Newspapers: government approval of stories in, 220; ownership and control of, 222, 231; printing ANS stories, 230; profit margin of, 228
Newton, Isaac, 14
Nickels, Greg, 170
Nike, 104, 123
Niman Ranch, 196, 430
9/11: architectural design for site of, 152; restaurant established by survivors of, 143–144; September Project commemorating, 305; shopping after, 6
9/11 Commission, 151–152
No Child Left Behind Act, 255, 273–274
No Sweat Apparel, 122–123, 422
Nogueira, Ana, 234
Nongovernmental organizations (NGOs), increasing number of, 24, 332nn41–42
Norquist, Grover, 19
Norris, Tyler, 176
Northeast Organic Farming Association (NOFA), 428
Nutrition Action Health Letter, 499
Nyerere, Julius, 52–53

O

Oberlin College, local food served by, 213, 427
Obesity: cost of illnesses related to, 185, 198; high-fructose corn syrup's contribution to, 188; increased rates of, 187, 198, 211; McDonald's salads and, 102
Ode magazine, 447
Odier-Fink, Eric, 122
Odier-Fink, Mandi, 122
Odwalla juice, 201
Ohio: community policing in (Cincinnati), 291–292, 444; criminal rehabilitation efforts in, 286, 288; study circles in (Lima), 173
Oil consumption: with corporate globalization, 128–129; with globalized food system, 214–215
Opelousas, Lousiana, low-power radio station in, 240
Openflows Networks, Ltd., 432
Oregon, GMO labeling initiative in, 191–192, 372n32
Organic Consumers Association, 427
Organic farming, 202–203, 377n82
Organic foods: campaign against, 192–193; cost of, 206, 378n88; farmer cooperatives producing, 200–201; at McDonald's in Sweden, 102
Organic Valley, 200–201, 428
Orion magazine, 447
Oroville, California, low-power radio station in, 241, 435
Orwell, George, 313

P

Pacific Institute for Community Organization (PICO), 363n9, 364n27, 407
Pacifica Radio, 435
Paine, Kevin, 270, 271
Paine, Tom, 231
Palast, Greg, 60, 176
Parenting, "surrogate," to prevent crime, 293–295
Pariser, Eli, 238–239
Participation: increasing, of citizens, 152–154, 180–182; in power, 35; in

problem solving, 44, 161. *See also* Citizen organizations; Citizens' movement
Pataki, George, 54
Pauli, Günter, 97
Paulino, Rita, 275
Paying attention: to economic choices, 147–149; as essential for Living Democracy, 47, 128, 314–316
Pennsylvania, corporate rights vs. local townships in, 90–93
Pennsylvania Environmental Network (PEN), 34, 45, 409
Pension funds: as corporate shareholders, 99–100, 347n66; union, active stewardship of investments of, 127
Pepsi, 96, 126, 190
Peretz, Louis, 301–302
Perkins, Barb, 204, 205
Perkins, David, 203–205
Perkins, Jeffrey, 314
Perkins, Perry, 37
Pesner, Jonah, 155
Pesticides, 198
Pfister, Don, 295, 296
Pharmaceutical industry, 59, 81, 336n14
PICO California, 364n27
Pimentel, David, 214
Political advertising, 223–224, 229, 383n30
Political parties: alternatives to current system of, 57–58; Americans lack of affiliation with, 176–177; Americans working for election of, 7; corporate giving to, 18, 58–59; decline in citizen involvement in, 152–153; limited dialogue by, in Congress, 15–16; news sources' affiliation with, 231; two-party system of, 52–53. *See also* Working Families Party
Politics: citizen participation in, 152–154; Internet communication's impact on, 177; as topic in news media, 221–222; as war, 17–18
Pollution: air, 8, 80; animal waste, 199; water, 81, 199
Portfolio preparation, 261–262, 263
Portland Office of Neighborhood Involvement (OR), 437
Poverty: among working Americans, 8, 66; death associated with, 8; effect on life expectancy, xi, xiii, 325n1; hunger associated with, 8; as moral concern, 26; number of Americans living in, 21; relationship between crime and, 282–284
Powell, Larry, 291–292
Powell, Lewis F., 65–66, 89
Powell Mercantile (Wyoming), 138–139, 420
Powell, Michael, 227, 247
Powell, Zawadi, 251–252, 260, 261, 262, 272, 274
Power, 29–47; from arousing compassion, 41–42; beliefs about engagement in community and, 29–31; of corporations, 77–78; in discipline, 40–41; of expectations, 106–107; humor in, 39–40; knowledge as, 38–39; of organized citizens, 39, 151–152; over food, importance of, 183–184; positive conceptualization of, 34–36; public impact of personal choices as, 32–34; relational, 35, 161, 163; relationships as, 36–38; views of, in public life, 42–43
Power shopping, 105, 117–123; for clothes and other products, 121–123; for food, 118–121
Powerful people: assumed knowledge and competence of, 38–39; becoming, as learning process, 46–47
Powerlessness, 5, 35
PR Watch, 432
Predatory lending, 165–166, 366n37
Press freedom, 219–220, 230
Preventing Violence (Gilligan), 282
Prisons: children with parents in, 281; number of people in, 278, 280–281;

recidivism after time in, 281, 286, 289; violence in, 284. *See also* Corrections
Private life, public life vs., 32–34
Problem solving: by citizens themselves, 44, 161, 181; increasing number of people involved in, 9; in study circles, 171, 174; through participation in power, 35
Processed foods: corporate profits with, 187, 370n7; cost of eating, 206, 378n88; health consequences of, 187–188
Profits: in food industry, 187, 197; increased corporate, 81; of media, 228–229; in prison industry, 280
Program on Corporations, Law and Democracy (POCLAD), 417
Project learning, 261–262, 263
Prometheus Radio Project, 239–240, 247, 433
Property crime, decreased rates of, 279, 397n10
Property rights: America's Founders' warnings on, 78; corporations' championing of, 15
Public Achievement, 439
Public Campaign, 411
Public Citizen, 59, 411
Public interest, in media, 225–227
Public land, sale of, with mineral rights, 80
Public life: private life vs., 32–34; reasons for entering, 45–46; reframing terminology for, 323; ways of viewing power in, 42–43
Publix Supermarkets, 140
Putnam, Robert, 153

Q

Quality Employment Through Skills Training (QUEST), 160–161, 423
The Quickening of America (F. Lappé and DuBois), xiv, 183, 274
Qwest, 88

R

Radio: American "consumption" of, 221; local, 237–239; low-power, 239–243, 431
Radio Preservation Act 2000, 242
Rahman, Ataur, 144
Rainforest Action Network (RAN), 71–75, 102, 126, 417
Rampton, Sheldon, 224, 230
Rathke, Wade, 164, 165, 316
Reagan, Ronald, 19, 64, 197, 226
Reclaim the Media (Seattle), 246, 433
ReclaimDemocracy.org, 417
Recycling, 96–97, 102
Red states, blue states vs., 26–27
Redefining Progress, 417
Redstone, Sumner, 233
Rehabilitation, in corrections, 285, 286–290, 401n48
Reilly, Thomas, 41
Relational power, 35, 161, 163
Relational self-interest, 45–46, 161
Relationships: as contributing to happiness, 29–30; economics as, 112–117; power as, 36–38; public vs. private, 32–34. *See also* Connection
Religion. *See* Faith-based community organizations
The Republican Noise Machine (Brock), 18
Resolve to Stop the Violence Project (RSVP), 287, 401n48, 446
Restaurant Opportunities Center of New York (ROC-NY), 422
Restorative justice programs, 295–297
Resurgence magazine, 448
Rice, Norm, 170
Ridley-Thomas, Mark, 172
Rifkin, Jeremy, 277, 305
"Right to know" law, 25–26
Robertson, Mik, 91–93
Robin, Vicki, 304
Rocky Mountain Institute, 97
Rooftop Films, 235, 435
Roosevelt, Franklin, 21, 22, 65, 331n29
Rosenblum, Marvin, 268–269

Ross, Blake, 243
Rowe, Frederick E., 100
Rowe, Richard R., 83, 85
Rubenstein, Robert, 125

S

SA8000 standard, 103
Safeway, 118
Saglio, Jan, 143
Saint Paul, Minnesota: Department of Planning and Economic Development, 437; neighborhood councils in, 169, 171
Salt Lake Vest Pocket Business Coalition, 137, 424
Sassaman, Hannah, 239–240, 242
School garden movement, 212, 429
School Mediation Associates, 440
School Redesign Network, 440
Schools: antidemocratic initiatives in, 255–256, 273–274; class scheduling in, 258–260; community-involvement programs in, 267–271; culture of connection in, 256–265, 273; examples of democratic approaches in, 251–252, 253–254, 255–256, 272–273, 274–276; junk food and, 210–212; local food in, 214; meaningful curriculum in, 260–262; mediation training in, 266–267, 276; negative results achieved by United States, 252–253; self-assessment in, 262–263; shared authority in, 263–264; size of, 258, 272; testing in, 255, 273, 274. *See also* Colleges and universities
Schumacher, E. F., 97, 138, 414
Schwartzman, Jay, 247
Schwarzenegger, Arnold, 286, 288
Seattle, Department of Neighborhoods of, 169–171, 438
Security, 277–307; connection as source of, 305–307; culture of fear and, 279–280, 303; foundation of, in Living Democracy, 278; innovative approaches to creating, 284–285; lack of, in chemical industry, 59; rethinking meaning of, 249
Self-Help Credit Union, 132
Self-Help Ventures Fund, 132
Self-interest: relational, 45–46, 161; selfishness vs., 43–46
Selfishness, self-interest vs., 43–46
Sentencing Project, 444
September Project, 305, 443
Service, as reason for entering public life, 45–46
Service learning programs, 268–271
Shame, culture of, 282–284
Shareholders: institutional investors as, 98–101, 347n66; intangibles of importance to, 101, 348n75; as owners of corporations, 87, 98; socially responsible activism of, 126. *See also* Employee stock ownership plans (ESOPs)
Shearin, James, 165
Shelby County Interfaith, 44, 408
Shopping: after 9/11, 6; organizations promoting, at local businesses, 135–137; power, 105, 117–123
Shore, Josh, 232
ShoreBank (formerly South Shore National Bank), 133–135, 317, 420
Shroder, Kerry, 215
Shultz, Mark, 215
Shuman, Michael, 131
Siemon, George, 200–201, 216, 316–317
Sierra Club, 225
Sifry, Micah, 177
Silent Spring (Carson), 24
Silver, Josh, 245
Silverstein, David, 298
Simple Machines Records, 436
Sizer, Theodore, 254, 260
Skocpol, Theda, 156
Small Is Beautiful (Schumacher), 97
Smith, Adam, 15
Smith, David, 260–261
Smith, Tim, 99

Smith, Trisha, 269–271
Smithfield, 197
Social Accountability International (SAI), 103, 417
Social Investment Forum, 418
Socially responsible investment (SRI): community banking as, 127, 131–135; financial performance with, 124–125; impact on corporations, 125; increase in, 123; shareholder activism as, 126; by union pension funds, 127
Sohn, Gigi, 226
Soil loss, due to current farming practices, 199
Soley, Lawrence, 225
Sony, 222
Sorenson, Bill, 69
The Soul of Capitalism (Greider), 99
South Shore National Bank. *See* ShoreBank
Spitz, Rene, 389n2
Spokane, Washington: community policing in, 290–291; low-power radio in, 238, 435
Standard Oil–Gulf Corporation merger, 21
Starbucks, 120, 348n78
States: campaign spending reform in, 60–63; corporate statutes of, 85–87. *See also individual states*
Staton, Eddie, 293–295
Stauber, John, 224
Stearn, Frank, 90–91
Steck, Diana, 45
Steel, Anim, 209–210
Steele, Cheryl, 290–291
Stewart, Ellen, 170–171
Stiglitz, Joseph, 115
Stoltzfus, Phil, 205
Stop & Shop, 118
Strey, Mike, 141–142
Study circles, 171–174
Study Circles Resource Center, 172, 181, 443
Sugars, in American diet, 187–188, 189
The Sun magazine, 448
Sunoco, 103
Super Size Me!, 236–237
Surowiecki, James, 174
Surpin, Rick, 143
Sustainability: Dow Jones index of, 105, 414; lifestyle emphasizing, 117
Sustainable Connections (WA), 135, 418
Sustainable Food Project, 212–213, 429
Sweden, McDonald's in, 102
Syngenta, 193

T

Taco Bell, 241
Talbot, James, 295, 296
Tate & Lyle, 195
Taxes: corporate vs. individual share of, 80; reframing terminology for, 323
Taylor, Gerald, 44
Taylor, Robert, 196
Teachout, Zephyr, 177
Teen courts, 297–298
Telecommunications Act (1996), 226, 245
Television: American "consumption" of, 221; as "appliance," 221; food advertising on, 190; lawsuit over beef disparagement on, 193; news on, 225, 229
Texas Interfaith Education Fund (IEF), 440
Thin Air Radio (Spokane, Washington), 238, 436
Thin democracy: lack of engagement in, 7–8; meaning of term, xiii, 309; weakness of, 6
Third World Majority, 433
Thomas Morgan, Alisha, 179
Thomas, Ted, 179–180
Thompson, Pauline, 36
Time Dollar USA, 444
Time Dollar Youth Court, 445
Time dollars programs, 299–302. *See also* Local currencies

Tocqueville, Alexis de, 29, 219, 220
Toomey, Jenny, 245–246, 247
Toxics Release Inventory, 25–26
Toys 'R' Us, 103
Training: job, 40–41, 159–161; mediation, 266–267, 276
TransFair USA, 118, 418
Transparency, citizen demand for, 25
Trillium Asset Management, 418
True, Jean, 34, 181
True Lies (A. Lappé and Marshall), 232
Trust: as dissolving fear, 303; lack of, in antidemocratic premise of Far Right, 279; money as substitute for, 302
TruthOut, 436

U

Unions: democratic capitalism and, 145–147; new alliances of, 158; number of workers protected by, 81; reframing terminology for, 323; stewardship of money invested by, 127; Working Families Party and, 55, 56
Unionwear, 418
United Nations: Genuine Progress Indicator, 148; Global Reporting Initiative (GRI), 105, 419
United Students Against Sweatshops (USAS), 104, 105, 419
United Students for Fair Trade, 119–121, 419
University of Arizona, 122
University of Michigan, 121
UPS, 140
Ury, Bill, 74
U.S. Congress: letter writing to, 7; limited dialogue in, 15–16; voter interest in elections for, 7
U.S. Constitution: corporations and, 79. *See also specific amendments*
U.S. Department of Agriculture: dietary guidelines of, 191; safe meat handling labeling requirements of, 191
USA PATRIOT Act, 20
Utne magazine, 448

V

Valeo, Buckley v., 60
Values, reforming corporate, 70–75
Values boundaries, 67, 94–98, 158, 310
Velez, Esteban, 288
Verité, 103, 419
Verizon, 242, 243
Vermont Community and Restorative Justice System, 445
Vermont Valley Community Farm, 204–205, 428
Vest Pocket (Salt Lake City), 137, 424
Viacom, 222, 225; Infinity, 246
Viertel, Joshua L., 212–213
Violence (Gilligan), 282
Violent crime, decreased rates of, 279, 397n10
Vivendi, 222
Vocabulary, for Living Democracy, 315, 321–324
Voter turnout: with clean election reforms, 60; in presidential elections, 7, 178–180
Voters: congressional elections ignored by, 7; Internet communication's effect on, 177
Voting: fusion, 54, 57; instant run-off, 58; shareholder, 87

W

W. L. Gore & Associates, 140
Wages: CEO vs. worker, 88, 283; living, 66–67, 157–158, 164, 167; minimum, 8, 54–55, 66, 146, 322; stagnation of, 81; at Wal-Mart, 81, 106–107, 141; with worker-owned corporations, 140, 141, 143
Wal-Mart: anti-unionism of, 147; as country's largest grocer, 188–189; expectations enabling, 106–107; law-making influenced by, 90; low wages at, 81, 106–107, 141; per-

centage of retail sales controlled by, 78; size of limited by local governments, 95; wealth of family owning, 64, 337n25
Walden Asset Management, 422
Wallis, Jim, 155
Walton family, wealth of, 64, 337n25
Waltz, Catherine, 296
Washington: community policing in (Spokane), 290–291; criminal rehabilitation effort in, 289; low-power radio in (Spokane), 238, 435; neighborhood councils in (Seattle), 169–171, 437; retirement benefits in ESOP companies in, 140; Sustainable Connections in, 135, 418
Washington State Institute for Community Oriented Policing, 447
Water pollution, 81, 199
Waters, Alice, 212
Waters, Fannie, 212
Wealth: concentration of, and market, 64–66; disparity in, and crime rate, 283; retirement, with ESOPs, 140, 142; trend in distribution of, 8, 21; trust as, 302; of Walton family, 64, 337n25
Weapons of Mass Deception (Rampton and Stauber), 224
Webb de Macias, Carolyn, 172
Well-being index, 148
Wellner, Tana, 139
Welsh, Patrick, 55
Weyerhaeuser, 73–74
White Dog Café, 111–112, 351n1, 423
Whole Foods, 118
Wicks, Judy, 111–112, 148, 351n1
Wickstrom, Todd, 238
Wild Oats, 118
Wilkinson, Reginald, 286, 288
Williams, Armstrong, 273–274
Williamson, Summer, 268
Wilson, Mark, 159
Wilson, Steve, 194, 429
Wimsatt, Billy, 179
Winfrey, Oprah, 193
The Wisdom of Crowds (Surowiecki), 174
Witt, Susan, 138
Wolfowitz, Paul, 17
Wood, George: on connection, 256–257; firing of, 276; on internship program, 268; on self-assessment by students, 262; on sharing authority with students, 263–265; on testing, 274
Woodward, Jeanne, 286–287
Worker Rights Consortium (WRC), 104, 105, 419
Workers: compensation of, vs. of CEOs, 88, 283; increase in work hours of, 81; as owners of companies, 139–145; protected by unions, 81
Working Families Party (WFP), 54–57, 66, 153, 316, 411
Working Films, 236, 244, 436
Working poor, 8, 66
WorldCom, 88
WorldWatch magazine, 448
Wright, Bonnie, 132

Y

Yale Sustainable Food Project, 212–213, 429
Yes! magazine, 448
You Have the Power (F. Lappé and Perkins), 314
Youth: job training for, 40–41; media projects run by, 244; Missouri rehabilitation efforts for, 288–289; restorative justice programs for, 295–297; teen courts for, 297–298; time dollars programs for, 300–301
Youth Action Program (New York City), 40–41, 442
YouthBuild USA (Boston), 41, 442